SEA OF DANGERS

SEA *of* DANGERS

CAPTAIN COOK AND HIS RIVALS
IN THE SOUTH PACIFIC

GEOFFREY BLAINEY

Ivan R. Dee   Chicago   2009

www.ivanrdee.com

First published by Penguin Books Australia Ltd., Victoria.

Library of Congress Cataloging-in-Publication Data:
Blainey, Geoffrey.
Sea of dangers : Captain Cook and his rivals in the South Pacific /
Geoffrey Blainey.
p. cm.
Originally published: Camberwell, Vic. : Viking, 2008.
Includes bibliographical references and index.
ISBN-13: 978-1-56663-825-8 (cloth : alk. paper)
ISBN-10: 1-56663-825-9 (cloth : alk. paper)
1. Cook, James, 1728-1779. 2. Explorers—Great Britain—Biography.
3. Oceania—Discovery and exploration—British. 4. Pacific Ocean—
Discovery and exploration—British. 5. Voyages around the world—
History—18th century. I. Title.
G246.C7B65 2009
910.9164'8—dc22
2008052623

Contents

Maps

Preface

THE VOYAGE of James Cook in the *Endeavour*, his first long voyage, was one of the most remarkable in recorded history. He not only sailed around the world, following the most difficult route any navigator had ever attempted, but he changed the maps of the world. In heavy seas he made a more thorough search for the missing continent—believed to lie somewhere between New Zealand and South America—than had previously been made. He was the first to explore most of the coast of New Zealand.

He was the first—so far as we know—to explore a vast stretch of the east coast of Australia, and the first to explore the longest reef in the world, the Great Barrier Reef. Thanks to his talented naturalists, Joseph Banks and Daniel Solander, more plants of novelty were found during this voyage than in any previous expedition in world history. In Jakarta and Cape Town, and in the seas between them, Cook lost one-third of his crew through tropical illnesses after earlier success in saving them from the killer of the sea, the disease of scurvy. The ship in which he circled the world was not much larger in area than a tennis court.

Some forty years ago I wrote briefly about this voyage in a book called *The Tyranny of Distance*. My curiosity was later quickened after chancing to visit many of the landmarks and seamarks of the *Endeavour*'s voyage. To look down on the coral reefs and mill races where that ship was almost wrecked on three occasions, to see the waves dash on lonely Booby Island, where Cook and Banks landed at their western exit from Torres Strait, and to approach from the ocean such harbors as Cape Town or such headlands as Cape Kidnappers in New Zealand, made me turn belatedly to Cook's detailed journals and those of Joseph Banks. New insights or unexpected strands of information appeared. After slowly reading Cook's long journal I was surprised to discover that on three occasions he ran into trouble when sailing near the coast under the seductive light of the full moon; he did not seem to learn his lesson from the early escapes, and on the third occasion his ship was almost wrecked.

So I began to write a book about the *Endeavour*'s voyage in the years between 1768 and 1771, concentrating especially on Australia. Soon I decided to widen the book to include his little-known French rival, Jean de Surville, who, exploring the South Pacific at the same time, was only a few miles away from Cook at a crucial stage of the voyage. De Surville was almost in sight of the sandstone cliffs near Sydney Harbor half a year before Cook. Not that I think the very first sighting of a coastline, whether by French or Portuguese or Dutch or British ships, is always significant; I try to explain this view in the Postscript on page 287.

De Surville's voyage in the *St. Jean-Baptiste* throws light on Cook's. Both searched for a missing continent. De Surville believed that the continent might contain a colony of Jewish traders, and his large ship was packed with textiles that he hoped to sell to them. His long voyage, which began in the port of Pondicherry in India, was gravely impaired by the onset of scurvy—in essence, a deficiency in Vitamin C. Indeed if Cook's seamen and Marines had suffered from scurvy as severely as de Surville's crew, the *Endeavour* might not have reached New Zealand and certainly not Australia. De Surville made his own practical discoveries, mainly of sea routes, but he has not received his share of praise.

Cook had other rivals. Banks, while a congenial and alert companion, was a rival in the same ship, month after month, for the two men pursued very different goals. A Polynesian navigator they recruited also became a rival. French and Scottish geographers were, in a sense, Cook's rivals as well as his promoters. The sea itself was an arena of international rivalry, and during the voyage Cook encountered Dutch, Spanish, French, and Portuguese rivalries and suspicions.

I acknowledge my debt to many historians, but especially to two New Zealanders: to the late Professor J. C. Beaglehole, who carried out the huge task of editing the separate *Endeavour* journals by Cook and Banks, and to Professor John Dunmore, who edited journals kept by de Surville and his second-in-command, Labé. My precise debt to them and to other historians is expressed in the Selected Sources.

For valuable comments on several chapters of my manuscript, I especially thank John Foley, a Torres Strait pilot and a historian too, and Keith Farrer, a Melbourne food scientist and historian of food technology. I thank John Windholf, who corresponded with me on Torres, the Spanish navigator, and my youngest brother, Don Blainey, a round-the-world yachtsman, who discussed the implications of de Surville's inability to calculate his longitude in the Coral and Tasman seas. For other advice or information I thank Michelle Atkins; Rosemary Balmford; Eleanor Collins; John Day; Bill Gillies, Sr.; Richard Hagen; Kate Hatch; Thomas Healy; David Hume; Stephen Pruett-Jones; Andrew, Chris, and Tim Warner; and various helpful librarians in Melbourne, Sydney, and Auckland. For translating documents I thank my wife and daughter, Ann and Anna Blainey. I was fortunate to have an excellent editor, Nicci Dodanwela. For errors and faults in the book, I alone am to blame.

SEA OF DANGERS

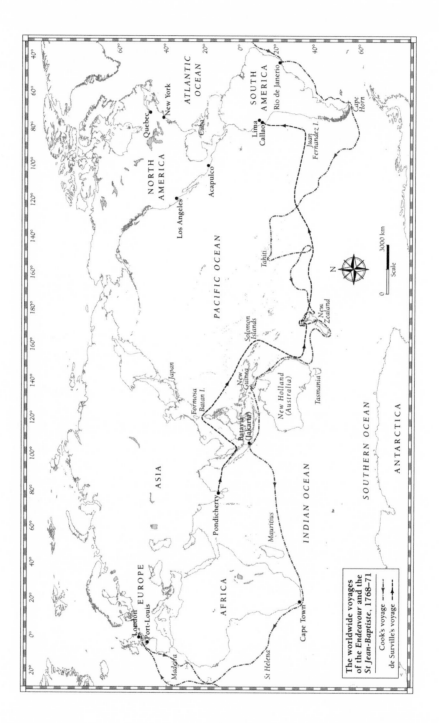

The worldwide voyages
of the *Endeavour* and the
St Jean-Baptiste, 1768–71

Cook's voyage ---◄---
de Surville's voyage ───◄───

1

Toward the Land of the Long Canoes

◢ IN JUNE 1767 clusters of islands were discovered by an English ship exploring the emptiness of the South Pacific. The most tantalizing of the islands was Tahiti, one of the homes of the long-distance navigators, the Polynesians. Their leisurely way of life, abundance of food, and apparent abundance of sexual activity excited the sailors from the *Dolphin* during their brief stay.

The discovery of the island was to have far-reaching consequences. Here at last, thanks to Captain Sam Wallis and his *Dolphin*, was a base from which this largest ocean in the world could be further explored. Many questions were still unanswered. How large was the ocean, and how many undiscovered lands did it hold? Way out in the ocean, not far from Tahiti, did there lie a mysterious continent? Surely, if it existed, it would be inhabited, perhaps densely inhabited. That was the prevailing view of the most learned Europeans. Almost certainly it would enrich the European nation whose sailors first discovered it.

The idea that such a continent existed was not new. It had been discussed since Greek and Roman times. Now the existence of this land seemed to be confirmed by reports brought to England by the *Dolphin*. A mountainous corner of the continent was reportedly glimpsed in the distance by some of her crew, just after they sailed away from Tahiti and the Society Islands. George Robertson, the master of the ship, was especially stirred by the glimpses. At first he saw high land to the south, but "the weather being so thick and hazy," others on deck at that moment could not be sure whether it was land.

At sunset two days later they thought they saw in the distance what Robertson called "the long wishd for Southern Continent." Another day passed, and they were "fully persuaded" that the continent lay not far away.

That the new continent must already be inhabited was the belief of many of these British sailors, because it was perhaps only a day's sailing time from islands that were as thickly populated as any land they could recall. Earlier, on first approaching Tahiti, their ship had sailed slowly past one island where some eight hundred men riding in a flotilla of canoes watched this unusual ship, while next day the long shore was "lined with men women and children all the way": a cavalcade of spectators using the beach as a grandstand.

How far from Tahiti was the mysterious continent? Robertson estimated that the crew of a long canoe leaving Tahiti at sunrise could reach the continent by sunset. He added that "the same trade wind will Bring them back next day if they want to come." Those who today read the journal that Robertson kept during the voyage might be inclined to conclude, from his random use of capital letters and eccentric spelling, that he was not well educated; but he was more literate than most naval officers of his day. His curiosity was intense; his mind was exploratory. He was convinced, for reasons that will emerge later, that between Tahiti and the mysterious continent a flourishing trade went on. It was dominated, he thought, by a race of people of paler skin than the copper-colored Tahitians. He glimpsed these people as they were conveyed in style in their double canoes, with canopies over their heads. He decided that they had "a great resemblance to the Jews."

It would have been easy for the *Dolphin*, in the space of a fortnight or a month, to investigate the question that fascinated Robertson. Captain Wallis, however, had been ill and was eager to commence the long homeward passage. Less inquisitive than Robertson, he was at heart only half an explorer.

The mountains that Robertson thought he saw were not necessarily seen by everyone aboard with quite the same confidence. Maybe the suggestive shapes on the horizon were banks of clouds rather than mountains? The *Dolphin* reached England by way of the East Indies and Cape Town with this doubt unresolved. In Robertson's eager opinion there were also spices and perhaps precious metals in Tahiti, and possibly in the whole region. Certainly pearls were found on the beaches. These promising hints fanned excitement in Europe, because the missing southern continent was the kind of topic on which, facts being few, the imagination was allowed a free rein. In the eyes of some geographers the unfound land might be as rich in silver as America, and the home of the strangest animals and plants. Some geographers of the eighteenth century called this mysterious continent the Great South Land.

Later generations have forgotten the allure of this missing continent. The intense and widespread search for it, and the ardent belief in its existence, have been almost erased from learned memory. Latter-day Australians have often adopted for their own land the title of the Great South Land or its Latin version, *Terra Australis*. The Latin language is no longer read widely, and so we have lost sight of the old distinction between the real *Terra Australis* or Australia on the one hand, and the unknown continent called *Terra Australis Incognita* on the other. That distinction, however, was real to scientists and geographers living in the eighteenth century. They knew of one southern continent, now known as Australia but then called New Holland by the Dutch and even by the English. But somewhere, out in the vastness of the Pacific Ocean, lay another and richer continent, which, they believed, was just waiting to be discovered.

In their view the missing continent, likely to be found in the vast ocean between Australia and South America, would be more fertile than Australia and its desolate coastline that had been seen by passing Dutch ships. When finally discovered, it was expected to yield new tropical fruits, new vegetables, new spices and drugs as well as sugar, cinnamon, tobacco, diamonds, silver, gold, and other tropical products already found in India and the East Indies, and Brazil and the West Indies. Accordingly Robertson of the *Dolphin* was entitled to feel jubilant when, in that secluded bay of Tahiti, he thought he saw Jewish faces and later, in the nearby sea, he thought he saw high and distant mountains that might belong to the missing continent.

From the northern hemisphere, after this exciting news was carried back by the *Dolphin*, two ships set out to search for this land beyond the clouds. One was a French armed merchant ship, sailing from the Indian port of Pondicherry with a magnificent cargo of trading goods. The other, a small British naval vessel, set sail from the English port of Plymouth carrying scientists rather than silks.

The *St. Jean-Baptiste*, commanded by Jean de Surville, and the *Endeavour*, commanded by James Cook, each made a remarkable voyage. The French ship was almost within sight of Botany Bay and Sydney Harbor months before the British ship arrived there. The two ships were about to meet, for the first time, on the coast of New Zealand when a gale separated them. For many days, unknown to each other, the ships were close, and on one day they were possibly in sight if telescopes had been carried to the highest lookout in one of the ships. Each ship traversed coasts on which no European or Asian had previously landed. As a result of their exploring, the lives of tens of millions of people would be drastically altered and the map of the world would not be the same again. But the land they were initially searching for, a place more important to them than any Australia, was to provide a very different story.

THE RISE OF SEAMAN COOK

James Cook, the captain of that English ship, was born on October 27, 1728, in a thatched cottage in the Yorkshire village of Marton-in-Cleveland, about fifteen miles from the North Sea. His mother was from Yorkshire, his father from Scotland. To be born in Scotland was an advantage, for the Scots were probably the most literate people in the world at that time, and it is almost certain that Cook's father could read and write. The father was a farm laborer and eventually a kind of manager or farm foreman in Yorkshire. For some years his son James was able to attend school, an incalculable advantage on which he built. In due course he became, largely by his own efforts, almost a scholar among sea captains. He was one of the few prominent Britons of his era to rise so high from such a humble background.

The Cook family's cottage was later dismantled, shipped to Australia, and rebuilt in public gardens in Melbourne; it is popular with overseas tourists, especially Japanese and Chinese. The two-story cottage with its walls of mottled red brick is charming and cozy. It has small windows, low ceilings, and a steep roof with a prominent chimney, but is less cramped than the typical farm worker's cottage of that era. It is not the cottage in which James and his seven brothers and sisters were born and raised. Erected in the year in which Cook joined the Royal Navy, the cottage was the parents' home in their later years, after the family had shrunk more through deaths than departures.

As a boy James Cook must have worked often in the fields, shooing away birds and helping with the harvest. By the age of seventeen he was living in the small fishing port of Staithes, about fifteen miles from his birthplace, and working long hours in a shop that sold groceries and haberdashery. After a year he went to the larger port of Whitby where he was apprenticed to John Walker, a wealthy Quaker who owned ships and was busy in the coal trade. The coal was shipped mostly from Tyneside to London, a city whose kitchens and foundries annually burned more coal than those of any other city in the world. Whitby's craftsmen built ships, and many of its seamen went in the town's coal ships or in the whaling ships to northern seas. On a river estuary, at the foot of high cliffs, the cramped streets were bustling in daytime, and their little cottages housed families from which at least one person typically went to sea.

Cook's first voyage from Whitby was in the *Freelove*, a brand-new collier, or coal ship, built at Great Yarmouth and carrying a crew of nineteen, of whom ten were apprentices or "servants." In the course of the next ten years Cook saw far more of the world than any of his ancestors would have seen. He often visited London, he sailed in the Irish Sea and the far north of the North Sea, and he visited the Baltic and called at one or more ports in Norway. He so impressed the shipowner that in 1755 he was offered the position of captain of the collier *Friendship*. Why Cook refused the post and its greater income is slightly puzzling. The likely answer is that, extremely competent in his seamanship, he was determined to make something of it. To sail in the Royal Navy was his ambition, and he signed on at the London riverside suburb of Wapping in June 1755.

His initial naval home was the *Eagle*, a ship of sixty guns, moored at Spithead. Soon he was promoted from able seaman to master's mate, the master himself being in charge of navigation. With a quill pen Cook began to maintain those daily records and diary that were such a part of naval life. His spelling lagged well behind his mathematics, and in the logbook he refers to stores carried aboard for the ship's purser as "Stoars for Pursser," while a newly arrived warship, named after the celebrated rock at the mouth of the Mediterranean, is recorded by him as the "Giberalter." He was in the navy for less than a year before war broke out between France and England, after which much of his time was spent intercepting or chasing enemy ships going to or returning from distant French colonies. At times the *Eagle* was packed with French seamen who had been taken as prisoners of war and were on their way to captivity in England.

The war between Britain and France was fought in scores of straits and sea routes extending across half the globe, but Cook's own war, and much of Britain's war, was in American seas. There France's most valuable possessions, the sugar islands of Guadeloupe and Martinique in the West Indies, were eventually captured by British forces. Cook spent much of the war in the sea lanes leading to the French strongholds in the Canadian towns of Quebec and Montreal, along the St. Lawrence River. To protect the entrance to the St. Lawrence estuary the French had built at Louisbourg, on Cape Breton Island, a powerful fort, which gained additional protection from the thick fogs often blanketing these seas. Cook, now master of the new sixty-four-gun ship the *Pembroke*, served in the naval force that blockaded the fort of Louisburg and tried to prevent French supply ships from arriving and French warships from leaving. In July 1758 the mighty fort surrendered. A year later Cook's ship was part of the large English fleet that sailed slowly along the St. Lawrence for some four hundred miles in order to besiege the cliff-top fort of Quebec. The French fort surrendered in September 1759, and a few days later Cook was transferred to the seventy-gun ship the *Northumberland*.

Cook's flair for mathematics—he was often studying textbooks and handbooks in his free time—guided him into the practice of surveying. He was partly responsible for compiling the large and detailed chart of the St. Lawrence River, which, consisting of twelve sheets, was engraved and placed on sale at a leading map shop and printery at Charing Cross in 1760. The most accurate map so far drawn of that mighty estuary, it was not viewed by Cook as the last word. The attitude of this perfectionist, now in his early thirties, is visible in the comment he wrote on a manuscript map of that long strip of the St. Lawrence estuary between Green and Pilgrim islands: the chart was "not so correct as I would wish." Lack of time had forced him to supplement his own observations and calculations with information gathered from other mariners. Sometimes those he questioned simply did not know the facts they should have known; and Cook regretted that an exact knowledge of one hazard in the river, the so-called middle bank, was possessed "by no one person I have yet conversed with."

On his return to riverside London he courted the twenty-one-year-old Elizabeth Batts. It was Napoleon who later claimed that England was a nation of shopkeepers, and Elizabeth's mercantile family mostly belonged to that shopping and trading sector, being neither rich nor poor. The marriage took place in a parish church four days before Christmas 1762. Fewer than four months later Cook went to sea again. Their marriage was to consist of a succession of farewells while his homecomings often did not occur within months of the time when she had been told to expect him. Elizabeth in her own sphere was probably as competent and as self-contained as he was in his. She was to outlive him by more than half a century.

After the Treaty of Paris was signed in 1763, marking the beginning of a period of British dominance, it seemed that opportunities for promotion in the British navy would be few. Such a large fleet would no longer be needed. And yet it proved to be a fortunate time for Cook's promotions toward the higher rungs of the naval ladder. Although scores of experienced captains could effectively fight a naval battle, not many could match Cook in what were primarily the peacetime skills of mapping and surveying. As commander of the schooner *Grenville*, he surveyed Newfoundland in the warmer months, ascertaining the depth of coastal rivers and the seabed in countless places, and then spent the colder months either in the freezing port of Halifax or in London, filling in his maps. The Atlantic coast of Canada had been busy with naval, fishing, and merchant vessels for more than two centuries; but the charts of its coast, estuaries, and bays, and the warnings of the shallower seas and submerged rocks and the effects of the tides, were far from adequate. Cook set out to improve the charts or to create them for coasts where no chart existed. One shipboard accident might have ended his naval career. In the *Grenville* in 1764, a horn of gunpowder exploded while gripped by his right hand. He was in acute pain, and his thumb was in some danger until the ship reached Halifax, where the surgeon of a French ship treated the wound, which was still gaping between the forefinger and thumb. The scar remained.

Immersing himself in Charles Leadbetter's manual, *A Compleat System of Astronomy*, and reading some pages again and again, James

Cook was becoming an astronomer. In the summer of 1766 he was ready to employ a brass telescopic quadrant and other instruments to observe an eagerly awaited eclipse of the sun. He was then at the southwest extremity of what he called "New-found-land," and the clear sky of August 5 favored his meticulous measuring. His brief paper setting out his calculations of the beginning and ending of the eclipse, down to the nearest second, found its way to an English physician, a lover of astronomy, and he approvingly read Cook's paper to a meeting of the most learned scientific institution in Britain, the Royal Society.

Cook, his ship now bobbing about the Atlantic, would have loved to hear the applause and murmurs of approval at that meeting in London. He could not yet imagine that one day he would be a master of observations made at sea. Five years later, not far from the equator, he saw yet another eclipse of the sun, and he wrote in his journal the cavalier comment that he observed "the Eclips" merely for the sake of observing it.

While computing the ship's latitude—the distance from the equator—was relatively easy for a sea captain of the 1760s, the ascertaining of longitude often remained the devil's own task. In the oceans far from Europe the exact longitude of many important headlands, reefs, and islands was not known with accuracy. Sometimes at sea a captain reading his chart in broad daylight was little better informed about the longitude of a well-known headland than if he had been navigating without a chart in thick Newfoundland fog. With the aid of a reflecting telescope assigned to him, Cook slowly learned how to compute longitude with more accuracy than most captains in the Royal Navy.

In London in 1768 the Admiralty were searching for a mariner capable of carrying out an unusual mission in the Pacific Ocean. They wanted a leader who could manage his crew when they were under pressure and display skill in astronomy as well as in navigation. Cook was a likely choice. The fact that the ship assigned to this expedition was much smaller than those commanded by senior naval captains increased the prospect that he would receive the appointment. Not yet a lieutenant, he was promoted to that rank once he was appointed to lead the expedition. Thereafter, aboard the ship, he was usually called captain simply because he was the captain.

Now aged thirty-nine, Cook was tall and strong boned. Probably he was just over six feet in height, which in his generation was unusually tall. Portraits painted a few years later show bushy eyebrows, a longish nose, a strong but not insensitive mouth, and thin lips. The jaw, very noticeable, conveys an air of command. The hair is long, receding very little at the forehead, and tied at the back with a ribbon; perhaps it is a powdered wig. The brow is white, as if he usually wore a cap or hat, but the cheeks are ruddy. As depicted in later oil portraits by James Webber and by Nathaniel Dance, he is not easily inclined to laughter. There is a slight tenseness about him, which would fit the known fact that on occasions he was spectacularly angry, even though the anger soon vanished. One detail in Webber's portrait is significant but easily overlooked: Cook's right hand—the hand scarred by the explosion off the Canadian coast—is covered by a glove.

If Cook had been painted in his street clothes, without the naval hallmarks of gold braid and sword and leather gloves and white waistcoat and trousers, he might have passed for a yeoman farmer—he had that independent and outdoors air. As described a few years later by James Boswell, a man of letters, Cook was "a grave, steady man, and his wife, a decent plump English woman." One of Cook's younger contemporaries summed him up as a mixture of audacity and caution. Knowing when to apply the caution and when to apply the audacity was to be one secret of his success.

THE TRANSIT OF VENUS—A MOMENTOUS EVENT

Cook's first task as captain was to sail his ship to the Pacific and observe a happening of only a few hours' duration: the transit of the planet Venus across the face of the sun. It was not the first time the transit had been carefully observed, but it would be the last opportunity for more than a century. As every important nation wished in its own way to take part in the observation and was eager to send its observers on long journeys, this would be costlier than any previous investigation carried out in the name of science.

The English astronomer Edmond Halley, after whom the celebrated comet was named, had been the instigator of this research project in 1716. He argued that if a meticulous observation were made of the transit of Venus across the face of the sun, that most important fact—the distance separating the sun from the Earth—could at last be revealed. One single observation was not enough; the same transit of Venus had to be observed in scattered parts of the world. If the time taken by Venus to cross the sun could be measured exactly in hours and minutes and seconds, and if the exact distance between just two distant places of observation could be ascertained, then the distance of the sun from the Earth might be measured accurately. Such a measurement would prove vital for navigation and many other activities. Halley's logic was beyond dispute. The problem was to organize the various long-distance expeditions needed to observe the transit from different points of the globe.

A transit was to take place on June 6, 1761, and costly and diligent attempts were made to measure and time it. One ship left England with ample time to escort two astronomers, Charles Mason and Jeremiah Dixon, to the East Indies where they were to watch the transit from Sumatra. Alas, there was a naval battle and other mishaps along the way—the war with France was still being fought—and the two scientists had to be content with observing the transit from the observatory in Cape Town. Later they made a reputation in British North America by surveying the state boundary known as the Mason–Dixon line. Today the evocative musical word "Dixieland" commemorates the astronomer Dixon.

On the day of the transit of 1761, about 120 little groups of observers were scattered across the northern hemisphere, ready for their long-awaited hours of watching. In Madras in India a clergyman was waiting; in Bologna an Italian professor; and in Newfoundland the Harvard professor John Winthrop—Harvard still being the university of an English colony. In distant Lapland in northern Europe and in Tobolsk in Siberia, visiting astronomers were ready to see Venus glide ever so slowly across the face of the sun.

In some places the sun had not quite risen when Venus began its passage, and in other places the presence of thick clouds marred the day. In Cape Town the sky was not quite clear, and Mason and Dixon timed the end of the transit but not the beginning. When months later the results arrived in London and Paris from all these distant sightings, there was consternation. In most recordings the entire transit took just under six hours from the left side of the sun to the right; but as to the exact number of minutes and seconds, the astronomers in Siberia and Stockholm and Calcutta strongly disagreed. Even in the city and suburbs of London several independent observers, men of competence, disagreed with the Royal Observatory at Greenwich.

Part of the failure came from the inability of some of the parties to determine the exact longitude of their place of observation. Another learned observer concluded that there were insuperable obstacles: peoples' eyes were different, and their telescopes had varying degrees of magnification. Meanwhile he concluded that Venus lay 68,891,486 miles from the sun. As for the distance from the Earth to the sun, he estimated that the Earth would have to travel for nearly 23 years, and at a speed "142 times as great as the velocity of a cannon-ball," in order to reach the sun!

The next transit of Venus was expected to take place eight years later, on June 3, 1769, after which there was to be an unusually long gap of 105 years. Therefore the observations in 1769 had to be accurate; this opportunity could not be lost. In London the Royal Society, the most esteemed of Britain's scientific institutes, made careful plans for parties to observe the transit in North America, in Norway, and in northwest Ireland where Mason himself was to be the official observer. The Royal Society was a driving force behind the plan to send a naval vessel to the Pacific in order that the transit could be observed there. It also inspired King George III to think of providing £4,000 to enable the purchase of a vessel for carrying Cook and an official astronomer to the South Pacific where the rare event could be observed, it was hoped, under a favorable sky.

The entry of the king was a vital step, for which he rarely receives the credit due him. In middle age he was to play his part in losing the North American colonies, and in old age he was mad and blind, but when a young monarch he was an enthusiast for science and technology. In the opinion of his latest biographer, Jeremy Black, he was more impressive intellectually and culturally than some of England's best-known prime ministers of the eighteenth century. In his late twenties, his tall physique and his light auburn hair and blue eyes made him a distinctive horseman when he rode from his home in Richmond to transact affairs of state in London. He was also distinctive among the monarchs of the world because he had studied physics and chemistry a little, was curious about the workings of clocks, of which he owned a large collection, and was one of Europe's keenest buyers and binders of books.

During the active years of his reign, George III was a patron of astronomy. He loved to see the night sky through the finest telescopes, and when in his forties he would finance the world's largest telescope, consisting primarily of a tube nearly forty feet in length. Through it he jubilantly crawled, before the glass was installed. In Kew he was looking forward to seeing the transit of Venus himself, from the brand-new observatory given him by his mother as a birthday present. Meanwhile he gave to the Royal Society the £4,000 without which Cook's voyage might have been impossible.

Captain Cook had already been chosen when Samuel Wallis reached England in the *Dolphin* late in May 1768 with the news that he had found the ideal island in which to set up an observatory. It was King George III Island, now known as Tahiti. There, Captain Wallis confidently advised, the skies would be clear on the vital day, and moreover the native inhabitants, he explained with not quite the same confidence, were likely to be friendly. In June the Royal Society accepted his advice.

Cook's timetable required him to be in Matavai Bay in Tahiti a couple of months before the transit of Venus occurred. After the transit he was to open his secret instructions. While the voyage to Tahiti was public knowledge, Cook's subsequent search for the missing continent was intended to be a secret. The competitive game of colonial expansion called for secrecy.

A CAT AND A COLLIER

The ship selected for the voyage was not glamorous. She was a mere carrier of coal, renovated for other purposes. In shape she was more like a compact shrub than a tall tree. When sailing along with a favorable wind she must have been a pleasing sight but not, to a connoisseur of sailing ships, a magical one.

The *Endeavour* met the distinct guidelines set down by the Admiralty. She was not heavily rigged, and so the sails on the three masts could be handled by a relatively small crew. She was capable of safely entering bays which, being shallow, might endanger a larger ship. In fact, when fully loaded, she could safely cross a river bar with only fifteen feet of water underneath her. At the same time, while not large, she had the capacity to carry the voluminous supplies that were needed in a voyage expected to last at least two years. She was slow, but that did not matter because she might later be engaged in the very slow task of exploring the shores of an unknown continent.

Shipyards and repair facilities were not likely to be found along the *Endeavour*'s route. Accordingly, if she ran onto a reef or sandbar and suffered damage, she had to be capable, after reaching the safety of a nearby harbor, of being laid on her side so that her bottom could be repaired. In essence she was the kind of ship that the Royal Navy would not dream of building or buying for fighting purposes.

Originally known as the *Earl of Pembroke*, the *Endeavour* had been built in the Yorkshire port of Whitby for the coastal coal trade. In the eyes of some nautical observers, she was of stolid styling. She was square at the stern, and her bow was not very pointed and supported no ornate figurehead; she could not be called streamlined. She belonged to the category called not ships but barks. Her length was a mere 106 feet, and the lower deck was just under 98 feet long. As her breadth was just over 29 feet, a sailor could walk right across the ship at her widest point in just ten or eleven steps. Her purchase price was £2,800, substantially less than the sum provided by the king, but her refitting would be very expensive.

The tiny size of this vessel, bound to encounter wild seas, would astonish us if we were able to view her from the vantage point of a seat in a sports stadium. On the playing surface of an ordinary soccer pitch, a total of twenty-three *Endeavours* could be fitted, according to my calculation. If the pitch were flooded, these identical ships could come advancing along it, seven abreast, with the front line of seven being followed by a second line and then a third. There would still be room for another two *Endeavours* to float in the unoccupied space. Cook himself did not choose this ship of such small dimensions, though he was pleased when he saw her, especially since he had worked as a seaman on similar colliers and knew their merits.

In the shipyards at Deptford, downstream from the city of London, the *Endeavour* was refitted for her long voyage. For her own defense she had to be fitted with ten carriage guns and a small number of light swivel guns. Her bottom had to be strengthened for the months spent in tropical seas, and so an extra layer of thin wooden boards, and tar and felt, was laid like a protective skin over her bottom planks. In the hope that the tropical sea worm would not eat too easily into the wood, a thin armour of nails, each with a wide head, was hammered in to reinforce the ship's bottom.

How many seamen should the ship carry on an arduous voyage of exploration? When carrying coal she employed a crew of no more than twenty. More seamen, however, would be needed for a long voyage of uncertain duration. As deaths were likely, especially if scurvy set in, a ship exploring in unfamiliar seas had to carry her own replacements. It also became clear that soldiers were needed as well as sailors, for the ship might anchor among hostile peoples. So a sergeant of Marines, John Edgcumbe, who was known as "very much of a gentleman," came aboard along with a corporal, a drummer, and nine privates. The first intention was to carry no more than one scientist, who was Charles Green, a professional astronomer. Then the ever-present Royal Society suggested that several natural scientists and their helpers should join in the voyage, and so a further enlargement of the ship's interior and the fitting out of the big cabin at the stern had to begin.

When the ship was on the point of sailing from the Thames to Plymouth, her last English port, more than eighty men were aboard, and more were to come. Most were below the age of thirty. A few were experienced officers and sailors who had already sailed around the world in the *Dolphin*, and several were boys intent on a naval career. One was Isaac Manley, a Londoner aged twelve, who eventually became an Admiral of the Red, outliving Cook by nearly sixty years. Another who was to become a senior captain in the Royal Navy was Isaac Smith, then aged sixteen. His kinship more than his experience gained him a position, for he was a cousin of Cook's wife.

The *Endeavour* was a hotel, a workplace, a means of transport, a warehouse, a mobile fort, and a farm—all in one. The tiny farm, rather exposed to the weather, consisted of poultry and edible animals, including a nanny goat that had already been around the world with Captain Wallis in the *Dolphin*. The hotel was more crowded than any on shore. Room eventually had to be found for more than ninety sleeping places, though not everyone slept at the same time. The solution was to roll up the hammocks in the morning and store them. The Marines or naval soldiers also had their own cramped quarters, and the midshipmen and servants too. In contrast, the senior officers and scientists were allotted cabins or shared them.

Most of the crew lived and slept in the mess deck, which was the biggest living space in the ship. There at night the hammocks or swinging cots, hung from the ceiling, occupied much of the space. For the ordinary seaman the hammock was only fourteen inches wide. He was so cocooned in his cramped hammock that the ship could roll from side to side without him falling out. A pillow was provided and a blanket gave some warmth. When the seaman was called to work, his hammock and blanket and pillow had to be rolled up so tightly that the round package could pass through a circle of a certain size. The hammock served another purpose: if a sailor died, he was wrapped in his hammock for burial at sea.

In the daytime the mess deck—home to about sixty of the seamen—was more spacious. In effect a big cabin, with no view of the sea, it occupied the stern of the ship and ran from one side to the other. Compared to most of the spaces in the ship its ceiling was surprisingly high, and even the tallest man could walk about with a little space over his head. Much of the floor space was occupied by sturdy tables arranged in a row. Here the men ate their meals, yarned when their watch was over, and read—if printed matter was available and if they were able to read.

Nearby was the ship's galley or kitchen, a tiny space with no partition to conceal it from the men's tables. The heavy stove, made of iron, was large and elaborate. To prevent fire from spreading, the stove rested on a bed of smooth, thinly sliced rock, which in turn rested on wooden decking. The stove burned short, sawed-off pieces of firewood, which made up a large item of the ship's cargo. As insufficient space could be set aside for the neat stacks of wood, the ship was obliged periodically to call at a harbor and collect more, in addition to filling casks with fresh water. Firewood had to be used frugally while the ship was at sea, so the stove was alight for only a few of the twenty-four hours each day.

Pork or beef, usually salted rather than fresh, was cooked and served on Tuesday, Thursday, Saturday, and Sunday. Bread or porridge was served on virtually every day. Thin soups mixed with peas or oatmeal were served on those days when no meat was in the ration. Occasional puddings or duffs were made with suet and raisins and sugar and flour, and of course each seaman received a daily ration of beer and spirits. For many, this was the incentive that persuaded them to go to sea.

The main cooking process, especially of salted meat, was boiling; and at the front end of the stove were two round copper receptacles for liquids. On the other side was the open fire where fresh meat and fish, when available, might be grilled. At least one professional cook was aboard the *Endeavour*, but it is dubious whether today he would be called a chef. The navy gave preference, when appointing cooks, to their own disabled sailors. After meeting the *Endeavour's* proposed cook and confirming that his right arm was missing, Lieutenant Cook asked instead for the appointment of a man who was physically fit. From the Navy Board came the stern reply that it presently could name no other convenient ship in which the one-handed man could serve. After coming aboard, John Thompson showed that his useful arm could stoke and operate a stove with skill.

For the purpose of eating, the seamen formed themselves into small teams. Allocated their daily ration in a woven bag, they kept it separately from the rations of every other team, and Thompson cooked it separately. The elected leader of the team or "mess," who usually served for a month at a time, brought the cooked food to the table, apportioned it more or less equally, and cleaned up the bowls, spoons, and mugs at the meal's end. Every man owned his own simple utensils, including the large spoon that was used at every meal. In the course of a voyage these messes often became tightly knit companies of men.

The careful conserving of space was evident in the hard seats that stood on each side of the mess table. The seats were actually the closed lids of oblong wooden chests in which each man kept his spare clothes and other personal possessions. Each sea chest was shared by two men.

On August 19, 1768, the seamen assembled on deck in Plymouth Harbor to hear the reading aloud of what in effect were their conditions of contract. To all but a few seamen the rules, known officially as the Articles of War, were familiar; they were intended to prevent or restrain desertion, cowardice, mutiny, profane oaths, drunkenness, provocative speeches, and even disturbances provoked by unwholesome food. Cook, after making his short speech, was pleased with the seamen's cheerful response and their "readyness to prosecute the Voyage." A high official came aboard and paid two months' wages in advance to the crew. Meanwhile all kinds of provisions were brought aboard for immediate eating or for stowing—bread, fresh beef, beer, rum, salt, and water. As the cask and barrel were the normal storing places, even for bread, the ship carried an astonishing variety of wooden barrels.

After those prominent scientists, Mr. Joseph Banks and Dr. Daniel Solander, came aboard, having hurried down the road from London, nearly all was in readiness for the ship to sail. The carpenters and shipwrights carried out their last tasks and departed. On the afternoon of Friday, August 25, in Cook's own words, the *Endeavour*, with ninety-four persons aboard, "got under sail and put to sea." Next morning at six, the familiar Cornish headland called the Lizard was seen across the sea, and all sight of England slowly faded away. A few days later the first gale was encountered, and heavy rain too, and a small boat was washed overboard. At this stage the ship was a traveling farm, with cats as mousers and dogs as hunters, along with goats and sheep and poultry in their pens, for no food was so prized as fresh meat during a voyage. Alas, in the gale the wooden pens holding three or four dozen poultry were washed overboard and not recovered.

THE SEAMAN AND THE SCIENTIST

The voyage of the *Endeavour* would not have been so fascinating but for the presence of two fine botanists and their entourage. It is doubtful if any previous European voyage of exploration, especially one conducted over a long period, had carried such fine all-round observers as distinct from nautical observers. Moreover the two naturalists—Banks and Solander—had a sense of fun and an acute eye for everyday happenings.

Joseph Banks was an affluent bachelor, aged twenty-five when he came aboard. The only wealthy person in the ship, he paid the salaries or expenses of a large contingent including Dr. Solander. As his clerk and personal secretary, Banks recruited Herman Spöring—"a grave thinking man" from a seaport in the Swedish province of Finland—who was also a skilled watchmaker and draftsman. Banks also brought with him two young British draftsmen, the equivalent of today's photographers: Parkinson, who specialized in drawing topics from natural history, and Buchan, who painted grand scenes. On top of this, Banks brought four servants and miscellaneous helpers, of whom two were black men. Banks was not an aristocrat but belonged to the landed and mercantile gentry, and his main fortune was inherited from a merchant who, trading from the east coast port of Hull, imported iron from Sweden and exported English lead.

While he had received an expensive education—Harrow School, Eton College, and Oxford University—Banks had not always made the most of it. Fortunately at the age of fourteen he was captivated by botany. After bathing in the Thames River one summer evening, he was returning to Eton along a rural lane when his eyes were captured by the color and variety of the flowers he passed. At Oxford he did not complete his degree but enriched his time by resolving, since no teaching in botany was available, that he would enlist a botanical teacher himself, which he did. After riding in a stagecoach across country to the rival university, Cambridge, he recruited there at his own expense an effective young lecturer, Israel Lyons, at whose feet he sat when he could divert time from his social activities at Oxford. Although Banks had enough money to be a playboy—and at times he was—he also wanted to be a scholar of nature. Steadily he built up his knowledge of botany, adding zoology too. At the age of twenty-three, determined to see the plants in other lands, he took part in a long expedition that crossed the Atlantic to Labrador and Newfoundland, returning by way of Lisbon.

This was a golden age for botany. The learned Swedish scholar Carl Linnaeus was revolutionizing the subject and guiding the collection and description of new plants. Banks seized the opportunity to see, on the far side of the world, lands that were unfamiliar to Linnaeus or to any other European botanist.

Cook must have been struck by this distinguished youngster who, with all his followers and staff as well as two handsome greyhounds, climbed aboard the *Endeavour* at the port of Plymouth. A worry for Cook was whether his personality would clash with that of Banks, and whether his own authority in the ship might be slightly undermined after the initial phase of mutual politeness was over. Would the two men succeed, month after month and even year after year, in living amiably side by side in the cramped spaces of the ship? Furthermore, would the demands of Banks as a scientist conflict with Cook's imperative to carry out his astronomical mission and then to undertake such additional exploration as might prove possible?

During the voyage both men would keep journals, but neither was tactless enough to describe on paper the personality and habits of the other. Soon Cook came to think well of Banks, who was much younger, much wealthier, socially superior, but less experienced. For his part Banks came to respect Cook, his experience of men and seas, his willingness to learn about new fields of knowledge, and his sheer competence as navigator and leader.

Banks, when on mother Earth rather than a windswept deck, usually dressed with style. The portrait by the celebrated Sir Joshua Reynolds, painted after Banks's return in the *Endeavour*, shows him wearing brown breeches and a long russet coat with fur around the collar. His white shirt is of expensive lace, and his brown waistcoat has many buttons, the last few of which are undone to give space for what may well be a slight paunch. His is a lean, sensitive face, white and mostly clean-shaven but almost in need of a shave around the chin and upper lip. He wears his wavy hair—or perhaps it is a wig—just long enough to cover his ears. It could almost be called an eager face: keen to please but also capable of momentarily taking offense. He is seated, close to a globe of the world and an inkwell holding a quill pen. He almost conveys the impression that the world is his.

Banks's friend Dr. Daniel Solander was at least ten years his senior and also a bachelor. His presence on the *Endeavour* made Banks's botanical mission almost certain to succeed. A protégé of Carl Linnaeus, Solander was so highly recommended that he would have become a professor at St. Petersburg if he had not already decided that his opportunities and friendships in London were more appealing. He made friends easily, and retained them. Portraits or medallions of him suggest that in his public appearances he was rather a dandy, with his hair arranged in an ornate ponytail and his chubby face looking as serious as possible for one who liked to laugh. Those few who saw their "dear Dr. Solander" enjoying what they called "a cheerful glass of wine" had a most favorable impression of him. The smaller numbers who saw him enthusing over and sorting botanical or zoological specimens at a big table marveled at his diligence. As one Londoner exclaimed in his letter to the distant Linnaeus: "Solander is very industrious in making all manner of observations to enrich himself and his country with knowledge in every branch of natural history."

Which country he was enriching did not really matter. Internationalism was floating in the deep blue sky. The voyage of the *Endeavour* was an international quest for knowledge, the benefits of which would accrue to seamen and scholars everywhere. But they would accrue mostly to England, already the greatest naval power but far from the leading colonial power.

While France held nearly three times the population of the British Isles and fielded much larger armies and hoarded far more wealth, England was stronger at sea. The maritime map of 1768, however, did not yet show England's dominance. In the Mediterranean the only English harbors were Gibraltar and the sheltered Port Mahon on the island of Minorca; farther east there was no Union Jack to be seen on any shore of the Mediterranean. England was strong on the Atlantic seaboard of North America and in the West Indies, with fine harbors extending from Jamaica to New York and the noble estuary of the St. Lawrence, but controlled no harbors on the Pacific Coast of the Americas. Spain was still dominant in that continent as a whole, controlling Chile and Peru and Mexico and Cuba, laying claim to the Falkland Islands, and controlling strategic places as far apart as the tropical isthmus of Panama and the bleak Straits of Magellan.

England was still relatively weak in Africa, except in those West African ports where its ships collected cargoes of slaves. In India the dominance of the English over the French was growing but far from complete: Pondicherry was only one of the French ports in India. And in the wide Indian Ocean the French possessed the isles of Mauritius and Reunion whereas England held no strategic island. Along that vital sea route between western Europe and India, the French and the Dutch held significant harbors that English naval men could only envy.

From Cape Town extending east, the Dutch were a strong presence in ports of western India, Ceylon, and the islands of the Dutch East Indies. Even Australia displayed their imprint, being called New Holland. In what later became the Far East, England was a nonentity, owning not one port of call. It had no harbor in China, though the Portuguese did, at Macao. In Japan the English ships were banned. In the long Malay peninsula, England held no harbor. The busy Malay trading post was at Malacca, where the Dutch were in control and Chinese merchants were already busy.

The simplest sign of the wide gaps in England's empire was that south of the equator she owned only two ports. One was St. Helena, which did not even operate a shipyard worthy of the name, and was such a lonely place that less than half a century later the Emperor Napoleon could be safely sent there to live his last years in exile. In the southern hemisphere the only other English port, eventually to be ceded to the Dutch, was Bencoolen in west Sumatra. Guarded by coral reefs, a low-lying, unhealthy place in which houses stood on bamboo posts, it was a kind of Singapore before its time and only a fraction as effective.

Half a century later England was dominant in most seas, and that dominance was derived in part from Cook's voyage in the *Endeavour*. But in 1768, when Cook was about to set out for the far side of the world, he realized that on the main part of the voyage he could, in an emergency, expect help from no English governor or harbormaster. If, on the other hand, he had been a Spanish or Portuguese or Dutch captain, he could at least have anticipated, somewhere along the way, a fortified port flying his country's flag and providing all the supplies, gunpowder, and new masts and sails he needed.

TO THE SEA OF BUTTERFLIES

Almost as soon as the *Endeavour* reached the Bay of Biscay, the scientists looked overboard, hour after hour, and rejoiced in the sight of porpoises, crabs, insects, shoals of little fish, and even the floating sprays of seaweed. Joseph Banks's sense of exhilaration was temporarily erased by almost a week of seasickness while the ability of his artists to draw the nautical specimens netted or hooked from the ocean was restrained by the rocking and rolling of the ship—so much so that Sydney Parkinson, a young Scottish Quaker, could hardly align his pencil with his white drawing paper before a violent motion of the ship tugged it in another direction.

Reaching the latitude of North Africa, the *Endeavour* sailed west toward the Portuguese-owned island of Madeira. A strand of homesickness appeared in Banks's journal, and he expressed his sadness at leaving behind his friends. He and Solander, he lamented, "took our leave of Europe for heaven knows how long, perhaps for Ever." The capital "E" for the word *ever* emphasized the dangers they faced, when left "alone to the Mercy of winds and waves."

Banks's long journal is a treasure. Eccentric, spasmodic, and engaging, it is strenuous in its enthusiasms and dislikes. It is almost as important as Cook's journals with their overwhelming emphasis on rigging and sails, points of the compass, longitude and latitude, gales and calms. Whereas Cook's daily journal was at first a duty, Banks's journal was often a display of pleasure and wonder, expressed with an unusual combination of the dignified and the carefree. Banks wrote in an era when English spelling, punctuation, and maybe grammar were not yet uniform. The creation of a first-class dictionary of the English language helped encourage a uniform way of spelling; but Samuel Johnson's *Dictionary* had not appeared until 1755, and its influence was slow to spread.

Of numerous questions of prose and grammar, Banks and Cook took no notice. They were content to deprive such nations as "england and spain" of their capital letters. In compensation they would donate a capital letter to a word that had no right to one. Sometimes their capital letters were like leaves carried aloft by the wind and then dropped anywhere. But what riveting detail about the voyage sits in many of those sentences! They obviously read each other's journals or discussed what they would write on certain events, but many happenings they saw through completely different eyes.

Their first port of call was the island of Madeira, where they spent five days in sight of the vineyards arranged on the steep slopes. Receiving the warmest of hospitality, Banks and Solander were hailed as masterminds. In a convent garden they were asked where precisely a well should be sunk in search of fresh water, and then questioned enthusiastically in the hope they could predict the coming of thunder and lightning. All the time the nuns chattered, and "there was not the fraction of a second in which their tongues did not go at an uncommonly nimble rate." Alongside the rough country roads, many unfamiliar plants and seeds were collected by the scientists, giving rise to hopes that they would gain an even richer harvest of plants, fishes, and insects in Brazil.

During the passage from Madeira to Rio de Janeiro, Banks and Solander spent day after day, along with the diligent artists and secretary Spöring, in recording and describing plants found at Madeira and not previously known by professional botanists in Europe. To increase their knowledge of the sea Banks made full use of the many days when the ship was becalmed near the equator, and was rowed about in a small boat hour after hour so that he could gather specimens. Rarely had scientists been so handsomely equipped for such pursuits. According to an English friend, "they have all sorts of machines for catching and preserving insects; all kinds of nets, trawls, drags and hooks for coral fishing," and even an astonishing telescope which in clear water could, he claimed, view the seabed if it were not too deep.

They looked forward to tropical Brazil and its vegetation, which so far had been described meagerly in the books of botany. Rio de Janeiro, however, was a frustration. The Portuguese viceroy refused to allow the officers and scientists to come ashore and virtually confined them to their ship for three weeks. In the sun-beaten, landlocked harbor "we sometimes have hardly had a breath of air," lamented Solander. He was lucky enough to sneak ashore, traveling with the boat that replenished casks with fresh water. Many of the native plants that Banks saw came his way by chance, being carried aboard in the grass and hay purchased as fodder for the sheep and other livestock fenced on the deck. Meanwhile, day after day, the botanists looked longingly at the forbidden shore and its tall palm trees, standing within easy swimming distance. They presumably had never before seen palm trees in the wild, and here they were forbidden to touch them or even approach them.

The tropical fruits, purchased ashore on behalf of the ship, were also a disappointment. While the watermelons were delightful, the mangoes tasted of turpentine, the sweet pineapples lacked flavor, the grapes and apples were inferior, the oranges were deficient in tartness, and the peaches—well, they were "abominable." It says something for the exotic plants that were being successfully grown in the few hothouses built for wealthy people in London or for the botanical garden at Kew that Solander had tasted bananas and plantains before he crossed the equator. Therefore he felt entitled to throw scorn at Brazilian fruits, which were "very little better than those you might have tasted at Kew."

Cook formed an even lower opinion of the Portuguese viceroy. He received little help and the barest courtesy from him. It was understandable that the high official was suspicious of Cook because his converted coal ship did not resemble a British warship. Nor was Cook's explanation that he was voyaging to observe the transit of Venus at all convincing, for the governor had not heard of that forthcoming astronomical event. Cook retaliated in his own way. Although his ship anchored in the harbor was always watched by armed men, Cook quietly took the most detailed notes, for the benefit of the British navy, of all the forts inside the harbor.

On December 7, 1768, Cook said his farewell to the Portuguese pilot who escorted the *Endeavour* from the harbor of Rio to the open ocean. Just over five weeks later, the ship was close to one of the more southerly points of South America. The scientists shared in Cook's sense of satisfaction, to which they added a touch of elation. On a memorable day, moths and butterflies and other insects landed on the deck like an invasion from an unseen land, and Banks paid sailors to gather the tiny specimens sprawled on the wooden decks. Soon Banks was able to venture out in a small boat and point his gun at albatrosses and other sea birds.

Making a shortcut through the narrow Strait of Le Maire, near the southeastern tip of South America, the *Endeavour* sailed slowly toward the smoke of native fires curling above the shores of Tierra del Fuego. Anchoring in a bay rarely visited by European ships, she halted there in January 1769 for some chilly days while Banks and Solander and their servants landed on a bleak beach and went inland with all the merriment of picnickers. Then a snowstorm set in. Two of their black servants, Thomas Richmond and George Dorlton, weakened by their quick gulping of a bottle of rum, succumbed to exposure from the extreme cold. They refused to be saved. Solander was lucky to escape with his life.

Alexander Buchan, Banks's scenic painter, was with the party who were surprised by the summer snowfall, but he did not paint that tragedy. His first "view" of this new land was the scene at the anchorage, called the Bay of Good Success, where ship's parties had gone ashore to explore but especially to cut firewood and to fill large wooden barrels with water from a narrow and fast stream. He painted the native peoples, who, wearing warm cloaks, had come down to see the ship, and the Marines with their muskets sloped on the shoulders of their red longcoats. He painted the sailors, each wearing a brimmed hat and the special winter jacket assigned to him, busily rolling the heavy barrels along the ground while two cooks tended a fire that was burning beneath a big black pot. Buchan, an epileptic, and afflicted in addition with a malady in the bowel, was to die three months later, leaving all the artistic work in the hands of Sydney Parkinson.

And now the ship, all of her ten guns having been stored in the hold, was ready to commence the first dangerous leg of the voyage, the passing of the spray-soaked Cape Horn and the passage toward the wide Pacific Ocean. The real voyage of exploration was about to begin, venturing into cold seas that few ships had ever entered.

2

A Missing Continent

🐦 THE PACIFIC OCEAN dwarfs every other ocean. Even the Atlantic, extending almost from North Pole to South Pole, is only half its size. In area the Pacific is larger than all the lands of the globe added together. At its widest points, not far from the equator, it stretches for twelve thousand miles from east to west. At its deepest points it is deeper than any other ocean and also lonelier. Vast expanses hold no land, but that was not known when Cook set out. Other expanses hold a sprinkling of volcanic and coral islands rather like stars in the Milky Way, but elsewhere a ship in distress could be a long way from help. Such a vast ocean embraces a variety of prevailing winds, such hazards as icebergs and fogs, and a myriad of islands. The early European navigators, like the Polynesian navigators who preceded them, had to learn by accident or chance where the islands lay.

Compared to the widest plains in the world, which at least were dissected by rivers and marked by changes of vegetation, this vast plain of the seas offered few landmarks or visible signposts. As ships had trouble in determining their longitude while at sea, their ability even to pinpoint an island was retarded. A group of islands as extensive as the Solomons had been found by Spaniards in the sixteenth century, only to be lost again for two centuries. Where exactly they were, nobody was sure. The Frenchman de Surville was to elucidate the mystery on his way to search for a Jewish colony in the southern Pacific. Cook himself, about to enter the Pacific from the other direction, was to encounter many islands marked on no European map.

CAPE HORN TO TAHITI:
FROM TURMOIL TO PARADISE

The voyage from the Atlantic into the Pacific lay ahead. Near Cape Horn the sea was expected to be high and the winds strong, even though it was summer. The *Endeavour* had to face winds and waves coming toward her from the west, often with such force that they were almost a wall.

At last Cape Horn and its "very high round hummocks" were sighted, though Cook could not feel certain that it actually was the now-famous landmark since no previous navigator had described it so accurately that it could be identified from a passing ship. Carefully he made lunar and solar observations to determine the exact position of this citadel of the oceans. It was a sign of the difficulty of determining the longitude from the deck of a rocking ship that he fixed Cape Horn's position as nearly forty miles west of its true position. In all, nearly five weeks were spent in crossing the seas at the foot of South America.

It was now Cook's resolve to explore some 250 to 300 miles farther southwest before steering toward the tropics. Entering seas previously seen by perhaps only one other navigator, he reached a position about 59 degrees south of the equator. He hoped that here an outreach of the missing continent—perhaps its most eastern shores—might be intercepted. At the end of February 1769 the *Endeavour* was well inside the Pacific Ocean and encountering seas that did not merit the name of "pacific." In dark weather or sunshine, in gales and in hail, she began to make her way to the northwest and to a calmer sea.

No land was seen, no hint of it. After the gusty southwesterly fell away, Cook observed that the high sea continued to roll in from that same point of the compass, even thirty hours after the wind had fallen. This persuaded him that no large landmass could possibly lie in that direction.

The *Endeavour* entered warm waters. On April 4, only eighteen degrees south of the equator, once more she was close to land. During the long voyage even the personal servants and young boys pulled their weight; and it was one of Banks's servants, Peter Briscoe, who was the first to see the land ahead. Cook named it Lagoon Island, but the Polynesians living there already knew it as Vahitahi. He felt slightly apprehensive when men carrying wooden clubs paraded along the shore as if "they ment to oppose our landing." In the next week more islands were passed. There was delight and relief when the high peaks of Tahiti, discovered by Wallis in the *Dolphin* two years earlier, came into sight.

In a sheltered bay of this mountain-topped island, Cook's sailors were astonished at what they saw. Polynesian men, with vivid tattoos on their hips and buttocks, arrived in large canoes, some carrying tall sails. Men of finer physique than the typical Londoner, a dozen of them could be seen excelling in a sport unknown in Europe. They were surfers. Sometimes clinging to a wooden plank, they rode the tops of pounding waves of such immensity that no watching European would dare swim in them. "We stood admiring this very wonderful scene for full half an hour," wrote Banks.

On the island the food was so plentiful that the *Endeavour* men lived as much on tropical fruits and vegetables and fish as on the barrels of food stowed in the ship. Soon they were full of vigor. Curiously the scurvy, briefly present, had vanished from the last sufferer just when the port of Tahiti was in sight. Another disease was about to take its place.

They had been prepared by Wallis's stories and those of his officers and seamen, but the reality of Tahiti was more remarkable. There was so much to marvel at. The women were shapely and seductive, and most of the visiting seamen were so eager to seduce or be seduced that at least half suffered from venereal disease in the following three months. Perhaps it could be called a form of justice, since other seamen, French or British, had earlier introduced the disease to Tahiti.

Cook was taken aback by one Tahitian skill—the art of borrowing or thieving. The Britons believed that the right to private property was one of the great and respected rights, and at first were careless with their possessions. On the first day Solander, while dining and of course conversing, looked down and found that his opera glasses had vanished. Monkhouse the surgeon turned around and, lo and behold, he could not find his snuffbox. Such boxes were usually ornate and valuable, apart from the precious snuff inside, and so were attractive to the Tahitians. It was a disappointment that such affable, noble-looking people could be so light-fingered. To compound the annoyance, Cook lost a pair of stockings kept under his pillow, and Banks lost a horse pistol. These were novel temptations, unknown in Polynesia. On a rural excursion, Banks had the misfortune to "lose" a white jacket and waistcoat, beautifully decorated with silver frogs. The new owner must have presented a dashing sight with his handsome coppery skin robed in ornate white.

Thieving was less likely if the novelties prized by the Polynesians could be obtained by barter. Soon the bartering between seamen and islanders was vigorous. English iron nails had high value, for the local Polynesians had no iron ore and no knowledge of metallurgy. The British seamen were not averse to stealing nails from their own ship in order to clinch a transaction. In effect the *Endeavour* had brought its own trade fair to Tahiti. At first, however, there was little agreement on trading rules and on the punishments for disobeying rules. Early on, an islander stole a musket and, while running away, was shot and killed. Parkinson was shocked that his shipmates while firing at the thief showed "the greatest glee imaginable." Banks, trying to be the peacemaker, did much to induce the islanders to resume friendly relations.

Cook was both a pacifier and a punisher. The more severe way of maintaining discipline among his seamen was a flogging, twelve lashes on the bare back being the punishment for serious breaches of the rules. To this happily chaotic island, for so it seemed, he reluctantly imported the same punishment. He ordered a flogging for a Polynesian who thieved. His punitive stance was understandable. In an orgy of thieving, one or two shining astronomical instruments would be the targets, and so the main purpose of the voyage could be endangered.

THAT SCIENTIFIC SATURDAY

The sky, not the sea, was the prime reason for the *Endeavour*'s voyage. Now it was time for the astronomer, Charles Green, to do his part in preparing to observe the transit of Venus. Son of a Yorkshire farmer, Green had advanced steadily in his learned profession, becoming assistant to the Astronomer Royal at the Greenwich observatory, serving as an official observer of the 1761 transit from Greenwich, and traveling on a mission to the West Indies with Nevil Maskelyne, the

Astronomer Royal. Dedicated to his profession, Green was already a frequent aid to Cook in computing the ship's longitude by the lunar method and in teaching that skill to a few eager midshipmen and seamen. He had his less predictable side: he liked the bottle, and he had a tendency to postpone those long-term tasks that could be shelved without arousing Cook's ire. It was fortunate that Cook was in charge of the entire astronomical project.

An observatory had to be built in readiness for the day when Venus would cross the face of the sun. A fort too was needed to protect the observatory and the valuable scientific instruments that had to be on shore. Called Fort Venus, it consisted of stone walls and surrounding ditches and fences, as well as two heavy guns mounted on carriages and smaller guns on swivels. It was really a village of tents and a couple of solid buildings, with a tent for the officers, another for the Marines, round and capacious tents for Banks and his party, a tiny observatory, and places where the ship's cook, blacksmith, and the makers of sails and barrels could carry out their daily tasks.

The fort was guarded—or at least that was the aim. On the first night, however, a Tahitian entered the compound, crept past the Marine on guard, and stole a vital quadrant. Eventually the damaged pieces were found some distance away, and urgent repairs made by Spöring, who had been a watchmaker in London. Weeks before the time of the transit, nearly everything seemed ready. In prime place stood the special clock to record the time and the two reflecting telescopes, each as long as an arm. But not everything was running quite according to plan, for astronomer Green was still having trouble working out the precise longitude of the observatory itself, a measurement critical for the final result. Even the latitude gave him trouble. Observing sun and stars, he and a few colleagues calculated the latitude of the makeshift observatory at Tahiti a total of forty-eight separate times. The slight variations in the results were disturbing.

Saturday June 3 dawned clear and blue. Although the main telescopes had a power of magnification of 140, the first crucial sighting of the transit was not completely clear. At 9:21 A.M. Venus commenced her long-awaited entry onto the face of the sun. A "dusky shade" prevented an exact measurement being taken, and what should have been a sharp clear line was fuzzy. Venus continued to move imperceptibly across the sun, a black dot on the golden ball. Midday came, and the temperature soared to 119 degrees in the shade. Three o'clock arrived and the air was even hotter. Now all eyes were alert for that final minute when the black dot reached the far edge of the sun, for the exact second of its final departure had to be recorded. They had crossed the world to measure that moment. It arrived at about 3:27 P.M.

Cook, Green, and Solander, the three official observers at Fort Venus, gave nearly everyone the feeling that the observation had been satisfactory; but Cook later declared that the precise time when the transit was complete "could not be observed to any great degree of certainty, at least not by me."

Other trained observers were working on nearby islands. Worried that a cloud might hover over Matavai Bay at the crucial time and blot out their view of the sun, two parties had traveled elsewhere to make their own observations with less expensive equipment. Banks went with one group, not as an observer of Venus the planet but rather as a devotee of Venus the goddess. A turban of Indian cloth wrapped around his head, he must have been a fine sight as he divided his time between a coral rock, where the telescope was fixed on Venus crossing the sun, and the seashore, where many Tahitians had come to inspect him. That evening "3 handsome girls" were enticed, without much effort, to stay the night in the tent occupied by Banks and several officers.

In seventy-six other parts of the globe on that same day, European scientists were observing the same transit of Venus. Cook was not necessarily the most remote—a French expedition had traveled across the narrow isthmus of Panama and then by sea to the southern coast of California—but he was essential. A remote site in the southern hemisphere was of crucial importance to the final result. The data from the observers, finally assembled a few years later, were to be analyzed for years. The measure of agreement by all the astronomers was much closer than in the previous transit; but in the end there was a feeling of slight frustration.

Several lifetimes passed before the main source of this frustration was identified. All the astronomers had been accustomed during their working life to observing the sky in the cool of night. They did not realize that in the full light of a warm day the ground was hot, and the sun beating down on the mirror of the reflecting telescope caused a fuzziness or blurring at the two crucial points where the transit of

Venus had to be so meticulously observed. All this was finally appreciated in the twentieth century when a new technique gave startling results: by bouncing radar echoes off the surface of Venus, so much that was puzzling at last became clear.

THE SEALED PACKET

Cook left England not only with specific instructions, given to him verbally, but with a sealed packet that set out, under tight secrecy, further instructions, to be opened and read when he was ready to leave Tahiti. He carried another letter which he was to show to the captain of any English naval vessel trying to intercept or detain him. That letter, also carrying the signatures of the three lords of the Admiralty, insisted that other English captains and flag officers must not "demand of him a sight of the Instructions."

Cook was instructed to sail south from Tahiti, where there was reason to expect "a Continent or Land of great extent." He was to explore as much of its coast as possible, sounding the depths of the sea, marking the shoals and rocks, fixing the position of the headlands and harbors, and observing the directions of tides and currents. The soil and sea and their products, "the Beasts and Fowls that inhabit or frequent" the land, and the seeds of grains and fruits and trees were all to be observed by him. As he might find valuable minerals or even working mines he was to bring home to England specimens of the main minerals as well as any precious stones. Living plants he should also bring home, in pots, for examination. As for the native inhabitants he should try to make friends with them by displaying "every Kind of Civility and Regard" and presenting them with such "trifles" as pleased them. If the "Southern Continent" did prove to be inhabited, Cook had to claim for King George III such portions of it as seemed important: a harbor here, a strait there, and perhaps any enticing cluster of adjacent islands.

If Cook was to make his name and even win fame, the phase of the voyage lying ahead was his opportunity. It is not denigrating his achievements since leaving England to explain that for all but a few weeks he had been sailing in known seas. Even in the ocean west of Cape Horn, the British commanders John Byron and Sam Wallis and various others had sailed ahead of him, including a forgotten Dutch lawyer who had shown the way almost half a century before. Jacob Roggeveen had come from the handsome Dutch port of Middelburg, the capital of the province of Zealand, and was obsessed by the sea and its mysteries. In July 1721 his three ships set out from Amsterdam to search for the missing continent. After calling at the Falkland Islands, but not landing, his little fleet ventured into the strong seas southwest of Cape Horn. Sailing closer than did the *Endeavour* to the hidden Antarctica, and following for many days the cold latitude of sixty degrees south, he had then sailed to warmer seas, discovering Easter Island on Easter Day in 1722 and, far to the west, the prominent island of Borabora near Tahiti. But scurvy devoured his crew; one small ship, the *African Galley*, was wrecked not far from Tahiti, and the other two ships were seized when finally they reached Java, their crime being to encroach on the maritime monopoly of the Dutch East India Company.

Cook's instructions meant facing what were likely to be strong seas and unfavorable winds. In contrast, all previous European ships in this part of the globe had sailed northwest toward the equator and, harnessing the favorable winds, made their way toward the Solomons and New Guinea and the Dutch East Indies before passing the Cape of Good Hope on their way home. Whereas Roggeveen and Wallis and others had followed routes that were studded with tropical islands, many of which had long been located, Cook was about to sail into unfavorable winds and a temperamental ocean, where no lands lay on the maps but many lay in the imagination.

A CONTINENT TO BE FOUND

The argument in favor of the missing continent was simple: why should there be so much land in the northern hemisphere and so little in the southern hemisphere? Why should oceans dominate the southern hemisphere? Unknown lands must exist somewhere in the vast seas south of the equator.

As Europe, the Middle East, North and Central America, and Asia were entirely north of the equator, and as Africa was mainly north of the equator, and such large islands as Greenland, the Philippines and Japan were also north of the equator, the imbalance was extreme. Should a world presumed to have been designed by God be so lacking in balance and symmetry? Somewhere in the vastness of the Great South Sea, especially in the southern waters between Australia and South America, there must be a large hidden land. When the *Dolphin* reached England in the summer of 1768 with reports that the high mountains of the great missing continent had probably been seen just to the south of Tahiti, the evidence seemed overwhelming.

In Britain, Alexander Dalrymple was the most articulate advocate for the missing southern continent. Born in Edinburgh in 1737, he had sailed to Madras to work for the East India Company and, fascinated by the Orient, became highly knowledgeable about the region even in his late twenties. Not a regular seafarer, he was formally placed in charge of a schooner that visited Canton in 1759. He was a keen buyer of books, able to read Dutch, French, and Spanish, and one of the first Britons to learn of the existence of Torres Strait, which divided Australia from New Guinea. His knowledge of that strait came from rare books he bought privately in India and in London, including two that had once belonged to the library of the French bureaucrat Jean-Baptiste Colbert.

On a visit to France, Dalrymple met the geographer and essayist Charles de Brosses, who supported the view that at least one unknown continent was waiting to be discovered somewhere in the immensity of the Pacific. A fine coiner of words, de Brosses gave to the world two long-lasting names: Australasia and Polynesia. In Europe he was a high provincial official, being president of the parliament—more judicial than legislative—that met regularly at Dijon. He was a scholar of distinction: his field of study stretched from the South Seas to the ancient ruins of the harbor city of Herculaneum, destroyed by the eruption of Vesuvius in Roman times. De Brosses would have become a member of the French Academy in 1770 but for the famous philosopher Voltaire, who disliked him. De Brosses was more scholarly than Dalrymple, and since 1756 his two large volumes on exploration in *Terres Australes* had been a repository of firm knowledge and brave but untested theories. His inescapable defect in the eyes of many Britons was that he was a Frenchman, and so the English-speaking world hailed not him but Alexander Dalrymple as the expert on the missing continent.

Now living in England, Dalrymple was seen by some, including himself, as the kind of world geographer who should be appointed to captain the *Endeavour* on her voyage to the South Seas. The Royal Society favored his appointment. Not a naval officer, and not very experienced as a navigator, he was finally rejected by the Royal Navy as ineligible to captain the *Endeavour*. Understandably disappointed that Cook received the appointment, Dalrymple remained a keen advocate of the voyage but a potential critic of the man who commanded it.

One year after the *Endeavour*'s departure, Dalrymple gave his emphatic opinion on the extent of the missing continent. From west to east it would span 5,323 land miles. Virtually as wide as Asia, it would be the equivalent of all the land extending from Turkey to "the eastern extremity of China." The west coast of New Zealand, he believed, formed the western rim of the missing continent, which would extend nearly all the way to South America. Its more favored regions would probably imitate the climates of the Mediterranean. A continent of contrasts, its colder zones might well be like the climate experienced in the Falklands. But if the warmer regions of this huge missing landmass were found to extend close to tropical Tahiti, as Robertson of the *Dolphin* predicted, the new continent might be a paradise of tropical products as well as those of the temperate zones.

It is no wonder that in the 1760s the missing southern continent—sometimes called Terra Australis Incognita—was viewed as both a colossus and a jewel. It was believed to be the largest piece of unsold real estate in the world. In the imagination of many it would be as fertile and as productive as the Americas. That continent and its nearby islands in the West Indies already produced for Europe a volume of raw materials ranging from tobacco to cotton, coffee to sugar, silver to gold, and many timbers and dyes. It was the assumption of de Brosses and Banks that the missing continent, being so isolated from the other landmasses, would provide a unique collection of flora and fauna.

There was another reason why the missing continent, especially if it happened to have a warm climate, might become a commercial wonderland. Whereas today many tropical lands are retarded in their economic life, in 1770 certain tropical islands were exceptionally vigorous and progressive. The slave economies, especially in the West Indies, experienced fast economic growth, even matching Britain in the first era of her industrial revolution.

As colonies of Britain, France, and Holland, these enslaved tropical lands displayed an economic vigor and an accumulation of wealth not matched in cooler New England and Canada with their independent-minded free settlers. In 1770 Britain's thirteen colonies on the Atlantic coast of North America produced exports averaging, for each person, just over £1. Indeed much of New England's foreign trade depended on the West Indies. In contrast, the slaves and their supervisors in the various English and French colonies of the Caribbean produced, for each person, six times the amount of export wealth that came from New England. Spanish Cuba, by some definitions, made infant New York seem like the Third World.

One sign of the wealth generated by the sugar islands of the West Indies was the price they were willing to pay for slaves shipped from West Africa. The price of slaves boomed. It increased even more rapidly than the price of sugar. Slavery was brutal for the slaves and highly profitable for the owners. Sugar, the chief export of the West Indies, was the maker of fortunes, most of which flowed to British, French, and Spanish plantation owners, merchants, and shippers.

We are so accustomed to viewing an enslaved or tyrannized workforce as the kiss of death that we have lost sight of the fact that in the eighteenth century the combination of tropical sugar and slavery was producing what seemed to be an economic miracle. While we marvel at the rate of economic growth in China today, eighteenth-century economists marveled at the booming sugar islands of the West Indies. It was through the window of the West Indies that geographers enthusiastically envisaged the missing continent of the South Pacific. If much of that new land happened to lie in a temperate zone and enjoy a climate similar to Virginia or South Carolina, it could well become—perhaps with the aid of slavery—a booming part of the globe. And if its native inhabitants were energetic, then no slaves would be needed.

Would this missing continent necessarily be inhabited? Dalrymple had not the wisp of a doubt. "The number of inhabitants in the Southern Continent," he wrote, "is probably more than 50 millions." Such a high total—according to my calculation—would equal the combined population of France, the British Isles, Holland, and Portugal in that year. And these inhabitants, so Dalrymple assumed, would be "civilized."

The president of the Royal Society was James Douglas, the fourteenth Earl of Morton, and he was inclined to share Dalrymple's optimism. A graduate of Cambridge with a fondness for physics and astronomy, Morton was a considerable figure in the patronage of science. In his home city of Edinburgh, one of the most intellectual cities in Europe, he was the first president of the Society for Improving Arts and Sciences; in the House of Lords in London he was an authoritative speaker on many matters; and in Paris he was one of the eight foreign members of the French Academy. He hoped that the *Endeavour* would find the missing continent, and to that topic he had already devoted much thought.

Morton had no doubt that the continent would be peopled. If the continent proved to be very large, it would probably be densely populated. In the informal instructions which, as president of the Royal Society, he prepared for Cook, he put forward two emphatic propositions:

> 1. "The most populous Nations are generally found on large Continents."
> 2. "Populous nations are commonly the most civilized."

It was Morton's view that if the missing continent proved to be "well inhabited," its people would probably show distinct progress in the arts and sciences, and in technology and astronomy. They might even have a "method of communicating their thoughts at a distance." Thanks to Cook, Morton's name was to be prominent on the map of another land: "Moreton Bay" in Queensland honors his name, though Cook had his own way of spelling it.

Would the people of this new land be white? There was an intuition, a hunch, that these people would be like Europeans. Reports and rumors sometimes arose that in newfound lands in the warmer parts of the Pacific Ocean, white people had been seen. The supposition was that they had emigrated from a continent lying farther south. From the decks of the *Dolphin* at Tahiti, Robertson thought he had heard light-skinned visitors speaking Hebrew. Decades earlier, at tropical islands lying near New Guinea, a Dutch navigator reported that the inhabitants had the same white complexion as Europeans "except that they were a little sun-burnt." In the 1570s Juan Fernandez the navigator was said to have found a rich continent of white people, peaceable and civil and "mighty well disposed." Presumably the continent had then disappeared from sight, to await its next discoverer. The stories were enticing and romantic.

The European nation that discovered this missing continent, with unique plants and animals and commodities, might well become the great trader of the southern hemisphere. Indeed that European nation would need a large fleet to carry on the trade with such a distant colony, and so would quickly build up its overall maritime strength. As Dalrymple argued of Britain: "Our navy, undoubtedly, is superior to all others at present, because our colonies are so." But what if the French were to find the missing continent and reap the rewards? Cook did not know that a French navigator was on his way to the same stretch of sea that he was about to explore intensively.

A PRIEST CLIMBS ABOARD

In Tahiti it was almost time for the *Endeavour* to begin the search for the missing continent that mesmerized Lord Morton, Alexander Dalrymple, Charles de Brosses, and hundreds of other people of intellectual standing. It was almost time to commence the adventure that was no longer a secret to Cook's crew—if ever it was a complete secret. In preparation, the *Endeavour* had been overhauled while anchored at Tahiti. During the repairs, all provisions and most of the other stores had been carried onto land, and now they were brought back and restowed. A ship on a long voyage was like a big warehouse, and as the voyage went on and the warehouse became emptier, the use of space could be replanned. Now an area of the ship's deck was almost jammed with pigs, hens, and other livestock bought in Tahiti.

Aboard were two special Polynesian passengers: Tupaia and his young friend and servant. Eager to see the world, they rejoiced that they had been chosen ahead of the scores of other Tahitians who wished to travel in this glamorous ship carrying so many sails. The decision to invite the two Polynesians was made reluctantly. Cook at first did not want them, but Banks thought they would be a vital source of information about the islands, their peoples' way of life, and even the missing continent if it were found. They would also be a public sensation when at last the ship reached England.

Banks knew that in England he would have to pay for the upkeep of the two Polynesians, but he already supported numerous servants and supernumeraries in London and on his large Lincolnshire estate. Defending Tupaia, Banks pointed out that some of his own friends at home "kept lions and tygers at larger expence than he will probably ever put me too." In due course, it was hoped, the two Polynesians would return to their home islands in another exploring ship. To his credit, Banks agreed to provide from his own stores in the ship some of the necessities and luxuries that Tupaia would require for the voyage. The two men were to become friends and equals, or almost equals, for Tupaia was proud and reluctant to bow before anybody. Banks was not unlike him.

On July 13, the day of departure from Tahiti, Tupaia cried a few tears when he saw the farewelling canoes grow dim in the distance. But soon he was at home in the ship and almost an officer in the respect he commanded and the privileges he received. All the sailors came to know him—he became a center of attention—and most pronounced his unfamiliar name as *Too-bai-ah*. Around the ship he was a friend, a fountain of advice, a source of merriment, a chef who showed onlookers how to kill a dog and eat the baked flesh, a fisherman of some ingenuity, and also a capable pilot. A priest, reared on the priestly island of Ra'iatea, he was ready to pray for favorable winds. He was a geographer too, with an impressive knowledge of many islands that did exist and maybe a few that didn't. Under the tuition of astronomer Green, he quickly learned to speak more English, and taught others to speak his own language with its swift succession of sounds that were not all picked up with ease by Britons.

Before sailing south in search of the missing continent, the *Endeavour* sailed to other nearby islands, some of which were collectively christened by Cook as the Society Islands—less in honor of the Royal Society of his homeland than because they formed a cluster or society. In nearly every direction were other islands, all smaller than Tahiti, and in negotiating the narrow entrances to their shallow harbors or lagoons, Tupaia already proved valuable. As always, Cook employed skilled seamen to stand on the platform at the side of the ship and cast the long line weighted with a lead, so that, falling to the bottom, it indicated the depth of water and even the texture of the seabed. At the entrance to the island of Huahine, however, Cook was taught an easier method. Tupaia called on a local man to jump from his canoe and demonstrate whether the channel would allow the *Endeavour* to glide safely through. Diving several times into the narrow channel, the man swam under the keel and rudder of the ship and cheerfully surfaced with vital information, which Tupaia translated for the benefit of Cook and the seaman at the wheel. Man for man the Polynesians were more experienced swimmers and divers than the Europeans. How many in the *Endeavour* were able to swim we do not know but, at a guess, nearly every Marine and more than half the sailors could not swim.

On August 9, 1769, nearly four months after reaching Tahiti, the *Endeavour* was ready to sail away in search of the missing continent. On this day Tupaia was seen as such a vital guide that when the ship sailed into the open, unmapped ocean, Banks confided in his journal that the ship was now "in search of what chance and Tupaia might direct us to." There was a feeling that this confident guide, so conversant with the geography of the region, might even guide them to distant mountains which would turn out to be the missing continent. Steering to the south, in keeping with the secret instructions, after some four days the *Endeavour* reached Rurutu, the very last of the cluster of islands, where Cook hoped to obtain local hints or advice on the whereabouts of the missing continent. But the only advice he received, from islanders armed with wooden spears and lances, was to "go away."

Tupaia made it known that he thought the *Endeavour* should be sailing west rather than on its present southerly course. But southward sailed the ship, with Cook closely following his naval instructions. Not far beyond the last of the clustered islands, there were several hours of elation when a big land seemed to be in sight. Tupaia even knew the name of it. The ship changed course to inspect the new land, which in due course converted itself into a low-lying cloud. The long-awaited continent, so eagerly anticipated, continued to hide itself.

On August 25 came a happy anniversary: one year since the commencement of the voyage in England. Officers and gentlemen in the big cabin celebrated with a cask of London-brewed porter and a round cheese from Cheshire. This was a meek substitute for the celebration likely to take place when the continent itself, that new America, came into view.

The ship ventured almost to forty degrees south—as far south as Cook's secret instructions had ordered him to sail. Tahiti was now almost fifteen hundred miles away. The winds became chillier, for August was the coldest month in the far southern hemisphere. In the wild expanse of rolling waves, not an island was to be seen—not even a bank of clouds that looked like an island. In compensation, on evenings when the clouds were few, the sky was magnificent. The Southern Cross seemed closer than ever. On one memorable night near the end of August there appeared, aloft, another brilliant spectacle: a bearded comet. First seen at 4 A.M., it stood to the north, sixty degrees above the horizon. During several other dark mornings it was viewed with awe by all the men on duty and was vividly described by midshipman Matra as lying very close to "the bright star in Orion's right foot." Charles Green, the astronomer, probably informed those who were still slightly homesick, after their taste of the Cheshire cheese, that the wonderful comet might well be visible in the British skies by their friends at home; and indeed it was.

At night that same comet was viewed with wonder by the seamen in a large French ship that was crossing the Pacific Ocean also in search of a missing continent. The French ship, approaching from warmer seas, would come closer and closer to the *Endeavour*, and a fortnight before Christmas would almost be in sight.

3

A French Floating Bazaar

◆ ON JUNE 2, 1769, the day before the transit of Venus, a ship left her anchorage in the Indian port of Pondicherry. Flying the French flag and carrying a large crew of sailors and a small contingent of Marines, she slowly disappeared with the aid of the southeast breeze.

In this little French corner of India there was much guessing and a flurry of rumors before the ship passed below the horizon. Since she was known to carry ample supplies of salted meat, dried biscuits, flour, rice, wine, and other provisions, and since many members of her crew had received six months' pay in advance, she was assumed to be leaving on a long voyage. The belief of the local French officials was that she would call at distant ports, including Canton in China, Manila in the Philippines, Jakarta in Java, and maybe even Japan. In fact the captain carried instructions so tightly guarded that even his first officer did not know of their intended destination.

The ship, just two years old, had been built at the busy port of Nantes, on France's Atlantic coast. Bearing a biblical name, *St. Jean-Baptiste*, she was trading along the coasts of India and Ceylon before her captain agreed to make a far longer voyage. She was well suited for that voyage, though the manner in which she rolled in wild weather upset the stomachs of some seamen. Of 650 tons—how those tons were computed is not clear—she was much larger than Cook's *Endeavour*, which was registered as 369 tons burthen. Her arms too were superior. The French ship carried twenty-four twelve-pounder guns, twelve other guns, and scores of handheld muskets. It was hoped that the heavy guns on deck would enable her, "as soon as news is received of a declaration of war," to capture the typical English merchant ships and even outgun the larger ships of England's powerful East India Company. Most pirate ships had little hope against her and would be quickly sunk if the French gunners were accurate.

The ship's captain, Jean-François-Marie de Surville, stamped the deck with his authority. He came from French families that belonged to the sea, but it could almost be said that the sea belonged to them. Many of his relatives were officers in ships trading in the Indian Ocean or patrolling far and wide for the French navy. He himself was born on January 18, 1717, at Port-Louis, in Brittany; his hometown stood on the same estuary as Lorient, a newer port created to accommodate the warehouses and shipyards of the growing fleet of the East India Company of France. Going to sea as a boy of ten, and visiting places as remote as China, he eventually attained the post of captain in a merchant ship and then in a naval vessel. Twice a captive in English ships during the warfare in the mid-1740s, he received rapid promotion in the Seven Years' War, winning in 1759, in the Bay of Bengal, the Cross of St. Louis for bravery during a naval action in which he was wounded.

In the French port of Nantes he married Marie Jouanneaulx. She gave birth to two sons who in childhood did not often see their father. De Surville spent much of his time at sea or in the ports of overseas France, especially in the Indian Ocean, where he knew Madagascar and Mauritius and Réunion, on which island he had his own farm. He was also well known in Pondicherry and other French ports on the Coromandel Coast of India. Pondicherry, from which he set out on his remarkable voyage of exploration, was a trading post on that two-hundred-mile strip of coast where there was not one natural harbor. Along that coast the commerce in textiles was so large that the French and Dutch and Danish and English all had their own distinct town-ports. They called them ports, but on that flat coast, where the surf boomed during the northeast monsoon, they were open roadsteads posing as ports. The deep-sea ships coming from Europe usually anchored a small distance from the shore and were loaded by catamarans and other small boats buzzing out from the port.

Pondicherry, so familiar to de Surville, was a minor prize in Europe's naval wars. The Dutch had captured it in the seventeenth

century, and the British captured it three times in the next century—
once when de Surville was living there. Indeed his youngest son, an
army officer, died from injuries received during the siege of 1778.
But after the peace negotiations it was invariably handed back to
France; and it was still their possession in the middle of the twentieth
century, several years after the British finally granted independence
to India. The long naval and commercial rivalry between France and
England shaped de Surville's life.

What de Surville looked like, and whether he was sinewy or
brown-eyed or walked with a swing of the arms, we do not know. He
is said to have been witty. He also knew when to say nothing, and
aboard the *St. Jean-Baptiste* he confided to no one the secret instructions in his possession. They came from the owners, of whom he was
one, and from French colonial officials, who were also shareholders
in the voyage. They were both written and verbal, and the written
copies have vanished.

If a European committee had been set up to select one navigator to
explore the Pacific Ocean, de Surville and not Cook might well have
been the impartial choice. His experience of dangers and adversity
was wider. He knew the prevailing winds and currents of much of the
South China Sea, the Bay of Bengal, and other tropical seas, whereas
Cook had not seen the tropics until his *Endeavour* made her voyage
toward Tahiti. De Surville's record in war and peace was exceptional,
and a note in the French archives praises him as "a great sailor, a fine
soldier, suited to great enterprises." While he did not draw pains-
taking charts, a craft in which Cook excelled, and while he was not
masterly in calculating his exact position at sea, he was at this time
far, far more experienced than Cook in commanding a ship in peace
and war. Aged fifty-two, he was eleven years older than Cook, and his
promotion had come early in his career, so that in December 1759 he
was captain of the *Centaure*, a warship of sixty-four guns, when Cook,
not yet a lieutenant, was publishing his very first map. Like Cook, he
was brave and determined. He was capable of managing his ship, his
officers and crew, and all the complexity of detail involved in a long
voyage through strange seas with calmness and competence.

Toward his sailors and Marines de Surville was not as strict and
punitive as Cook. On occasions he vexed his fellow officers by trans-
ferring scarce food from their table to the plates of sick seamen. Feel-

ing some kinship toward the native peoples whom he met, he thought it was usually—but not always—sensible to treat them as worthy human beings. Late in the voyage, officers would be rather dismayed to see the captain invite a Pacific islander to sit at the dining table in the officers' cabin, and have him served first of all and given larger helpings than were set on the plates of the senior Frenchmen at table.

Captain de Surville, his second-in-command, Guillaume Labé, and other members of the ship's company were shareholders in this voyage by the *St. Jean-Baptiste*. Among other investors were French merchants and officials living in western France and in eastern India, including Governor Lauriston of Pondicherry. The large sums they invested were visible in the variety of cargo that Indian laborers had carried aboard and stowed, not very efficiently, in the ship's hold. There were packages holding nutmeg, cinnamon, pepper, cloves, and other spices. Below were enough bales of material to fill a dozen street bazaars: Bengal cotton cloth, Madras taffeta, printed cloth from Pondicherry and other ports on the Bay of Bengal, shirts and embroidered cuffs, tablecloths, barbers' towels, and costly hand-painted handkerchiefs. India was then far ahead of Lancashire in the production of stylish fabrics, and a busy exporter of textiles to England. Indeed the names of calico, chintz, and muslin were Indian in origin. While most of the ship's cargo came from India, some novelties came from distant ports—including three hundred bottles of brandy from France and various carpets from Constantinople where the French were ensconced as the main European traders.

The ship was so crammed with items for sale or barter that scant space was left in several of the officers' cabins. The first officer could barely stretch his legs and arms, such was the stack of his personal goods and supplies. On the main deck stood a small barnyard of bullocks and goats, to be replenished by poultry and livestock bought at the early ports of call.

The crew numbered close to two hundred, or more than double that of the *Endeavour*. Just over half were Frenchmen, mostly from the ports of Brittany, with a few Germans and other Europeans, while the remainder were Africans and Indians. The majority of the crew and all the officers were Christians, but on board there were also numerous Muslims who were mostly known as Moors—so named after the Islamic inhabitants of North Africa. One Muslim, born in Bengal, supervised the Indians working on deck and also served as the lamp attendant. Known as "the cassobe of the lascars," he was to die just when the ship entered the unexplored Coral Sea.

THE SEARCH FOR A COLONY OF JEWS

According to de Surville's orders, his first task was to trade with ports on the far side of the Bay of Bengal, to the east of India. His second and all-important task was to find the lost but ever-inviting continent and to trade there. This faraway land, or an adjacent island, was believed to house a colony or group of Jewish traders.

English navigators exploring the Pacific were the main source of the reports and rumors that inspired de Surville's expedition. Captain Wallis in the *Dolphin* had not only discovered Tahiti but had glimpsed, it was believed, an adjacent mass of land in the South Pacific. Of that landmass the French merchants living in Pondicherry heard secondhand reports. Possibly the reports came to them from Cape Town, where Wallis's ship had anchored during her return passage to England and where certain of his crew had gossiped about the elusive land they had seen or almost seen. Merchants and sea captains at Pondicherry were especially excited by this gossip. Their port, they knew, was much closer than London and Paris to the new southern land, vague as its position was.

We know something about the enticing reports reaching Pondicherry. On the next-to-last day of 1768 a letter from Jean-Baptiste Chevalier, a high French official in India, reported that an English ship exploring the South Pacific had been blown off course. She had eventually reached "an island which did not figure on the charts." The news was initially kept secret as long as possible, as were the results of nearly all voyages of discovery during that period, but when the ship returned the news was leaked. According to the French official, "certain people from this ship have been so enthusiastic about this discovery that they were unable to stop themselves from gossiping." That France rather than England should exploit the discovery was vital. As the official confided in his letter to the minister for marine in distant Paris, he felt "honor bound to sacrifice everything to make it succeed," such was the potential worth of the discovery "for our nation." To the question, where exactly was the discovery?, the French informant was not completely certain.

The fascination with this island was gilded by another rumor: that it was inhabited by Jewish traders. The belief in the presence of Jews seemed to have a basis of fact. George Robertson, the master as well as one of the more experienced men in Wallis's ship, claimed to have seen, in several double-canoes arriving at Tahiti, an impressive, fair-skinned people who had "a great resemblance to the Jews." They were fairer than any other people he had seen in the islands. They were also stout, "Jolly fatt well made people." They had holes in their ears, as if they were accustomed to wearing "some sort of Jewelry when at home." They were the masters, and the darker-skinned paddlers of the double-canoes were their obedient servants. Befitting their status, the stout ones sat together beneath a canopy that sheltered their skin from the sun. The stately scene reminded Robertson of the grand ceremonial barges favored by the grandees of the city of London, though the canoes were "not so finely decorated."

Their long-bearded, venerable leader wore a white turban and finer clothes than the others. He spoke a foreign language, several words of which were not entirely strange to Robertson, who wrote them down; later the paper blew away or was misplaced. Robertson gave his opinion that these fair-skinned people greatly resembled those tribes of wandering Jews "which are Scaterd through all the knowen parts of the Earth." His deduction was that the Jewish-like people came from the high lands in the southwest, originating—in his view—in that "Southern Continant."

A minor happening strengthened this mysterious image of the lordly Jews. Their double-canoes had arrived at dusk, on the evening before the *Dolphin* was finally to sail from Tahiti. There was no time to send a boat across to investigate the canoes, and no time in which to arrange a meeting with these exotic people. Questions were asked of bystanders, who replied that they had never before seen these visitors. So the *Dolphin* sailed away, carrying this tantalizing, unsolved mystery.

Sketches of the arriving Jews were penned by Robertson in his journal, which for decades remained unpublished and read by few. But what he saw or thought he saw, others aboard saw too, and no doubt they freely discussed or debated the mystery of these Jewish inhabitants of the South Seas. Such talk probably found its way to the port of Cape Town, where Captain Wallis's *Dolphin* called in February 1768 and remained long enough for some of the ship's gossip to circulate in those taverns where rum and brandy were sold and rumors changed hands. The same rumors presumably also surfaced in London, though Cape Town, being closer to French India, was probably the source of the first stories to reach Pondicherry.

Alexis Rochon, later a chronicler of French voyages, was present in Pondicherry when he heard of this episode. As he pithily recorded it, "the rumor spread that an English vessel had found in the South Sea a very rich island where, among other peculiarities, a colony of Jews had been settled." One aim of de Surville's voyage was "to search for this marvelous island" and do business with its Jewish traders.

For more than a thousand years Jews had been trading in those Asian ports where they could gain official permission to settle. They were trading with the Chinese in Canton as early as the ninth century. Three centuries later Jewish traders were reliably reported to be busy in Aden in the Red Sea and in bazaars at the mouth of the Persian Gulf. A few centuries later they were prominent in the Indian port of Cochin, which was on a finger-shaped island running parallel to the west coast. There they were trading cloth, pepper, and other spices probably before the first Portuguese arrived along the new sea route they had opened by way of the Cape of Good Hope. In Cochin their Paradesi synagogue, built as early as 1568, can still be visited. Its clock tower was erected and the blue-and-white Chinese-willow tiles first decorated the synagogue's interior during the same century as de Surville set sail from India. While most of its congregation consisted of so-called Black Jews, some were new traders attracted from Constantinople and Syria. Wealthy families, they lived in style and some splendor. An English visitor of the 1770s praised the grand house of long-bearded Isaac Surgun, with its precious tableware and, nearby, its spittoons of pure silver. Here Jewish hospitality was dispensed with "all the profusion that wealth can command and generosity display."

Shipowners, financiers, and traders, these Jews of Cochin were renowned for their wealth. After the Dutch supplanted the Portuguese as the rulers of Cochin, several of the local Jews lent large sums to the Dutch East India Company. Their web of contacts was wide, and to Cochin they imported copper from Japan and textiles from China. Two other Jewish settlements with their synagogues, one founded in about the year 1200, flourished and waned near Cochin. Therefore the idea that other Jews might be living and trading in the remote Pacific was not bizarre.

Jews were widely known as wanderers, as people of enterprise. Perhaps those reported to be living in the South Pacific had been expelled from colonial ports in South Asia or South America, thus forcing them to find other havens, or perhaps they had set out on their own initiative for what were then called the South Seas. Even New Guinea was said to be a home for wandering Jews. William Dampier was the English authority on this mysterious island, and a map of his voyages around the year 1700 pointed to Jewish people—thought to be descendants of the ten tribes of Israel—living there.

De Surville obviously saw a distinct advantage in a distant Pacific land possessing its own colony of Jewish traders. Having mastered the resources of that region, these traders would have acquired for their shops and warehouses such local commodities and handicrafts as were tradable. If there were gold and silver in the district they would be trading in it. These possibilities inspired de Surville's syndicate. Whereas Cook was an explorer and chartmaker, de Surville was an explorer and trader, and his ship was packed with goods that would sell quickly. The wealth that he hoped to carry back to Pondicherry—in exchange for his cargo—would presumably be pearls and other jewels, and ingots and ornaments of silver and gold.

THE MYSTERIOUS CAPTAIN DAVIS

Here was a French expedition designed partly out of rumor and speculation. What London knew about Tahiti and the surrounding seas was also a mixture of astute observation, rumor, and rosy speculation, but London had the advantage that one of its ships had actually discovered Tahiti. In contrast, the French in Pondicherry had to rely on garbled secondhand reports and rumors.

The rumor of the recent sighting of the Jews somewhere in the South Pacific was quickly merged with another enticing theory. This was the hope that a land first seen in the preceding century by an Englishman named Davis, and not seen since, might well be the land inhabited by these enterprising Jews. Davis Land—sometimes called David Land—was a floating dream. More than eighty years earlier a British buccaneer and sea captain, Edward Davis, had glimpsed the coast of a supposedly big land in the southeastern quarter of the Pacific Ocean. Sailing past the Galapagos and heading toward the stormy tip of South America after a fight with the Spanish in 1686, Davis had reportedly passed a sandy island and then seen a long stretch of high land running to the northwest. Irrespective of whether it was a distinct land or a mountain-shaped cloud, irrespective of whether it was closer to the coast of Chile or of Peru, it came to be known as Davis Land. William Dampier publicized it in his much-read book *A New Voyage Round the World*, first issued in 1697. He offered the exciting hypothesis that it could be the missing continent.

Davis Land is now viewed as a fairy tale. But it was not necessarily a fairy tale at the time. Wallis in the *Dolphin* spent about eleven days searching for it in 1767. The search was soon renewed by two French ships, which we will meet in a later chapter. It was just when Davis Land was being so energetically sought that the rumor of the remote Jewish outpost reached India. Jean-Baptiste Chevalier, governor of the French colony at Chandernagore, which was within sight of England's growing port of Calcutta, wrote to the government in Paris expressing the view that the mysterious Jewish land was probably "the one seen by the Englishman David." To many French listeners, Davis and David were the same.

France, having lost Canada at the end of the Seven Years' War, was eager to acquire new trading worlds—and Davis Land was one of them. Most geographers believed it lay closer to South America than any other known continent. The common view was that Davis Land lay about twenty-seven or twenty-eight degrees south of the equator. Its longitude, however, was not known, and that was the cause of the unceasing speculation, for it sat in the widest ocean in the world. Some observers believed that Davis Land was not far from Easter Island. Others believed it might be closer to New Zealand. Wherever it was, it was perhaps the homeland or the adopted land of those Jewish-like visitors arriving in their canoes just when the *Dolphin* was about to depart from Tahiti.

The expectation in Pondicherry was that Davis Land would prove to be rich in gold. In the opinion of Pierre-Antoine Monneron, who was a clerk aboard the *St. Jean-Baptiste* and a minor shareholder in the ship's cargo, the mysterious land lay on the same latitude as Capiazo, "where the Spaniards get gold from in immense quantities." The west coast of South America, especially Peru, was then the world's main mine of precious metals, and its geography gave rise to a widespread theory—which was partly accepted by Joseph Banks—that precious metals were more likely to be found on certain east–west lines than on others. Perhaps Davis Land lay on that golden latitude. Monneron in his private journal summed up all these snippets of information then circulating in moneyed circles in Pondicherry: "What they heard about this island was so extraordinary that it deserved the whole of their attention."

Before de Surville sailed away on his search, he must have known that the British were sending another expedition to the Pacific, ostensibly to observe the transit of Venus but perhaps also to look for the lands that so excited him and his financiers. News from London and Paris was slow to reach Pondicherry. But there was ample time, before de Surville set sail, for reports to arrive from Europe that the *Endeavour* was actually being fitted out to make the voyage. As Pondicherry would be an important French site for observing the transit of Venus in June 1769, some of its citizens eagerly awaited further information about the British plans to observe the same transit in the Pacific Ocean. Would the British expedition also look for the mysterious lands that so excited Jean de Surville? This was an additional reason for de Surville to accelerate his search.

A VOYAGE TO EVERYWHERE

De Surville's ship, the *St. Jean-Baptiste*, was really a French floating bazaar when, leaving Pondicherry behind, she crossed the wide Bay of Bengal toward the Malay Peninsula. On the way de Surville intended to learn whether Denmark had founded a trading settlement on the isolated Nicobar Islands; but reaching the islands near midnight and facing unfavorable winds he did not venture toward them. Calling instead at the Dutch port of Malacca, he waited while rudder and tiller were repaired. Further along his course, while halting to take on fresh water, the ship lost an anchor, which embedded itself in the coral reef.

Hoping to trade on the east coast of the Malay Peninsula, de Surville favored the river port of Trengganu, but it was not marked clearly on his maps. Eventually he was guided there by the captain of a small British vessel. In hot and steamy weather de Surville steered his ship up the river, congested with tiny fishing boats, and finally reached a straggling settlement consisting mainly of palm-thatched houses and muddy streets, of which the only walkable one was the Chinese street. When the daily market and bazaar was opened at 3 P.M., he saw how eagerly the Malays bought his red and green and purple fabrics and a fine, light-woven cloth which, being black, they donned when in mourning.

Nine hundred miles to the northeast, in the South China Sea, de Surville reached one of the Batan Islands, halfway between the Philippines and Taiwan. He was probably guided by the writings of William Dampier, the English navigator who had visited the islands some seventy years earlier and reported the presence of gold. Alongside the incoming French ship, more than seventy local canoes from Bashee Island jostled for position. The islander men, their haircuts reminiscent of French Franciscan monks, were happy to buy a very simple item: the strips of linen cloth cut from Indian-made trousers. In turn, most of the French seamen and Marines bought the local liquor made from sugar cane, and were drunk by the end of the day.

The *St. Jean-Baptiste* sailed away with three islanders. They had been kidnapped, partly in the hope they would replace Breton sailors who had run away at the last port of call. It was assumed that the kidnapped Filipinos would quickly learn the French language and would impart vital knowledge about Bashee Island. The ship also carried away seventy-seven pigs and about as many young goats, payment for them being made with new knives.

Already 11 weeks into her voyage, the ship was about to enter seas which few Europeans had crossed. She was sailing toward the Solomon Islands, which had been discovered by the Spaniard Mendana 201 years earlier and not located since. They were really another version of Davis Land—a land found and then lost again. There was the similar hope that the Solomons, like Davis Land, would yield gold and spices. Indeed they were called the Solomons because they were believed to have supplied the beaten gold with which King Solomon adorned his temple in Jerusalem. Solomon had built a navy on the shore of the Red Sea, and his servants had set forth for Ophir, from which were returned, every three years, a consignment of gold and silver, ivory, apes and peacocks, all made memorable in John

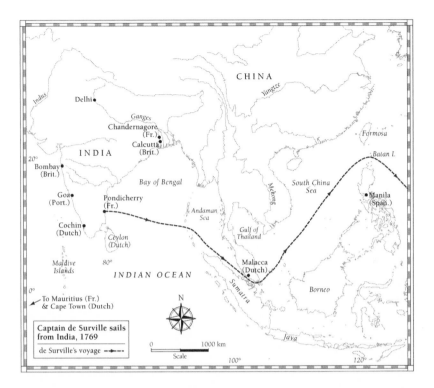

Masefield's poem "Cargoes." From Ophir came also precious stones and sawn sandalwood, which was said to have been part of the new temple in Jerusalem. Many French and British merchants believed that biblical Ophir lay somewhere in the west Pacific.

Following a southeasterly course, the *St. Jean-Baptiste* crossed tropical seas toward the northern coast of New Guinea and the Solomon Islands. She "is laboring heavily," wrote the captain, as she rolled awkwardly in strong cross-seas and her masts and deck timbers began to creak unduly. "The sea was frightful," he recorded on Friday, August 25. After the storm, the same comet that Cook saw in the South Pacific appeared in the clearing sky "a little above the horizon." The bearded comet that was so brilliant in the Pacific night sky on the last days of August 1769 and has not been seen since was eventually named Napoleon's Comet, having first appeared in the month of his birth.

A new comet was often seen as an omen of bad luck. It seemed to be an ill omen for de Surville, who sailed slowly toward the east, making little headway in the tropical seas. Often becalmed, the *St. Jean-Baptiste* succeeded in covering a mere eighty miles in all during the last six days of September. The hot, steamy atmosphere vexed many of the crew, the rats and cockroaches and other pests multiplied, and the first signs of scurvy were detected amongst seamen.

If scurvy spread, it could ruin the voyage. The symptoms of the disease included swollen and even putrefied gums, foul breath, teeth so loose they fell out, a sallow complexion, swollen arms and legs, spots on the limbs, and stiffness in the knee joints. Many men experienced vomiting. As Captain de Surville must often have observed, many sufferers lying in their hammocks felt inwardly that they were strong, but as soon as they tried to walk they felt extreme weakness and langor; it was hopeless to expect work from them. Sometimes the disease set in slowly, but at other times it was swift, ending with pneumonia. In some ships, after scurvy set in, virtually none of the sick recovered—so long as the ship was at sea. Once the ship reached a port, and fresh fruits and vegetables and meat were added to the diet, recovery of many of the sick sailors could be quick.

Alarmed at the spread of scurvy, de Surville was eager to find a harbor surrounded by fertile soil and luxuriant vegetation. After more than seven weeks at sea, the *St. Jean-Baptiste* anchored off the western end of Santa Isabel Island in the Solomons, near an inhabited, island-fringed bay which he christened Port Praslin in honor of a French minister of the day. That he was among the Solomon Islands he did not realize, though his maps and journals were to play a vital part in later defining where the long-lost Solomon Islands really lay. Indeed some of his officers believed that they were at the very eastern end of New Guinea.

De Surville assumed that if the sick could go ashore during the hours of daylight and eat fresh food and breathe "the land air," they would recover. But fresh flesh was not to be found. De Surville saw no livestock, and his men caught virtually no fish because the jagged coral rocks in the bay prevented them from using their nets. When they stepped ashore they were able to gather very few of the coconuts, figs, and bananas that flourished on the island. Fortunately they did gather the tender and edible heart of about 100 cabbage palms that they chopped down, and they heaped their longboat with firewood and filled 196 casks with fresh water. But the price of all these acquisitions was high.

While ashore, out of sight of the anchored ship, a French boating expedition was taken completely by surprise. Armed islanders appeared—several hundred of them. The French sergeant of Marines was fatally wounded, at least three sailors were hurt, and Labé, the officer in charge, was hit twice in the thighs by lances; the wooden point of one lance remained buried in his thigh, festering. While hopelessly outnumbered, the French possessed the surprise weapons of gunpowder and firearms. The islanders did not know what do in the face of such mysterious weapons and were almost massacred. When Labé went to inspect the site, he found that thirty-six to forty had died and that other corpses had been carried away on the shoulders of their kinsmen. "All around this place," he wrote, "one saw nothing but blood." There was further retaliation that night. In the light of the moon, two canoes were fired on, and several islanders must have been killed, drowned, or severely wounded.

Captain de Surville was highly indignant when he heard of the episode. He accepted overeagerly the assurance that the islanders had treacherously attacked his men. He christened the islands the Arsacides, or the land of the assassins. In short, he named them after those well-known Muslims—virtually "terrorists" in the eyes of medieval Christianity—who had once made suicidal attacks from their fortresses in Lebanon. So that he could learn more about these islands— just in case any future Frenchman was bold enough to return—his crew kidnapped a boy aged thirteen or fourteen. For some time the boy lay on the deck "shamming death without opening his eyes," and then came to life after the surgeon made him drink a reviver. Quickly the boy learned French and became a useful member of the crew. Useful seamen were increasingly needed, for perhaps half a dozen had died of scurvy even while the ship was in the Solomons.

IN THE SHADOW OF SCURVY

Here were two ships, exploring in the Pacific Ocean, far apart but converging on the same goal. In the following two months the *Endeavour* and the *St. Jean-Baptiste* would come closer and closer. But their success, even at this stage, depended on the health of their crews.

In the French and English navies during the preceding hundred years, more men had died from scurvy than had died from battle wounds. In the merchant navy, probably more sailors and passengers died from scurvy than from shipwreck. In voyages of exploration, and they were always long, scurvy was a regular killer. George Anson, in circumnavigating the globe in the early 1740s, lost perhaps eight of every ten men to scurvy. In the 1760s Samuel Wallis, on his voyage to and from Tahiti, also had to combat serious scurvy among his crew.

What actually caused scurvy was a topic of long debate in nautical and medical circles, and it was not until the twentieth century that Vitamin C was firmly identified as the cure. In the era of Cook and de Surville, a few talented medical men had already glimpsed the cause. Foremost was the Scottish doctor James Lind. Learning from the experience of a few other mariners, especially on the route between Europe and India, he thought lemons and oranges were a potential cure. In 1747 he snatched the opportunity to conduct his own experiment in a British warship, the *HMS Salisbury*, which was cruising in west European seas. After many of the sailors became sick with scurvy, Lind selected pairs of men and gave them different treatments in order to see which pair responded and which pair languished. A brilliant experiment, it was ever so simple. To one group of sufferers, Lind handed out daily palliatives as diverse as slightly alcoholic cider, elixir of vitriol, and seawater. These "cures" achieved nothing. The startling results came from the group provided with fresh lemons and oranges. Until the supply of fruit ran out, they "ate greedily," and much of their health and vigor returned. Six years later in Edinburgh, James Lind published his findings in a book entitled *Treatise of the Scurvy*.

In the 1760s he tested his cure in the large naval hospital that he conducted at Haslar in the port of Plymouth. The navy ensured that he had plenty of scurvy patients, for the malady was common at sea. Lind's remedies, however, were not easily applied. Lemons and oranges could be imported to England only at certain times of the year. And even if a consignment of citrus fruits was to be loaded into ships about to sail on voyages of exploration, the fruit was not likely to stay fresh for a year. There were many ports on the far side of the world where fresh lemons and limes were procurable in no month of the year. Moreover Lind did not succeed in persuading ships' surgeons that his naval hospital near Plymouth was a huge success in treating scurvy. It was widely argued that typical scurvy patients, once they reached land, had a fair chance of recovering, no matter what treatment they received.

A version of Lind's remedy, supplied to Cook by the Admiralty, came in the form of syrup. Loaded into the *Endeavour* were kegs of syrup derived from boiling down the juice of lemons and oranges. It was known as "rob of lemon," "rob" being the Arab or Persian word for syrup. Unfortunately the process of boiling destroyed nearly all the vitamin in the lemon. Nonetheless a few scientific men on board, even the surgeon, retained some faith in this dubious remedy. While Cook eventually lost his faith, Banks retained his, partly because he had the good luck to carry a cask or two containing a special mixture. It consisted of lemon or orange juice—not ruined by boiling—and a lacing of brandy.

The navy sent aboard the *Endeavour* no copies of Lind's book but several copies of an updated book by David MacBride, a Dublin physician who held other ideas. He thought that malt made from barley was the miracle cure for scurvy, and through his influence the *Endeavour* was supplied with enough malt to create, in hours of crisis, a fermented mixture that could be fed to the sick. Called "sweet wort," it contained only a smidgeon of the vital Vitamin C. Even Captain Wallis, who had already tried wort during his long voyage to and from Tahiti, doubted its worth. During his three years in the *Endeavour*, Cook retained his faith, and during his next voyage of exploration he was still an exponent of wort.

The *Endeavour* also carried another proposed cure for scurvy. The Admiralty had provided casks of the German fermented cabbage called sauerkraut, and the ship carried enough to allow everyone a twice-weekly serving when the ship was at sea. As Cook expected to be at sea for much longer than one year, he had to conserve his supplies. Several seamen were only too pleased to dispense with their own serving, for the taste was sour and sharp, but Cook compelled all—for the sake of their health—to eat it. Medical opinion, in time to come, would endorse his faith, for the white cabbage in its natural state held almost as high a proportion of Vitamin C as did the juice of lemons and oranges. Whether the French ship carried casks of sauerkraut we do not know. The answer is probably no.

Aboard the *Endeavour* another kind of cabbage was eaten eagerly by the few who had access to it. Carefully prepared in London, each iron-bound cask contained leaves of fresh cabbage, preserved between layers of salt, pressed down tightly, and finally topped up with more leaves and layers of salt. The first cask was not opened until the ship had passed Cape Horn. The cabbage tasted fresh, at least to those palates which had recently tasted no other fresh food; and in the opinion of Joseph Banks, who sometimes expressed himself like a salesman, it was "as green and pleasing to the eye as if it was bought fresh every morning at Covent Garden market."

Cook also imposed his own hygienic regime on the crew. Probably he was influenced by his knowledge of other voyages, including Commodore Anson's voyage from the Atlantic to the Pacific only a generation previously, when the crew suffered terribly from scurvy, perhaps because they were crammed into a tight space. Believing that fresh air and cleanliness might ease the adverse effects of overcrowding, Cook periodically lit wood fires inside his ship, especially on the lower deck where most seamen lived and slept. The smoke was believed to be a purifier, eliminating putrid smells; and presumably damp wood or a little grass was burned to increase the volume of smoke. Cook insisted that the men should occasionally air their bedding, try to dry their clothes as soon as possible when they came in from the rain, and wash themselves with cold water regularly: hot bathing water was unknown in the ship.

In trying to keep scurvy at bay, Cook also trusted in a concoction called "portable soup." A recent predecessor in Pacific exploration, Lord Byron, had given his crew a similar soup. In the *Endeavour* on those days when no meat was served—Monday, Wednesday, and Friday were called the "banyan days"—a watery soup was prepared by the cook. He added carefully weighed portions of boiled peas or oatmeal, greens when available, and a special ingredient called portable soup.

A kind of meat extract, portable soup consisted of oblong slabs or cakes, of which half a ton had been carried aboard in England. They were grey-white on the outside with flakes of golden brown inside. We know a lot about them, because a few slabs manufactured in 1771 and carried on Cook's second voyage to the Pacific Ocean were preserved long after. Several soup slabs were analyzed by two scientists, almost on the eve of World War II. Still soluble and still edible, they turned into a pale yellow liquid when water was added. Alas, they were almost devoid of taste and aroma. They were probably devoid, too, of vitamins.

While some of Cook's precautions—in particular the serving of sauerkraut—probably reduced the risk of scurvy, the disease finally appeared in his ship. This onset of scurvy is not mentioned in his daily journals; it has rarely been noticed even by his notable biographers. The first signs of scurvy appeared in the sailors, and it became visible during the long leg between Cape Horn and Tahiti.

A twenty-eight-year-old sailor named Richard Hutchins was medically examined on March 1, 1769. He did not feel exhausted or excessively weary, but one of his ankles displayed sores. Furthermore his gums, he explained to surgeon Monkhouse, felt painful though they "were still adhering to the teeth." During the following three weeks, William Wiltshire, a Marine, and Sam Jones, a seaman, reported aches and other symptoms. Even the surgeon's mate reported telltale signs and recorded that "an unusual languor and lazyness had infested me; no posture was as easy as lying down." A sore in his left leg was painful, and weeks later he could still see the spot clearly marked by a circle of deep blue surrounded by a halo of light yellow.

The surgeon's remedy was sweet wort, which tended to loosen the bowels of the sick. His other advice to the sick was to consume plenty of the portable soup and to eat flour in place of the ration of salted meat. He was doing his best, in light of current knowledge, but neither of his remedies was probably useful. Cook must have been fully aware of the surgeon's concern. He kept his fingers crossed and, in the face of the onset of scurvy, did not confide the news to his journal. Perhaps he was confident that the sickness would go away once he reached a harbor and a supply of fresh food.

A CAPTAIN IN A HURRY

We do not know how well the *St. Jean-Baptiste* was equipped with palliatives for scurvy. Did she carry wort of malt and barrels of sauerkraut? Probably she did not. There was also a view in some French seafaring circles that citrus fruits were desirable. Certainly her second-in-command held in his cabin a supply of lime juice. If it was fresh rather than boiled into a syrup, it would have been more efficacious than the rob of lemon in Cook's ship.

De Surville understood the danger of scurvy. As an experienced captain he must have encountered it often. He knew the value of fresh greens, but on this voyage so far he was in too much of a hurry to spare adequate time ashore in search of them. His was a trading mission. As speed was considered essential—time was money—he rarely halted long. In retrospect his failure to halt for more than two and a half days at Bashee Island, near Taiwan, was unfortunate. There the fruit was mostly out of season, and he took aboard only a minor load of potatoes and pumpkin, and ignored the chance to buy the yams, maize, sorghum, and small beans that the islanders boiled and ate. In addition, pigs and baby goats were bought and placed in pens on the deck, and greens were carried aboard for them rather than for the seamen.

Fresh livestock and fresh water were de Surville's first priority. Unfortunately no water well or spring was easily accessible at Bashee. If there had been water he would have stayed longer. At the next port of call in the Solomons, the inhabitants, perhaps short of food themselves, were so defensive that virtually nothing could be bought or bartered; fresh food could be safely collected only with the aid of an armed guard. It was de Surville's misfortune, at this crucial harbor, to encounter inhabitants who were more unfriendly than any facing Cook in the first year of his voyage.

By mid-November more than five months had passed since de Surville had sailed from Pondicherry. Nowhere had he been able to take aboard an adequate supply of fresh vegetables and fresh water. And another cause of the widespread scurvy in his ship seems to have been beyond his control. His crew included many African and Indian seamen who—for a reason not known—proved to be highly susceptible to the disease. Dozens of them were too ill to take part in the daily tasks. Until he could find a harbor where fresh greens were easily supplied, their health was endangered. And without the services of a healthy crew, his whole voyage was at risk.

Now de Surville was in the Coral Sea and sailing south. He was in uncharted waters, and no island was in sight.

4

Young Nick's Day

A FEW WEEKS after sailing south from Tahiti, Cook had changed course to the west. It was a zigzag course, at first to the northwest and then to the southwest. He knew that if he found no land in the next few weeks, and that if he continued to make his way west, he would eventually reach the land that Abel Janszoon Tasman had discovered in the previous century. This was New Zealand, named after a province of Tasman's own Holland. Only a fraction of the coastline of this new land had been inspected by Tasman. Therefore it was even conceivable—and Cook toyed with the idea—that New Zealand might prove to be an extension of the elusive continent.

IN THE WAKE OF THE FLYING DUTCHMAN

Tasman had begun his voyage of discovery in 1642, his mission being to find the mysterious southern continent for which Cook was now searching. Tasman's Holland was then at the height of its commercial power. The flat little land of two million people had a voice in the affairs of much of the world. It had supplanted Portugal as the main carrier of spices from East Asia to Europe. It was becoming the main carrier of slaves from Africa to the American plantations. It owned ports in India and the Indonesian archipelago. It possessed sugar islands in the West Indies and was building at home the largest sugar refineries in the world. In North America—seventeen years before Tasman sailed—Holland founded the town of New Amsterdam on

Manhattan Island and shipped away the beaver, bear, and otter furs that were boated far down the Hudson River.

The Dutch knew more about the Australian coast than did any other European seafarers. The north coast they discovered in 1606. The west coast was close to their new outgoing route from Amsterdam to Java and its spices; and in the decades after 1616 they saw from the safety of their ships—or occasionally on land, when shipwrecked—far more of the western coastline than they wished. Much of the land near the coast was dry, and wells had to be sunk to find fresh water. The more fertile country around the Swan River and Perth was eventually explored by the Dutch, but no part of western Australia then had attractions compared to those of New York, Japan, Java, and other places where the Dutch traded and even governed. The west coast did offer one tempting advantage: potentially it could provide a port of call for Dutch ships making the long outward voyage from Holland to Java and the Dutch East Indies. But in 1652 that port of call was established on the shores of a noble South African harbor. Once Cape Town was flourishing as a halfway house, there was no need for another Dutch port near Perth.

In these seas remote from Europe perhaps there was somewhere more enticing than Australia. At the very height of Dutch prestige, Abel Tasman was told to find it. He was the servant of a rich Dutch trading company, and his ships carried textiles and other merchandise. There was some anticipation that he might also find gold and silver mines, for the Dutch East India Company suspected that precious metals lay buried in an unknown land far west of Peru and Chile, those great Spanish possessions.

From Batavia, the present-day Jakarta, Tasman sailed to Mauritius, which was then a Dutch outpost, as its name suggests. He then ventured south toward the roaring forties of the Indian Ocean and, he hoped, the coast of the missing continent. Old maps suggested to the Dutch that the missing continent lay some fifty degrees south of the equator. Tasman sailed far south into a cold, windy ocean but saw no sign of land before turning toward the east. His two ships were small, their combined tonnage not equaling that of the *Endeavour*, but they coped with the high winds and waves. It was on the eve of summer, but now and then the snow almost whitened his ship, and sleet lay on the slippery decks. There was much praying in the face of danger in the little Dutch ships.

Tasman found the west coast of Tasmania, where he named two mountains after his ships, the *Heemskerck* and the *Zeehaen*. He did not go ashore. The surf and the ferocious westerly winds were shields keeping away any sensible navigator. Two and a half centuries after his discovery, the busy silver field of Zeehan—the Dutch word for sea cock—was to arise on the narrow button-grass plain at the foot of one of the pointed mountains that Tasman had seen.

After reaching the quieter east coast of Tasmania and sending a few men to examine the shore, he crossed the sea that now honors his name, the Tasman Sea. He discovered the west coast of New Zealand in December 1642. He was hoping to see gold. It was not far away. Rich gold, though he had no means of knowing it, lay in the hills and gullies a score or two of miles behind the shore he first sighted. More than two centuries later the port of Hokitika, a mere aperture through the surf, was bustling with gold-diggers arriving in small steamships.

Never perhaps in the history of exploration had a navigator, discovering two distinct lands in successive months, twice made his actual landfalls at places rich in minerals. The first place he sighted in Tasmania held hidden silver, and his first in New Zealand held gold. Remarkably, the officials of the Dutch East India Company, hoping for such discoveries, had issued Tasman stern instructions not to encourage the native peoples to think for one moment that he and his crew were really interested in precious metals. He was to pretend to be lukewarm at the sight of a bar or trinket of gold. Thereby he would dissuade the native peoples from asking too high a price for their gold. The official advice he received was not to hint to the native peoples that he valued the gold more than the humbler metals such as copper, lead, and spelter. Be clever and cunning, he was told. Put on an inscrutable face, "representing yourself to be not eager." Unfortunately he himself was to see neither gold nor silver in the course of his remarkable voyage.

Eventually anchoring in a sheltered bay near Cook Strait, Tasman's ships were approached by a small fleet of Maori canoes. He tried to entice aboard a few of the canoeists by displaying white cloth and other merchandise. When they refused to come he sent a boatload of sailors to meet them. The Maori in one canoe attacked the Dutch, killing four. The other sailors, escaping, swam back to the ships. The bay, christened Murderers' Bay with much indignation, is now politely known as Golden Bay.

Sailing along the west coast of New Zealand in light rain that sometimes became a "dark, gloomy" drizzle, the two Dutch crews celebrated Christmas at sea. Killing two pigs and feasting on the pork, they enjoyed an additional ration of wine. On January 4, 1643, they passed the northwest tip of the north island of New Zealand, naming it Cape Maria van Diemen after the wife of the good governor in Jakarta. Anchoring off a nearby island on January 6, which in the Christian calendar is called "Epiphany" or the "Day of the Three Kings," Tasman gave that exotic name to the rocky islands.

Those who pass the Three Kings today in rough weather find them slightly forbidding, as did Tasman. The main island, volcanic and high and not much over a square mile in area, is hit by strong seas and winds at certain times of the year. Even when the sea is sunlit and blue, the scatter of lesser islands, as seen from a passing ship, reminds one of a row of broken teeth sticking up above the foam.

An attempt by the Dutchmen to row ashore to the big island to collect fresh water and greens was a failure. On the shore and hills of the main island assembled hostile Maori—it was wisest to assume that they were hostile, even if they were benign. Close to the rocky shore was a dangerous surf. It was more sensible to talk than to act. As was the custom, the white flag was raised in one ship, inviting the officers in the other to a conference; and aboard the decision was reached to search no more for the great missing land in the southern seas and instead to sail north toward the equator.

Tasman's two ships returned to Jakarta by a roundabout route, discovering the island of Tonga and two of the main Fijian islands before passing the north coast of New Guinea on their way. The voyage of exploration had been carried out with speed—almost too much speed—for Tasman and his governing committee were usually more eager to sail away than to investigate. And yet it was a remarkable achievement. Rarely if ever has one voyage found such a dispersed collection of large islands, though they were of no value at that time to the Dutch in Jakarta. And yet Tasman, the stay-aboard captain, did not once step ashore on the main islands he discovered.

Cook was well informed about Tasman's voyage of long ago. He felt reasonably confident that, by sailing west, he would soon be within sight of Tasman's land, though probably it would be a part of the coast that the Dutchman had not seen. Tasman's chart indicated only part of the west coast of New Zealand, whereas Cook was sailing toward the east coast. Indeed, if New Zealand was of any size, that east coast might soon come into sight.

As we now know the shape of New Zealand, we forget that European explorers in 1769 might legitimately have expected it to be a much bigger land. Tasman's chart suggested that it was not a couple of islands but a single and elongated land, roughly running from south to north. What if it proved to be as wide as it was long? What if it turned out to embrace the squarelike shape of Greenland rather than the skinny, attenuated shape that we now know it to be? A New Zealand that was not only a thousand miles from north to south—its actual dimension—but also a thousand miles from east to west, would be huge. It would be one-third the size of Australia, or far larger than the largest countries of central and western Europe. Cook and Banks had no opinion on this matter of shape. But they were entitled to conjecture that the strip of western coast that Tasman had charted might form just one of four sides of a landmass or archipelago capable of equaling, in combined area, the present France, Germany, Spain and Portugal, Belgium and Holland, with the British Isles thrown in.

OUR LAND OF PROMISE

There was no reason to put the field glasses away. The most exciting part of the *Endeavour*'s voyage might lie over the horizon. What excitement and anticipation now invigorated the daily discussions below deck! The missing continent was discussed almost daily. Would it be the home of unfamiliar creatures—maybe man-eating animals and fat pythons? Would the land be mountainous and forested or as flat as the fens of Banks's own Lincolnshire? No doubt there were rival views, with distinct opinions predominating in different quarters of the ship. Would it be another Tahiti with more of those shapely, amorous women who were regarded by most of the seamen as a cut above their own English women? Or would the inhabitants be well clothed and living in houses?

Would the people in the missing land be white? Many explorers and geographers believed the answer to be "yes." Even the courteous, "brisk and lively" inhabitants of New Britain, northeast of New Guinea, were reported by one Scottish anthologist of voyages, John

Callander, to be white. Toward the very end of his nineteen-hundred-page series on the little-explored Pacific and the unknown south land he wrote: "All the inhabitants of these islands were white, and differed nothing in their complexion from Europeans, except that they were a little sunburnt." He signed off his third volume at Craigforth, near Stirling, just half a year before the *Endeavour* sailed from Plymouth. His fellow Scot, Alexander Dalrymple, preaching at the very same time the same faith in the existence of the missing southern continent, hinted that the white-skinned folk found in tropical islands in the Pacific probably originated from the missing continent.

As the *Endeavour* sailed closer and closer to what might prove to be the mysterious continent, the first sight of land was awaited more eagerly because scurvy appeared again. While not spread so widely as to cause alarm, it was sufficient to summon special remedies carried from England. Banks himself had brought with him Dr. Hulme's Essence of Lemon Juice, of which he served a helpful dose to his fellow botanist, Daniel Solander. In the opinion of the beneficiaries of this private medicine cabinet, Dr. Hulme's miraculous potion tasted almost like fresh lemon juice.

The crew had lived on the fat of the land in Tahiti, and now their daily diet was less attractive. The flour and oatmeal and even the preserved meat were edible, but the weevil-infested biscuits were irking everyone. Even fresh fish were a rarity. As for fresh meat, not many livestock remained in the roofed pens on deck. The seventeen sheep, a couple of goats, the English boar and sow and their piglets, the few remaining Tahitian pigs, and the small assortment of fowls and Muscovy ducks were primarily for the officers and for Banks and his circle.

The alcohol supply was, fortunately, not in jeopardy. The officers and scientists were still served from the casks of beer and porter brought all the way from London and fitted with taps; Banks vowed they were "as good as I ever drank." For some sailors there was occasionally alcohol in profusion. After the ship sailed from Tahiti, the boatswain's mate, John Reading, drank the best part of a bottle of rum in one thirsty rush before falling "speechless"—not the first time this convivial young man had been in a stupor. He died from a surfeit of alcohol.

A sight of land was expected almost daily by the more exuberant of the gentlemen and sailors, and even by many who were usually sober in mood. At the end of September there was quiet jubilation when pieces of seaweed were seen drifting past the ship. A hand net, dipped into the water, plucked up specimens of the weed which, on examination, were declared by Banks "not to have been long at sea."

An intermittent rivalry between Cook and Banks was sharpened by this all-engrossing question: where exactly is the missing continent? Banks was even more eager than Cook that it should be found, and more optimistic of success. Any clue suggesting that land might be close—whether in the shape of the clouds or seaweed floating in the sea—created tension between the two. But Cook, who was pragmatic, did not usually change direction merely to follow up the kind of clues that excited Banks.

Now the coastline, in Banks's opinion, is close. He catches sight of a bird with a short bill, which he declares must be a land bird, and his journal pulses with enthusiasm about the place he calls "our Land of Promise." The most traveled of mariners, Lieutenant Gore, seeing a brownish skualike bird that flaps its wings like a crow, swears that it is a Port Egmont hen and a sure sign that land is nearby. Every clue pointing to the presence of land is seized upon, as well as a few clues that are deceptive. On October 3, a calm morning, an instant squall shakes the ship for five minutes, summoning the crew to attend to the topsails. Banks affirms that this sudden shift in the weather must be a sign of nearby land. Cook maintains his poker face. He is not committing himself.

Banks, on a day when he is full of contentment, paints a charming picture of the big, well-lit cabin at the rear of the ship. He portrays himself sitting at his bureau, dipping his pen in the ink and writing his journal, and Solander sitting at the cabin table and penning his descriptions of the new marine objects found almost daily—not least the seaweed and the barnacle-encrusted piece of wood that he suspected had floated from a shore close by. "Now do I wish," writes Banks, with his exotic spelling, "that our freinds in England could by the assistance of some magical spying glass take a peep at our situation." The English friends, if only they could see "our lips move very often," might even guess the topic of conversation. No, it was not the seaweed, and not the driftwood. We were, said Banks, "talking about what we should see upon the land which there is now no doubt we shall see very soon."

Two days later the exciting news sprints up and down the ship, hustling into every hideaway: land is on the horizon. The message arouses doubt as well as acceptance, and for three hours there is argument whether this is solid land or just a fairy floss of clouds. In the end the clouds win. Banks, with his sense of fun overriding his sense of dignity, concedes that again he has been tricked by what he calls his familiar enemy, Cape Fly Away. The land that seemed to lie on the horizon has flown away.

Around the ship from time to time, scores of porpoises leap from the water to form a long procession, reminding Banks, in the way they keep together, of a pack of hounds hunting a fox. After they almost disappear into the distance their trail of foam can still be seen, like breakers. Every eye is scanning the horizon for land. The occasional glimpse of fur seals, asleep on the water, convinces some seamen that land must be near. Cook sees the seawater becoming paler, which makes him think that land might be close. His men constantly sound the depth of the water, thinking that shallow water will denote the proximity of land. But the ocean remains deep.

LAND!

Cook had sharpened the eyesight of almost everyone by offering a reward to the first person who saw land. The prize was a gallon of rum and maybe the promise that a bay or headland in the newfound land would be named after the winner. Who won would be partly a matter of luck: it depended on who was on duty, and who happened to be at the masthead, at the hour when the ship came within sight of land.

Nick Young had come aboard the *Endeavour* possibly as one of Banks's servants or even a servant of a servant. He does not appear in the records until the ship is in Tahiti, but clearly he was not a Tahitian. His age was perhaps twelve. The only reference to his character, to his capacity to annoy and maybe also to dispense a childlike charm, is an impetuous outburst in an anonymous journal kept on board the *Endeavour*: "N Young is a son of a Bitch," wrote an angry shipmate. Nick must have held some compensating virtues because, after the ship returned to England, he remained in Banks's service and traveled with him to Iceland.

Young's alert eyes were on duty at around 2 P.M. on Friday, October 6. Suddenly he called out, "Land!" His boyish cry was heard below, for there was no strong wind to muffle his voice. An officer must have climbed up to join him on the masthead. He saw that Nick Young was not mistaken.*

The buzz around the ship must have been electrifying. Men who were lounging or half asleep or just finishing a meal came running up the ladders. The side of the deck facing the land was lined with men, shading their eyes in the hope they might glimpse the shore; but from the deck it was not yet visible. None was more elated than Banks. Surely this was the long-awaited continent. He climbed aloft to see it, and again was aloft when the sun was sinking over the land just visible across the sea.

At sunset those on the deck could at last see distant mountains close to where the sun was setting. The ship continued to approach the far-off land until midnight, when extreme caution was required, for reefs might be hidden. Slowly, slowly in the morning light the ship again glided on calm seas toward Nick Young's nameless land. Smoke could be seen, suggesting strongly that the land was inhabited. What kind of people lived here? The discussions on board can be imagined.

The captain, as the discovery of land unfolded, displayed few twitches of excitement in his daily journal. And yet he realized that this was not a small island they had found. At about 5 P.M. on the following day a large harbor came into view. In his own words Cook saw "the opening of a Bay that appear'd to run pretty far inland." For the remainder of the night the ship marked time, marching up and back, many of the crew busily handling the sails.

Banks was on his own form of sentry duty earlier that evening. His diary—his own listening post and watch-house—recorded his happiness: "all hands seem to agree that this is certainly the Continent we

---

* While the shore time was October 6, the ship's own time was already October 7. Cook in his journal used the ship's way of measuring time. The ship's day began at noon and ended at noon, twenty-four hours later. Accordingly in the afternoon and evening the ship's time was one day ahead of the shore time. In the morning the two times were the same. When Cook's journal described events after midday on what he called December 25, this was December 24 in shore or civilian time. Banks, on the other hand, tended to use shore time in his journal, though not always.

are in search of." As the discovery of a new continent is a rare event in human history, many of those in the ship must have felt they were on the verge of the happening of a lifetime. Did Cook think it was momentous? One suspects that it was far too early to tell. Moreover he knew that if it was a continent, its western coast had already been discovered by Tasman.

On the following morning the new country stood out in all its charm with mountain ranges in the background, green and wooded hills in the middle distance, and steep white cliffs on the shore, where people could be seen. In the bay, riding the swell—the bay was not sheltered—were canoes. Were their crews eager to trade with the visitors, or were they waiting to defend their homeland?

The canoes began to mesmerize the English sailors watching from the ship. Fifteen men might be paddling on each side, and the way they lifted their paddles in unison, the speed of their strokes, and the dextrous skill with which they again dipped the paddles, were a marvel. The canoe moved not in jerks but with "incredible swiftness," almost as though the rowers were "animated" by the same soul; so Banks wrote. As the voyage went on, the size of the largest canoes evinced admiration, one being sixty-eight feet in length and five feet in width. In the opinion of Cook it could carry as many men as the *Endeavour* held, though its storage space was small.

The dilemma now facing Cook was whether he should show constant friendliness to these strangers and offer them gifts or whether, when mistrust arose, he should threaten them and eventually fire warning shots to show them who was really the master. While Cook hoped to do no harm, he was alert for the possibility of a surprise attack by these Maori. He ordered the sailmakers to make canvas covers that would protect from the weather the swivel guns to be placed in some of the *Endeavour*'s accompanying boats.

On the first day the pinnace and the yawl—small auxiliary vessels—set out for the shore. The visit began in an awkward and even tense atmosphere. Before long a few Maori seized the yawl. The seamen in the pinnace came to the rescue. Muskets were fired over the Maori heads, a spear was raised in defense, and a man was shot dead. His body was examined by the Englishmen, after his Maori comrades had dragged it a short distance, and one oddity was noticed at once. His skin was marked by sharply defined tattoos, but his were on the face whereas in Tahiti the tattoos were usually on the chest and buttocks.

Like the Tahitians, these tattooed Maori were intent on stealing captivating items. This was not surprising; the Englishmen were intent on stealing fresh water and greens and firewood without making the kind of payment that Banks would have demanded if a party of Dutchmen had crossed the North Sea and landed, uninvited, on his Lincolnshire estate with their axes and water buckets and vegetable baskets.

The second day began warily. Along with the armed Marines, formally carrying a Union Jack, Cook and the vital Polynesian interpreter went ashore and soon came within earshot of the New Zealanders on the opposite bank of the river. As soon as Tupaia spoke to the Maori men they recognized his words. To Cook's surprise "they perfectly understood him." In the entire history of global exploration it must have been most exceptional for an interpreter traveling so far from his own land to find that his language was understood by utter strangers.

A common language was not enough to ensure harmony. Understandably the Maori were suspicious. They had never before seen firearms or foreigners. They had never seen a ship of this size, never seen men with white but weather-beaten faces, and certainly not witnessed the strange European habit of rowing a boat with the men's backs, and not their eyes, facing the direction in which they were heading. Did these palefaced oarsmen have eyes in the backs of their heads?

Once again Maori mingled with the Britons. Lo and behold the small swords or "hangers" worn by Gore the officer and Green the astronomer were stolen. Shots were fired, and one Maori was killed. Worse was to follow. That afternoon another three or four were killed and others wounded. Cook and Banks returned to the safety of the ship, feeling guilt and even shame. Banks, one of those who had fired a musket, thought it the blackest day of his young life.

One puzzle to them was that some of the younger Maori did not seem angry or indignant. Two teenagers and a boy who were temporarily brought aboard stayed the night and ate large helpings of the ship's bread. At times they were extremely cheerful, even singing a part-song rather like a psalm tune. Their delight was transparent in the morning when they were dressed up, complete with necklaces and bracelets.

Cook's first impression was not as hopeful as this fertile land deserved. The horseshoe bay where his men first landed and fought in New Zealand was christened Poverty Bay. The unjust name was conferred, after Cook ended his stay, because "it afforded us no one thing we wanted." He had hoped to ferry from the shore fresh casks of water and bundles of fresh greens and perhaps fresh meat and fish but, through one mishap and another, he gained nothing. He had also hoped to initiate friendly relations with the inhabitants. That failure, as much as anything, was his reason for denouncing a bay and a landscape, in whose quiet beauty and richness the earlier and later inhabitants rejoiced.

Cook wrote one other name on the new map that he had begun to draw. At the south end of Poverty Bay was a headland which, to the delight of the juvenile discoverer, was henceforth known as Young Nick's Head. In the eyes of the white New Zealanders of a later century the headland, so romantically named, served almost as sacred ground: the beginning of what they saw as the history of their New Zealand. To the Maori, it came rather to be seen as a twilight of their way of life.

Four days after leaving Poverty Bay, with the intention of exploring the coast to the south, Cook saw a new line of Maori canoes in sight of the bare white cliffs of Cape Kidnappers, near the present port of Napier. Friendly acts of barter in which smoked fish were exchanged for Tahitian cloth were followed by unfriendly acts on both sides. Taiata, the boy traveling with Tupaia the interpreter, was snatched away by Maori canoe-men. Soon he was rescued, frightened and unharmed, but only after shots were fired at the Maori canoes by one of the big guns on deck. After such affrays it was too dangerous for the English Marines and seamen to scout around and to see how many Maori were killed and how many wounded, but this clash of October 15 cost several lives.

Cook, like the Dutchmen in the previous century, had instantly established poor relations with the Maori. But as the weeks passed he was favorably impressed. The people were active and strong and physically impressive. Though he did not say so, he implied that they were slightly taller than the English. Parkinson was even more impressed, insisting that most were "tall, well-limbed, clever fellows." Moreover they had more energy than the Tahitians, who were regarded by the first Europeans as slightly lazy and leisurely.

On the other hand Tupaia soon decided that the Maori as a people were inferior to the Polynesians in his corner of the Pacific. Eventually he was to conclude that they were inclined to be liars, and one old man in particular not only lied but lied "too much." That they were cannibals also disgusted Tupaia, though it should be added that his own people had abandoned that practice only a few generations earlier. He actually looked down on the Maori, viewing them with sterner feelings than those held by Cook, Banks, or Solander, who were the offspring of one of Europe's more tolerant centuries.

In the following months Banks and his colleagues were determined to learn everything they could about these people with whom they had clashed. Banks decided that Maori people were brown but no browner than a sunburned Spaniard. They were not frequent bathers whereas the Tahitians were probably cleaner than the English. As an adornment the Maori spread fat on their hair; if the fat was rancid, the hair smelled. With a mix of ochre and oil the women so reddened their faces that, if they were kissed, the telltale signs remained on Banks's nose. In due course the women and their soft voices impressed that roaming admirer of females, and were livelier and more "laughter loving than the men." Compared to the Tahitians they were decent in talk and "modest in their carriage," but some were not altogether averse to sex with a stranger if asked persuasively, the request being accompanied by a gift.

MERCURY BAY AND RIVER THAMES

After exploring the coast some distance to the south of his landfall, Cook turned the ship around and began to steer north. There was sometimes a grandeur to the scenery—a chain of snow-capped mountains and forests with clearings on the lower slopes, and a picturesque coast—but he still had no idea of the size of the land he had discovered. He felt it likely that this was the land that Abel Tasman had found, but it was too early to be certain. Curiously the name of Tasman does not appear in this part of Cook's journal. It was possible that this might be the missing southern continent, but who could tell?

Cook set out to tell. The *Endeavour* followed the coast of what we now know is the North Island of New Zealand, passing the pale cliffs of East Cape and its little knob of an island where a lighthouse now stands, and sighting various Maori canoes whose crew were surprised to see this large ship with such an abundance of sailcloth.

It was now the start of November, and an anchorage had to be found and soon an observation place secured on shore so that the transit of Mercury could be observed. Mercury, a small planet only three times the size of the moon, was rarely visible with the naked eye from English soil and would represent only a tiny spot as it slowly crossed the sun. Like Venus, it was always on the same side of the sun as the Earth is. Unlike Venus, it made its transit frequently. To observe it accurately offered one pronounced advantage, for it would provide Cook with an exact longitude for the place where it was observed.

Near the Bay of Plenty, Cook found an ideal inlet with a sandy beach. He remained there for eleven days—longer than he intended. Ashore, the local celery grew in plenty, and after being boiled on the big stove in the ship it was fed to the crew every day. The sailors set out to collect shellfish, and on one day the longboat sank low in the water, so pressed down was it by the weight of oysters. The Maori were happy to trade fish—mackerel on one day and loads of cockles, clams, and mussels on another. Cloth was the British item they craved.

At first everything was more or less peaceful. But on the crucial day when Cook, Green, and Lieutenant Hicks were ashore to make their observations of the transit, five canoes came close to the *Endeavour*. A dogskin cloak was being eagerly traded for a large piece of cloth when, suddenly, a Maori hurried away with the cloth without fulfilling his side of the bargain. Lieutenant Gore, who was temporarily in command of the ship, pointed his musket at the fleeing man and shot him. Whether he intended to kill was irrelevant. As Cook pointed out, the deadly penalty imposed on the Maori was out of all proportion to the offense. Curiously, the numerous Maori who were present did not think the punishment unjust. In an odd gesture of compromise, the dead man was allowed to keep the cloth he had stolen. It was buried alongside him.

Fortunately the day of the transit, November 9, was blessed with "light breezes and clear weather." Cook was proud that on the sandy beach he was able to establish his longitude exactly. This would be a boon to later mariners, partly because Abel Tasman's own determination of the position of New Zealand had been so inaccurate, for in determining the longitude of the northwest headland of the North Island he had been astray by 116 miles! The lonely bay where Cook observed with such precision was christened Mercury Bay. It became one of the symbolic points on his own chart of the voyage, and here on a shoreside tree his men carved the date of their visit while he duly claimed the area, but not the whole island, for His Majesty King George III. But there is no village, city, or port at Mercury Bay to this day.

The British, though they were on a scientific expedition, were also keen to find commodities that might form useful items of trade. Banks saw promise in a tall hardwood tree, "as big as an oak in England" and perhaps capable of providing the timber for masts and for the big cogs of the millwheels or waterwheels that were increasingly used in the English industrial towns. Even more attractive to him was the New Zealand flax, called *harakeke* by the Maori, who used its broad, rushlike leaves to make string and ropes, and the linen for their clothes. Observing that it grew on the hills but positively flourished in the deep bogs, he thought it would grow well in the northern hemisphere, thereby supplanting the European crops. Vast areas of farmland in northern Europe, especially along the Baltic, were devoted to the growing of hemp and flax, whose fibers went into the manufacture of rope for ships, coarse cloth for the making of sails, and fine linen for clothing. The efficient New Zealand plant, if cultivated in Europe, might provide a raw material that was vital for every naval power. In the shaping of Banks's opinion Dr. Solander was probably influential, for he knew the Baltic coast. This native flax, called *Phormium tenax*, was later to be a vital export for New Zealand.

Another potential prize, which Cook first saw on the beach at Mercury Bay, was a transparent resin or gum originating from the big kauri trees and washed down to the sea by the river. A few weeks later the first French explorer to see the resin guessed that it was rather like amber, the fossilized gum from the Baltic forests. When lumps of this kauri gum were set alight they gave off a bright flame and a sweetish scent. The Maori had long realized the worth of the noble kauri tree, selecting its trunk when making their long canoes, and using its gum as an ingredient in the pigment that gave the blue-black or the green color to the pattern of tattoos painfully chiseled in their bare skin. In the kauri forests of the warmer parts of the North Island, a century later, the gum was to be dug from the ground on a large scale and exported to Europe for the making of varnish.

Perhaps the most appealing quality of the new land was its soil and grasses. They suggested that one day Europeans might settle here. With new farming methods they might make the soil infinitely more productive. In the island-studded bays not too far east of where the city of Auckland now stands, Cook and Banks could see how pleasing was the soil, whether covered with grass or with tall trees growing close together. They were so taken with one wide river, the rural scenery along its banks as well as its width and tidal currents, that they nostalgically named it the Thames.

In the Bay of Islands the fine root-crops growing in small Maori gardens were further testimony to the rich patches of soil. Ashore on a summer night, three sailors used spades or sticks to dig up potatoes in these unguarded gardens. Cook, conscious of the need for amicable relations with people whom he had just fended off with muskets and even warning shots from a cannon, ordered that the three culprits each receive one dozen lashes. To Cook's surprise one of the young men, Matthew Cox, persisted in saying that he had done no wrong; next day, as a penalty for his defiance, he was further punished with half a dozen lashes. A brave "bush lawyer" from Dorset—probably a mere twenty-three years old at the time—he was to initiate a legal action against Cook on his return to England. Although it was a brave tilt at a naval captain's authority, his lawsuit was bound to fail.

The thought does not appear in their journals, but it must some-times have occupied their minds: New Zealand, as seen so far, was a land of the temperate zone, and for that very reason it was slightly disappointing. Cook and his British sponsors had hoped to find a warmer land. Admittedly it was still feasible that New Zealand was the missing continent and that it extended much farther—perhaps even a thousand miles—north of Mercury Bay. No European, not even Tasman, had explored the vast area to the northeast of Mercury Bay; and so, for all Cook knew, New Zealand might extend, like a long peninsula, as far as the Tropic of Capricorn. But within a few weeks, as he sailed in a northerly direction, he would find that the country became ever so narrow and then ended abruptly. It was not to be the tropical or subtropical land that most European geographers had wished for.

THE SNARE OF THE MOON

On the evening of December 5, 1769, in the Bay of Islands, Cook weighed anchor, intending to make use of a favorable wind to sail farther north. The wind, however, fell away to a whisper, and in the ensuing stillness a current began to drive the ship toward an island. The bottom of the sea, just here, seemed too unpromising for an anchor to be dropped, and, minute after minute, the ship was quickly swept closer to the surf near the shore. She was so near the waves breaking on the beach that those on deck could hear the Maori people shouting from the shore, their voices rising above the "roaring of the breakers."

Parkinson the artist, marveling at the force of "the eddy-tide" and the seeming helplessness of the ship, depicted the mounting danger in his journal. He remarked how the possibility of disaster "threw us into a panic, and occasioned great confusion." As the ship was driven toward the shore, Matra the midshipman thought the cannibals might now be standing in readiness to kill or capture the crew. He saw or imagined them "flourishing their weapons, exulting at our dangers, and expecting us for their prey." As more Maori men had gathered in this vicinity, close to Point Pocock, than in any other part of the coast so far visited, the sheer weight of their numbers heightened the fear among the *Endeavour's* men. Banks wittily reflected on the situation after the crisis had passed: "the almost certainty of being eat as soon as you come ashore adds not a little to the terrors of shipwreck."

As an experienced seaman Cook was probably not so agitated by the danger facing his ship in the grip of the tide, but even he had his nervous moments. His solution, adopted at the last moment, was to lower the pinnace and join it by a cable to the bow of the *Endeavour*. Rowing with skill and vigor, the crew of the pinnace towed the ship back toward deeper water. An offshore breeze sprang up, easing their efforts. At last, having towed the ship a safe distance from the dangerous coast, they could loosen their grip on the oars. The sense of peril was succeeded by gratitude that the breeze had saved them. Banks felt elated: "We were all happy in our breeze and fine clear moonlight."

The drama seemed to be over. It was time for bed, and Banks went to his little cabin, sat down on his cot, and began to undress. Suddenly he felt a jolting and jarring. "I felt the ship strike upon a rock, before I could get upon my leggs she struck again. I ran upon deck but before I could get there the danger was over." The ship escaped undamaged.

Cook sometimes had to face serious risks when exploring an unknown coast where winds and currents were unpredictable. After the risks had been safely overcome, he tended to downplay them in the official record that he kept for his masters in the Royal Navy. That night he minimized the risk facing his ship. In contrast, other observers who left a record of the episode thought it was a narrow escape.

The whalelike rock that the *Endeavour* rubbed against late that night had already been seen in daylight, but, being viewed from a distance, had not been labeled as a rock but as a strange marine creature—a whale or grampus—splashing in the sea. That evening the rock was visible from a closer distance but was detected too late. In the moonlight it was not seen with the clarity that would have been available in the light of day. This was not the last time that Cook would be seduced by the light of the moon.

5

The Sea of Surville

◪ WHILE COOK was exploring an unmapped coast, de Surville, not too far away, was exploring a vast expanse of ocean known to no previous European. One of de Surville's instructions from the French authorities had been to search for new lands. After leaving the Solomon Islands he began to sail south, passing through the middle of an unknown zone of the Pacific. Most of the perimeters of this zone were unexplored. Its eastern borders were New Caledonia, Norfolk Island, and New Zealand. Its western borders were mainland Australia and Tasmania. This sea extended from about 10 degrees south of the equator, where the seas were often smooth, to the rolling waves and biting winds of the roaring forties, about 42 degrees south. Covering about 2,200 miles on a north-south line, it was a larger expanse than the Mediterranean, the Black Sea, and the Baltic Sea combined. This expanse is now called the Coral Sea in the north and the Tasman Sea in the south. It is too late to alter these names, but the entire sweep of sea almost merits the name the Sea of Surville.

What resources might be fronting such a vast expanse of sea? The unexplored line of coast might well contain gold, silver, spices, and other precious commodities. Of the many thousands of miles of coast that bordered this Sea of Surville, so far only a few hundred had been seen by a visiting European. That coastline marked roughly on Tasman's chart was as much the squiggles of his hand as a careful delineation.

The French ship sailed south into this sea, partly in the hope of avoiding unfavorable winds near the equator. Her captain also hoped to find harbors where he could quickly obtain fresh greens and perhaps fresh meat for those seamen afflicted with scurvy. Above all, he was on his way to search for the mysterious land, irrespective of whether it was Davis Land or that island home of Jewish-like merchants. Perhaps, in the eyes of the mariners from Pondicherry, Davis Land and the Land of the Jews were one and the same. Probably the easiest way to reach this seductive region was to sail in a southerly direction toward a position on the map lying some twenty-eight degrees south, and then change course and sail due east, thereby voyaging in the general direction of South America.

Despite the sickness and death among the crew, the *St. Jean-Baptiste* continued to sail south. She sailed out of sight of New Caledonia, which lay to the east. No European had yet seen that large island with its rich deposits of nickel—a mineral of no value in the eighteenth century. With a little luck de Surville might have discovered New Caledonia, though he would have halted there only briefly. He was a navigator in a hurry. Southward his ship slowly sailed, day and night. Within a few days Australia to the west would become the nearest land worthy of the name of land, though it was still far away.

All the time de Surville and his crew longed for a sight of land. At one time it seemed to be close, partly because of the abundance of those black Pacific swallows, nicknamed "wing-beaters" because their wings were always flapping. On November 14 many birds were flying around the ship, while toward evening the air was speckled with butterflies, perhaps blown out to sea from some land lying to the east. A tantalizing glimpse of driftwood, seaweed, and other evidence hinted that land might not be too far away. A week later, just south of the Tropic of Capricorn, seamen saw red-beaked birds, their tail feathers displaying the color of fire. Having seen similar birds in the French colony of Mauritius, in the Indian Ocean, they wondered if their presence signified the proximity of land. In the ship's makeshift sickrooms the news of the birds, and the hope pinned to them, was heartening.

"We are going very slowly," wrote de Surville on November 17, "and each day someone dies." The ship barely held enough fit men for the tasks of altering the sails as the winds rose, fell, or changed direction. On the evening of November 21 the light wind died and a "flat calm" descended. As the ship had to pluck a breeze from somewhere, the studding sails, which were used alongside the square sails in fair weather, were put in place. Some seamen carrying out these tasks could barely climb the ladders, fix the ropes, or lift the heavy sails. The ship was retarded further when the wind began to blow from the south, accompanied by a swell. During four days and nights she covered a mere 150 sea miles. On one day, in which she met heavy seas running from the east, she sailed only 17 miles.

More sailors, soldiers, and servants fell ill or, while able to walk, felt pain or stiffness in their limbs. Exaggerating a little, Labé wrote, "The entire crew is attacked by scurvy." Those officers with compassion wished they could help the sick and the dying. Although fresh food was seen as one palliative, nearly all the livestock, once so numerous in the cramped pens on the decks, had been killed and eaten. Fortunately Labé retained a shrinking hoard of luxuries, which he had purchased in distant Pondicherry for his own use, and to his credit he handed out lime juice and other remedies or delicacies to the sick, whom he visited daily. "I suffer to see the poor wretches in such a deplorable condition," he wrote.

On most days a death was reported. A surge of hope was felt when two successive days went by without one death. As the ship sailed farther and farther from the equator, de Surville hoped that the cooler weather would restore those sailors lying helpless with the scurvy.

TOWARD AUSTRALIA: A MOMENT OF DECISION

Even with the benefit of hindsight and the latest charts, we cannot be certain precisely where the *St. Jean-Baptiste* was at noon each day. The officers themselves had more trouble than did Cook in calculating their longitude with accuracy. When in the Solomons, the ship was actually three hundred nautical miles to the east of where they thought she was! Moreover they did not necessarily have a clear grasp of the geography of the vast Pacific and of the islands already on the map. When the ship was close to the Tropic of Capricorn, the first officer revealed his geographical confusion: "May God grant us the favor of finding among our discoveries some good islands where we could get supplies and restore our sailors and other men. I would be glad indeed to be able to land in New Zealand or at least in Easter Island or other places where the people or islanders might welcome unhappy travelers." In fact Easter Island was far, far away, and Australia was the closest land.

The ship's southerly course ran more or less parallel to the coast of Australia. On November 21 the ship was almost to the east of what is now the port of Rockhampton. Standing out of sight, between the ship and the coast, was the southernmost part of the Great Barrier Reef. With the winds blowing often from a southeasterly direction, the ship's progress continued to be slow. About November 26 she was a few hundred miles from the surf beaches of what is now the famous holiday resort of the Gold Coast. On the following day the nearest land—perhaps two hundred miles away—was at Byron Bay, the most easterly point of the continent where a tall lighthouse now stands.

Several officers suspected that land was near because they saw "large flights of wing-beaters." It was de Surville's view that the birds were in pursuit of fish just below the surface of the sea. "I have never seen these birds very far from land," he remarked. At about 10 A.M. the following morning, the wing-beaters disappeared, suggesting to de Surville that land had perhaps been passed unseen. At sunset of the same day, close to the northern rivers of what is now New South Wales, he felt that land might soon be sighted, and so he "furled the studding sails from below to be more prepared to maneuver in case of some sighting."

At this point the coast changed direction, veering more to the southwest, and so the *St. Jean-Baptiste* no longer continued to close steadily the gap between ship and shore. Nonetheless the coast, now running somewhat parallel to the course of the ship, was probably so near that it could be reached in little more than a day of sailing if the wind were favorable.

For a few hours, probably on November 29, the ship had invisible land standing on both sides. To the west stood the Australian coast near Port Macquarie. To the east stood the two volcanic peaks of uninhabited Lord Howe Island and, nearby, the tiny rocky island now known as Ball's Pyramid, its steep cliffs a nesting home for seabirds. The gap between these isolated islands and Australia is only about four hundred nautical miles, and the ship was probably close to the middle of that gap.

As the ship sailed farther from the equator, the weather became cooler. The active sailors, who normally worked in bare legs and bare feet, were allocated shoes and stockings to counter the chill. For the African seamen, less accustomed to the cold, the warm footwear was especially welcome. Possibly as a result of the cool weather, some days passed without a death, but the time of hope was brief. In the last three days of November, five African and Bengali seamen, along with one man from Prussia and a Frenchman from Brest, died in quick succession. "I do not know what will become of us," wrote Labé on December 1. He wondered whether the ship could survive if, in the end, not enough sailors possessed the physical health needed to work the sails, heavy anchors, and pumps.

The ship was very close to Australia, but de Surville had already made up his mind to change course, even choosing the point on the sea chart where he would act. Just after his ship crossed the Tropic of Capricorn, he had briefly discussed with Labé something he rarely divulged: his plan of action. Unwilling to retreat, he confided that he had no intention of sailing back toward the equator and so to the Dutch East Indies or the Philippines or even China, where there was a chance of selling the precious cargo. Instead he proposed to steer, before long, toward the North Island of New Zealand, that "being the land nearest to us." In fact de Surville was not only closer to Australia but also coming closer each day.

In favoring a visit to New Zealand, he was drawing on Tasman's experiences, for the *St. Jean-Baptiste* carried at least two recent French books that outlined what Tasman had observed. According to de Surville, Tasman had described New Zealand as "an attractive country, well populated." Moreover Labé had the feeling that New Zealand might produce "gold or silver." Those precious metals, if already mined and smelted, could then be bought by the French in return for the Indian textiles, clothes, and other goods stored in the hold of their ship. Here was the possibility that the French could trade all or most of their cargo at a profit before even finding the distant Jewish colony. New Zealand's other advantage was clear: it could supply food and fresh water and a few weeks of rest for the sick crew.

On the other hand the inhabitants of New Zealand were said by Tasman to be "ferocious and bloodthirsty." Therefore the French Marines and sailors might have to confront them forcibly, holding them at gunpoint in order to acquire fresh supplies. But surely, the Frenchmen argued, it was wiser to fight the Maori ashore than to be stranded in a drifting ship in which, eventually, no sailors would be fit enough to handle the sails.

De Surville had received Labé's blessing for his decision to sail farther south, traveling—without realizing it—almost parallel to the nearby Australian coast before changing direction toward New Zealand. Favorable winds, fortunately, hastened the ship's passage to the south. In four days and nights she covered a total of over four hundred nautical miles—far more than in any earlier span of four days. Soon she would reach the same latitude as de Surville's intended destination—the coast that Tasman had briefly glimpsed in northern New Zealand. The ship could then change course and sail due east in the certainty that Tasman's land would be found.

In following his plan, de Surville was conforming to a practical seafaring tradition. Setting out for an unfamiliar land by aiming to reach a specific latitude and then sailing along that latitude was a familiar tactic of navigators when in strange seas. The success of this plan rested on unassailable facts. Seamen knew that they could rely far more on their latitude, which they could easily calculate each noonday when the sun reached its zenith, than on their longitude, which they could not easily compute with accuracy.

THE SEA-BLOWN SCENT OF AUSTRALIA

On Monday, December 4, 1769, several hours before sunrise, the *St. Jean-Baptiste* was not far from Sydney Harbor. At 3 A.M., de Surville wrote, "several of our men could smell land, but only intermittently and then nothing." De Surville had been asleep at that hour—his report relies on other witnesses—but Labé was probably awake. He testified with confidence that the strong smell of land came from the south or south-southwest. He insisted that for more than three hours "we smelt a scent of meadow, like dry hay." This haylike aroma, blown by the offshore wind, usually signified that invisible land was very close, perhaps a mere twenty to forty miles away. To those sailors who, coming from rural France, knew the summer odors of freshly cut or fast-drying hay, the scent must have been nostalgic. After six weeks at sea, here at last was an opportunity to send men ashore.

It was almost a commonplace in the era of sailing ships that land could be smelled by sailors even before it was in sight. The fabled Captain Ahab, navigating his whaling ship in what he called a mild wind, smelled South American land, though he could not yet see it. He vowed that "the air smells now, as if it blew from a far-away meadow." The mowers, he announced, "have been making hay somewhere under the slopes of the Andes." So Herman Melville, author of *Moby Dick*, which recaptures his own life as a Pacific seaman, evoked an episode experienced by thousands of others in the era of long sailing-ship voyages.

The smell of land is a crucial clue intimating that the French ship was tantalizingly close to Australia. Fortunately another French officer kept his own neat journal of the events of that week. Those pages have never been published nor translated into English. An inspection of his daily entries for that week reveals that he and many others in the ship smelled the land at approximately 3 A.M. According to Lieutenant Jean Pottier de l'Horme who was third-in-command, the *odeur de terre* was strong and persistent.

The time would soon come when this coast of Australia was settled by Europeans, and more and more ships would arrive each year. Again and again, passengers and sailors in those ships would distinctly smell the country before they even reached it. Coming from the British Isles, after several months at sea, they first sniffed the Victorian coast—especially when a north wind was blowing from the shore. The points of the Australian coast they first glimpsed in the palmy era of the sailing ships were near the entrance to Bass Strait and the sea approaches to the port of Melbourne.

In September 1852 William Howitt, aboard a ship bound from England to Melbourne, suddenly realized that the long-awaited Australian coast must be close: "On opening the scuttle in my cabin, I perceived an aromatic odor, as of spicy flowers blown from the land." Leaving his cabin he heard another passenger call out excitedly, "Come on deck, and smell the land!" Howitt noted in his journal that the wind was blowing briskly from a shore that was not yet visible. To Howitt it was the scent of a field of hay, though less sweet and more spicy than hay. As the nearest region of Australia held no cultivated ground, no hayfield, and probably not even an abundance of dry grass because it was still springtime, the scent reaching the ship was possibly from the blossoms of wattles and other flowering bushes. Whatever the source, the scent was powerful and distinctive.

For long-distance passengers approaching Australia the aroma of land was to become less frequent when, more than a century later, steamships began replacing sailing ships. The heat and odor from the burning of coal and oil in the engine room tended to taint the air around a big ship, and the scent rising from the earth could not compete. But even today, just out of sight of the Australian coast, yachtsmen sometimes pick up the aroma that tantalized seamen on duty in the *St. Jean-Baptiste*.

Eyes as well as noses indicated that land was probably not far away. Birds usually associated with coastal rather than deep waters were seen. In the *St. Jean-Baptiste* birds had rarely been seen in recent days but now, on occasions, they were flying past or around the ship, in ones and twos or in flocks small and large. On the morning when the smell of hay filled the air, "great numbers of birds named velvet sleeves" were seen by Labé. Probably they were red-footed boobies, skilled in diving headlong into the water with a splash. In his opinion such birds did not usually stray more than sixty or seventy-five miles from land, but—it should be added—occasionally they have been reported several hundred miles from land. The boobies are likely to have been attracted by the prospect of catching the small fish feeding in the warmer waters of the continental shelf that stretched twenty or more miles from the coast.

Other clues positively suggest that the ship was near the Australian coast. "The sea seemed," wrote de Surville, "a little different to me at dawn." Was it shallower, was it sandier? He did not elaborate. Many jellyfish, usually creatures of the coastal waters, were seen swimming or drifting past the ship for just a quarter of an hour. A few brown bundles of seaweed floated by. At least two white cuttlebones slid past the ship. They were the solid remains of the cuttlefish, on which the albatrosses still feast in season within the coastal waters near Port Kembla, just south of Sydney.

The crew of the *St. Jean-Baptiste* had, for forty-eight hours, been preoccupied with the weather. The wind and sea were fickle. In the darkness the weathervane on the mast suddenly glowed, after an occurrence of the electrical discharge known by sailors as St. Elmo's Fire. The weather formed an unpredictable mosaic: a burst of clear sky, squalls and light gusts of wind, claps of thunder. Now a high sea running from the southwest was pummeling and shaking the ship, and there came sudden rushes of wind so powerful that the mizzen topsail was torn. All men on duty were no doubt alert for a glimpse of land, because in such weather the ship could be blown perilously close.

On the afternoon of December 4—using the civilian calendar—the clouds cleared and the visibility must have been pleasing. Whether clouds hovered above the Australian shore and the inland ranges is not certain, but the men taking turns in the lookout would probably have seen the land—if there was land to be seen—at some time during the course of the long hours of daylight. Australia was probably at least twenty miles away, perhaps fifty. The officers' own reckoning of the longitude of the ship cannot be relied upon, but the reported latitude—of which de Surville's calculations were pretty reliable—was in line with Sydney Harbor and the nearby coast. The spicy, grassy aroma, blown from the shore, might well have wafted across the sea from the cliffs and escarpments in the vicinity of the Bulli Pass, Botany Bay, Sydney Harbor, or what are now the northern beaches.

As most of the suffering crew craved a taste of fresh food and a time of rest ashore, there was an argument in favor of seeking refuge in the nearest Australian harbor. The idea must have been contemplated by de Surville and then dismissed; he had no wish to take it seriously because he had already made it clear that he was not in the least attracted by Australia. All the available European literature, from explorers and commentators and historians and strategists, and all the relevant books in his cabin, emphasized that Australia was not to be compared with New Zealand as a potential source of food, let alone a potential source of trade.

De Surville carried the large and learned book *Histoire des Navigations aux Terres Australes*, written by Charles de Brosses and published in Paris only thirteen years earlier. In volume two de Surville could read about the bleak impressions that Australia had made on the many Dutchmen who had sailed much of its coastline and occasionally waded ashore. All agreed that the terrain was dry and infertile, drinking water was hard to find, and many parts of the coastline were hazardous. What warning could be clearer than this sentence, translated from the French: "The inhabitants are brutish, stupid, incapable of work and unfamiliar with commerce." The whole essence of de Surville's expedition, planned so carefully in the merchants' warehouses and governor's residence in French India, was that it would find a distant land where commerce was already advanced. That was why the prospect of meeting Jewish traders somewhere in the South Pacific was so enticing. The French wanted a virtually instant market, but such a market could not be supplied by Australia and its nomadic inhabitants.

De Surville was also familiar with the voyages of William Dampier and respected him as an explorer, having recently followed his route to Bashee Island. Dampier's opinion of the faraway western coast of Australia, which he had depicted in widely read books, was not encouraging. De Surville therefore assumed, rather rashly, that the eastern coast would resemble the west.

On what might be expected if a European landed on Australia's coast, Dampier's warning was stark. Water was so scarce that wells had to be dug. The trees were small, and the soil sandy and dry. Birds were few, fish not easily caught, and the tiny bush-flies were a pest, crawling into nostrils and even mouths. The inhabitants, tall and thin and "coal black" in color, tended to vanish as soon as a stranger appeared on the beach.

Indian or European textiles had no appeal to these Aborigines, for they lived almost naked except in cold weather. As they kept no livestock and no farms, they were unlikely to supply newcomers with fresh meat, fish and eggs, greens, yams and potatoes, or fruit. But the French were traveling as traders, intent on quick transactions, and they had no wish or time to gather their own food. Furthermore most of their crew were now too weak to do arduous physical tasks. An intelligent reading of Dampier's book would have quashed almost any hope that a foreign ship urgently seeking fresh supplies would find them on the Australian coast. This is the most likely explanation of why de Surville, when so close to Australia, had no thought of examining it.

The remarkable fact is that for at least seventy-two hours the ship was very close to a strategic point of the eastern Australian coast. During that time she sailed from the latitude of Terrigal and Gosford, just north of Sydney Harbor, to the latitude of Botany Bay, just south of Sydney Harbor. In the course of the three days and nights her progress to the south was less than 40 nautical miles. Her longitude—always difficult to determine—was estimated to be roughly the same at the start as at the end of that period of slow headway; but during the three days she had maneuvered and zigzagged so that the distance sailed was almost 140 miles, all in order to advance less than 40 miles in a straight line. Were these maneuvers dictated by sailing conditions or by the belief that land was so close as to be dangerous in certain winds? An answer is not easily offered. During those three days and nights there was a strong southerly swell, along with variable winds that ranged from very light to very strong, even compelling sailors to strengthen a mast. We cannot be sure what went on in the mind of the captain during these days when the coast was close. He must have been tempted, if the sea and wind became more favorable, to send a boat to inspect the nearby shore. After all, he at first speculated, as did Labé, that this might prove to be the coast of New Zealand rather than Australia.

About six or seven hours after the aroma of Australia could no longer be sniffed, the decision was confirmed to sail toward New Zealand. "At midday Mr. Surville after consulting me stood S.E.," wrote Labé. De Surville resolved to sail a short distance southeast toward the latitude of thirty-five degrees, then change course.

THE DAY THAT MIGHT HAVE BEEN

What might well have been one of the most momentous days in the modern history of Australia passed uneventfully. It could all have been so different. If there had been a tiny change in the winds or currents during the previous week, this would have been sufficient to drive the *St. Jean-Baptiste* ten or twenty miles closer to the coast. Accordingly, when the sun rose across that strong sea on Monday, December 4, the entrance to Botany Bay or Sydney Harbor or the mouth of the Hawkesbury might have been glimpsed from the deck or masthead.

From such a vantage point the coastline near Sydney would have been tempting. There stood high sandstone cliffs, through which ran narrow but relatively safe entrances into two of the finest natural harbors in Australia. Measured by the needs of the navigators and fortress engineers of the eighteenth century, the entrances to these two harbors were impressive. Sydney's harbor, once a ship was safely inside, was superb. The first European naval officer to venture inside was to marvel at its magnificence. Along the whole Asian coast from China to India and Arabia, there was probably no natural harbor to surpass Sydney. Even Cape Town, standing on the sea route from Europe to Asia, did not have an entrance as safe and negotiable as Sydney's. As for India, it possessed no superb or natural harbor, whether controlled by the French or British, Portuguese, Danish, or Dutch.

If de Surville had come close to Australia's coast at this point, he might also have been attracted by the sight of the Blue Mountains, rising in places to a height of more than two-thirds of a mile. Whereas the west coast of the continent had seemed flat and featureless to the Dutch, here on the east coast a few stretches of the landscape were more dramatic. Here rose the most prominent mountains—not high by European standards but the highest Australia could provide.

It so happened that high mountains formed part of a theory of the most influential of European naturalists, Comte de Buffon, who was the curator of the royal museums, gardens, and zoos in Paris and the author of an ambitious, fifteen-volume work not completed when de Surville departed France for India. Buffon, who possessed the schol-arly eminence that Banks was later to achieve, argued that the sav-ages tended to inhabit the coastal lowlands while the civilized people would inhabit the higher mountains of Australia's interior. This argu-ment, based on the history of the Aztecs and Incas of America, was neatly summarized, and a few of its key sentences quoted, in a book available in the *St. Jean-Baptiste*: "One presumes that in the interior of Australia the more civilized men will be found in the high country from which the rivers flow to the sea." De Surville was therefore en-titled to think that this region of Australia might, after all, be more at-tractive than the far western coast derided by the Dutch and despised by Dampier. But the Frenchman had decided in advance: he did not wish to inspect any part of eastern Australia.

If the *St. Jean-Baptiste* had been blown a few miles closer to the coast, de Surville might, through sheer curiosity, have lowered a boat and sent it to examine one of these Australian harbors. And if the preliminary reports from the French boat were favorable, he might have steered his ship through the guardian headlands to shores where his crew could recuperate for several weeks. Even if he had found that no stream of fresh water and no edible plants were near the harbor's entrance, and even if, as a result, he had resolved forthwith to sail toward New Zealand, his lightning visit to Australia would have been recorded in his journal, or on a makeshift monument or plaque on the shore itself. Accordingly, France and not England would have been recognized as the discoverer of this part of eastern Australia.

On the other hand, if de Surville had laid claim to Sydney Harbor and Botany Bay, they might not have remained as French possessions. In the long term, the discovery of a fine harbor means little if the harbor is not eventually settled and occupied by the finders. The Dutch discovered dozens of bays and rivers and headlands in western Australia and even called the whole land New Holland, but after two centuries it slipped silently from their possession. Likewise, if Sydney Harbor had been named Port Surville and been marked on the maps as a French possession, it still might eventually have passed into British hands, either peacefully or in time of war.

After sailing southeast from the Australian coast, de Surville's ship turned east. New Zealand, and the coastline that Tasman had explored, lay in that direction. De Surville's route across the Tasman Sea was now aided by the strong westerlies. On Wednesday, December 6, a gale began to drive the ship toward New Zealand at a heartening speed; and during one period of 24 hours the ship covered 170 nautical miles. In the cooler, fresher air the deaths from scurvy diminished: for six consecutive days not one death was recorded. Perhaps the morale in the sickrooms was lifted by the news that the ship was approaching a land where fresh food could be gathered.

Fortunately the killing of the last pigs supplied a little fresh pork for the sick, and giblets for the broth being heated in the ship's galley. The officers, to their credit, demanded no priority in receiving this more nutritious food. Their meals, however, were now becoming gloomy social occasions. "God knows what will become of us," wrote Labé, two days after parting from the aroma of Australian soil.

In these strong seas, with their pronounced hollows and crests, the rolling of the ship opened tiny gaps in her timbered sides. The intrusion of saltwater dampened about two hundred sacks of rice and wheat stored in the hold. So much water found its way inside the ship that the healthier and fitter of the sailors were employing much of their physical strength to work the pumps. Others were busy laying out the food soaked by the seawater in the hope that it could be dried.

Eventually the winds subsided. The groaning and creaking of the ship's timbers grew less noisy. The *St. Jean-Baptiste* crossed the Tasman Sea so quickly that the coast of New Zealand was soon to be expected. Only five days after the French officers had smelled the Australian bush they were inclined to conclude from their own calculations, using the rough-and-ready Tasman and Vaugondy maps set out before them, that the New Zealand coast lay just 41 nautical miles ahead. In fact it lay 390 miles ahead. A day or two later Labé wryly acknowledged that, on the basis of his previous calculations, his ship must now be resting on dry land in the interior of New Zealand!

The morning of December 12 was foggy and the sea was still. After the thundering seas and howling winds of the Tasman, the silence was eerie. Suddenly the quiet was broken by shouts from the lookout. High land could be seen. The news was spread around the ship and carried down ladders to the quarters of the sick. The coastline, seen with increasing clarity, was sandy; and its dunes, according to experienced French seamen, resembled those lying to the north of Cape Town. The narrow harbor of Hokianga came into view. But, guarded by a sandbar over which the waves broke, it was quickly condemned by the officers as too unsafe for the ship to enter.

Farther along the bleak coast a search was made for another landing place. In the following three days and nights, however, the wind and the sea were hazardous and deterred the captain from approaching close enough to inspect the coast. Meanwhile more seamen were dying from scurvy, and those few sailors who were still strong enough had to carry out, as best they could, the tasks called for in that dangerous predicament.

Four days after the first sighting of the coast, with a strong wind blowing and rain squalls beating on the sails, the *St. Jean-Baptiste* made her way toward the northwest tip of New Zealand. Help was almost in sight for all those seamen who were working but aching, or lying below in fear of death. Perhaps the help would come from another ship, for this was the eve of one of most remarkable coincidences in the history of exploration.

De Surville was entitled to believe that he was thousands of miles from the nearest European ship. In fact he was less than a hundred miles, as the crow flies, from Cook's *Endeavour*. The *St. Jean-Baptiste* was now sailing around the top headlands of New Zealand in a clockwise direction while the *Endeavour* was approaching from the opposite position. It seemed certain, or almost certain, that the two ships would meet.

IN THE GRIP OF THE GALE

The *Endeavour*, having left her anchorage in the Bay of Islands on December 5, sailed in a northerly direction. Tacking often to enlist the winds blowing from an unwanted direction, she passed close to native canoes whose riders were surprised to see this monster ship arriving from some mysterious port. Inlets and headlands, sandy beaches and open bays were passed. One was Doubtless Bay, a curve in the coast where de Surville was soon to find shelter. Cook so named it, presumably because it was, without doubt, a bay, though he did not bother to sail inside to investigate it.

On December 13 the rains fell and the wind whistled, flapping the sails of Cook's ship. A squall grabbed the main topsail and tore the canvas as if it were just an old handkerchief. Fearing that his ship might be driven against the shore, Cook headed out to the relative safety of the open sea; and for almost the first time since reaching New Zealand, he could see no land. He also reasoned or half-guessed that, even if he clung to the coast, he was coming to the end of the land. Eager to discover the northernmost headlands and capes in New Zealand, he was about to find them and meticulously pinpoint their position.

When the gale began to blow, Cook had been separated from de Surville by only that narrow peninsula in which northern New Zealand tapers into the sea. De Surville's ship was on the west coast of the peninsula, close to what is called Ninety Mile Beach, and Cook's was on the east coast. Surely the two would meet as they passed the top of the peninsula.

The French ship, "laboring heavily" in the strong seas, at last reached the northwestern capes of New Zealand. On December 15 she approached the sand dunes of Cape Maria van Diemen, long ago named by Tasman during this same season of the year. For the first time in 137 years a European was revisiting one of Tasman's many landmarks on the shores of Tasmania and New Zealand. De Surville, soon changing his ship's course toward the east, was about to follow for the first time a shore that Tasman had not seen. But the sea seemed determined to halt his plan. "We had a strong gale all the afternoon and evening yesterday," de Surville wrote on December 16. "We were under the major sails and the mizzen topsail, everything double-reefed. In this way we resisted very strong rain and wind storms." The same gale would affect his rival, Cook, even more.

At sunrise on December 16, Cook was fewer than fifty nautical miles northeast of de Surville, and the French and English ships were sailing toward each other. For his part, Cook was eager to calculate accurately the position of the North Cape, seeing it as one of the vital navigational markers in this part of the world; and, as soon as the weather improved a little in his corner of the ocean, he would sail toward the cape from the open sea.

The fierce storms dictated whether the two ships would meet or not meet. In the preceding week the summer gales had driven the *Endeavour* away from the coastline that the *St. Jean-Baptiste* was following. At the beginning of this day when their paths were most likely to converge, Cook's ship was still out of sight of land. He recorded that he was using his "utmost endeavours to keep in with" the land, but the large swell from the west coupled with the southwesterly gale made it too dangerous to come close, especially to a coast that was uncharted. Indeed many of the *Endeavour*'s sails, already weakened by storms, were beginning to rip apart.

The same wild westerlies that thwarted Cook favored de Surville. He had to make many maneuvers to cope with the high seas and strong favoring winds, but his ship made quick headway during December 16, passing the northwest tip of New Zealand sometime after sunrise and approaching the North Cape or northeastern tip soon after noon. His crew was exhausted, but his ship sailed on. By about 2:30 that afternoon the *St. Jean-Baptiste* "was weathering round" the North Cape.

North Cape was also Cook's goal that day, but his men did not see it until the following morning. How far away was the *Endeavour* when the French ship approached and rounded the cape? If both ships had posted men constantly at the masthead they might well, at some time on December 16, have seen the masts and sails of the rival ship. But surely the weather on such a stormy day would not have aided such clear visibility? A reading of Labé's journal shows that, despite the high winds and seas, there were times when the sky was clear. Just two hours before reaching North Cape, Labé could still see the peak of one of the Three Kings Islands some fifty nautical miles to the west.

Without doubt the two ships were incredibly close. Possibly for one hour of that summer day, only twenty-five or thirty miles were between them—no farther than the channel that separates England and France. Neither captain had an inkling that the other was also exploring in this corner of the Pacific Ocean, let alone that they were in such proximity.

6

Two Ships Went Sailing By

After rounding the northeast corner of New Zealand and passing the prominent North Cape, the *St. Jean-Baptiste* reached a point on the exact route the *Endeavour* had passed while sailing in the opposite direction during the previous week. The French ship, on many occasions during the next day and night, was to cross the zigzag route that the English ship had so recently made. Although the two captains had fought with opposing navies in the Seven Years' War, any coming together would have been amicable as long as one captain was not pressed hard to disclose vital details about his voyage and its aims. Both were pledged to secrecy. They would have remained tight-lipped except perhaps when they discussed their common enemy, the scurvy, and that eternal enemy and ally, the vast ocean and its winds and currents.

THE COMFORTS OF DOUBTLESS BAY

Instead of meeting an English ship, de Surville met Maori canoes. On the morning of December 17 he saw them emerge one by one from the nearby coast. After half an hour, four of the finely carved canoes were clearly in view, and soon the brown faces of their crew could be seen—eight or ten men in each canoe. There must have been some nervousness on the French quarterdeck as the leading canoes drew near. Tasman had denounced the Maori as murderers, and most of these canoe-men—with their reddened hair tied in a topknot—were obviously well armed.

This first encounter was friendly. All but one canoe carried freshly caught fish, which were eagerly bought by the Frenchmen; the first basket of "excellent" fish was exchanged for a length of white cloth and a knife. In the *St. Jean-Baptiste* everyone who was well enough to eat, whether sailor or soldier or servant, black man or white, received an ample meal. Close to two months had passed since the sailors had been given a large plate of *fresh* food.

Meanwhile several barefooted Maori were invited on board, including one who seemed to be the chief. The French lieutenant who was third in the line of command, Jean Pottier de l'Horme, has left behind a charming account of the first meeting between members of two contrasting races and cultures. Climbing up toward the deck of the *St. Jean-Baptiste*, and seeing her towering masts and hearing the voices of foreigners, the Maori leader or chief was at first nervous: "When he arrived on the deck he appeared astonished and shivered. We patted him a great deal and the Captain embraced him and led him to the quarter deck cabin, and gave him food and liquor. He made him a present of a jacket of heavy red cloth with green Bavarian lace and facings and red trousers. This man let the jacket be put on him."

The chief must have looked a little comical, wearing the bright jacket but no breeches. The red trousers he had not put on but held in his hand. What he thought of his new role as a kind of male model we can only guess, but he responded graciously by presenting the French captain with his own knee-length cloak made from dog skins sewn together. It is not clear whether de Surville put on the cloak, thereby also assuming the role of a fashion plate.

The Frenchmen, contemplating their puzzled guest, decided that he was still not dressed quite according to Parisian protocol. Escorted to the big cabin, the chief allowed himself to be dressed afresh, with a shirt next to his skin and the ceremonial red and green jacket worn on top. Back in his canoe, however, he decided that these bright clothes were not as comfortable as his grey dogskin cloak. Indeed his French garments might well cause ridicule and derogatory laughter among his kinsfolk. So he began to take them off. To remove a shirt with its long, entangling sleeves is not easy when attempted for the first time, and seamen aboard the ship engaged in a little merriment when they saw him across the water, in his canoe, wrestling with those sleeves.

That night, just after sunset, the *St. Jean-Baptiste* was safely inside a deep bay and riding at anchor on a seabed that had been thoroughly tested for soundness and depth. Cook, when recently sailing past the wide and exposed entrance, had named it Doubtless Bay; but de Surville preferred a French name, calling it after Baron Lauriston, the governor of Pondicherry in India.

The following morning, not long after sunrise, canoes came across the harbor to the side of the French ship. Baskets piled with fresh fish were hauled aboard, in exchange for small lengths of white and blue cloth, which the Maori decided should be worn across their shoulders. After eight or more canoes came alongside, the French "had enough fish to feed four hundred men," or nearly three times as many as were aboard.

There was faint risk of the New Zealanders storming the ship as long as the Marines were on guard. For the Frenchmen, stepping ashore was riskier. Outnumbered and on unfamiliar soil, they could easily be taken by surprise and massacred. De Surville therefore planned with care his first arrival on shore. Into a boat were crammed ten soldiers, eight oarsmen each armed with a sword, and the captain himself serving as coxswain. On this overcast, breezy morning the boat sailed through the surf to the beach, where its arrival was watched intently by Maori men and women coming down from the nearby fort with its ramparts and palisades. De Surville either waded ashore or was carried on the shoulders of sailors. Someone of high rank was there to greet him. "He received me graciously and offered me his nose; it is their way of kissing," recalled the captain.

The Frenchmen were guided to a little stream of fresh, very drinkable water tumbling down to the sandy beach. Slowly they filled ten water barrels. Along with the firewood cut and collected on shore, the barrels were carried safely back to the ship. Soon fresh greens were also being gathered in large quantities—green cress and wild celery and the same plant that Cook and Banks had called scurvy grass. It has been said that de Surville had no real knowledge of how to combat scurvy, but these episodes refute the accusation.

The fresh greens were boiled, together with meat or fish, in the pots in the ship's kitchen, or sometimes on campfires ashore. Wild

'SOUTH SEA'

Three
Kings Is.
North Cape
Doubless Bay
Cape Maria van Diemen
Bay of Islands

35°   35°

Hokianga
Harbour
Mercury Bay
Cape Colville
Firth of
Thames
Cape
Runaway
Bay of
Plenty

TASMAN SEA

North Island

Poverty
Bay

Hawke
Bay

40°   40°

Cape Farewell
Tasman
Bay
Queen
Charlotte
Sound
Cape Turnagain

NEW ZEALAND

Cape Foulwind

Cook Strait
Cape Palliser

South Island

Banks Peninsula

Canterbury
Bight

Milford Sound

45°   45°

Gore's
✗ 'Imaginary Land'

Dusky
Sound

'SOUTH SEA'

Foveaux Str.
Stewart
Island
The
Traps

N

The English and French rivals
in New Zealand, 1769–70

Cook's voyage
de Surville's voyage

0   200 km
Scale

50°   50°

cress and parsley, especially beneficial, were sometimes eaten raw. Fruit was sought in the nearby countryside but not found. Near the beach was erected a tent where the sick who were capable of wading the few steps from the rowboat to the shore—and those who were carried—could lie in comfort for much of the day. To spend the night ashore was considered unsafe.

Whenever the chief came aboard the ship he was not only welcomed but also watched intently, for he was inclined to thieve. "He wants everything he sees," was the complaint made privately by the French. For his part, the chief thought the French were stealing his people's supply of fish, greens, firewood, and water whenever they came ashore. To his credit, de Surville realized that he was the trespasser. He thought that he and his seamen should try to be just and considerate toward these "people who are in their own country and have never thought of coming to disturb you in yours."

De Surville was the kind of man who thought it important to be generous but also to be the first to shake his fist, if fists were to be used. As there might be a confrontation between the two peoples, he decided to make it clear that the French would prevail. A lesson had to be taught them. One day, in the presence of the chief, the soldiers aboard fired a cannonball from one of the ship's big guns. With some amazement, the chief watched the ball fly through the air and splash into the bay, sending up a spout of seawater. While other Maori spectators were frightened by this display of force, he was not; when the cannonball hit the surface of the sea, "he gave a loud exclamation and spoke to his people."

After a while the supplies of fish and fresh vegetables sent in long canoes to the ship, to be traded for calico, began to decline in quantity and regularity. Perhaps the daily catches of fish were sometimes inadequate when they had to feed about 140 visitors as well as the local inhabitants. It is also possible that the Maori leader decided to apply sanctions against the overfrequent visitors. Soon the Frenchmen had to catch their own fish.

Ashore the French officers and crew stepped warily. The order had been sent around the ship that the situation, if the crew were careless or impetuous, could become explosive, endangering their lives and even the safety of the ship. When Maori were lining the hill near the fort, the Frenchmen ashore were careful not even to look at them—this was the captain's instruction.

So far the contact ashore had been mainly between the men. Now a few Maori women came forward. Making "extremely lewd gestures," they seemed intent on enticing some of the visitors into the bushes. The sailors and soldiers, though obviously aroused or interested, obeyed their captain's orders not to follow the women. The women continued their friendly gestures, with little result. Labé was surprised at their boldness in conspicuously displaying "gestures that are not made even in brothels, going so far as to lift up the bird skin that covers their nakedness."

Days later, three young women made a final attempt to entice the Frenchmen by indulging in "very lascivious and immodest dances" that reminded Labé of the Spanish dance known as the Mosquito. The captain was their special target. On one of his last visits ashore, de Surville was grabbed round the waist and squeezed hard by a woman who "made the most lascivious movements against me." But the captain was not to be seduced: "I shook her off and we went about our tasks."

Most of the Frenchmen retained a lingering fear that the New Zealanders might take advantage of their officers and crew, and suddenly switch their intentions from making love to making war. The armed men might appear out of hiding and launch a surprise attack or take a hostage. But the ship's chaplain, perhaps naively, had no such fear. Wandering away from his French countrymen one day, he walked some distance from the shore before realizing that he was far from help and that armed Maori were following him. He felt even more in peril when other people came "out from amongst the ferns." There was now a risk that they might be tempted to snatch his musket or perhaps attack him with a lance, a stone spatula, or other weapons. He turned around and set out for home, which he reached safely. Other members of the crew were bold enough to climb the hill to inspect the Maori fortifications. In all these adventures, no visitor was attacked or seriously threatened. The Frenchmen had first landed on these beaches in trepidation. Their fear, derived from Tasman's experience and the violent death of four of his men, seemed to be misplaced.

By Sunday, December 24, the Frenchmen and their African and Asian sailors and servants were more relaxed, a feeling shared by the Maori. "They are beginning to believe we mean them no harm; they are no longer on the alert," Labé said of them. The exchange of gifts fanned friendships. De Surville, hoping that the Maori might become keepers of livestock—they owned only dogs—presented them with a male and female pig and a white, leggy rooster and hen, his only remaining poultry. He expressed the wish that the pigs and poultry would soon multiply. He also donated seeds of wheat, rice, and French peas, and gave instructions on how to cultivate them. His gifts were generous but did not lead to new ways of farming.

Although they had no common language, both peoples were skilled and patient with their signs and mimicry. Each side learned much about the other, though naturally they did not always understand what they saw. In the history of early relations between very distant and dissimilar peoples, these meetings were rather unusual. Respect and incessant curiosity were displayed on both sides.

The contacts between French and Maori in this wind-exposed bay probably formed the longest and smoothest relationship so far forged between foreigners and natives in the vast area fronting the Coral Sea and the Tasman Sea. Along all the coast stretching from New Zealand and Tasmania to New Caledonia and the islands of Torres Strait there had probably been no contact so harmonious, or so prolonged. In contrast, Tasman's crew had spent only a couple of days ashore, disastrous days, while Cook in New Zealand had spent so far no more than eleven successive days in the one place. Even those days spent at Mercury Bay were not cordial.

A FIRST CHRISTMAS

In the arrival of Western civilization into New Zealand, the French were to the fore. The first Christian service to be held was, in all likelihood, conducted by the Dominican chaplain traveling in de Surville's ship. The Reverend Father Paul-Antoine Léonard de Villefeix was a native of the village of Etouars, about eighty miles northeast of Bordeaux. A priest of intellectual stature, now in his early forties, he had refused the offer of a lectureship in theology at the institution where he was trained, the Convent of St. Jacques in Paris. At sea he had to perform many duties because all or nearly all the officers and most of the able seamen in the *St. Jean-Baptiste* were French Catholics, and even some of the Asians were Christians. Those who were ill were especially in the chaplain's care.

Presumably de Villefeix performed mass on Sunday, December 24, 1769, and again on the day that followed. Whether the ceremonies were held in the ship or on shore is not clear, but certainly they were in the present territory of New Zealand. At that same Christmas, in contrast, no religious service seems to have been conducted in the *Endeavour*, which lay a mere sixty or so miles away.

Cook's crew had already celebrated, riotously, one Christmas since sailing from England. While in the roaring forties of the South Atlantic they had celebrated the sacred time so wholeheartedly that the ship, according to Cook, was not being steered quite in the right direction. All good Christians in the ship, added Banks, were so "abominably drunk that there was scarce a sober man in the ship." Fortunately the wind on that day was not strong, otherwise "the lord knows what would become of us."

A year later the *Endeavour*'s second celebration, off the New Zealand coast, was a time of calm sandwiched between gales. "As it was the humor of the ship to keep Christmas in the old fashioned way," wrote Banks, "it was resolved of them to make a Goose pye for tomorrows dinner." The first task was to find a substitute for a fat goose. The sea on Christmas Eve was smooth. A rowboat was launched, and Banks shot enough long-necked gannets—sometimes known as solan geese—to enable the baking of a special pie in the little kitchen.

It was the happiest of celebrations. The breeze from the southeast, being gentle, required the workaday skills of very few sailors until midnight, when the *Endeavour* had to tack. Meanwhile the goose pie gave pleasure, and sufficient alcohol was available to make nearly all hands "drunk." Cook in his journal chose not to record at all the presence of Christmas, leaving it for Banks to describe the general hangover felt on the following day when "all heads achd."

OUR SICK WENT WALKING

The French had much to be thankful for. In the opinion of de Surville the air on land had a healing and wholesome quality that was absent in the salty sea air or the putrid atmosphere below deck. Faith was a small part of the cure for scurvy, and to be on firm land was part of the faith. At first, however, there were suspicions about the spartan diet of greens. Those sick seamen who ate the wild cress became flushed in the face, and for an hour or so they had some trouble breathing. Some said their mouth tasted of blood. After they ate more salad, their breathlessness returned, though it did not last long. Monneron, the young ship's clerk, had no doubt that the meadow cress and the wild, long-leaved cress were part of the cure for scurvy. With surprising speed the disease diminished. Most of the sick regained a little of their strength, and after one week they were able to go wandering. When "our sick went walking in the plain and on the hills," the Maori took no advantage of their weakness.

On several mornings one sailor, probably close to death, was carried ashore from the rowboat as if he were a helpless child. Others were too ill to be carried. Soon a few miracles of recovery were recorded in the Frenchmen's journals. One sailor, his limbs grossly swollen, his mouth "absolutely rotten," his strength so undermined that he could hardly crawl, briskly recovered. Others who had recently been at death's door turned their back on the door and resumed daily life, at first feebly and then firmly. Perhaps forty of the crew were still sick, whereas double that number had been ailing and aching when the ship had arrived in the bay.

Nearly sixty men had died since the ship sailed from the harbor in the Solomons, but now a typical day passed without one death. In the week beginning December 21 only one seaman died, on Christmas morning. Aged twenty-two, he was one of those Filipinos who had been kidnapped from Bashee Island. With the new diet and the rising morale, the ship now held almost a sufficient number of able-bodied men to perform, up the rigging and at the capstan, the more arduous seafaring tasks. Soon the voyage could be resumed, if de Surville so wished. But he did not yet wish it. His men needed at least another fortnight of resting and relaxing, and a diet of fresh food, before the ship could safely sail away.

It was the weather, not the Maori, that forced de Surville to consider resuming the voyage earlier than he had intended. Soon after Christmas a gale sprang up, and the wind and waves tumbled into the exposed bay from the northeast. The broad entrance to the harbor permitted the waves to roll in, thus depriving the *St. Jean-Baptiste* of shelter. The waves broke against her side, washed over her decks, and pressed through tiny gaps in her timbering. Three anchors were now needed to prevent her from being swept onto a reef near the shore.

The pressure grew on the cables linking ship and anchors, so strong was the wind and so "mountainous" were the seas inside the harbor.

The ship began to drag on her anchors and drift closer and closer to the reef and its foam-spattered rocks. At one moment, in the words of an observer, she was only a musket shot away from the reef. A few minutes later she was only a revolver shot away—as everyone knew, a revolver could not fire very far. At the moment of highest peril, the ship was only as far away from the reef as the combined length of two longboats standing end to end. Many sailors in the ship must have been waiting for her to be crunched against the rocks. The crisis was sufficient, wrote Labé, "to make our hair stand on end."

In the face of the gale and thundering waves, the ship carried too much sail, and that also helped propel her toward the rocks. Somehow the few fit sailors managed to adjust the sails. The foresail was the first to exploit the wind and, almost by magic, drove the ship from the vicinity of the reef fast toward a slightly more sheltered anchorage not far away. But danger would persist if the gale continued.

The crew were "terror-stricken." Mostly frail or unfit, they could not necessarily carry out the tasks that might be required to save the *St. Jean-Baptiste*. Even those seamen who were marooned on shore by the swift onset of the gale could see that their ship, at times, was wallowing helplessly in her new anchorage. Lieutenant Jean Pottier de l'Horme, in charge of those sick men who were stranded ashore, walked to the high point of a cove and, looking out over the white-capped waves, saw the ship and feared for her safety in her new place of refuge. She seemed very close to the land and was "side on to the wind and rolling heavily." Not a sail was to be seen, just the three masts standing like "bare poles."

As the rain fell, much of the shore could not be seen from the ship, adding to the crew's sense of peril. It was also difficult to stand up on deck, for the ship was pitching and rolling. Part of the cargo broke loose. A few water barrels, dislodged from their neat alignment, rolled drunkenly around the deck, threatening to break the legs or arms of any careless sailor. Meanwhile the pressure on the precious kedge anchor, the sole survivor of the large anchors, was acute.

All the time every eye watched for any sign of a welcome change in the wind and sea. The waves continued to pummel the deck. The ship was still at the mercy of whatever Nature decided to do. At last the wind appeared to be changing direction, from northeast to north-west and finally to the west, leaving the ship and the mouth of the harbor no longer so exposed.

During the first of those stormy days, various active sailors re-mained stranded on land, along with a group of the sick. About forty-five in all, they had been boated ashore just before the gale struck. Aboard the ship, fears were voiced about their safety. Had they drowned? Were they in danger of attack from the Maori? Or if they were temporarily safe, could those who were seriously ill survive such drenching rains and such cold?

On the first night of the storm, many of the missing seamen had sat in the open boat near the wind-whipped beach, with only a square of sailcloth to protect them from the rain. Next morning, on leav-ing their boat, they were presented with dried fish by a Maori living nearby. "This good man," wrote the ship's clerk Monneron, "feeling pity for the pitiful state in which he saw our sick ones," pressed them to come to his hut. Many of the sick, though not all, accepted his invitation to sit on the hut's earthen floor where they felt safe from the worst of the weather. They hoped soon to be rescued, but in such a sea it was impossible to send a boat from the *St. Jean-Baptiste* to shore. Forced by the turbulent seas to remain ashore for another night, they spent it in a makeshift tent. Next morning de l'Horme led the two boats which, bringing back his "whole flock," crossed safely from the shore to the ship at anchor. At least four of the sick did not recover from their ordeal. On the last Saturday and Sunday of the year two Pondicherry-born Indians, one "lascar" from Bengal, and a boatswain's mate born on the coast of Brittany, died of scurvy.

During the gales the *St. Jean-Baptiste* had lost four anchors and four cables. One large anchor had survived the storm. The dilemma was whether to try to retrieve some of the lost anchors or sail without them. The ongoing voyage would be infinitely safer if they could sal-vage the anchors; but even if the anchors were located at the bottom of the bay, sufficient men of muscle would be needed to retrieve them and then haul them back onto the ship. The biggest iron anchor was not only heavy but large, even its cross-beam exceeding the height of two full-grown men. Its size is known with certainty because it was recovered from the bottom of the bay two centuries later.

It was now feared that the boisterous weather was likely to per-sist. If the wind should again blow directly into the shallow bay, the

St. Jean-Baptiste would be exposed while riding at anchor. While de Surville knew it would be unwise to expose her to another storm, he had no alternative but to resume his voyage without the anchors. He chose to follow an eastward route where the winds were almost sure to be favorable and the ocean so deep that anchors might not be needed. On the way he hoped to find the Jewish enclave, in Davis Land. Later, in a faraway port in South America, new anchors might be purchased, and sails and spars carried aboard. Then perhaps, fitted out afresh and strengthened, the ship could resume her trading voyage.

De Surville's decision to depart hurriedly from New Zealand was hastened by an unfortunate incident. One of his dinghies had been lost during the storm, its rope having snapped. Now, with the aid of a telescope, he saw at the water's edge a group of Maori in possession of the dinghy.

Small rowing and sailing boats were vital to the success of the French voyage. The boats fulfilled countless tasks, including the measuring of the depth of the water when the big ship was about to enter shallow or rocky waters, the conveying of seamen from ship to shore, and the catching of fish. And of course they served as lifeboats. The captain was entitled to feel angry at the loss of his dinghy and the boldness of the Maori thieves who stole it.

Summoning about thirty sailors and soldiers, many of whom carried arms, de Surville packed them into his longboat and steered toward the beach in the hope of recapturing the dinghy. At first detecting no clues, he eventually spotted a trail marking its disappearance. The dinghy had been pulled along the beach and over the sand dunes, and hidden in the reeds of a lagoon.

The captain did not rush to carry out reprisals. Taking his time, he and his men ate a late breakfast consisting of smallish birds which had just been shot, and many pieces of wild celery, all cooked in a cauldron set up near the beach. "We had a heavenly meal," he wrote—a true eulogy from a Frenchman who rarely talked about food.

Resolving to teach a lesson to anyone else in sight, he led his men toward the local fishing village. There they burned the fragile fishing nets, set fire to numerous family huts, and destroyed two Maori canoes. Another canoe, seized as a replacement for the stolen dinghy, was towed back to the *St. Jean-Baptiste*. The punishment of the villagers went on. Even a storehouse in which they kept their precious hoard of fern roots was set alight. The fire, blown by a boisterous wind, spread so quickly through the dry grass that the smoke could be seen from the deck of the French ship in the bay.

A Maori leader, Ranginui, was arrested, his hands were tied, and he was bundled into the longboat waiting near the beach. This was less an act of revenge than a cool decision to capture a knowledge-able Maori who, in the following weeks, could be questioned about the way of life and the natural resources of his people. That, at least, was de Surville's way of thinking. Frightened for his life, Ranginui cried piteously when he was carried aboard. His plight attracted the sympathy of those who recognized him as the stranger who had gen-erously offered food and shelter to them when they were marooned on shore during the gale. The low-roofed hut where they had taken refuge was presumably one of those buildings that had been burned to the ground.

In appearance, Ranginui was not as commanding as most of his kinsmen, being squarely built and about five feet two inches in height. His longish hair was tied in a topknot, and his copper-colored flesh displayed an array of tattoos. He was temporarily placed in irons and manacles for fear that, like the men captured in the Solomons, he would try to jump overboard. Lieutenant Jean Pottier de l'Horme was "touched with the greatest compassion" when he met Ranginui aboard. Here was their kind friend, living in fear. The Maori did not know "what his fate would be." He fell at one officer's feet and kissed them. He then "got up and wanted to kiss me too, with tears in his eyes," wrote the lieutenant. Meanwhile he was "saying to me things that I did not understand."

Four Pacific captives, including Ranginui, were now living in the ship. The two Filipinos—a third had died—did no work around the ship and preferred to talk with each other rather than learn French. In contrast the mischievous young Solomon Islander was learning French and becoming part of the crew, even if not yet an active sea-man. These three seem to have been treated sympathetically, and their daily ration of food was not skimped. But they had no words with which to convey this reassuring news to Ranginui.

To be clasped in irons was an indignity for Ranginui; but to be whisked away from his homeland, against his will, was bewildering. His heart sank as the ship sailed into the open, windswept sea on this last day of the year. Just before sunset he must have seen—whenever he was allowed a glimpse of the sea and shore—the long land receding. Slowly the grassy hills and the frothy-white shoreline grew hazy. But in his mind they remained vivid. Probably he was the first New Zealander in hundreds of years to leave his homeland.

It could be argued that the French, by the reprisals they carried out on their last day ashore, had wrecked their prospects of making an effective settlement in New Zealand. They had thrown away the welcome offered to them and jettisoned their chances of ever returning safely. De Surville would not have agreed with such an argument. He thought that, until the last day, he had been kind and considerate to the Maori. He had also impressed on them that, compared to him, they were lacking in boldness and "enterprise." He believed that his deck guns and portable muskets, along with his own personal strength, gave him complete control of the situation. In his eyes the French, if they wished, could return to New Zealand safely, for the Maori had been taught a lesson.

De Surville did hope to return someday. He felt attracted to this wide bay where he had found shelter and to the fertile patches of soil in its hinterland. Here ran streams of fresh water, here lay plenty of firewood, and in the bay the fish were often abundant. He even contemplated Port Lauriston—his name for Doubtless Bay—as the site for a permanent French settlement, a base from which settlers could explore the countryside and perhaps even discover "great riches."

Admittedly the bay suffered from one grave defect. Ships at anchor were dangerously exposed when a strong wind blew directly into the bay from the open sea. But if a ship possessed adequate anchors, de Surville believed she could withstand those punishing winds and waves while riding in the bay. He spoke from experience, being a mariner of the Coromandel Coast where, harbors being rare, ships had no alternative but to ride the incoming sea. He believed that Refuge Cove, the corner of Doubtless Bay where he had finally found shelter, provided "good holding ground" for anchors, and it was here that the last of his anchors had held firm during the gale. His confidence about the ultimate worth of this harbor was not shared by his first officer Labé, but then, being subordinate, Labé's opinion did not count.

De Surville expected that a more sheltered anchorage would eventually be found in another part of Doubtless Bay. On his last day in New Zealand he had intended to sound out and inspect the mouth of a river that ran into the bay, but the theft of his dinghy and his attempt to punish the thieves had halted his inspection of the promising harbor. "It was too late," he wrote, "I could not go." A century later that corner of the bay, Mangonui, was to be a small port.

Jean de Surville sailed away on the last evening of the year. As his ship was passing out of sight of the northern coast of New Zealand, he called together his officers and explained the choice facing them. Although his ship had lost too many of her anchors and too many of her crew, he had no thought of retracing her path back toward the equator and sailing by way of the Solomon Islands to the Spanish port of Manila or a Dutch port in Java where they could sell all their unsold textiles. Readily the officers accepted his plan to sail toward South America, initially crossing seas which, to the best of their knowledge, no European sailors had ever visited. The westerly wind would surely aid them on this route. And they were accompanied by the hope that the mysterious Jewish presence, perhaps in Davis Land, might be found along the way.

7

Wild Musicians and Wilder Seas

THE FRENCH SHIP and the English ship, fewer than a hundred miles apart, each suffered from the weather after Christmas. The gale breaking into Doubtless Bay eventually compelled the Frenchmen to resume their global voyage. The same gale caught the *Endeavour* when she was close to the most northerly points of New Zealand. Near the Three Kings Islands she was battered by a sea that was "prodigious high." The clothes of the English sailors were dripping wet, for frequent orders were issued to reef this sail or lower that sail in what Cook called these wild and "rowling" seas.

To read one of the private logs kept by an officer of the *Endeavour* for the week beginning at noon on December 27 is to be immersed in storms. On that Wednesday the moderate breezes and the haze over the water both disappeared. The log for Thursday began with the pithy words: "Hard Gales, dark, Cloudy, Squally Rainey Weather." Friday dawned with strong gales and squalls, but then the weather turned fair. Saturday deteriorated into hard gales and then softened, after which the wind blew afresh. On Sunday, the last day of the year, and Monday, the first day of 1770, there were gales again. The sailmaker was constantly at work, stitching the damaged sails.

In a gale a large sailing ship gave out distinctive sounds. A shrill note—likened by some sailors to a troubled hiss—arose from the tops of the waves as they were sliced into spray by the wind. Now and then a thumping sound was heard as a heavy wave broke against the ship's wooden side. Joseph Conrad, the novelist who served as an officer in the final days of the tall sailing ships, recalled the strange sound of the wind blowing against the high sails and spars. He recorded with words the "weird effects of that invisible orchestra." In a storm an experienced sailor listened consciously or unconsciously for such sounds, for they warned him that the ship might be carrying too much sail, thus endangering the masts or spars. It was important, wrote Conrad, for "a seaman to have nothing the matter with his ears."

Cook's ears were sharp. He could hardly believe that here, in summer, his ship was being buffeted by a wind blowing so strongly and for so long. He could not remember such a wind in the North Atlantic or the North Sea. Much worse than the weather near Cape Horn, this was perhaps equal to the wildest he was to encounter in his entire voyage around the globe. He thought it safest to remain many miles from the nearest land during the succession of gales and strong seas, "otherwise it might have proved fatal to us."

In such seas the *Endeavour* made little headway. For three weeks, constantly zigzagging, she advanced only a mere thirty nautical miles along the route that Cook pursued. The slow progress came partly from his sense of duty. He was determined to find the true position of those great nautical signposts, the North Cape and the Cape Maria van Diemen, because only by fixing them accurately on his chart would he be able to guide the next generation of seamen sailing in these seas. And yet the risk of approaching too close to the capes, and the need to retreat to the open ocean when the gale blew afresh, hampered his duties. On January 7, 1770, the *Endeavour* was, as the crow flies, barely thirty miles west of the bay recently abandoned by the French.

A HAVEN AT QUEEN CHARLOTTE SOUND

Now the *Endeavour* was sailing south again, tracing the stretch of coast visited by Tasman. Parts of the coast were barren until there strode dramatically into view Taranaki, or Mount Egmont, as Cook named it. A tall volcanic cone, its sides were capped with snow, making it resemble an iced cake rising almost out of the earth.

On January 14 Cook saw what he later realized was a wide strait. On the following day, towed by the rowboats into a narrow inlet on the southern shore, his ship anchored within a short swim of the land. This narrow inlet he named in honor of the king's young German wife, Queen Charlotte. Not often did Cook select a woman for such honors. With its steep timbered hills and stream of fresh water near the anchorage, Queen Charlotte Sound was an excellent place for replenishing supplies and for refreshing the crew. Celery and scurvy grass were cut for the salads, and fresh fish were caught with lines and nets. The ship was restocked with firewood, and casks of fresh water were carried aboard. Even twigs were cut and brooms made by the boatswain and his helpers. After the six weeks spent in howling winds and swelling seas, this inlet was almost a paradise.

At 1 or 2 A.M. on the first morning, sailors on duty in the ship heard songs coming from the darkness. A day later Banks was awakened by a choir of what he called the "bellbirds." He marveled at the music of these small honey-eaters: "the most melodious wild musick I have ever heard, almost imitating small bells but with the most tuneable silver sound imaginable." Eagerly he looked for them when he went ashore, soon finding them perched on trees, their curved beaks wide open. The reason why their song was so loud and enticing was not discovered for another century: here the female and male bellbirds sang their own distinct songs, whereas among most of the songbirds of Europe, only the males sang.

With the Maori living close by, friendly relations were slowly established, and visits and gifts were exchanged; iron nails and pieces of English cloth were bartered for smoked fish. One day Cook and Banks and Tupaia visited a campsite where they noticed that a dog had just been cooked in an oven. Two bones in a provisions basket—not the bones of a dog—also caught their eye. The leftovers of a meal, the bones were partly covered with cooked flesh and scratched by the gnawing marks made by human teeth. Tupaia, on questioning the people, was told that they were "the bones of a man," an enemy who had arrived in a canoe. Have you, Tupaia enquired, eaten this human flesh? Their answer was yes. "Have you none of it left?" Their answer was no. The seamen who had rowed Cook ashore stood around and listened, their faces expressing dismay or horror as Tupaia interpreted. Tupaia was often Cook's mouth and ears and eyes, and he must sometimes have misunderstood slightly the questions that he was invited to ask the Maori. But the accuracy of this exchange could not be in dispute. To many seamen, this place was henceforth known as Cannibal Bay.

Seamen with a few hours of leisure made social calls on Maori families living near the ship. Banks and Solander, while busily shooting shags with their muskets, were invited to visit a large family and their dogs. Banks particularly relished "the numberles huggs and kisses we got from both sexes old and young," as well as the fish received in exchange for ribbons and beads. Later he called again on this extended family. Their behavior "was so affable, obliging and unsuspicious that I should certainly have accepted their invitation of staying the night with them" but for his knowledge that his ship could be about to sail away.

The crew's working holiday at the sheltered anchorage, extending over three weeks, was almost at an end. Hay had already been cut as long-term fodder for the livestock on board, but it could not yet be safely stored inside the ship because—as every farmer knew—wet hay might begin to smolder and eventually catch fire. Meanwhile Banks and Solander delighted in the daily songs of their magical birds. How they admired their persistence in singing through all weathers! On one of the last days of January, even the blustering northerly wind and the pelting rain were not enough, Banks affectionately wrote, to disturb "the concert of our little musical neighbors." But two days later the heavy rain almost succeeded in silencing "our poor little wild musicians."

During the downpour a neighboring stream, swelling into a torrent, washed out to sea about ten small kegs filled with fresh water. The thick rope holding the ship to the shore was snapped by the force of the wind, and an anchor had to be dropped to safeguard the ship.

Here and there Cook erected signs to inform later Europeans that he had first been here. On one hill he built a small pyramid of stones with musket balls and other identifiably European items perched on top. In another ceremony on a small island a pole was erected and suitably inscribed, the Union Jack was hoisted, and the adjacent lands were claimed in the name of King George III. Various trinkets and small silver coins were handed to Maori people in the hope they would retain possession of them and so provide unmistakable evidence that the British had once landed there.

The formal claiming of the land was as much a prior claim against other European naval powers as against the local Maori. And what lands, exactly, was Cook claiming? Even he could not answer that question precisely. If his own unfinished map of New Zealand had been drawn on paper that day, it would have depicted a land with little geographical resemblance to the one that is now the home of more than four million people. The exploring of the most rugged shores of New Zealand lay ahead of him.

THE LIEUTENANT'S IMAGINARY LAND

After climbing a steep hill in company with his two botanists and gazing down upon the hazy expanse of land and sea, Cook had confirmed that he had made a valuable discovery. In front of him was a narrow strait separating him from what is now called the North Island. The existence of the strait, he wrote, was "the greatest probability in the world." But which two lands did the strait actually divide? Did it divide the island in the north from a continent in the south? That was the puzzle. Was he now standing on a large unexplored continent? Several scientists and officers still had great faith in the existence of the missing continent, though the cautious captain himself was silent on this question.

In the hope of solving these riddles, the *Endeavour* set sail from Queen Charlotte Sound on February 6, 1770. But Cook first had to explore the nearby waterways. After meeting an unexpected current that almost drove his ship onto rocky islets called the Brothers, he sailed through the strait he had found. He was persuaded to give it his name. It was probably the most important feature he had found so far in his new career as global explorer.

The strait was a small prize compared to the continent that was now sought to the south. It was an axiom that the mysterious continent must possess inhabitants, and at first the southerly coastline followed by the *Endeavour* was definitely inhabited. Near the Kaikoura Peninsula—south of the present town of Blenheim—four double-canoes appeared. Banks, who was in a rowboat and eagerly shooting seabirds, did not notice the quiet canoes until they came so close as to startle him. When the canoes and their fifty-seven men arrived within a stone's throw of the *Endeavour*, an invitation was shouted to several canoe-men to come aboard. The invitation was refused, and even gifts were rejected. Their conduct conveyed the impression that they had not known, until that day, that a foreign ship was visiting

New Zealand. Intensely curious about the ship, they delayed their departure until late in the afternoon. At sunset they could be seen in the distance, paddling their canoes toward their homeland.

Was their homeland a peninsula of the missing continent? From the ship, the land in sight seemed large. The coastline, viewed from the masthead, ran far south in a relatively straight line until it bulged out near the site of the present city of Christchurch. The sheer length of this south-stretching coast, slightly hazy on these pleasant summer days, encouraged hopes that it might be part of a big land.

A few days after meeting the canoes, Lieutenant Gore, in charge of the morning watch, glimpsed something exciting. He thought he saw another mass of land across the sea. Cook, on deck at the time, looked closely, calling for his telescope before concluding that the illusion of land came from clouds banked low on the horizon. He was correct. As the sun rose higher and the air became clear, the new land disappeared.

Next day on the quarterdeck, Gore reopened the topic, insisting that he *had* seen land the day before. Gore's opinion had to be taken seriously. Slightly younger than Cook, he knew the Pacific more intimately. In fact he was more knowledgeable than almost any living English mariner about the endless seas of the South Pacific because he had been master's mate in the *Dolphin*'s earlier voyage when Tahiti and other islands were discovered. In his time he had seen numerous unmapped islands emerge above the horizon. Cook, faced with such enthusiastic disagreement from a fellow officer, was in a quandary. While clinging to his own opinion, he was determined that nobody, in some distant year, should accuse him of being merely a halfhearted explorer who neglected his opportunities. Moreover the thought must have come to him that, while Gore's eyesight and deductive powers seemed astray on this occasion, he might just prove to be correct. What if, a decade later, the missing continent was discovered by another explorer, and in the very direction where Gore's finger was pointing? Reluctantly giving in, Cook ordered the helmsman to change course and sail in the direction of what he later called "Mr. Gores imaginary land."

At the prospect of any major discovery there was excitement in the ship, though not in every ladderway and every cubby. Many of the crew were beginning to ache for home. They no longer wished to see the missing continent. The finding of it would call for months of investigation on its shores, delaying the crew's return home to the pleasures for which they were already pining. In the colorful phrase of Joseph Banks, the crew had begun to "sigh for roast beef." In the British Isles in that era, roast beef was too costly to be eaten often by the average family but was widely viewed as a vital source of national strength and a fancied symbol of the solid virtues of the British peoples.

From noon until 7 P.M. the ship advanced in the direction of Gore's mystery land. At the onset of dusk, a time when mountainlike clouds sometimes appeared on the horizon, there was no hint of land. Certainly Cook's powerful telescope, or "glass" as it was commonly called, could detect nothing. His telescope—long and thin like a wooden leg—can still be seen in the maritime museum at Greenwich in England.

In finding nothing, Cook showed just a touch of glee; and those who longed to enjoy a meal of roast beef at home shared it. The ship resumed her southward course, but Banks remained the optimist. He and a few shipmates had found "in some books" a hint—sufficient to stir his optimism—that the Dutch government in the preceding century had secretly despatched ships in order to follow up Tasman's discoveries, and that these ships had found a new land. Reportedly their land extended from New Zealand in a southerly direction until it reached the latitude of sixty-four degrees. If it really existed, that farthest point of land would be far more southerly, far more distant from the equator, than even Cape Horn. A new continent stretching nearly all the way from New Zealand to the Antarctic Circle could theoretically be as large as Europe. With such hints from the pages of old volumes, Banks kept alive his hopes.

What if Banks were correct? On this day the *Endeavour* might conceivably be sailing close to the very land that those Dutch mariners had once glimpsed. On February 19 Banks thought he saw an unusual formation of high land. His spirits soared: "We once more cherishd strong hopes that we had at last compleated our wishes & that this was absolutely a part of the Southern continent," he wrote. A few days later several seamen rallied to the support of Banks. They saw further clues across a stretch of sea. The day had been cloudy with a light wind from the south, but around sunset the sky brightened, revealing one distant peak and an expanse of rugged mountains running roughly between north and south. The height of the peak and the sweep of these distant mountains, possibly illuminated by the evening sunlight, hinted at something grand. Even Cook wondered whether it was a new land, not known even to the Maori.

The high peak stood out starkly before the night fell; it was real. Some weeks later, however, it became apparent that the peak belonged to New Zealand's southern alps.

The seamen felt the biting cold as their ship moved south. The weather became unpredictable. Gales that felled a top gallant mast and a studding sail boom were followed by quieter spells of weather. One afternoon the ship was actually becalmed, and Banks was rowed—or rowed himself—some distance from the *Endeavour* on another of his shooting expeditions. Taking aim, he shot two dark-brown Port Egmont hens, each as large as a Muscovy duck.

The presence of the hens intrigued Cook. As it is probable that he had last seen similar birds five months earlier, on the eve of first sighting New Zealand, he wondered whether they were a sign that another new land lay just over the horizon. This was almost the last time during the voyage that he publicly showed a hope that he might find the missing continent in this part of the globe. Banks did not give in so easily, but even his optimism faded a little. In a self-mocking moment he once claimed with exaggeration that only he and one "poor midshipman" were keeping their hope alive.

From time to time more land came into view. Smoke, a sign of human habitation, was seen. On another day Lieutenant Hicks saw in the distance a fire so fierce that he thought, mistakenly, that it was a glowing volcano. On March 5 the debate was waged between the team named by Banks as "we Continents," of whom he was the captain, and the larger team called the "No Continents." The team game, however, was almost over. What we now know as the South Island of New Zealand—and not the missing continent—was taking shape on Cook's expanding chart.

By the time the *Endeavour* had come to the end of the South Island, and sailed long detours far from its coast, the space remaining in this ocean for the mysterious continent had shrunk. Soon, in the presence of his colleagues, Banks was to comment sadly on what he called his "aerial fabrick," his hypothesis that southern New Zealand was part of this lost continent. On March 10 he admitted that such a hypothesis was virtually demolished. He confessed that his faith in its existence had arisen less from hard evidence than from an intuition so intense that he was puzzled by its very intensity. He still believed that the continent existed. But he conceded that it was likely to be "prodigiously smaller" than he had previously thought. Thousands of miles to the east, Captain de Surville was also doubting whether the continent existed in his part of that same sweeping ocean.

A FORTUNATE ESCAPE

As Cook was not close to the coast, he thought it safe, at night, to continue sailing whenever the moon was bright. Not far from the point that he was to name South Cape he decided to sail ahead, for "the weather was fine" and the glowing moon was lighting up the ship's now-westward course. As the ship was possibly nine or ten miles from the shore, he was entitled to assume that she was in no danger of encountering unseen reefs. But there was danger. Not far ahead stood an isolated ledge of rocks, against which the waves dashed high. Protruding a foot or two above the surface of the sea, the rocks did not become visible that night until the *Endeavour* was dangerously close. She actually passed them "at no great distance." Whether those asleep near the big cabin were told of the near miss is not clear.

After seeing the ledge, the seaman at the helm quickly changed course, steering away from the coast. Sailing about 18 miles from what is now known as Stewart Island, the ship seemed to be safe. But suddenly, in the pale light before daybreak, the moon having disappeared, danger again approached. A man who had climbed to the masthead shouted a warning that waves were breaking over another ledge or "parcel of rocks" just ahead. According to a few observers, the rocks lay three-quarters of a mile away, but one midshipman judged that they were even closer to the approaching ship. He estimated that the rocks were "about half a mile forwards and extending a-cross both our bows." The crisis fortunately summoned all of Cook's seamanship and decisiveness. He tacked rapidly, a maneuver assisted by a change of wind at just the right time. The ship quickly changed course by more than 120 degrees, avoiding the rocks.

The *Endeavour* had been extremely unlucky to run so close to two separate reefs, far from the shore. On the other hand she was lucky to escape. If the breeze had been a little stronger and the ship had been sailing a little faster, she would have reached the second ledge of rocks during darkness rather than in the first pale phase of daylight, thereby heightening the risk of disaster. At that earlier hour the rocks probably would have been invisible until the ship was perilously close. James Matra, a midshipman, gave silent thanks because in his view the presence of a different wind and a different light during the dark hours of that morning "would have occasioned our certain destruction." Parkinson the artist, no doubt echoing what seamen had told him, also thought it was a lucky escape. Being religious, he did not like to use the word *luck*, preferring to record that all men and boys aboard were saved by "the good providence of God."

Cook named these two quite separate ledges of rock the Traps. They were waiting to trap unwary sailors, and his was the first big ship that had ever passed them. He confessed that "we had a very fortunate escape." If the ship had struck the rocks and the sea had become rough, most of the men might have been drowned. Even those who succeeded in reaching the nearest shore would have been marooned. Help from England could not be relied upon. Perhaps three years might have passed before a ship, eventually sent out in search of the *Endeavour*, would have reached Tahiti. Whether it would have then continued the search in the direction of New Zealand is far from certain. Even if it did finally reach New Zealand, it might not necessarily have found the survivors on that long, wave-swept coastline.

A feast was prepared for later that day, after the Traps had slipped below the horizon. Designed to celebrate the birthday of an officer, it might also have been a celebration of a fortunate escape. For the party a Tahitian dog was killed, and the meat was carefully apportioned. The hindquarters were roasted, the forequarters were sliced and cooked as a pie, and the entrails formed the basis of a Scottish haggis. Presumably only the officers and scientists and Tupaia shared in this feast; the flesh of one dog could not feed the whole crew.

Now there arrived, in full view of the ship, what seemed a consolation prize. Gleaming white veins could be seen in rocks ashore, the white so bright and smooth that it almost seemed that this desolate shore was "paved with glass." To Cook, the rock seemed like marble when caught by the strong sunlight. In fact the rock itself was probably valueless granite, and part of the Fraser peaks. In the following century gold-seekers sailing to the new gold port of Dunedin would set eyes on these same glassy slopes. Banks was correct when he argued that this must be a country "abounding in minerals," for gold was not far away.

Changing course, the *Endeavour* began to sail along the west coast of New Zealand. Buffeted by the westerlies and towering waves of the Tasman Sea, each crest followed by a deep hollow, the ship kept well out to sea. Mists and fogs, like curtains, sometimes veiled the wooded mountains on the coast, but inlets were glimpsed here and there. The scientists longed to go ashore and seek minerals and snip samples of the native plants, of which they now had four hundred species, but Cook sensibly refused. He must have expressed his views forcefully, for they were long remembered. He explained how easy it was to sail in and anchor snugly in an inlet, but how difficult it might be to sail back to the open sea in the face of the southwesterlies.

There was something Norwegian about the height of the coastal mountains and the fjords or "sounds"; but Cook did not see the narrow entrance to Milford Sound, one of the most majestic scenes of the entire Pacific. He glimpsed a glacier and stretches of snow but saw no sign of habitation—not even a wisp of smoke from a fire. The only prominent creatures were the albatrosses, with their white faces expressionless as they followed the ship at a distance. Then they effortlessly glided forward, even hovering above the masts. For four days in succession Sydney Parkinson, filled with the glory of the sea and earth, thought the western coastline of the South Island was "as wild and romantic as can be conceived." He might have succeeded in sketching the "mountains piled on mountains to an amazing height" if his grip on the pencil had not been weakened by the rocking of the ship.

Rarely in the voyage was the crew of the *Endeavour* so close to land for so long but not allowed to go ashore. The fog came down like a cloak, and then the winds began to roar before calm descended, after which the ship made little headway. The weather on one gloomy day, though not the worst, "put us all out of spirits," lamented Banks. For nine days in succession he spent only a couple of minutes, if that many, in writing up his journal. Even Cook, the stoic, was not altogether pleased. The main headland on that west coast he christened Cape Foul Wind.

The last fortnight spent off the coast of New Zealand was almost an anticlimax. There was nothing more to see. Unfavorable winds did not enable Cook to find a harbor for his final preparations before leaving New Zealand. When at last he saw an anchorage on the southern shore of Cook Strait, near the home of the bellbirds, the wind came from an unfavorable direction and rain pummeled the ship. "The sea," wrote Banks on March 25, "is certainly an excellent school for patience." Spending his first day ashore after a long absence, he found no new plant. On another day he pushed his way through ferns as high as his head, to find only three new plants, whereas Tupaia was able to fill his small boat with a day's catch of fish. Banks could not foretell that the most stirring months of his life—a period of triumph such as only a few botanists had ever experienced—were just ahead of him.

Cook could already look back on one triumph. New Zealand was his first memorable achievement as an explorer. Admittedly Abel Tasman had discovered it, seen part of its rugged west coast, and fixed—with a very wide margin of error—its position on the globe. It was Cook, however, who saw every prominent cape, discovered that there were two main islands, and fixed their position on the map with impressive accuracy.

Of the six months the *Endeavour* spent around New Zealand, Cook was able to spend only a total of seven weeks ashore, including days when he was on land for only a few hours. In all he had landed at six different points on the North Island but only two on the South Island, both of which lay at the northern end. He proved beyond doubt that New Zealand was not an elongated arm of the mysterious, long-sought southern continent. With patience Cook had mapped a land almost as large as Italy, making only two major mapping errors, both in the South Island. Through lack of time, he mistakenly thought that Banks Peninsula was an island, and he thought that Stewart Island, at the very south, was a peninsula.

Keeping in mind the gales and other contrary winds Cook met, his mapping was incomparable. The big headlands and capes and harbors he positioned almost exactly, for the benefit of all future sailors. Several years later the French explorer Lieutenant Julien-Marie Crozet, while sailing along the coast of New Zealand, was in a position to judge the charts that Cook had made. Their precision,

Crozet later wrote, "astonished me beyond all powers of expression, and I doubt much whether the charts of our own French coasts are laid down with greater precision."

On the eve of his departure from New Zealand, Cook concluded that it was a noble country, with plenty of local timber suitable for every purpose except perhaps the masts for ships. The country contained expanses of fertile soil, excellent fish and oysters, and lobsters more delicious than any the sailors had tasted elsewhere. Under normal conditions Cook thought that Europeans could settle there with ease, and by importing their own grains, seedlings, and livestock they might win a better living than was won by the Maori. Which was the finest place for Britons to settle, if that should "ever become an object"? His answer was the Bay of Islands or the valley of the Thames, both of which offered a safe harbor.

Here in Cook's own hand was the first draft of a prospectus for any ambitious Briton intent on founding a distant colony. If such a place had been found along the Atlantic coast of North America, the excitement felt in London would have been intense. But New Zealand was on the far side of the globe and therefore not so enticing.

Would the Maori resist newcomers? Cook did not underestimate their qualities. They were brave and warlike and also seemed to be devoid of treachery. On the other hand, he thought they were too divided among themselves to display effective opposition to an inflow of white settlers should they arrive in the years ahead. On this question—could the Maori defend their land—he was to alter his opinion.

THE KIDNAPPED PASSENGER

Captain Jean de Surville by now was far away. The *St. Jean-Baptiste*, after spending a fortnight in proximity to Cook's ship near the North Island of New Zealand, had sailed in the direction of South America. De Surville was steering toward that same zone of the southern ocean which, unknown to him, Cook had partly traversed.

The South Pacific was vast, and de Surville correctly assumed that wide tracts were not yet explored. The Jewish colony or Davis Land might be found along the way. The missing continent with its high mountains and its untapped mines of silver and gold might be waiting too. Perhaps the missing continent and Davis Land and the Jewish enclave were other names for the one place. De Surville's deputy had already confided to his journal his optimism toward "our search in the east." He prayed that their crew, once the scurvy had been conquered, might be "more fortunate in finding islands rich in metals in exchange for our goods." He trusted that God might guide their ship toward a harbor worth entering. "God is merciful, He does not abandon his children."

The French ship had sailed from New Zealand with a new passenger, the kidnapped Ranginui. Bewildered after leaving behind the lands of his tribe, the Ngati Kahu people, he was frightened that he might be killed and eaten by the French seamen: "From time to time he is afraid that we will open his stomach and then eat him." Liberated from his irons and manacles, he could see the open sea. His spirits, rising a little as he employed his freedom to move about the ship, could not rise too high because he hardly knew whether he would ever see his own sandy beaches and fishing grounds again.

In due course the daily routine, governed by the ship's bell, began to absorb Ranginui. No work was demanded of this favored guest, and he relished each mealtime, which he spent in the company of the officers. According to the first officer, maybe with some exaggeration, "he no longer seems sad, laughs with everyone, drinks and eats well and sleeps well." Ranginui felt as happy as anyone could feel after being dragged aboard a foreign ship bound for an unknown destination. Possibly he gained consolation, later in the voyage, from the hope that he would eventually be returned to New Zealand.

The voyage across the Pacific was longer than expected. The winds at first were not favorable, and so the ship, in order to harness the west winds, veered into colder seas, at times entering the verge of the roaring forties. The French deliberately went farther south than Cook had sailed in that vast sea to the east of New Zealand. "By this latitude," wrote Monneron, "we experienced, in general, heavy weather which decided M. de Surville to have the body of the vessel tied up with ropes on the quarter-deck to prevent it from getting loose."

No island, not even a sea-splashed rock, was discovered. The growing scarcity of drinking water, there being no port at which the casks could be refilled, harmed sailors whose diet already was heavily salted. As no fresh food was collected, scurvy and other illnesses began to weaken members of the crew. Fortunately the scurvy, which was raging when the ship was in the Coral Sea and Tasman Sea, was no longer so devastating. The seamen who were most vulnerable, especially the Africans and Indians, had already died, and most of the survivors were hardier. The French officers and other officials were the least affected, and only one of the eighteen was to die from sickness in the course of the entire voyage.

Despite the sickness, de Surville stuck to his plans. A formidable figure, he was in full command. Week after week, thinking his own thoughts, he kept the ship on her eastbound course. Usually following close to the latitudes of thirty-four and thirty-five degrees south, he occasionally reached the edge of the roaring forties. In sailing so far south of the equator he was virtually emulating Cook's secret instructions.

Each daybreak, when the crew on duty looked into the rising sun, they were alert for land. Once the land was found, de Surville would be able, he hoped, to sell to the Jewish traders his barrels, crates, and packages of precious textiles and other goods. There must have been many hours when the distant clouds on the horizon resembled low mountains. Again and again when crossing the lonely and landless expanses of the South Pacific, one clearly sees from the deck of a ship these rounded banks of white cumulus clouds that can easily be mistaken for high, snow-topped ranges, especially in the last hour of daylight.

Now sailing far to the south of Tahiti, de Surville entered seas that neither Cook nor any other navigator had entered. From the longitude of about 147 degrees east to the longitude of 120 degrees east, a distance of some 1,500 miles, the *St. Jean-Baptiste* plowed through the South Pacific, sometimes encountering majestic waves that must have seemed frighteningly high even to experienced sailors.

On their voyage from New Zealand they saw no barren rock, no half-submerged reef. Day after day the seamen on watch scanned the horizon but glimpsed no canopied vessel carrying Jews and their merchandise. The French ship was crammed with cottons and silks awaiting a buyer, but there was no buyer in this empty sea.

A MONTH TO REMEMBER

It has not been recognized that the short time between mid-February and mid-March 1770 marked a significant occasion in the geographical history of the world. In the South Pacific the European search for the missing continent had been prosecuted with hope and vigor for more than two hundred years. Now, at the end of the southern summer of 1769–1770, the exciting part of the search was over.

Both Cook and de Surville had shared in this momentous occasion. The British mariner was near the South Island of New Zealand and proving to his complete satisfaction—and eventually convincing even Joseph Banks—that the missing continent would not be found in that region. The French mariner was sailing far to the southeast of Tahiti and proving that the missing continent did not exist there. Admittedly it was still theoretically possible that a habitable continent might be found somewhere in the roaring forties and foaming fifties of either the Indian or the Pacific oceans, especially in the region beyond forty-five degrees south. But much of that land, if it existed, would be situated in a less hospitable climate. Even the sunnier provinces in such a continent—if it existed—would not provide the hot climate and tropical products so eagerly sought by European navigators.

In the eyes of the merchants of this day, a cramped sugar island in the West Indies was preferable to a Tasmania or a New Zealand. During the negotiations for the Treaty of Paris, which ended the war between Britain and France in 1763, the Englishmen had strongly argued that it would be wiser for their country to keep the French sugar island of Martinique than to keep Canada and its vast territory. It was Lord Morton, president of the Royal Society, who in 1768 had stressed how vital it was that the southern continent should have a warm climate. Having once owned most of the bleak windswept Orkney and Shetland islands, to the north of Scotland, he could write from experience when he advised Cook in 1768 that the missing southern continent was hardly worth finding if it lay in a cold latitude, far from the equator. He wrote that such a continent "in a rigorous climate, could be of little or no advantage to this nation."

As we now know the results of these British and French explorations in the South Pacific, it is easy to feel some superiority toward those geographers and scientists who had been so mistaken about the existence of a huge, warm continent lying somewhere between Australia and South America. Indeed Charles de Brosses of France thought there might be several such continents. But we should not smile for long at their misunderstandings. At that time the knowledge about even the world's *known* continents was peppered with error. In 1771 the first volume of the first edition of the *Encyclopaedia Britannica* mistakenly explained that America was "by much the largest part" of the world, and much bigger than Asia. The second volume, though more accurate, vastly understated the area of both the Americas and Asia. Similarly the encyclopaedia, reflecting the latest knowledge, proclaimed that the Andes were "the highest mountains in the world." It was not yet realized that Mount Everest and other mountains of central Asia were far higher. In such a fragile state of geographical knowledge, the belief in a missing continent was not extraordinary but rather a rational attempt to explain a puzzle.

8

Where Are All the People?

⚑ Cook's last day in New Zealand was spent in Admiralty Bay, not far from Queen Charlotte Sound where his voyage around the South Island had begun. Fresh water and firewood had been taken aboard, and rigging and sails had been repaired. He was about to commence his long homeward passage; but which way should he sail? Should he return to the east and so to Cape Horn, or should he continue to the west and eventually reach South Africa and Cape Town and the mouth of his own Thames?

THE CAPTAIN'S DILEMMA

As Cook was halfway around the world, these alternative voyages were of similar length. He quickly dismissed a direct westerly voyage to South Africa, partly because that route offered little hope of finding the missing continent. Many Dutch explorers and merchant ships had already sailed much of that ocean but had found no signs that a large unmapped land might exist, let alone that it might occupy a favorable climatic zone. Cook might have also offered another valid reason for rejecting the South African route: to sail that way would be to face unfavorable winds for much of the way. But he did not yet realize the persistence of the westerly winds in the colder regions of the southern hemisphere.

The more attractive route, in theory, was to sail east from New Zealand and cross the expanse of the Pacific Ocean to Cape Horn,

sailing along those high latitudes where there was still hope of finding the missing continent. That route would fit in with Cook's own
secret instruction—that he must not be "diverted from the Object
which you are always to have in View, the Discovery of the Southern Continent so often Mentioned." Unknown to him, this was also
the route being followed by the *St. Jean-Baptiste* after leaving New
Zealand.

Cook, however, now doubted the existence of the missing continent, unless it was nearer the South Pole than the equator. He had
learned enough in the last year to conclude that the famous prize was
less glittering than he had anticipated when he left England. The
magic of the missing continent in the eyes of the believers was that
it would lie mostly in the tropics and so would be a source of exotic
commodities and maybe precious minerals too; but Cook's recent
experience made him think that if the continent existed it would be
more like a Canada than an India in its climate.

Cook had another reason for refusing to sail toward Cape Horn:
the *Endeavour* would have to approach it in "the very depth of winter," the worst time of the year for such a passage. Moreover the ship
had been buffeted by windy seas during the last five weeks, and her
sails were much damaged. The seas and winds might be even wilder
and more damaging if he approached Cape Horn. Cook firmly rejected this route. Thereby he was imitating a decision made in similar
circumstances three years earlier by Captain Wallis, soon after his
discovery of Tahiti. Wallis had lamented that his *Dolphin* "was leaky,
that the rudder shook the stern very much," and that the bottom of
the ship was damaged, making it unwise to attempt to reach Cape
Horn or the Straits of Magellan in winter.

As both the routes to Cape Horn and the Cape of Good Hope were
unsatisfactory, Cook devised a third option: the *Endeavour* would sail
home by a longer, roundabout, and completely new route. She would
cross the Tasman Sea to what Cook believed was the southeastern
extremity of Australia. On reaching that coast the *Endeavour* would,
in Cook's words, "follow the direction of that Coast to the Northward
or what other direction it may take untill we arrive at its northern
extremity." Eventually it was hoped that she would find her way to a
Dutch port in Java where more supplies could be obtained before she
continued her voyage past South Africa to England.

At this time Cook could not tell whether the eastern coast of Australia ran roughly south to north, or whether it had a vast indentation cutting into the interior like another Great Australian Bight, or even a long promontory stretching eastward into the Pacific. Here lay an enormous area of sea and land waiting to be explored. As for the existence of Torres Strait at the very northeast corner, Cook had his ideas and speculations but no firm opinion.

An attraction of this tropical route was that the sugar and tea, salt, tobacco, wheat and bread, spirits, and other foodstuffs that were now scarce inside the ship's hold could be replenished eventually at warehouses and shops in Jakarta. The reality was that the *Endeavour* lacked adequate supplies of almost everything except salted meat, wheat, and biscuits, and maybe rice. A further virtue of Cook's chosen route was speed. It was probably the opinion of Cook that the ship, once she reached tropical seas, would reach Jakarta quickly with the aid of the southeast monsoon prevailing in that area for most of the year.

The final plan was elaborated on by Cook in the big cabin. He did not positively discourage discussion, but no officer dissented. What is now called Australia would be the first destination. He expected that this would be the safest route for ship and crew. Contrary to his expectations, it would prove to be highly dangerous.

On March 31, 1770, with favorable winds, the *Endeavour* sailed from New Zealand. She was not long out of sight of land when the cold southerlies faded. A slow ship in nearly all weathers, she could only dawdle in the light winds that prevailed during the following four days and nights. The distance she traveled was a mere eighty-three miles. The calm sea and the warm days, however, enabled the sailmakers to mend the sails that had been damaged in earlier storms. A tent was cut into pieces to provide new canvas.

After experiencing weeks of cold weather in New Zealand seas, the crew began to complain of the Indian summer. The air was so humid that some objects began to mold. At daybreak the ship's rigging was almost dripping with dew. On April 9, the sea being "as smooth as a millpool," the crisp sound of Banks's musket was heard as he was rowed around in search of marine life.

On April 15, Easter Sunday, the calm was swept away. A southerly blew up, and big waves rolled in from the southwest and west.

ABOVE Abel Tasman, his second wife Janetjie, and daughter
Claesgen. Their portrait was painted in Amsterdam in 1637,
before Tasman returned to the Dutch East Indies where he began
the bold voyage of discovery that paved the way for Captain Cook.
The painting is probably by Jacob Cuyp.

BELOW The bark *Earl of Pembroke*, later *Endeavour*, leaving
Whitby Harbor in 1768. The painting is by Thomas Luny.

ABOVE Port-Louis in 1776,
three years after the return of the *St. Jean-Baptiste*.

OPPOSITE Captain Cook,
as painted by John Webber in 1782.

ABOVE The Yorkshire cottage in which Captain Cook's father lived in his later years. Its stones and bricks were shipped to Melbourne and re-erected in the 1930s.

OPPOSITE An impressive full-scale replica of the *Endeavour*, launched in 1993. She can usually be seen in Sydney Harbor.

BELOW A family of Tierra del Fuego, their heads "smeared with brown and red paint," were sketched by Sydney Parkinson, one of the *Endeavour*'s two artists, near the southern tip of South America.

ABOVE One of the *Endeavour*'s boats and a small local canoe, in sight of one of the many Maori coastal forts on the North Island of New Zealand.

OPPOSITE The rugged Three Kings Islands, near the northwest cape of New Zealand. This was the only landmark visited by the first three European explorers in these seas: Abel Tasman in 1643, and Jean de Surville and James Cook in the summer of 1769–1770.

BELOW Doubtless Bay, where de Surville spent a busy fortnight, is a mosaic of sandy beaches guarded by fortified seafront hilltops. In this wide, exposed bay his *St. Jean-Baptiste* was almost wrecked in 1769.

ABOVE A modern deep-sea diver examines one of the heavy French anchors lost in the 1769 storm in Doubtless Bay.

BELOW Through two low headlands, the *Endeavour* sailed into Botany Bay in April 1770. Cook praised the safety of the bay for ships, but it was more exposed than he realized to the strong wind and swell from the Pacific Ocean.

ABOVE Point Hicks, where Cook first saw the coast of Australia in April 1770, remains a lonely coastline—except for the lighthouse.

BELOW On the Australian coast the *Endeavour*'s first important zoological discovery was the bustard; it was later followed, farther north, by the discovery of the first kangaroo.

ABOVE The *Endeavour*, after hitting a coral reef, was repaired on the sloping river bank at what is now the North Queensland port of Cooktown; engraving by William Byrne, 1743–1805.

ABOVE Parkinson made this sketch near Cooktown;
he titled it "Two of Natives of New Holland Advancing to Combat."
They wear the "bowsprit yard" in their noses.

BELOW Lizard Island in the foreground.
Here Cook and Banks climbed a hill to seek a gap in the coral barrier.

ABOVE Corals of the Great Barrier Reef, near Cairns.
In the bright sunlight the different shades of blue and green
usually denote the depth of the water. By sailing at night in
these treacherous seas, Cook was misled by the moonlight.
His ship crashed into a barely submerged coral reef.

ABOVE The voyage of the *St. Jean-Baptiste* was inspired by the belief that Jewish or other merchants were already in the South Pacific. William Hodges's panel, painted during Cook's second voyage (1772–1775), evoked a foreign presence there. Called "View of the Province of Oparee," it shows the shores of Tahiti.

ABOVE Tropical diseases swept through the *Endeavour* late in the voyage. Among the dead were Sydney Parkinson the artist (left), and Taiata the Tahitian lad (right), as drawn by the artist. Taiata had been eagerly looking forward to the sights of London.

ABOVE William Hodges's painting of Cape Town, November 1772. A year earlier the *Endeavour*'s visit to this prosperous Dutch-owned port gave Cook and Banks a new vision of what might be achieved at Botany Bay.

ABOVE Sir Joseph Banks, as painted by Antoine Cardon in 1810. Long outliving Cook, Banks had a deep influence on the early British history of Australia.

The gale and the strong swell shook the ship, and one towering wave swirled over the deck and almost "washed several of us overboard," reported Parkinson. At the mercy of wind and waves, the ship was both pitching and rolling. This was the weather they had expected to meet if they had sailed toward Cape Horn, the route they had rejected because of their fear of the tempestuous seas.

IN THE WAKE OF TASMAN

In the past quarter-century a new intellectual trend, especially in Australia, has tended to dethrone Cook. It is said that in exploring the east coast of Australia he possibly used the maps and the information gathered much earlier by the Portuguese or the Chinese. In fact there is only frail or tentative evidence, so far, to indicate that he was following in the path of the Portuguese, and no evidence that he was gaining from a map drawn by Chinese navigators. Cook, however, did sail in the path of an earlier navigator. His name is well known. Just as Abel Tasman's flimsy chart had guided Cook toward New Zealand, so it now guided him toward eastern Australia.

As Cook approached what he hoped would prove to be the east coast of Australia, he did not think he would be the first to discover the major part of a new land. He believed that Tasman had discovered not an island but the southeast corner of the Australian mainland. At that time the existence of the wide strait separating Australia from Tasmania was not known. Indeed, Tasman himself had no specific reason to think he had discovered a separate island rather than a remote corner of the continent. Significantly, in naming his discovery Van Diemen's Land, he had selected the word *land* to signify a region or province rather than to claim that it was a separate land. He was merely copying the naming practices of earlier Dutch navigators who gave to northern Australia—New Holland, to be exact—the name of Arnhem Land and to other regions such names as Eendracht Land and Southland.

Cook's aim, in sailing from New Zealand, was simply to reach the coast that Tasman had found. He would have been surprised if he were informed that one day he would be honored as the discoverer of the east coast of Australia. In his eyes Tasman had already found that coast, at its coldest end.

ZACHARY'S LAND

From the decks and masthead of the *Endeavour*, signs of Australia were eagerly sought. In the belief that the sea might become shallow as the ship approached land, Cook had begun to use a long leadline. It measured the depth of the sea down to 130 fathoms. "We kept the lead going all night," he wrote, "but found no soundings."

Aboard ship the discussions about signs of land must have been absorbing. The prospect of discovering land again was almost an obsession. Joseph Banks, a sounding board for theories and speculations, heard affirmations that the squalls now hitting the ship—and wetting people's hair—must be a sign that Australia was just ahead. He was also half-persuaded that sudden changes in the wind from one point of the compass to another were heralds of land. This kind of weather, he wrote, "is often met with in the neighborhood of land so that with this and the former signs our seamen began to prophesy that we were not now at any great distance from it."

At daybreak on Easter Tuesday the sea was wild and the sky dark and hazy. For a few hours the wind quieted and the sun and moon could be glimpsed, enabling the taking of observations to determine the ship's precise position. Unwilling to lie down, the wind resumed its puffing and blowing, and sailors busied themselves on the top gallant yards. Gale-driven clouds scudded by, squalls thrust rain into the faces of seamen at work, and the westerly swell tossed the ship about. This was equal to the wildest storm the *Endeavour* had experienced in the course of the voyage.

Alert to the possible closeness of land, and feeling the full force of the gale, Cook tried to mark time. Soon after dark he reported that "we wore and stood to the Southward" until midnight, wore and stood to the northwest for another four hours, and then, with a fresh southwesterly gale arriving, stood to the south. To "wear" was a kind of tacking. In essence, the head of the ship was guided away from the wind instead of being brought up to the wind, and this expedient saved stress on the sails and rigging.

Already the seamen observed the presence of birds which, they believed, did not fly far from land. One small bird, of the land rather than the sea, even perched in the rigging until one or two of the ship's boys clambered aloft in pursuit. The sparrowlike bird flew away "and was never seen after." Captain Cook, not regularly a bird observer, saw a gannet and a tern flying close to the ship, and later the sight of Port Egmont hens further convinced him that land was near. The sad spectacle of a butterfly stranded on deck was another hint. Tupaia, keeping his lonely watch, saw a large piece of seaweed float by; it might well have come from a nearby shore.

The wild weather engulfed the ship. Although the gale freshened and then abated, it was still worthy of the name of "gale" on its third day. Then the wind began to moderate a little. In retrospect it was as if the new land, just out of sight, was about to be unveiled. In the early light of the morning of April 19, around 6 A.M., a faint outline of a coast was picked out. Standing some fifteen or eighteen miles away, it was not easily seen. The visibility at first was restricted by haze or a touch of fog, but by 10 A.M. the discovery was clear. Contrary to what Cook had expected, the coast did not seem to run from south to north but more from the northeast to the west.

Lieutenant Zachary Hicks, on duty, was the first to see the land. In his early thirties, probably of Cornish descent but born at Stepney near the London docks, Hicks was noted for his sharp eyesight. Weakened by tuberculosis but carrying out all his duties, he had a good sailor's intuition for distant vistas. He was not easily deceived, as were some of his shipmates, into thinking that a sharply etched bank of cumulus clouds sitting on the horizon was land itself. The land he saw that morning was real. Whereas Cook, half a year earlier, had offered an attractive bonus of rum to the first person to set eyes on New Zealand, he offered no high incentive here; none was needed, in his opinion. Tasman's simple chart—and Cook's skilled reading of it—had indicated that land might be expected any day.

Hicks's journal for that day of discovery, running in the shipboard manner from the previous noon, was simple: "Fresh gales and squally. At 6 P.M., handed ye topsails. At 12 midnight, lay to; no ground 130 fathoms. At 1 A.M., made sail. At 6 A.M., saw ye land making high ..." This entry, marking the most famous day in his short life, ended at noon with the crisp phrase: "a fresh gale and cloudy."

This Australian coastline, now inspected through every telescope in the ship, was rugged. The most prominent cape, once known as Cape Everard but now Point Hicks, was dotted with granite boulders while its sandy beach was studded with several big rocks, awash at high tide. Behind the cape rose a distinctive peak with sandy slopes, but the adjacent ranges, not very high, were densely timbered. As the coast was dangerous, a lighthouse was erected on the cape a century later, and its light was seen twenty miles out to sea.

Cook, without knowing it, had been sailing directly toward the strait severing Tasmania from Australia, and for two hours he sailed his ship farther toward the strait before turning around and following the coast in the other direction. With a favorable wind the ship sailed briskly, parallel to the coast. At about 1 P.M. on that first day in Australian waters there was excitement. A call went up, summoning Banks and Solander from their quarters. They saw that the sea was agitated, with spray rising high. Three water spouts were at work, each in a different place, as if nature were making its own spectacle to welcome the ship.

After the two spouts disappeared, the surviving one whirled and danced on a patch of troubled sea not more than three miles away. Standing upright but slightly shaky, the spout was like a thin column of water stretching upward and becoming transparent near the top. Swaying as if wrapped up by the wind, it reminded Banks of a slippery "tube of glass." It was almost as if a cloud were dangling this glass like a puppet, and manipulating it "by very quick motions." A minor version of a tornado or tropical cyclone, it rotated effortlessly.

As the *Endeavour* followed the coast, the appearance of the land improved. On the following morning Banks awoke, not far from the present border of Victoria and New South Wales, and inwardly rejoiced: "The countrey this morning rose in gently sloping hills which had the appearance of the highest fertility," he wrote. On the sides and top of each hill were trees of "no mean size." Cook was even more impressed, calling it "very agreeable and promising" and depicting the more open patches as "small lawns." The two botanists, already convinced that the daylight was clearer and sharper in the southern hemisphere, marveled at the landscape unfolding.

With the coast as close to the ship as Cook's sense of safety would allow, the chatter in various parts of the ship must have been intense. A new land could bring them women. It could bring fruit, fresh meat, and a change of diet. It could also endanger human life. The crew might be ambushed in their first hour ashore, or their ship could be wrecked, for this seductive coast was entirely uncharted.

Would the local inhabitants be like the South Americans or the enticing Tahitians or the fearless New Zealanders? And what language would they speak? Would their words—like those of the Maori—be intelligible to the indispensable Tupaia? In the private journals kept in the ship there is no hint of these questions, but they must have been asked again and again as the sailors yarned with one another.

"WE SAW SOME SMOKE"

Around noon on this second day spent on the coast, Parkinson "saw some smoke ascending out of a wood near the sea side." Was this a sign of human activity or the result of a lightning strike? In the evening Cook saw "the smook of fire in several places," convincing him that human beings lived there. Temporarily hiding themselves from his prying telescope, the inhabitants would surely soon appear. Five distinct fires could be seen burning in the forest after darkness set in, leading Banks to deduce that the country must be rather more populous than he had at first concluded.

The next day the *Endeavour* was running with a gentle breeze close to the coast when people were seen on the beach—at first with the aid of the field glasses and then with the naked eye. Cook wondered whether they were wearing dark clothes, but Richard Pickersgill thought they were black-skinned and naked. Others, not to be outdone, insisted they were "very naked." In Banks's eyes they were not only black but "enormously black." Obviously they were not like the brownish people of Tahiti and New Zealand. From the ship the fascinated seamen finally counted five people sitting near a fire on the beach. The term given them in the ship's log was "Indians," that being a general name for the dark inhabitants of new lands.

On the strength of this first sighting of people, Banks reached tentative conclusions. On the bookshelves of the big cabin were copies of William Dampier's two books, of 1697 and 1703, which inclined Banks to argue that the Aboriginal people he was watching were the same as the "coal black," African-like people whom Dampier had rather pityingly seen on the far western coast of Australia.

Banks soon had second thoughts. He no longer felt sure these people were connected with those whom Dampier had observed more than two thousand miles away. "So far did the prejudices which we had built on Dampiers account influence us that we fancied we could see their Color," he wrote. In fact "we could scarce distinguish whether or not they were men."

These dark people seemed to pursue a different way of life to those he had met in New Zealand. For example, the fires he saw burning here and there were not large. They were not the great blazes seen near Tahiti or New Zealand, where fires were lit with the aim of clearing bushland in readiness for planting vegetables. No doubt after earnest discussion with his friend Solander, Banks was beginning to think that these dark people—whom he optimistically called "our future friends"—lived the simplest of lives and were probably not even diggers of the soil or planters of gardens.

It was a surprise to the *Endeavour*'s men, after coming from New Zealand, to reach a shore where armed men did not launch a large canoe and race out to inspect this intruding ship! Perhaps, implied Parkinson, the people of this new land did not even know how to build a boat. He was tempted to conclude that "they live upon the produce of the earth, as we did not see any canoes, and the coast seems to be unfavorable for fishing." In short, they could not even catch fish.

This Sunday was one of the more eventful days in the history of the world's exploration, though it is not yet regarded as such in the mainstream accounts written on the history of Australia. For the first time the inhabitants of a vast extent of Australian coastline were examined from afar by strangers, and their way of life was to be analyzed thoughtfully, though speculatively. This day was really more important than the day, earlier that week, when Lieutenant Hicks had first sighted the granite coast. He had discovered a coast already known or assumed to exist. Now his shipmates were discovering a people of whom little was known. In the course of the following four months the men in this ship would record, to the best of their ability though with many mistakes, far more about the Aboriginal Australians and their way of life than had been recorded on all the previous voyages by Dutchmen and others.

As the *Endeavour* sailed slowly north, evocative hills came into sight. North of Bega, near what is now the cheese-making town of Tilba Tilba, Cook had named a high mountain—which rather resembled a camel from certain angles—Mount Dromedary. In Australia this mountain was never to become a national landmark, and appears on no single-page map of the continent, but for Italian scholars it became the most familiar landmark of the entire continent. In Venice in 1774 the publisher of the first global map to include the *Endeavour's* discoveries decided to print—for a reason known to him alone—only one name on the entire Australian coast: that of the cape at the foot of the mountain, Cape Dromedario.

Naming is an ever-present task of a maritime discoverer. Names had to be given not only to coastal peaks but also to prominent headlands and bays. Bateman's Bay was named after the master of a ship in which Cook had served in Canada. Near what is now the town of Ulladulla, Cook noticed a peak that resembled the top of an English dovecote or pigeon house, and he christened it the Pigeon House Hill. A little to the north stood Jervis Bay, named after an English naval hero, though Cook himself did not name it. And a procession of more obvious names was assembled: Red Point, Red Cliff, Long Nose, and Hat Hill, which is the present Mount Kembla.

On most days the only hint of the presence of Aborigines was the smoke from fires burning in forests or in more open country near the shore. The seamen's view—arrived at quickly—was that these fires were for warmth or cooking rather than for burning off the country. One morning, when Banks saw large fires being lit not far from the sea, he exercised his sense of mischief by supposing "that the gentlemen ashore had a plentifull breakfast to prepare." In fact, whether lighting a fire for the purposes of cooking food or for heating themselves in cold weather, Aborigines were not extravagant in their use of firewood. Like all sensible cooks they preferred a moderate fire near which they could stand or kneel without scorching themselves.

The passing ship apparently aroused no excitement among the Aborigines who chanced to see the sails from the shore. This was one of the most remarkable happenings—that they showed no *visible* signs of curiosity. No one saw Aborigines waving to the ship or pointing weapons toward her. When the ship was near Bulla, however, Parkinson "saw several fires along the coast lit up one after another," causing him to wonder whether the Aborigines were trying to signal to the ship. In the light of later knowledge his theory was probably mistaken. If they were signaling with the use of flames or smoke, they were probably signaling to one another.

Every day the visitors were eager to land. In New Zealand they had landed almost at once, but on this coast they often encountered a strong southeasterly swell rolling toward the shore, with waves breaking noisily on the sandy beaches and against the rocky headlands. Several times Cook thought of lowering a boat and sending it to examine the shores in the hope of finding a safe anchorage for the *Endeavour*; but, observing the direction of the wind, he shelved his plan each time.

At last his opportunity came. As the ship was just two miles from the shore and the shape of the nearby coast was favorable, his seamen set to work to lower the pinnace. Seawater slipped through the gaps in the pinnace's timbers, however, and it had to be hoisted back on board for repair. Instead the smaller yawl was lowered, and Cook took his place in this wooden boat along with Banks, Solander, and the four seamen who were to work the oars. Tupaia also went as interpreter. They hoped that any people they encountered would speak the language of the New Zealanders.

While the yawl was being rowed toward the coast, two Aborigines were clearly seen walking on the beach, while two more carried on their shoulders a tiny canoe. It had been doubted that the Aborigines possessed a vessel of any kind, but now three or four flimsy canoes could be seen lying on the beach. For some minutes there was hope that they would turn toward the sea and paddle out to meet Cook. They made no attempt.

The Aborigines on the beach did not seem to be interested in the *Endeavour* riding the swell nearby, though she was much larger than any man-made structure they had ever seen on sea or land. They even seemed indifferent to the approaching yawl and its eight passengers and oarsmen who were eager to meet these people whom Banks now decided were "exceedingly black."

Separated by only a short expanse of sea, an encounter between the two peoples seemed certain. At the last moment, however, the Aborigines ran away. Cook thought of reaching the beach and following them on foot, but he realized that the surf made such a landing dangerous. For a time, in the bobbing boat, everyone peered intently at the countryside into which the Aborigines had disappeared. It was almost like a park, with no undergrowth, and the most conspicuous trees being the tall native palms known as cabbage trees. The beach where this first encounter almost took place was just north of Port Kembla, now an industrial city.

The curiosity of Cook and the scientists, now intense, could be satisfied only by landing on another beach. At daylight next morning, Saturday, April 28, they found a convenient bay, sheltered from most winds. Today Sydney's main airport stands on the northern shore and the long runway extends into the shallows of this bay.

A DAY OF EXCITEMENT

As the bay had a narrow opening and might also be shallow, Cook was not certain whether the *Endeavour* could enter with safety. Therefore at mid-morning the pinnace entered the harbor while the ship rode in the open ocean, exposed to a southerly breeze. From the ship, telescopes were directed to the shores of the bay where a little smoke was rising. About ten Aborigines could be seen standing or sitting near a fire; after a while the group moved to a hill from which they could survey the strangers in the bay. Through the telescope Banks saw two canoeists paddle to the shore and eventually join those on the hill. There stood the largest group of people the crew had seen since the *Endeavour* had reached the Australian coast.

When at last the master of the pinnace returned to report that the harbor was deep enough for the *Endeavour* to enter, he was eagerly cross-examined about the Aborigines he had seen. It appeared that, as the pinnace came toward them, they had walked down to a small cove inside the bay "and invited our people to land." While their gestures seemed to be welcoming, their hands carried weapons. As the boatmen were outnumbered, they had no intention of leaving the pinnace and wading ashore.

The Aborigines were close enough to be clearly seen. Their naked bodies were painted vividly with a white clay or pigment; indeed they were "painted with broad strokes drawn over their breasts and backs" in such a way as to resemble the white cross-belts worn by the British Marines. Talking together with some intensity, these Australians were discussing the strange spectacle—not seen before in their part of the world—of a ship with whitish sails and men with whitish faces. From time to time, observed Banks from afar, they brandished "their crooked weapons at us as in token of defiance." One of the weapons was probably a boomerang.

It was already tense. The Aborigines were far more numerous than had been expected on the basis of the earlier sightings of them.

Would they be hostile or friendly? Were dozens of others hidden from sight?

At noon, as the *Endeavour* passed through the narrow entrance into the bay, seamen saw the Aborigines going about their tasks as if the appearance of a sailing ship were a monthly event. At the south entrance, almost in the surf, four men in small canoes were fishing with the aid of long spears. They barely looked up from their work or glanced sideways. The ship passed within a quarter of a mile of them "and yet," wrote Banks, "they scarce lifted their eyes from their employment." The rustling of the sails and the clap of waves on the ship's side must have been unfamiliar sounds, but they did not seem to reach the Aborigines' ears. Perhaps, it was thought, they were "deafened by the noise of the surf."

Two miles inside the entrance and on the southern shore, many of those on deck still fixed their eyes on the few Aborigines to be seen. A woman and three children, each carrying a small load of firewood, were walking casually from the bushy country toward the shore. The woman, to the seamen's surprise and probably their pleasure, was entirely naked. The Old Testament depicted the naked Eve wearing a fig leaf to cover part of her body in the Garden of Eden; but this woman, minutely examined by Banks through the telescope, did not even "copy our mother Eve."

The woman lit a fire so as to prepare a meal. The smoke and smell of food attracted more Aborigines. The children increased to six while the returning canoes contributed four men. They behaved as if the ship nearby did not exist. The woman also "expressed neither surprise nor concern" at the sight of the ship now riding at anchor barely half a mile away.

Once the early afternoon dinner had been eaten in the ship, several boats filled with officers, sailors, and Marines were rowed part of the short distance to the shore. Suddenly it was observed that the woman, children, and about half the men previously at the fire site were disappearing. Two men remained, standing up. Obviously willing to confront the approaching intruders, they held several weapons including spears much taller than themselves.

As Tupaia had been successful as an interpreter ever since he joined the *Endeavour*, he was inclined to assume that he could talk with the Aborigines. But of their words heard across the water he could recognize not one. Cook, having learned a little of the Polynesian language, hoped that he might understand a few Aboriginal words. But he also understood not a word.

Perhaps gifts would persuade where words could not. The English-made nails had appealed to the Tahitians—so much so that the *Endeavour* had been in danger of being pulled apart by nail thieves. Surely the same iron nails would appeal to people who, having never seen a sharp iron object, might instantly appreciate their value as working tools. Accordingly a few nails and beads were tossed across the narrow gap now separating the Aborigines on land from the foreigners in a boat. These beads and nails, intended to excite mild wonder like the gift of an Easter egg, at first seemed to please the Aborigines. In fact they were puzzled rather than pleased. Although their main cutting tool was only a sharpened piece of stone, that was preferable to the unfamiliar nail, and the Aborigines were indifferent to the gifts.

Cook had the distinct impression that the Aborigines now made a friendly gesture, inviting him and his men to land. The gesture was nothing of the sort. Here were two Aborigines standing firm in the face of boats that carried at least thirty strangers. Cook, however, had no intention of retreating. He wanted a supply of fresh water; at least one of his boats carried empty wooden barrels ready to convey water from shore to ship. In sign language the English tried to explain that they wanted water. The Aborigines did not care what the visitors wanted.

After a quarter of an hour spent in "parleying," Cook ordered his rowboat to proceed straight to the shore. He himself took up a musket and fired a shot, to warn rather than to wound. The sudden noise of the gunpowder forced one of the warriors to let fall his bundle of spears, but he soon picked them up again, making brave gestures. The defenders remained fearless. From a distance of about forty yards they threw a few stones toward Cook's open boat. In reply a musket filled with small shot was fired directly at one Aboriginal man. Hit on the leg, he soldiered on. Again the musket was fired at him, and he ran, slightly wounded, to a flimsy hut.

By now the Marines and seamen had landed on the flat shore. They were in a position to run forward and capture Aborigines if they so decided, but Cook was advised to be cautious. Banks suspected that the tips of their spears were poisoned, though sometime later he was to conclude that the local Aborigines did not employ poison as a fighting weapon. In truth, in some parts of the continent they did have a knowledge of native plants capable of producing a sedative or poison, but the poison was used against animals rather than people.

While Cook and his men were cautious, the Aborigines were bold. From a flimsy bark hut, a man emerged carrying an object not instantly recognized. It was a wooden shield, which, he assumed, would enable him to ward off the small pieces of lead shot fired by the muskets. At least one other man appeared with his own simple artillery, consisting of long spears, and threw them one by one toward the seamen. The spears landed harmlessly in the ground nearby. Several of the Marines replied by firing small shot, which entered or grazed the skin of the Aborigines. For perhaps a quarter of an hour a couple of defenders were brave in confronting two boats loaded with men. Eventually a final spear was thrown toward the Marines.

Descriptions of this encounter in the shipboard journals vary considerably, and the event was probably a little more damaging to the Aborigines than was reported in most journals. On the other hand a more dramatic version of the first encounter was recorded by Parkinson, who depicted the women and children giving a "most horrid howl" before hiding under some bark. His version describes a "lance" thrown dangerously near him and falling between his feet. He added that after one man was shot, his dark friends "were very frantic and furious, shouting for assistance, calling Hala, hala, mae." As these were Maori words, and unknown to the people of Botany Bay, his description is slightly suspect.

What the Aborigines thought we do not exactly know. One message does emerge, however, from the varied eyewitness accounts of this British landing: the Aborigines, while wary of mounting a vigorous defense, hoped that these visitors would quickly go away.

9

In Botany Bay

THE EXCITEMENT of seeing a new harbor and a strange hinterland was temporarily hushed by the death of one of the *Endeavour*'s seamen. Forbes Sutherland was about thirty years old and came from an island off northern Scotland. He was suffering from tuberculosis and perhaps was ailing even before he boarded the *Endeavour*. His disease reared up during the cold weather near Cape Horn, and he must have been an object of pity when the cold winds were blowing hard near the South Island of New Zealand.

By trade he was a poulterer, and on the ship it was his job to prepare poultry and game for the officers' tables or, when game was abundant, for the whole crew. He also carried out other duties—no one in Cook's ship could be entirely a specialist. He was familiarly known as Forby, a nickname used even by Cook.

He died at sunset. The following morning, May 1, 1770, Sydney Parkinson the artist penned one simple sentence: "On this day, Forbes Sutherland, a native of the Orkneys, who had departed this life, was carried on shore and decently interred." The same phrase "departed this life" was written by others in their journals. Presumably the Church of England burial service was read over his grave, near the sandy place where the ship's boats were already filling their casks with fresh water. A nearby geographical point was named after him, a rare gesture to an ordinary seaman. He was probably the first European to be buried on the eastern coast of Australia.

Only one keeper of a journal did not mention Forbes Sutherland's death or burial. That diligent recorder of events, Joseph Banks, was already out of sight on the morning of the burial, excitedly gathering and naming plants. It seems that even Cook eventually forgot about Sutherland's death. Months later, reporting by letter to the Admiralty, he rejoiced that during the whole voyage so far he had lost no man through sickness, not even one. His report possibly reflected the habit of naval captains to exaggerate the care they took of their seamen. Then again perhaps he regarded a death through tuberculosis as an act of God and quite beyond a captain's power to prevent.

A GAME OF CAT AND MOUSE

There was so much to see on the shores of the relatively smooth bay. Native dwellings had to be examined—a "kind of house or wig-wam" was the first description. The carpenters noticed that these huts had no windows or doors, no floorboards, and no inside fireplace. The simplest of shelters, they were made of large strips of bark and such light timber as could be found on the spot. Among these people, unsawn timber was king. Bricks, pottery, and iron were unknown. None of the naval observers publicly expressed the observation, though perhaps they thought it, that people who moved periodically from place to place "like Arabs," to use their phrase, probably preferred a simple shelter that could be built in the space of an hour rather than a more elaborate structure.

The native canoes lying on the beach were inspected with astonishment. They were so slender that a man sitting in them could dip one hand in the water to the left and the other to the right. Small wooden paddles were used simultaneously, one in each hand. Cook, that master seaman, could hardly believe his eyes when for the first time he examined a canoe. He called it "the worst I think I ever saw." Each canoe—and several were more than thirteen feet long—was made of a single piece of bark, "drawn or tied up" at each end. A little strengthening was provided in the middle of the canoe by a few horizontal sticks that extended from side to side, the sticks being held taut by the pressure of the sappy bark. Such sticks were too fragile to sit on.

The ship's carpenter led his team of woodmen into the bush where they sawed the native timber into small lengths fit for the ship's stove and then carried them back by the boatload. Seamen were also on shore with wooden barrels in which they collected fresh water from springs or from holes sunk in sand: "80 tons" was their measurement of the quantity of fresh water they finally stored in the ship. Day after day the ship's log carried the quaint entry: "Wooders and waterers on shore."

Other groups were also at their tasks: sailors cutting a store of grass-hay for the sheep and goats and pigs in the ship, sailmakers repairing or drying the ship's sails, and sailors cleaning away the marine life clinging to the lower parts of the ship. Meanwhile the so-called armorers were working at their forge, burning coal carried all the way from London in order to generate the heat with which they melted iron and manufactured nails.

Cook landed at one place where Aborigines had been camped within the hour. Small fires were still glowing and mussels were cooking in the ashes, the meal having been abandoned. At one or two of these deserted campsites the Englishmen's earlier gift of nails lay there, unwanted. Clearly the Aborigines had examined them before discarding them.

The local inhabitants were entitled to be wary. Where did this huge ship come from? Would she be followed by more, each with their fishing nets, so that few fish and oysters would remain for the Aborigines to eat? How many men were hidden out of sight in the ship, ready perhaps to take over the land? And where did these white faces come from? It was sometimes said that they were the spirits of dead Aborigines returning home. If so, were they friendly or hostile spirits? And what magic was inside their firearms? Why did they walk unthinkingly over sites that were hallowed ground? And where were the women and children? To some of these mysteries the Aborigines probably devised their own answers, just as Cook's men tried to explain away the mysteries they witnessed.

Every British seaman had an opportunity to go ashore one day or another. Boats were frequently rowed from ship to shore, or at least to the shallow water a few steps from dry land. Exploring parties went inland, but all tried to make a point of rejoining the ship before nightfall. Nervous about the Aborigines, they feared they might be wounded by a surprise attack. The decision that all should return at night was based on the knowledge that a ship was a fort and easily defended from an attack using simple weapons.

The first evenings were enchanting for those seamen attracted to exotic sights. From the deck of the ship, after darkness fell, fires could be seen along the edge of the bay and especially on the water. Long after midnight, points of fire could be seen—"fishing fires as we supposed," wrote Banks. The Aborigines in the bay were accustomed to place a small bed of clay on the floor of the bark canoe and there to keep alight a tiny wood fire while they fished at night. These pinpoints of light could be seen gently moving in the darkness, hour after hour.

On the Englishmen's second day ashore the local inhabitants emerged in large numbers. Seamen, busily filling barrels with water, were surprised to find sixteen or eighteen Aborigines assembled in what seemed a determined manner, only a hundred yards away. They appeared to be well armed, though it was not always easy to tell whether they held fishing implements or fighting weapons. While they did not threaten war, they were not friendly. Next day another ten visited the place where barrels were being filled. Cook hoped to speak with them, but even before he landed, they walked away. He followed them along the shore, but the sight of him, on his own and unarmed, did not allay their fears. They had no wish to go near him.

The game of cat and mouse went on. Aborigines suddenly appeared out of the scrub and stood close to small bands of visiting officers and seamen before they disappeared again. Lieutenant Gore was always eager for adventures. After boating to the far shores of the bay to dredge for oysters, he decided to return on foot with one companion, a midshipman. About twenty armed Aborigines, appearing from nowhere, followed Gore at a distance of only twenty or so yards. When he stopped and turned toward them, they halted too.

Surgeon Monkhouse had devised his own strategy for interacting with the locals. After approaching them he pretended to be frightened, and he and his men began to run or move away. For some reason their retreat aroused the "Indians," a few of whom took aim with those long spears that the British called their "lances." The wooden weapons, traveling a distance of about forty yards, were probably intended to warn, not to wound. From such episodes Cook came to the conclusion that the Aborigines had only one wish: "all they seem'd to want was for us to be gone."

The Aborigines could not enter the minds of the newcomers, nor could the newcomers enter the minds of the Aborigines. Each could only make guesses. Richard Pickersgill, seeing two Aborigines step forward from their accompanying group, wondered if they were challenging a seaman to fight a duel. Alternatively, thought Pickersgill, they were simply "commanding us to go away." The dark orators addressed the white men at some length, but the listeners could not understand a word of the "unknown tongue."

After almost a week there lingered a hope that if men from the *Endeavour* could meet the Aborigines face to face for a calm half-hour they would begin to understand each other. William Monkhouse, seeking personal contact, took risks. Not far from the stream or spring where the water barrels were being filled, he and a companion, walking in tree-dotted terrain, came across six Aborigines. His impression was that they were waiting for him. Fearlessly or rashly he approached them, hoping they would talk. Suddenly a "dart," thrown by an Aboriginal lad sitting in a tree, passed close to him. Having thrown his weapon, the boy slid down the tree and escaped.

There were various encounters between the locals and the Englishmen but they are not easily described with accuracy, for it was not known what the Aborigines were thinking. Without doubt they could have killed several seamen who were either not alert as a group or wandering alone. Although sometimes threatening, their manner was not starkly aggressive. On one occasion Cook, Solander, and Tupaia, with no Marines nearby to guard them, set out to make friendly contact with a few spear-carriers. Facing the Aborigines, they spoke to them, perhaps with simple Polynesian words. Alas, wrote Cook, "by neither words nor actions" could the Aborigines be persuaded to come closer.

The hope persisted that the local Aborigines might understand a few Polynesian words and phrases. As Tupaia's tongue had worked miracles in New Zealand, it was natural to expect the same miracle in Australia—if only they could all sit down and talk. Some even thought that if the right English words were spoken, the Aborigines would respond.

One day Tupaia was on his own, some distance from the shore. Quick to adopt such western ways as pleased him, he was firing a musket at parrots. The sound attracted nine "Indians." According to Tupaia's story, they looked just once at him before running away. In these brief encounters between whites and blacks, no one was killed or seriously wounded.

The Englishmen's desire to make contact with the Aborigines did not wane. Two days before the ship finally put out to sea, an English midshipman was wandering in the countryside near Botany Bay. Although he carried a musket, he would have been no match for Aborigines if they had attacked him in numbers. Fortunately he met only old grey-headed people and children. He offered them parrots he had shot, but they refused his gift emphatically, withdrawing their hands and simultaneously showing signs of fear or disgust at his behavior. That he had been walking alone shows how confident the seamen of the *Endeavour* had become. In Banks's opinion the crew had no reason to fear the Aborigines whom, rather harshly, he labeled as "rank cowards." But the midshipman eventually realized he was in danger. He saw, not far away, Aborigines fishing from their canoes and knew that he was hopelessly outnumbered—what if they paddled to the beach and, joining with those on shore, chased and attacked him?

But this meeting of young and old passed off peaceably. For the first time these representatives of two different worlds, the northern and southern hemispheres, had approached each other and almost touched hands. From the midshipman, when he reached the safety of the ship, came the first confident description of the Aborigines—their faces, hair texture, and the color of their skin, which was dark brown rather than black. That he was the only Briton to meet them face to face was the proof of how cleverly the Aborigines, since the arrival of the *Endeavour*, had kept their distance or simply vanished.

While the seamen in their short time ashore had learned much about these Aborigines, they were unable to appreciate the diversity of their skills. Cook and Banks did not realize that the wide array of vegetables, nuts, seeds, and fruits which the Aborigines gathered in the course of the year gave them a more varied diet than that of a typical English or Irish family. The newcomers had no means of learning that a nomadic society depended on its wide-ranging knowledge more than on its simple wooden weapons and utensils. It relied more on its skills and ecological knowledge than on its hardware. For their part, the Aborigines must have understood even less about the way of life, attitudes, and skills of the people who retreated to the anchored ship each evening.

No canoe came close to the *Endeavour*, and no person tried to climb the rope ladder and board the ship. Nothing was stolen on shore by the Aborigines. No gift offered to them, whether nails or ribbons or beads or mirrors or colored cloth, was of the faintest interest. The absence of a burning acquisitive instinct was in remarkable contrast to Tahiti and New Zealand, where thefts were attempted almost daily.

On the shores of the bay, if any people could be dubbed as thieves, it was the Britons who fished day after day in what the Aborigines regarded as their preserve. On one memorable day the big fishing net, hauled through the shallows, caught nearly one-seventh of a ton of fish, providing overloaded plates of hot fish for several consecutive meals. In addition, while ashore the Britons "confiscated" or "souvenired"—two words the Aborigines would have equated with theft—perhaps fifty or sixty spears and a variety of other weapons.

HERE COMES THE BANKSIA MAN

The *Endeavour*'s visit to Australia was one long picnic for Banks and Solander. Rarely in the history of recorded exploration can scientists have been given such an exciting opportunity. Moreover they had the pleasure of collecting in a golden age of botany, when the science of classifying and naming plants had, largely through the work of Linnaeus of Sweden, reached a new level of sophistication. Here grew hundreds of plants that had not previously been collected by a European. While some had been seen by Dutch men and women landing or shipwrecked on the west coast of Australia, they certainly had not been classified and named. Not only were new Australian plants gathered and dried for safekeeping at Botany Bay, but also new fish, animals, and insects.

As they explored further, the two botanists became bolder. After initially walking with armed parties, they starting working more by themselves. To travel inland was easy, for the country was open, lightly wooded, and rather flat. Frequently they halted to express their surprise before resting on their knees to collect plants they had never seen before.

Among the hundreds of plants unknown to Europe was one that, sturdy and strange, was almost fit for a botanical circus. It actually thrived on periodical bush fires, for the heat scorched the fruit, opening the odd-looking seed box and releasing the seeds so that the breeze could whisk them to new ground. A large shrub, its flowers were each like a clenched fist full of brightly colored, thin spikes. At times the flower resembled the busby—the fur hat then in fashion in England.

The color of these flowers ranges from lemon-yellow to deep orange and red and brown. So far more than seventy-five variations of this plant have been found, mostly in the southwest of the continent, but the first was found by Banks at Botany Bay and carried home to England, where it was later drawn in full color. He had first named the shrub "honeysuckle," for it was a favorite of the nectar-eating birds. Twelve years later it was honored with his own name and christened *Banksia serrata* by a Swedish botanist, the son of the famous Linnaeus. In these naming ceremonies Solander was not entirely forgotten: years later another variety of the banksia, distinguished by a fawn flower, was christened Solander's Banksia.

The naturalists' tasks were more difficult than in New Zealand, where their interpreter could glean knowledge about animals, birds, and plants from the Maori. Here they had to employ their own eyes, along with the cunning they had brought from Europe. When they approached an unusual bird or animal they had to command silence from their retinue of Marines or seamen if they were not alone. And when they crept close to a new bird or animal in the wild, they must have been careful not to look it in the eye. This was traditional advice recorded by Richard Jefferies, an English nature-lover and gamekeeper: "remain quiet, still looking straight before you as if you saw nothing."

Wild creatures, when they know they are being watched, usually stare intently and nervously at the eye and face of the potential enemy. It is "always the eye they watch." The human hunter or observer must pretend not to be looking at the wild creature he is stalking or intently observing. "This," affirmed Jefferies, "is the secret of observation: stillness, silence and apparent indifference." Banks and Solander had learned that lesson when they were boys at play in the fields of England and Sweden.

The fourth day ashore, May 1, was exhilarating for the scientists. In England that day was celebrated as the ripening of spring and the prelude to summer, a day when even the boys sweeping chimneys enjoyed a holiday. On the shores of this Australian bay, where the calendar was upside down and autumn was in the air, the day proved to be epoch-making, for Cook and the scientists made their only long excursion inland. Accompanied by seamen and Marines, carrying ten muskets in all, they walked and walked. Small flocks of bright cockatoos and parrots were shot at, and the brilliant feathers of the shot birds were plucked and their bodies gutted so that, back in the ship, the meat could be baked into a pie. Strange animals were glimpsed with gasps of astonishment. In the long grass a small creature like a rabbit was sighted by Dr. Solander, and noticed too by one of Banks's own greyhounds who set out in pursuit, only to lame himself by accidentally running against a stump that was concealed by the grass.

Like detectives, Banks and Solander examined the footprints and pawprints left by native animals on the sandy soil. Here were the signs of a wolflike animal, probably a dingo. Here was the ball of dung left behind by a large, grass-eating animal; maybe it was a kind of stag or deer, they thought. More likely it was a kangaroo. Curiously, in the course of that week, no kangaroo or wallaby was definitely reported.

On this day a far-reaching observation was tentatively made about the mosaic of parklike country and those patches of grassland that Cook called "lawns." The soil near Cook's River, though light and sandy, seemed fertile; between the well-spaced trees grew tufts or tussocks of "good grass." Cook could almost imagine an English farmer—perhaps his own father—arriving with his plow and instantly beginning work, for large areas "might be cultivated without being oblig'd to cut down a single tree." Banks, owner of a farming estate in Lincolnshire, was almost as pleased with the rural prospects, though his viewpoint was more that of a potential pastoralist than a sturdy farmer intending to harness a horse and plow the virgin ground. He exulted that "every place was covered with vast quantities of grass." That evening the exhausted wanderers, carrying their dead birds and their collections of plants and insects, returned to the ship.

Another daylong visit by Banks to the southwest of the bay was not as rewarding. The sandy soils and bushes growing only about as high as his knees reminded him of the moors of England. While not fit for plowing, they might frugally feed a small herd of cattle.

A disappointing fact was that most of the soil around the shores of the bay derived from sandstone and was not very fertile by

English standards. But here and there, especially along Cook's River, lay patches of fertile soil. A century later Chinese immigrants were to improve this soil with the aid of the "night soil" carted from nearby Sydney suburbs. Eventually their market gardens stood out like an oasis. This scene would not have surprised Banks and Cook. Almost certainly they assumed—but did not say so—that if the shores of this bay were to be settled and colonized, the daily work would be carried out by cheap imported labor, and probably by slaves rather than British settlers.

These first inspections of the shores were to have a profound influence on the decision, made some sixteen years later, to dispatch the British expedition that founded the first European settlement in Australia. Mainly the result of two days of walking inland and a few days of strolling along the beach of the bay, these inspections were not likely to be thorough. There remained the awkward question: were they inspecting this land at the wet or dry time of the year? Vital for a judicious assessment of the potential of this strange land, this question could be answered only if Cook's men were to spend several years here, for the climate was so variable.

If a few Aborigines had chanced to arrive in England for the first time that same month, and were not familiar with the vegetation and had no access to records of rainfall, they likewise would have been unable to assess the English climate. We can say that with confidence because we know how untypical the weather was in southern England that month. It so happened that the new spring of 1770 arrived late. The Reverend Gilbert White, a friend of Banks's, remarked on the unusual weather in his village in the south of England, noting "such a constant succession of frost, and snow, and hail, and tempest," that the regular springtime migration of the birds was retarded. The migratory swallows came to his village of Selborne, then disappeared again before returning to build their nests.

In Botany Bay the year-round climate was just as inscrutable to Banks and Cook. Weighing the few available fragments of evidence, they did try to come to a conclusion about the climate. They guessed that this was the dry time of the year—when in fact it was one of the wettest. Therefore they overestimated the agricultural prospects of the land near the bay.

Even the harbor and its advantages for visiting ships was not easy to assess. Years later it was realized that when the wind blew into the harbor from the east, the ships at anchor were not secure. Cook, however, thought the harbor was "safe and commodious," with handy anchorages near the south and north shores. A stream of drinking water ran nearby, and there were various other watering points. Everywhere firewood was plentiful. What more could a visiting sea captain desire? Indirectly he claimed possession of the harbor and the nearby countryside by displaying prominently the "English Colors," and by cutting an inscription on the trunk of a conspicuous tree, recording the ship's name and the date of her visit.

THE BAY OF THE STINGRAY

One fish in particular aroused curiosity. The stingrays were large, diamond-shaped, and rather flat, as if they had been shaped in infancy by a large flatiron. Appearing to arrive with the floodtide, they floated in water that came up not much higher than the men's knees. If accidentally trodden on—and on a shadowy day they were camouflaged—the stingrays were capable of inflicting a dangerous sting with their barbed tail.

The biggest stingray the men caught weighed 336 pounds even after its guts had been ripped out. To drag the whole stingray to the wood-burning fire of the ship's galley would have been almost impossible; it occupied too much space. The big fish had to be cut up outside the ship. Its wings, when cooked, were the most edible, but even the cartilage became soft and palatable enough. The flavor of the flesh, mostly pale pink or yellow–white, was delicate. Most present-day Australians who see a stingray on the sandy bottom of a beach would not dream of eating its flesh; but many do consume it, unknowingly, when it appears on a menu as sharkfin soup or fishcakes.

Cook initially decided to confer on the whole harbor the name of Sting Ray's Bay, for those fish were prolific. But after writing the exotic name in his journal, he hesitated to confirm it. As this was one of the finest harbors he had ever found, he looked for a happier combination of words. Maybe he should honor his botanists? But he had already assigned the names of Banks and Solander to the north and south headlands of the bay. And yet the whole bay deserved a name that smacked of flora. Seeing merit in Botanists' Bay he finally called it Botany Bay, not selecting the name until three or more months after departing from it. If by chance kangaroos had been seen near the bay, rather than later in the voyage, it might have been marked on the maps as Zoological Bay.

Solander and Banks, filled with astonishment, had already collected more plants than they could conveniently handle. When rain set in on the fifth morning, "we were well contented to find an excuse for staying on board to examine them a little at least," wrote Banks. Even when they had collected only one or two specimens of each novelty, the work of preserving and labeling them was formidable. The leaves and flowers had to be dried as quickly as possible, and that was more easily attempted in the open air than in the cramped spaces of the ship. The first task was to lay the plants on the drying paper they had brought in large quantities from London. Sheets of paper were laid out on a spare sail, and plants or clippings were arranged on the paper to dry slowly in the sun, with Banks turning them over every now and then. A small selection of plants was not dried. Kept fresh so that Parkinson the artist could sketch them or paint them in full color, they were wrapped in wet cloth and packed in tin chests. In the space of a fortnight Parkinson made ninety-four botanical sketches, "so quick a hand" had he acquired by virtue of long practice.

In this floral paradise the two botanists implored Cook to stay a few days longer. He heard their pleas with one ear. As many unknown seas and headlands, reefs and shoals lay ahead, he was not inclined to dawdle in the bay. On Thursday, May 3, he resolved to sail the following morning if the wind would allow his ship to pass out of the heads. Fortunately for the botanists, the weather was on their side. A northerly sprang up, which Cook announced "would not permit us to sail." So Banks was able to spend one more day in the countryside and then another in collecting specimens nearer the ship, with the mosquitoes biting him as he hurriedly wrote his descriptions.

Now everyone was aboard the *Endeavour* except poor Sutherland. No sailor had a wish to desert the ship and trust his luck in this strange land. Early on the morning of May 6 the wind at last was favorable. The ship passed slowly through the heads and into the open ocean.

As the *Endeavour* sailed close to the coast, nearly every member of the crew enjoyed a special midday dinner. "We dined today," wrote Banks, "upon the sting-ray and his tripe." The well-cooked tripe made most of the diners smack their lips, but some felt sick afterward. The leaves of an Australian vegetable, the freshly picked *Tetragonia—*

a kind of spinach—were served with the stingray. The prevention of scurvy remained high in Cook's priorities.

Just about the time they sat down to eat, the ship slowly passed the mouth of the promising bay that was to become the great harbor of Australia. Clearly in view were the two high sandstone headlands guarding the entrance, the very headlands which de Surville had almost seen only five months earlier. As the headlands are close together, the full expanse of the harbor—it veers and extends to one side—cannot easily be seen from a ship standing a few miles out to sea. From the *Endeavour* the twin headlands could clearly be seen; but just inside the harbor a rough sandstone ridge largely obstructed the view of the main arm of the harbor. It was given the name of Port Jackson, a name once familiar to most Australians but now little used.

The winds were light and the sea quiet as the *Endeavour* advanced slowly north. One morning Banks awoke to find the sails wringing wet with dew. On Tuesday, May 8, Cook regretted that the ship, owing to slight winds and an unfavorable current, had advanced "not one step to the northward" in the last twenty-four hours. The sea current that had favored de Surville was now Cook's opponent. But there were wonderful sights for those who had eyes to see. Thus one evening Parkinson saw two perfectly shaped rainbows with a strangely dark light separating them, and one rainbow so brilliant that its colors were reflected on the sea. There could be no clearer picture of the calmness of the sea in which the *Endeavour* sailed.

Sailing close to the coast, Cook passed the site of Newcastle without noticing the mouth of the Hunter River. A century and a half later, ardent admirers of this steelworks city observed that if Cook had actually seen the mouth of the Hunter and the pleasing harbor, the first British settlement would have been planted there rather than at Sydney. It was true that the Hunter twisted its way to the sea through river flats far more fertile than any soils near Sydney. And yet if Cook had been rowed to the estuary of the Hunter, he would not have praised its difficult entrance or anchorage. It is forgotten that Newcastle became a prominent port only after breakwaters were built.

Did Cook possess a blind eye when he passed fine harbors? His distinguished biographer once remarked that Cook "consistently missed the best harbors in those countries he deemed of most importance." Thus in New Zealand he did not find the entrance to Auckland, which was camouflaged by islands; and so for another half-century it was entered only by long Maori canoes. The narrow entrances to Wellington and Lyttelton, now important ports, he failed to discover; and he minimized Sydney Harbor and missed the river-mouth entrances to Newcastle and Brisbane.

In defense of Cook, he was primarily concerned with safety. Careful to steer some distance from the shores that he was inspecting, he could easily miss glimpsing the mouth of the safer harbors. Moreover those harbors considered to be the safest, especially in the era of sail, tended to combine a narrow entrance and a high adjacent coastline that often served as a windbreak. And so such harbors by their very nature were largely concealed from a high lookout in a ship in the open ocean. In addition, the east coast of Australia, by European standards, is deficient in safe natural harbors. Port Kembla and Newcastle, Hay Point, Townsville, and most of the bustling east-coast ports that now receive big overseas ships are man-made harbors with costly breakwaters of stone and concrete, or long jetties. And of those eastern Australian harbors capable of welcoming a ship as small as the *Endeavour*, most were river estuaries, and often guarded by a sandbar which could be a hazard even at high tide.

So Cook's converted coal-carrier sailed slowly along, the men on watch barely noticing port after port that would one day attract huge ships so cavernous that they could each carry three or four hundred times as much coal as the *Endeavour* had carried in her earlier life. By the year 2000 this long line of Australian coast would be one of the world's main suppliers of black coal, producing annually far more coal than the British Isles. But when Cook followed the coastline, the rich seams of black coal were of little worth. The age of steam was in its infancy.

Cook's seamen saw no sign of the coal from the ship or when venturing ashore. What they saw were miles of sandy beaches: white sand, pale yellow sand, and golden sand, with timbered hills and sometimes windblown sand dunes rising behind. In the fullness of time these beaches would become well known; and those sea passengers who today follow the route of the *Endeavour* now see the baby skyscrapers of Tweed Heads, Surfers Paradise, the Sunshine Coast, and other resorts, glorying in the sand that in its plenitude had almost dismayed Cook.

10

Into the Coral Jaws

To READ the daily diaries and journals kept in the *Endeavour*, and to learn of the sails so handled as to harness the varying winds, to hear the roughening of the seas, and to peruse the mishaps and alarms, is to glimpse a sense of purpose among the people crammed into those small wood-walled spaces. But ninety people, or more, are incapable of avoiding quarrels or forgetting their personal suspicions. Even the discipline imposed and the loyalty demanded by a firm captain cannot prevent the steam from rising and the kettle boiling over. Near the coast of what is now central Queensland the kettle not only boiled over but splashed hot water all around. Cook's personal clerk was the one scalded.

On Wednesday, May 23, having recorded the workaday details about the sails, winds, and seas during the preceding twenty-four hours, Cook added a few troubled sentences. The writing of them pained him. Almost under his own eyes, a scandal had taken place in the night.

His personal clerk, Richard Orton, had been drunk, and Cook recorded that a malicious "person or persons in the Ship took the advantage of his being drunk and cut off all the cloaths from off his back." That was not the end of the assault on Orton. His assailants "some time after went into his Cabbin and cut off a part of both his Ears as he lay asleep in his bed." Parkinson in his private journal was more dramatic. "This day the captain's clerk had his ears cut off."

It is unlikely that the clerk lost the whole of his ears but maybe he lost more than just the flabby flesh. Although no instrument was mentioned, it presumably was a knife. Blood must have flowed, and perhaps the surgeon was summoned, but the bleeding is not mentioned.

Throughout the congested spaces of the ship the news of the episode must have caused astonished chatter and speculation. When Orton next day appeared in sight of the ordinary sailors and officers, he was like a walking sideshow, and every eye must have turned toward the two mutilated ears. There were also glances at his clothes to see if they showed signs of the snippers. By then he had put on other clothes.

After Cook was told of the assault he began an inquiry. But all the questions asked yielded only silence or evasion. At first the culprit, whoever he was, had no intention of owning up. Soon the young midshipman, James Mario Matra, was named tentatively by Orton as the likely ear-cutter. Matra, aged about twenty-four and a native of New York, was enterprising and mischievous. Part of his ancestry was Corsican, which meant that, somewhat unjustly, he was seen as the offspring of southern European savages. He had been a frequent drinking friend of Orton's—"drunken frolics" was the description Cook gave to their partying. Moreover Matra had snipped off Orton's clothes on a previous occasion. No wonder he was viewed as the likely culprit.

Obviously the relationship of the pair was out of the ordinary. Matra had once been heard to say that he would like to murder Orton and that only a fear of punishment by the law prevented him from carrying out his wish. This in itself was powerful evidence against him. As the victim was so drunk that the snipping of his ears appears to have caused him little pain, and as he did not awaken fully from his stupor in time to see his assailant, he was of little help in answering questions. On the other hand he perhaps knew more than he was willing to tell about their emotional relationship.

After weighing the sparse available evidence, Cook felt uncertain. In his careful handwriting, in blacker ink than usual, he agonized over who had been the culprit. To make matters worse, Orton and Matra were not a pair of rough-and-tough seamen but members of the exclusive quarterdeck. Cook viewed the whole episode and the secrecy surrounding it as a blow to his prestige. What an insult, he thought, to "my authority in this Ship"! What a reward for his unfailing willingness to listen to all complaints and grievances! He rightly believed that he was the only one who should mediate in disputes and the only officer who should deliver appropriate rebukes and punishments, and yet here was an unknown person inflicting his own form of punishment. "I have always been ready," announced Cook, "to hear and redress every complaint." So he privately praised himself, and with some justification.

Discipline had to be maintained during a hazardous round-the-world voyage; it was vital for the safety of the ship. Therefore if the culprit could not be identified, a sacrificial lamb had to be found to atone for the assault on Orton. Young Matra, the well-known frolicker, was sent for, spoken to sternly by the captain, and virtually suspended from duty. He was forbidden to walk on the quarterdeck. In essence he had to mingle with the crew rather than the officers—a humiliating sentence in a status-conscious vessel.

It is feasible that Cook had additional reasons for suspending Matra. The young midshipman did not always pull his weight in the daily tasks of the ship, and his services were not necessary for her smooth running. In short he was "good for nothing." Three weeks later Cook, concluding that Matra had been taught a lesson, decided that he was not guilty of "the crimes" and reinstated him. At that time Cook possibly had an additional motive for forgiving and reinstating Matra: the *Endeavour* had run into danger, and young Matra must have pulled his weight during the crisis. That he was a person of potential was demonstrated in his later career, which included a long period as British consul in the North African port of Tangiers.

The episode of Orton's ears provides an insight into daily and nightly life in the ship. Space was tightly rationed; many of the ceilings were low, and partitions were not always noise-proof. Any privacy was precarious. And yet on this breezy night the rushing and swishing of the sea and the wind, and the creaking of the ship's timbers, had provided enough privacy for whatever took place in Orton's cabin. The drinking session must have gone on when many people only a few feet away and, separated by a thin partition, were still awake. The actual snipping of the ears took place in the time of night called the middle watch, which ran from midnight to 4 A.M. By then everyone on the quarterdeck—except the officer keeping the watch—was probably asleep, and so the violent act could more easily be accomplished. The fact remained that several people in the ship must have known with some degree of certainty who was the aggressor. That they refused to tell Cook was, to him, a vote of mistrust.

A DAY IN ANT LAND

Apart from the affair of Orton's ears, one topic was of riveting interest on board: would they meet the Aborigines again? If fertile land was encountered, surely Aborigines would be there. Two days before the Orton affair the shoreline had become more attractive, and at nightfall Banks vowed that it was as fertile "as any thing we have seen upon this coast." After anchoring overnight, the ship briefly passed another stretch of fertile land. Covered with palms, it savored of the tropics, which the *Endeavour* was steadily approaching. Smoke from Aboriginal fires became frequent. On a beach two Aborigines were seen walking and taking no notice of the ship. Presumably they observed it but thought it prudent to adopt the cunning stance of the hunter, looking straight ahead rather than at the strange marine animal following their coast.

The next morning, in a cold wind, Cook and Banks went ashore in warm cloaks, which they soon threw off. By mid-afternoon the sun was "almost intolerably hot." Mangrove trees and their strange roots fringed the lagoon, and pelicans "far larger than swans" strolled about. They were so shy that "we could not get within gunshot of them." In the salty shallows there was delight when edible shellfish and little darting fish came into view. Oysters, mussels, cockles, and even small pearl oysters were seen in the shallow waters.

The bushy mangroves on the water's edge provided excitement. On closer inspection they were seen to be concealing nests of ants. As soon as a branch was disturbed by Banks, the ants rallied in large numbers, taking their revenge and "biting sharper than any I have felt in Europe." Green, hairy caterpillars, feeding on the leaves of the mangroves, arranged themselves like soldiers in neat formations. If by chance they were brushed against and disturbed, they immediately stung, reminding Banks of the stinging nettles growing at home. He named these small green creatures the "wrathfull militia." Two centuries later an entomologist—not familiar with Banks's journal—reported that when these insects contacted the human skin they were capable of instantly causing "a painful sensation not unlike that produced by a stinging nettle." It was almost as if he had been reading Banks's words.

Meanwhile the Aborigines were nowhere to be seen. The ashes of their recent campfires were found, and one was still burning, with cockleshells and fishbones—the signs of a recent meal—littering the ground. Judging by the trampling of the soil near the cooking fire, the Aborigines might have been camped there for some days before they fled, presumably after seeing or hearing the seamen stepping ashore.

The place was bleak. Where, apart from a thicket of trees, could the Aborigines find shelter in a cold night wind? "We saw," regretted Banks, "no signs of a house or anything like the ruins of an old one." Tupaia, who had been rowed ashore in the hope that his language or his observations might at last prove useful, gave his scoffing verdict of the scene with just two Tahitian words. Cook interpreted him to mean that here were people leading a comfortless life that was beyond belief.

Throughout the day's visit no Aborigines were seen by those seamen wandering ashore. The officers and seamen who stayed aboard, however, were more fortunate. Across the sea they saw perhaps twenty Aborigines standing on the shore. The Aborigines looked for some time in the direction of the strange ship before departing "into the woods."

THE BUSTARD AND THE GRASSLANDS

The telescopes held to the eye in the *Endeavour* did not penetrate far into the interior of the continent. On the other side of the rib of mountains that ran parallel to the coast stretched grasslands, which in due course would produce more wool than any other country in the world.

This home of the stinging insects was one spot where grasslands came close to the sea. Here, near the Aborigines' abandoned camp fires, a few grasslands birds could be seen pecking at seeds and even seizing small reptiles on this late-autumn day. One bird was watched with curiosity. A bustard, it sported a long and slightly curved neck of white, and a head neatly capped in black. When it flew low and straight, with a slow and regular beat of its orange–brown wings, its wingspan was impressive, so too was its ability to fly long distances without food or water. Other parts of the world had their bustard— they belonged to the family called *Otididae*—but the Australian species was distinctive.

Long-legged, the bustard conveyed an independent and self-respecting air as it strolled along in search of food. Of the visiting seamen—indeed of every human being—it was wary. Therefore the Aborigines traditionally set out to hunt a bustard by concealing themselves behind a branch of a bush that they held in one hand while their other hand clutched a stick to which was attached, as bait, a live moth or butterfly. The fluttering of the moth attracted the bustard, which unwisely moved in the direction of the concealed hunter. If, however, the hunter was in clear view, the bustard took fright and flew away.

On this warm day the bustard, feeding near the banks of the lagoon, was caught off guard. It seems likely that the *Endeavour*'s seamen had rowed up the lagoon, sounding the depth of water here and there. As they did not resemble hunters, the bustard ignored them. In what proved to be a tragic day for his species, he was shot at close range, his plumage examined and his beak marveled at. Carried to the ship, he was weighed: the scales registered just over seventeen pounds, though Banks reckoned it at fifteen pounds.

Aboard, the bird was dismembered and cooked for dinner. The verdict, almost unanimous, was that the officers had eaten nothing to equal its flesh since leaving England. The Aborigines, we know, always enjoyed eating the bustard's dark-colored flesh, and later Australians regarded it as perhaps the most delicious of all native birds and willingly paid high prices for it at their markets. For decades the bustards were to remain plentiful. In many parts of the continent they assembled in big flocks at the start of the mating season, and one flock numbering a thousand was to be seen in 1897 near Hay in the Riverina where the mating call of the strutting males, a drawn-out "hoo" sound, boomed across the plain. But the day came when, on the grasslands of most Australian regions, the bustards became rare.

The place where this bird was killed was christened "Bustard Bay," and the name survives. During the voyage along the eastern coast, so far as can be ascertained, this was the only place to be named after a native bird or animal. A small tourist town now straggles near the lagoon where the stately bustard was killed. It is quaintly named the "Town of Seventeen Seventy."

THE WHITSUNDAY MAZE

As the *Endeavour* sailed north, the days became warmer and the landscape more forbidding. Near the mouth of the Fitzroy River the seamen noticed how the muddy outflow discolored the sea, but elsewhere the land seemed brown and dry. One arid shore, visited on May 29, was aptly named Thirsty Sound. The ship slowly crossed shallow seas. As it was too dangerous to sail at night, the anchor was dropped, and when the voyage was resumed in the morning a small boat was sent ahead to probe the seabed and verify that it was deep enough. Sometimes the warnings shouted from the boat came just in time to prevent the *Endeavour* from running aground.

To the naturalists, ashore or aboard, came diversions and bonuses. They rejoiced to see a swarm of butterflies covering three or four acres like a colored quilt and so close together that one swish of a seaman's cap would propel scores of them into the air. Banks and Solander marveled at snakes swimming in the clear sea, flying fish skimming over the still surface, a "shoal of fish about the size of and much like flounders but perfectly white," and beautiful parrots flying above poor country spotted with small gum trees. Eucalyptuses were observed in all their variety. Banks must have been one of the first botanists to use the now popular word *gum* to describe them. *Eucalypt*, a later name, was chosen not by the early Dutch and English navigators but by a Frenchman who did not visit Australia.

The land seemed fit for nothing. If questioned closely, Cook might have been forced to concede that this stretch of shore was the most forlorn he had seen since leaving the tip of South America; and yet it was to become a prolific producer of minerals. Close to the coast was the rich gold of Mount Morgan, from which came the income that in 1908 financed the first successful search for oil in the Middle East; and further inland lay hidden coalfields, which in time would supply Japan, China, and western Europe. Parkinson the artist actually saw these mineral riches in his imagination, and farther north he wrote of these "very high hills, whose bowels are probably rich in ore."

Close to the coast Cook reached a maze of islands, through which a passage had to be found. To fly over the islands today by helicopter, and to travel from Brampton Island to Hayman Island, is a quick journey of only about ninety-three miles, providing a clear view of the tangled geography. Cook had no such luxury. He had to find his own narrow channel past the islands.

On the larger islands were narrow sandy beaches and rocky headlands. Occasionally mountain peaks prevented seamen from glimpsing what lay ahead, and they must have been tempted to row ashore, climb one of the peaks, and snatch a spectacular view of the islands all around. If Cook had climbed the main peak on Lindeman Island he would have clearly seen, in the Whitsundays alone, several dozen of the seventy-four islands. Today they support a chain of holiday and boating resorts, but most of the islands remain uninhabited, out of bounds to campers, and as peaceful as they were when the *Endeavour* glided past.

ECHOES OF SPAIN

At this stage of the voyage, Cook's feelings took a new turn. In his journal on Sunday, June 3, 1770, he showed an acute religious awareness. For the first time he turned to Christianity for his list of landmark names. Christening a narrow strait between the maze of islands "Whitsunday's Passage," he explained that it was discovered "on the Day the Church commemorates that Festival." The festival of Whitsunday or White Sunday was a favored day for conducting the ceremony of baptism, and white garments were traditionally worn. On this same day, the fiftieth day after Easter, he also named a distinctive island as "Pentecost," the formal name for this holy day. Resembling the head and resting paws of a lion, the island deserved a name, but the choice of Pentecost emphasized that something unusual was at work in Cook's mind.

His belated burst of religious zeal is surprising. Cook's ship had celebrated two Christmases at sea and, as we have seen, they were riotous rather than religious occasions. The ship had passed through two Easters, the second one falling almost on the eve of the discovery of the east coast of Australia, but the shipboard journals make no mention of any celebration of that Easter and drop no hint that so far in the voyage Good Friday had twice come and gone. There is no specific record of Cook, in the course of the long voyage, conducting a Sabbath service or a burial ceremony, even though as captain of a naval vessel one of his duties was to uphold the principles and perform the ceremonies of the Church of England. The absence of evidence does not necessarily mean that these formal religious duties were neglected in the ship, and we do know that surgeon Monkhouse preached on several Sundays in Tahiti, his message being heard by many curious inhabitants. It is relevant to observe that in Whitby, when young, Cook had been under the influence of Quakers. Their religious feelings were expressed quietly and personally rather than through those rituals and that cycle of holy days dear to the Church of England and the Church of Rome. It is therefore odd that Cook should suddenly select holy days as names for his latest discoveries.

His desire to commemorate this particular Whitsunday, this day of Pentecost, is puzzling, until we also notice at this time his quickening interest in earlier voyages made in this region by Catholic navigators. On at least one voyage the Spanish had sailed somewhere on the sea that Cook was now approaching. He therefore had wondered, as he sailed toward the Whitsunday Islands, whether he might come across the land they had discovered and named. It was even conceivable that he might find relics of their expedition—perhaps the wreck of a small rowboat or a stone cairn built on a cape.

From their port of Callao in Peru, the Spanish had long been exploring the southwest Pacific. Their first such voyage, commenced in 1567, led them to the Solomon Islands. Their second voyage toward Australia, launched in 1595, failed to set up the Spanish settlement they had planned. The devout Portuguese-born pilot, Pedro Fernandez de Quiros, who had guided the ships on that disastrous second voyage, was determined to succeed again. Inspired by his pilgrimage to Rome in a holy year, he returned to Callao from which, in December 1605, he set out to pilot yet another Spanish expedition across the Pacific. Traveling with him were six Franciscan friars led by Martin de Munilla, who was said to be over eighty years of age. Also with them was the Spanish admiral Luis Vaez de Torres, who was later to discover and pass through the strait separating New Guinea from Australia and so find a route to the Spanish port of Manila.

The Spanish fleet of three ships eventually approached to within fifteen hundred miles of the eastern coast of Australia. Although de

Quiros believed that he had actually reached that coast, he had really found the largest island of the New Hebrides group, now the republic of Vanuatu. In a deep bight or bay, named in honor of St. Philip and St. James, the voyagers laid the foundation of their city of New Jerusalem, a city never to be built. There on Sunday, May 14, 1606, the day of Pentecost or Whitsunday, they went in procession from the beach to a new chapel thatched with plantain leaves. Laying claim to all the land spreading "as far as the South Pole," they called the land *Espíritu Santo*, meaning in English the Land of the Holy Spirit. This name they prefaced with the word *Austrialia*, because the royal family of Austria ruled Spain. By a process of alteration and attrition—so it is argued—the slightly shorter name "Australia" came into vogue two centuries later.

Cook knew most of the essential facts about the de Quiros expeditions. But the position of the land they discovered was uncertain, partly because the Spanish were secretive but more because their calculation of longitude was often astray. Nonetheless mapmakers did their best to pinpoint their discovery. One of the maps in Cook's possession boldly depicted de Quiros's new land. It confidently insisted that the land was not the present Vanuatu but lay on a part of Australia's coast that the *Endeavour* was fast approaching.

Drawn by Robert de Vaugondy in France, this recent map showed a rather straight Australian coastline suddenly bulging eastward in order to embrace de Quiros's discovery. Vaugondy's map extended northeastern Australia's real coastline several hundred miles to the east. According to his map, the proposed city of New Jerusalem was in almost the same latitude as today's Townsville.

Each day Cook must have been watching intently for signs that the coast, in conformity with Vaugondy's map, would belatedly begin to veer to the east. If the coast did veer, Cook might soon reach the site of the unbuilt city of New Jerusalem. Frequently thinking about the bold voyage of the Spanish ships in 1606, Cook knew the significance of the day of Pentecost, or Espíritu Santo, for de Quiros. And as Cook sailed toward that Spanish-inspired bulge so conspicuous on Vaugondy's map, and as he noticed on his calendar that this very Sunday was the day of Pentecost, he selected the names Pentecost and Whitsunday for landmarks on his new chart. That this was probably the first day in the course of his long voyage that he turned to the

Christian calendar reflects his thought that soon he might be walking in the seaboots of de Quiros.

Day after day Cook scanned the horizon, wondering whether the coast would bulge, but it refused. In fact, as it extended north, it contracted. Eventually, a week or more after passing the Whitsundays, he concluded that the Spaniards' land of Espíritu Santo must be well out of sight of the coast. Therefore de Quiros could not have discovered the coastline that the *Endeavour* was following. Eventually Cook was to write in his journal a final comment on de Quiros: "we are morally certain that he never was upon any part of this coast."

A DECEPTIVE COAST

To Cook the land currently in sight gave no sign that it would ever become a holiday-maker's paradise. Neither the navigator in him, nor the plowboy, was pleased with what he saw: most of this coast seemed to be barren. It was Banks who was a trifle more impressed.

Whenever he saw smoke rising from distant fires he inferred that the land could at least provide the Aborigines with food, water, and shelter. Occasionally, from the deck, he even watched "some very large smooks." Probably they had been lit by Aborigines in order to burn the dry grass and so encourage young shoots after rain.

One dark night Parkinson was entranced by a bush fire, its flames darting here and there—even jumping across creek beds and igniting bush on the far side. No smoke could be seen, only the licking flames and their "very grateful odor." Parkinson vowed that it was like the aroma coming from the burning of "the wood of gum Benjamin." Benjamin, or benzoin, was a resin collected by tapping trees in Sumatra and Java, and used for making perfume and incense. As it was also an ingredient of varnish, its odor was familiar to painters, many of whom likened it to the smell of vanilla. Here was one of the first recorded attempts to describe the sour-sweet odor which even today pervades some Australian cities on those summer days when smoke is blown by the prevailing wind from bush fires in the interior.

Pleasing patches of country sometimes came into sight. After passing the Whitsundays, Banks wrote with approval: "In the evening the countrey was moderately hilly and seemed green and pleasant." He was not committing himself—it only *seemed* green. During the opening ten days of June the ship passed close to a chain of alluvial plains and river valleys that were to become one of the world's major producers of cane sugar. She passed close to the Pioneer River where the sugar port of Mackay now stands. She passed near the fertile flats of the Burdekin River, south of Townsville, and what are now the cane fields around Ingham and the banana plantations of Innisfail, and was soon close to the present cane fields around Cairns and Mosman. But as nearly all of this fertile country was hidden from their view, the seamen were entitled to feel a little despondent at what they saw from the deck. And yet, Banks reminded himself, even Europe had its coastal wildernesses. When he passed infertile Magnetic Island and its tumbled rocks he decided that it resembled Cabo da Roca on the Portuguese coast.

Since leaving Botany Bay the crew had rarely gone ashore, and then only for a few hours. Few bundles of greens were collected and few fish caught. The scurvy was in danger of reappearing. Soon after leaving Botany Bay, Tupaia felt a soreness in his mouth and a swelling in his gums. For about a fortnight he remained silent and uncomplaining, for he did not realize that these were dangerous symptoms. After breaking his silence he was plied with extract of lemon.

Soon the ship reached Palm Island, where a party landed in the fading light. Here occurred one of those little incidents that was talked about for days. Banks longed to make his first close personal contact with Aborigines, and when he and Lieutenant Hicks and Solander were about to return to the waiting ship, "an Indian" silently appeared in the darkness. Quite invisible, he "shouted to us very loud." They searched for him. As so often had happened, he simply vanished. So this strange, ghostly land continued to puzzle the visitors. The sea, too, was about to puzzle them.

INTO THE CORAL JAWS

Once inside the tropics, Cook was likely to encounter coral reefs; but at first they were concealed by the sea. Sailing close to Hook Island, where coral reefs can be viewed today through the windows of a large underwater observatory, Cook saw no coral. He passed, at times, almost within sight of the main coral reef, the Great Barrier Reef, lying many miles out to sea; from the masthead, seamen occasionally

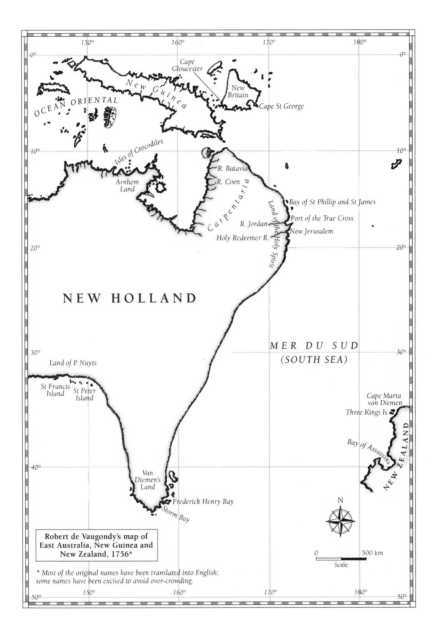

Robert de Vaugondy's map of
East Australia, New Guinea and
New Zealand, 1756*

* Most of the original names have been translated into English;
some names have been excised to avoid over-crowding.

might have gazed on the turbulent waters just above that massive reef. But there was no strong reason for them to deduce that it was a coral reef—indeed the largest in the world.

Coral reefs are numerous in the tropics. India and the Red Sea have their reefs, and Tahiti and the nearby islands are ringed by them. But not one of those reefs could match the maze of reefs that the *Endeavour* was now entering. The Great Barrier Reef runs for about thirteen hundred miles along Australia's east coast, sometimes near it and sometimes out of sight. Not impassable, it is a wall with many openings through which the seawater sometimes runs swiftly. At first its extent was incomprehensible to Cook. Although the corals grow best in water that is warm and sunlit and shallow, they can also grow at such a depth that they almost defy discovery. Two centuries after the *Endeavour* passed by, the Apollo spacecraft, looking down momentarily on North Queensland, would provide photographs of coral reefs that were not on the official charts.

As the *Endeavour* sailed north she entered a funnel, with the Australian coast on one side and the main barrier reef on the other. At first scores of miles in width, the funnel gradually becomes narrow. The Great Barrier Reef is not a single huge reef—it is misnamed— but a jumble of reefs running alongside the coast.

Into this half-hidden trap of jagged rocks the *Endeavour* groped her way. Shoals, shallows, and reefs lay just ahead or to the side. Some were isolated rocks that could be clearly seen, and others so near the surface that they forced the tide to swirl around them. White and yellow sandbars, the sand being of startling purity, were visible at low tide but completely covered as the tide rose.

So the ship advanced almost at snail's pace, while sailors constantly sounded the depth of the water. Often a small boat with oars or sails had to go ahead to determine whether the water was deep enough. On many nights the ship anchored securely, but the wind could be so fierce that some seamen wondered whether the ship would be driven aground if the anchors proved useless. Banks, not a seaman, was probably voicing the fears of others when he wrote: "we had nothing to expect but going ashore on some one or other of the shoals which lay around us."

Initially there was not a sign of coral in the tricky island-studded waters. Banks first identified a coral island near the present city of

Cairns on Saturday evening, June 9. He might have failed to identify the coral except for the fact that the ship dropped her anchor nearby. Although the nearby island was cloaked with rainforest, he recognized that the forest and soil lay "upon a large Coral shoal." Named in honor of the ship's astronomer Charles Green, the island served as a warning. Curiously Cook that day did not even mention the coral in his journal. Apparently he did not yet realize that many of the coral reefs, indeed the most dangerous reefs, were invisible.

11

A Seductive Moon

⚓ THE *Endeavour* was about to face calamity, and Cook's part in that calamity is not easily explained.

One secret of Cook's success so far was that he was not, like de Surville, on a mercantile voyage where time was all-important. He could spend months in the leisurely inspection of unknown coasts, though he still had to watch his time. He does not say so in his daily journal, but the food in the ship would become scarce if the voyage should be unduly prolonged. The scurvy too showed signs of reappearing. Moreover for more than a year he had been exploring where no European or Asian had sailed before; and so now a touch of emotional strain, some wear and tear, was no doubt present. He was approaching, he hoped, the end of the uncharted seas. Thankfully he might soon enter seas that had been somewhat explored by the Dutch and Spanish. He had good reasons to reach those seas as soon as possible.

THE CAPE CALLED TRIBULATION

On Saturday, June 9, the *Endeavour* was anchored close to the entrance to the present-day harbor and holiday resort of Cairns. Now the port receives an annual flood of tourists from Japanese, Korean, and other overseas cities, but on this winter day nothing was there to entice a visitor. Cook, Banks, and Solander were not in the least enticed. Having found no water at Thirsty Sound more than a week earlier, they hoped to find enough fresh water here to fill their casks. But mangrove trees, their roots sticking out of the mud, prevented them from stepping ashore on what is now called Mission Beach. Further along, the prow of the rowboat could not safely touch the shore because of the surf and the rocks. At Cape Grafton an attractive little stream of fresh water ran over the sandy beach, but the water casks, if they were filled, would have to be rolled or carried over rough ground back to the boat.

Cook abandoned his idea of spending another day examining the shore. That evening, when the moon rose from the surface of the ocean, he decided that it was a pity to waste its dreamy light. At midnight the anchor was weighed and the *Endeavour* sailed past tiny Green Island where that day the first coral had been identified. A faint breeze behind her, she resumed her course in a northerly direction. Although a few showers fell, the moonlight was sufficiently bright for the steersman to feel confident.

The wind, freshening before sunrise, assisted the ship. By 10 A.M. she had completed the crossing of the curve in the coast that Cook christened Trinity Bay, for the day was Trinity Sunday, the last name of religious significance he would invoke during the rest of the voyage. Soon he passed the headland of the present Port Douglas and was near the largest of the Low Islands, so named because at high tide they were partly covered by water. Cook perhaps did not realize that these were coral islands, enclosed by reefs.

The next cape on the mainland was a grassy hillock rather than a rocky headland. To sailors on watch it was visible only from certain angles and indeed was low compared to the conspicuous mountains that rose behind it. It hardly deserved a name, and yet Cook would soon christen it Cape Tribulation. Then part of everyday speech, and resonant with familiar biblical echoes, the word *tribulation* is now outdated and used mainly in the phrase "trials and tribulations." To Cook, however, it was a powerful word, and he used it to christen the cape because here—he afterward wrote—"begun all our troubles." His grammar was not quite correct, but what did that matter when the life of everyone on board was in danger?

On Trinity Sunday at 10 P.M. the ship continued to sail. Cook deliberately chose, as on the previous night, not to anchor, for he wished again to harness a moon so brilliant that it was turning the sea in front of him into an illuminated pathway. He passed close to

Pickersgill Reef, seeing it clearly because its surface of white sand was above the highest tide. He did not realize that another coral reef lay a few miles ahead.

"Having the advantage of a fine breeze of wind and a clear moonlight night," as he recalled, he had every reason to feel confident. As the breeze was blowing from the land, there was little risk of the ship being swept by tide or current too close to the coast. There was another source of reassurance: several of his skilled seamen were intent on heaving the lead and ascertaining the depth of water in which the ship was sailing, so that any sudden change in the position and composition of the seabed would be quickly detected. The scene seemed wonderfully serene in the soft light, with the gentle flapping of the sails, the air neither cold nor hot, and the moon smiling on the water. There was little noise except for the sound of voices as the men with the leadline regularly called aloud their information.

Suddenly the atmosphere changed. Tension crept in. The depth of the water began to alter erratically. Between 6 and 9 P.M. it had been quite deep. Now it became shallower, a mere eight fathoms, or forty-eight feet. While plenty of water still lay beneath the ship, the quick change in depth was ominous. Cook called everyone to his post in readiness to adjust the sails, drop anchor, and allow the ship to pass the night in a safe anchorage.

After 10 P.M. the men heaving the lead reported cheerful news in a loud voice. The water was becoming deeper again, being twenty-one fathoms. The depth declined a little toward 11 P.M., but the water underneath the ship was still deep enough to provide a feeling of comfort. What more could a captain want in the soothing light of the moon? Cook went to bed.

From the nearest point of shore the ship at times might well have been visible: gliding along at a gentle speed, carrying no sails except the double-reefed topsails, and thus ensuring that only a fraction of the gentle wind was being harnessed. Surely there would be sufficient time, if another shoal came into sight, for those on watch to shout a warning. But when the moment of danger arrived, no seaman shouted—so far as is known—even a word of warning.

At about 11 P.M. the ship ran into a reef. She did not just run into it; with her momentum, and the breeze behind her, she ran *on top* of it. There, after much grating and shuddering and jolting, the bow of the ship came to rest. The reef, consisting of sand and stones as well as a core of coral, was probably covered completely by the sea at the time of impact. Later, when the tide fell, part of the rock would lie above the water.

Alarmed at the noise and the shuddering, Cook ran up the ladder wearing only his long underwear. The other officers, jolted from their sleep, quickly appeared. Their fear as they hurried into the open air must have been sharpened by past experiences of a similar crisis and all the mishaps that might ensue. Was water flooding in? Had any seamen been knocked overboard or flung from the masthead by the force of the collision? Was their ship about to sink?

Banks left behind a record of his own astonishment: "scarce were we warm in our beds when we were calld up with the alarming news of the ship being fast ashore upon a rock." The ship, strictly speaking, was not ashore but on an isolated reef. The anxiety of nearly everyone was magnified by the sound of the wind and the tide, together beating against the ship, which was wedged on the reef. So violently did the ship shake that "we could hardly keep our legs."

A sense of purpose took over. The officers, it was observed, were "void of all hurry and confusion." Those who were first to arrive on deck knew or guessed, with the aid of the moonlight, how grave the situation was. Some wreckage, especially a few boards torn from the bottom of the ship, could be seen floating on the moonlit sea. It was impossible to assess the damage to the sides of the ship until boats were lowered. The yawl was let down first into the slightly swaying sea; the crew took to the oars, and the master examined the sides and bow of the ship from every available angle. The pinnace and the longboat were eventually lowered, though the sloping deck made the operation difficult.

A task of these boats, once in the sea, was to convey the light and heavy anchors to the positions deemed suitable for each. As the ship when anchored was more likely to survive the buffeting, and as the anchors would play a vital part in the physical tug-of-war needed to drag the ship off the reef, the careful selection of those sites for the dropping of the anchors was crucial. The placing of the anchors took some time.

In this rush of orderly activity the seamen aboard, and those seamen rowing the yawl in its urgent tour of inspection, were the frontline sailors. Often they could hear each other at work. Being sheltered from the open ocean by the outer wall of the Great Barrier Reef many miles to the east, the sea was not vociferous enough to muffle the human voices passing on orders, messages, and warnings. Nor was the wind strong—it would have been called a pleasant breeze if the ship were sailing along. Above the sounds created by the light sea and wind, the crew in the endangered ship could hear the handling of the ropes and sails, and the orders shouted to men aloft or in the nearby yawl. The commanding voice of Cook must have been heard from time to time. He was not known for his silence when urgency was in the air.

The *Endeavour* was carrying a light volume of canvas at the time she hit the reef. Nonetheless the wind, in blowing her sails, was inching the ship further onto the reef. Seamen climbed aloft to dismantle the tops of the mast and remove the yards and heavy sails. The main mast was not one solid length of timber but consisted of the stout basic mast, supporting overhead the separate top mast and then, right above, the top gallant mast. This superstructure of additional masts and yards and sails and innumerable ropes had to be removed for the safety of the ship. It was an intricate task, done step by step, with orders—when necessary—shouted up and down the eighty feet separating the skilled little teams on top from those on the deck. The main topsail yards alone weighed close to half a ton, not counting the canvas, and to lower them was awkward, for the sea and wind were jolting the precarious perches where the men were at work. The dismantling went on for hours.

Fortunately, as the tide fell the sea became calmer. The ship meantime was suffering further damage. Part of her bottom floated over shallow water and part lay flat on the coral reef, and a rasping, grating noise came regularly from the moving timbers rubbing against the sharp coral. In the early hours of the morning, as the tide fell, the ship settled even more firmly onto the reef.

Initially the damage was assessed as dangerous but far from disastrous. The full extent would be visible only when the *Endeavour* was finally pulled off the reef, if ever that happy event were accomplished. The next high tide was vital if the ship were to be liberated.

In the darkness of the early hours, about 4 A.M., the seamen set to work to make the ship lighter in the hope she might be lifted by the incoming tide and enabled to float away. The ship was still burdened by the numerous casks of fresh water taken aboard at Botany Bay. The water was emptied, and even some of the casks themselves were dropped into the warm sea. Firewood, stacked in quantities below, was carried up narrow ladders and thrown overboard, leaving just enough to cook a few more hot meals. Oil jars and staves of timber were jettisoned.

The ship carried New Zealand rocks as ballast, and they were hauled to the side of the ship and thrown overboard. Bars of pig iron, stacked largely in the bread room near the stern of the hold, were carried up, bar by bar, and thrown overboard. They served as ballast but were also the raw material for the ship's blacksmith, who must have regretted their loss. These tasks were carried out efficiently and almost cheerfully, for a lighter ship might float from the reef at high tide.

Banks was the breathless but vivid recorder of these activities. He set down what Cook, familiar with crises at sea, did not bother to record. He noted the absence of panic and the calmness of the common seamen: "no grumbling or growling was to be heard throughout the ship, no not even an oath." Some blasphemy and profanity—the careless or disparaging use of the names of Christ and God—must have been frequent enough in a ship and employed instinctively by many seamen in times of hardship; but Banks implies that their best behavior came to the fore. It was almost as if, for a few hours, the crew had been so conscious of the prospect of death that they thought it too risky to use God's name in vain.

ON THE BRINK OF DISASTER

Morning was just around the corner. In the first faint light the mainland could be seen. That was the good news. The bad news was that the land was actually a long way off. As far as could be seen there was no island that might serve as a haven at any point along the twenty-five or so miles separating ship and shore. As the light improved, a halfway island—a mere apology for an island—crept into view.

At 8 A.M. it was found that the ship had sprung a serious leak. Three pumps were set to work, all by hand. The fourth pump was not in a state of repair. An officer, name unknown, had failed in his duty. To keep all pumps in working order was one of the high priorities of safety at sea.

Many on board wondered what would happen if the wind and sea turned from light to moderate and the ship slowly broke into pieces. The *Endeavour* did not carry what today would be called lifeboats; the yawl, the pinnace, and the longboat doubled as lifeboats. But even if these three boats were filled—almost to the point of danger—with seamen as well as essential provisions, there might not be room for everybody. Some officers and men would be left behind, perhaps to drown.

High tide was expected at 11 A.M., and eagerly awaited. As the water rose, the ship, which had been resting steadily on her wide bottom, began to lean to one side. At the height of the new tide the level of the water was inadequate to float the ship. Disappointingly, the jettisoning of the precious water and other goods had not been enough. Physical might was now enlisted in an attempt to heave the ship from the reef; and groups of seamen took their turn to work the capstan, thus tightening the cable joined to the anchor. In this way the ship could be slowly tugged backward from the reef by sheer human strength. She was moved just a little.

To lighten the ship even further, most of the heavy guns—still vital if the *Endeavour* should meet an enemy warship on the way home—had to be sacrificed. Six of the guns standing on carriages in their normal place on deck—the other four were stored below—were unfastened. Each gun was six feet long and weighed more than half a ton. It was a heavy task to remove them and drop them into the sea. Buoys were fixed to each of the guns in the hope that each gun might be located and recovered if the ship were eventually saved.

More men were ordered to work the pumps. Banks, a gentleman and in effect a paying passenger, was not the kind of person who could normally be ordered to do anything, but his sense of duty compelled him to help. Even more potent than his sense of duty was his fear that the ship might sink—along with all his flora and fauna, geological specimens, native artifacts, drawings, and sketches.

At one time Banks thought all was lost. He went to the big cabin and packed such of his possessions as he decided were precious. If the ship had to be abandoned, he might be able to carry them ashore. Others who had the time or willingness to think of their fate saw little comfort. Even if they safely reached the shore they might, in the end, not be better off than those who drowned. They might land without the muskets and powder and shot with which to defend themselves. Banks, while at Botany Bay, had concluded that the "Indians" were cowardly. Now in the tropical north he feared they might turn out to be very brave when facing sailors who possessed few firearms and few portions of gunpowder.

Australia, which had seemed fairly fertile at a few places along the coast, now became, in his fearful mind, totally infertile—"barren we always found it," he said with exaggeration. Would the shipwrecked people be able to grow their own food? Even if they managed to save fishing nets from the wreck, could they survive on fish alone? At this stage Cook and Banks had reason to believe, though the belief was erroneous, that Aborigines lived largely on fish.

In these hours of peril, Banks consoled himself with the new speculation that the Aborigines on shore might turn out to be friendly and that sufficient food might be found for blacks and whites. But what consolation was that to someone who loved fine architecture, books, good company, wine, and spirits; who liked to write and receive letters; who took pleasure in adding to his zoological and botanical collections, enjoyed the renewing of old friendships, and relished an elegant roof over his head? In the imperiled ship, with the water swirling around her sides, he tried to envisage the miseries and spartan joys of a life of permanent exile on the tropical coast. There they would be the most miserable of shipwrecked creatures, "debarrd from a hope of ever again seeing their native countrey or conversing with any but the most uncivilised savages perhaps in the world." Hour after hour, Banks oscillated between misery and deep misery.

Would the next rising of the tide raise the ship from the reef? Everyone must have asked that question in silence, but few with words. Life and death floated on that question. In many faces could be detected the thinly disguised or open signs of anxiety. A little optimism came from Cook's belief that the high tide, occurring at night when the moon was full, would be especially high. In these situations his judgement and instinct were so often apt.

The night tide was rising; its swish and swirl could be heard and seen, and everyone hoped that it would lift the ship from the reef. "The dreadfull time now approachd," wrote Banks. The fear of death—Banks's own phrase—stared everybody in the face: "hopes we had none," he added, "except the hope of being able to keep the ship afloat till we could run her ashore." This was a halfway hope: the prospect that the ship, successfully raised from her bed by the rising tide, could limp into a shallow bay on the mainland or be pushed by the tide onto a sandy beach. Perhaps the ship would then be slowly pulled apart, and a smaller *Endeavour*—rebuilt from the salvaged materials—could be sailed to the Dutch colonial port of Jakarta. In sailing distance this port was relatively near, being only a couple of months away.

As the tide rose the ship, which was previously leaning to one side, righted herself. Alas, the hole in the bottom of the ship was exposed a little further to the seawater, which trickled in. The three pumps, into which enormous human effort was expended, could not cope adequately. Nearly every man, including even the genial and unathletic Dr. Solander, took his turn in working the pumps in short bursts of activity. Still the water rose in the bottom of the ship. "This was an alarming and I may say terrible Circumstance," wrote Cook. He feared that as soon as the ship was free from the reef, she might sink. For the ship had wedged herself neatly into the reef, and the reef was like a hard bandage wrapped loosely around the bottom of the ship, preventing too much water from entering through the hole in the timbers. Remove the ship from the reef and the life-sustaining bandage would be removed too.

At about 9 P.M. Cook made his bold decision: he would take the risk of totally dislodging the ship from the reef. His men—all those who could be spared from working the pumps—would make a super-human effort to heave the ship from the reef just when the tide was highest. Fortunately the high tide at night was higher than the high tide during the day. The combination of a very high tide and the application of human strength, coupled with the steadfast anchors, might dislodge the ship from what Cook called a "Ledge of Rocks."

The capstan was manned, each man heaving on one of the capstan bars and pressing it forward with all strength. The windlass, too, was manned. Anchors and ropes held firm, enabling the ship to be tugged by human muscle-power toward the anchors, inch by inch. The rising level of the sea aided the task. Little by little, with the ominous noise of broken or frail timbers underneath, the ship was tugged from her resting place on the rock. Finally free soon after 10 P.M., she floated. She had been on the reef for twenty-three tense hours.

The *Endeavour*'s seaworthiness, however, was still in doubt. Water was entering through holes in the ship's bottom or side. The level of water in the bottom was measured again; alas, it appeared to be rising more quickly than before. This surmise proved to be an error of arithmetic. In fact the water level was manageable as long as nearly all hands took their turn to work the pumps. The pumpers, in Cook's words, "redoubled" their vigor. By 8 A.M. the water level was lower. By 11 A.M. the seamen had raised aloft a top mast and yard, and the ship was ready to harness the light breeze and move slowly toward the coast.

Who could tell whether the damaged ship, with holes in the bottom, would survive? There did exist a technique for plugging the holes, at least temporarily. Although Cook himself had never experimented with it, one of his midshipmen—the young brother of surgeon Monkhouse—had applied it with success while sailing in a leaking ship from Virginia to England. Known as "fothering," it called for a large sailcloth to serve as a plug, rather as a heavy piece of towel might be used to block a hole in a tub of water. Wool and oakum—the teased remnants of old rope—were divided into smaller pieces and strewn over the sailcloth laid out on the deck. So that the pieces of oakum would stick to the sail, they were mixed with "sheep dung or other filth" collected from the pens in which the ship's livestock still remained.

The stinking sail with its shaggy surface then had to be applied to the hole—not from the inside of the vessel, which would have been easy, but from the outside. Hauled by a rope to a position directly beneath the starboard bow, the sail and its pieces of sticky wool quickly worked their way inside the hole in the timbers. Pressed tight by the rush of the sea, the sail and its coating served as a clumsy plug and reduced the ship's leaking. Now only one pump had to be at work, and for only part of the time, in order to expel the slow inflow of water.

The peril remained. With his acute sense of drama, Banks vowed that there was "nothing but a lock of Wool between us and destruction."

ISLES OF HOPE

When the ship was stuck on the ledge of rock, everyone had looked longingly toward the mainland. It seemed to be twenty or thirty miles away, with hills clearly visible behind the shore. That gap, however, would not be crossed easily by the smaller boats if by chance the crippled *Endeavour* sank. Fortunately between the ship and the mainland were low islands, one of which could be seen from a distance. "I have named them Hope Islands," wrote Cook. Now, as the patched ship sailed past them, Cook confessed that they were "a poor enough object of hope, mere bush-covered sand cays, small and low, each surrounded by a reef." He must have guessed, but did not say so, that they were unlikely to supply enough fresh water to keep men alive.

He urgently needed a harbor where the ship could be beached and her bottom inspected and repaired. The little pinnace sailed ahead, leading the search for such a harbor. A bay, later called Weary Bay, was found but rejected because it could not provide the fresh water needed during a long stay by nearly a hundred men. Meanwhile the *Endeavour* was at anchor at night, and sailing slowly northward by day, in reef-dotted seas. Then to the relief of all, a river estuary was conveniently found.

Although Cook could be short-tempered in a crisis and stamp his feet, he could now think of paying a proud tribute to his sailors and to that other group he called "the gentlemen." Everyone had answered the challenge: "I must say that no men ever behaved better than they have done on this occasion." It was the more meritorious because for more than a month the daily dangers facing the ship had created strain. To his old friend and employer, Captain John Walker of the Yorkshire port of Whitby, Cook later reported that he had travelled a total of twelve hundred nautical miles along this coast, and in virtually every hour the leadsman was measuring the water's depth. In addition one boat and sometimes two or three went ahead "to direct us" and give warnings of hidden danger.

Cook had taken many precautions, as he was entitled to tell his friends. But had he taken enough? If he had anchored for the night instead of sailing in the light of the moon, the ship would not have struck that coral reef. Was he wise then to have sailed ahead? To ask that question is not to deny his greatness as a navigator and explorer. To refuse, however, to ask it is to carry the veneration of Cook a little too far and almost to confer on him divine qualities, which are a heavy burden for any mortal being to bear.

For his conduct that night Cook has been largely exonerated by historians. One exception was Alan Villiers, who was himself an experienced navigator in the final era of the windjammers. Of Cook's conduct he wrote sympathetically, pointing out that on that "peacefully beautiful moonlit night" there stretched ahead "a silvery radiance." But he added that such a night perhaps exerted a lulling and complacent influence on "watch-keepers grown long used to intense vigilance." With this one sentence Villiers delivered a gentle smack, less to Cook than to the men who kept watch that night.

Alexander Dalrymple, the Scot who was a rival of Cook and virtually a competitor for the post of captain of the *Endeavour*, was to criticize the decision to keep on sailing. Cook's main biographer, the excellent J. C. Beaglehole, felt it necessary to quote this criticism though not to support it: "Dalrymple held that it was bad seamanship that took the *Endeavour* on to the reef, though there have been few to agree with him." The biographer was firmly on the side of Cook. He argued that Cook was blessed with those "ideal conditions for night sailing that he had exploited before," and so naturally he exploited those conditions again. This view is a little mistaken. In the preceding fortnight—until the evening of the accident—Cook had sailed only once at night and then only for half the night. The biographer's further defense was simply that Cook's "intention was not to risk danger," and that he faced no unusual risks. But if this assessment is true, how did his ship contrive to run aground?

It is valid to offer a defense of Cook. Ever since his ship had entered that long stretch of the coastline sprinkled with islands, he had taken nearly every precaution. Usually he had anchored before twilight fell. The evening of his departure from Trinity Bay was perhaps the first in which, during that whole fortnight, he had sailed in the hours of darkness; even then he sailed for no more than half the night. On his second successive night of sailing by moonlight, his night of disaster, he changed his mind at least once because the depth of the water was proving to be very erratic. In the end he became more confident than the conditions justified.

Cook's confidence is slightly surprising in view of the warning given to him that danger might be lying ahead. On the day before the *Endeavour* hit the reef, Banks noted that Green Island, near the present city of Cairns, was lying on a coral shoal. Its significance was clear to Banks, who reported that the island was "the first of the kind we had met with in this part of the South Sea." Moreover, low sandy islands farther east consisted of the same coral formation.

Obviously Cook had been informed by Banks that the ship was inside coral seas. The warning, so important in retrospect, was recorded by Banks but not mentioned by Cook in his own journal. A slight complacency or even impetuosity dulled Cook's sense of risk. Admittedly he was still taking precautions, being especially careful to sound the depth of the water, but he was not quite as alert as the situation demanded.

WAS COOK SLIGHTLY MOONSTRUCK?

Cook at that time was prone to take risks for another reason. The full moon seemed to lighten his spirits or, more likely, give him slightly more confidence than was justified. His loyal defenders do not realize that on two previous occasions he had sailed into trouble on moonlit nights. His ship, almost beached in the Bay of Islands, was saved only by his crew taking to the oars. At the other end of New Zealand she had almost run into those rocks called the Traps while sailing at night, initially by the light of the moon.

The hazard Cook faced at the Traps could hardly have been predicted because the *Endeavour* was sailing so far from the shore. But the hazard he faced off the coast of northeastern Australia was more dangerous, and predictably so. Cook had learned in the last thirty hours that coral islands were present and that coral reefs might therefore be concealed just under the water. He was sufficiently alerted to be taking regular soundings of the depth of the water. He learned that those depths were erratic and unpredictable. Therefore his decision to continue to sail slowly in the moonlight rather than to anchor for the night might seem to be rather optimistic.

For these reef-dotted seas a few broad rules were later formulated by experienced seamen; one century later the rules were set down in the official navy-sponsored books that pilots and other navigators used. From his own experience Cook would already have known much of this advice. One vital rule insisted on keeping watch from the masthead and not just from the deck. Whether Cook, however, had placed a man at the masthead on this moonlit night is not known with certainty. Another rule was that the man at the masthead was more likely to see a reef if the sun was either overhead or somewhere behind him rather than shining toward his face. Curiously there was no rule about the moon, but the present generation of experienced pilots who make their living by guiding huge deep-sea ships near the Great Barrier Reef believe that, on a moonlit night, a reef is more likely to be seen if the moon's light is ahead rather than shining from another angle. On this particular night the moon presumably was not shining from a favorable angle. Cook therefore was disadvantaged by his decision to continue sailing in the moonlight.

Cook magnified the risk that evening by discarding one of his normal precautions in these difficult waters. If he had followed his practice and sent several of the ship's boats to scout ahead, the reef would probably have been detected. Whether the boatmen's warning would have been signaled or shouted in time to allow the ship to change course and so avoid the reef is not certain. We can assume with some certainty, however, that late on this moonlit night the boats were not exploring out in front.

One other fact suggests that Cook would have been wiser to sail by daylight. A sign of the presence of a reef was the color of the seawater above it. This color could not be detected in darkness or even in moonlight; it was most easily detected when the sun was shining and the sea was ruffled by a light breeze. If only three feet of water covered the reef, the water was usually colored light brown. If the reef lay about six feet below the water, a different intensity of light turned the water a conspicuous clear green. As the water over the reef became deeper, its color usually changed to a darker and darker green. Over a patch of very dark green the ship could safely sail, for the reef lay deep. When the water became too deep to be measured by soundings, it was a deep blue.

Captain de Quiros, exploring in the Pacific in the preceding century, also knew something about this color code: "In short, if the sea is of any other color except the usual color of deep sea water, namely blue, the sight of it should be a warning to take due care." Cook himself, ever observant, must have begun to glean most of the elements of this color code as he sailed along the tricky coast. If he had chosen to sail in daylight, he might have been warned of this dangerous reef simply by observing, just ahead, the change in the color of the sea.

To raise these serious doubts is in no way to rob Cook of his greatness. It is to see him as a human being, performing remarkable feats. Cook's dilemma, with only one ship and uncharted seas ahead of him, was almost unique. Nearly every day, when land was near, he had to weigh decisions and take risks. His attention to detail, and his desire for perfection as an explorer, magnified his risks. If he had been like Tasman and had quickly sailed away after every discovery, rarely attempting to pinpoint accurately his ship's position on the map, his total achievements would have been noteworthy rather than remarkable. Instead Cook was willing to investigate deep bays and estuaries, to ascertain the longitude of the main capes and straits, to assess the land's fauna and flora, and to report on the native peoples. These duties imposed further strain on his limited stores of food and absorbed valuable time. It is not surprising that sometimes he was overeager to make up for lost time.

Cook could never avoid danger completely. Without confronting danger, there was no hope of a resounding success. As Lord Nelson was to explain during the French Revolutionary Wars one generation later: "If I had been censured every time I have run my ship, or fleets under my command, into great danger, I should long ago have been *out* of the Service." Success in naval exploration, as in naval war, called for boldness as well as cautiousness.

Among captains in the seas near Australia, Cook was not alone in allowing the moonlight to seduce him. Others had been enticed toward danger by its brilliance. Almost a century and a half earlier, on the western coast of Australia in June 1629, the Dutch merchant ship *Batavia*, in the last stage of her voyage from Holland to Java, ran onto a well-known reef after the moonlight deceived the captain. He had probably seen the foam arising from waves breaking on the reef, just ahead, but later he claimed that he thought the moonlight was creating the white streak on the sea. The most disastrous of many wrecks near the Great Barrier Reef was to be that of the passenger liner *Quetta*, which, steaming ahead on a moonlit night in February 1890, ran into an uncharted reef and sank in three minutes, with heavy loss of life. Significantly, both of these ships, like Cook's, were sailing north and were possibly facing the moonlight at an unfavorable angle.

In retrospect Cook should have sailed only in daylight along this hazardous coast. In the ship, however, there was probably no thought of blaming him. He might have led his crew into danger, but he brought them out safely. Their loyalty—even admiration—prevailed.

In nearly every mind the reef itself was to blame for the near wreck of the *Endeavour*. Parkinson the artist, who later penned a short, breathless letter to his cousin Jane in England, wrote of his ship's "many hair-breadth escapes on this coast." The coral, he added, was "so dangerous, that I am of opinion our account of it will deter any from going that way again." No ship, he predicted, would ever again tackle the coast near the Great Barrier Reef. While Cook did not make a similar prediction, he believed that no ship had ever passed through such a maze of obstacles.

12

In Cook's River-Camp

WHEN THE commander of the pinnace returned to the *Endeavour* he pleased every seaman with his confident report that he had found a suitable haven for the damaged ship. He had found a small bay leading to a navigable river. The sloping banks of the river, a short distance from the mouth, were miraculously suited for the tasks of unloading the ship and then beaching her so that the damaged timbers could be inspected at low tide.

The *Endeavour* resumed her slow course toward the newfound harbor. As Cook was wary of taking his disabled ship into the river, two boats were rowed ahead to confirm that the water was deep enough. Although shoals were in the way, the route seemed navigable. But then a wind sprang up. "By this time," wrote Cook, "it began to blow in so much that the ship would not work." On the reef, so much ballast had been removed in an attempt to lighten the ship that the rudder no longer responded readily to the helmsman's hand. Cook began to fear that he had strayed into a new peril soon after escaping the last. He was, in his own words, "entangled among shoals" and commanding a ship that was not completely under his control.

The ship dropped anchor close to the shore and the river mouth. All eyes watched—and some prayed—for favorable weather. But to Cook's dismay the wind, blowing from the southeast, became stronger than perhaps any wind he had encountered along the coast of Australia. Showers of rain whipped past, and the wind persisted. In the hope that the wind might subside and so enable the ship to sail safely through the wide mouth of the river, many alterations were made to yards and sails. The wind did not fall but the spirits of those on board did. Impatient at what Banks called "our tedious delays," everybody longed for the ship to enter the river.

On the morning of Sunday, June 17, 1770—a week after the reef disaster—the wind had quieted enough for Cook to prepare to sail his ship into the river. At 7 A.M. the anchor was weighed and, amidst silent cheers, the ship sailed toward the river's mouth. As buoys had been set up to mark the deepest channel through the wide and shallow estuary, the advancing ship seemed safe. An hour later she stuck in sand at the river's mouth; it almost seemed as if the coast were haunted. To Cook's pleasure, however, the ship soon floated free.

Again she ran aground while inside the narrow channel of the river. The muscular strength of her crew was called on, and she was warped inside. By early afternoon she was safely at a river bend on the south bank, at what they called Charco Harbor but is now known as Cooktown. Heavy cables and hawsers made of strong rope, and the anchors too, were conveyed to the appropriate places, thus securing the ship in case the river should flood or the incoming tide should prove too strong. A risky anchorage, Cook had no alternative but to accept it.

From the open sea there was no clear sign of the *Endeavour*. Aboriginal canoe-men venturing a couple of miles offshore would have seen, on looking back, only the long sandy beach fronting the river mouth and the tall hills that were lookout posts on either side of the estuary. The *Endeavour* herself was tucked away in a bend of the river. At first only the smoke coming from the sailors' cooking fires or the blacksmith's little forge would have been seen from the open bay.

Large tents were erected on the rising ground near the river, one being a store for the ship's provisions and cargoes. The ship had to be emptied of heavy items before she could even be examined, let alone hauled into the appropriate place for repairs to be made. Fortunately, deep water lay close to a fairly steep slope on the bank of the river, fully protected from the southeast gales that had been blowing day after day. Only twenty feet separated the ship from the sloping shore, and that gap was covered by a small gangway built of planks and spars. Soon a procession of men crossed the gangway, carrying or rolling items from the ship. Empty water casks were rolled ashore and arranged neatly on the high ground. Timber and sails were carried ashore by pairs or small groups of men. Nearly all the provisions were placed in the tent, where a sentry stood on watch.

The carpenter and boatswain, each having a corner of the ship where their special equipment and stores were kept, sent many items ashore, including a spare anchor and the precious gunpowder. Even the ballast remaining in the bottom of the ship was carried ashore. The last of the tidy piles of firewood, gathered at harbors along the coast, were carried from the ship and stacked. And what should be done with the four heavy guns that remained in the hold? Hauled from below, the four-pounders were mounted on the quarterdeck where, if necessary, they could defend the ship from attack. Almost on dry land, she was now highly vulnerable.

IN THE LIGHT OF THE LAMP

On the third day the ship was almost emptied of everything that had lain in her hold. At the very bottom of part of the hold, and almost untouched since the departure from England, was a row of water butts or casks. It was assumed that their timber was still sound, but an inspection revealed that they had been quietly rotting in the airless corners of the ship. Some were so fragile that "they would not bear the rolling." It was impossible, in the words of the old sailors' song, "to roll out the barrel."

Coal carried all the way from London, and still lying in the fore part of the hold, had to be carried ashore across the makeshift gangway and piled neatly on the ground. And as the level of coal in the hold slowly receded and the wooden bottom of the ship was almost within touching distance, there could be heard the sound of water flowing in. Cook had a stronger word: he later said the water was "gushing in." The hole in the ship was still concealed by coal, and the incoming water would be heard but not yet seen. The decision was made to remove the last layer of coal and carry it ashore in relays, nearly all hands being employed.

The ship now had to be moved to her final position on the river bank. High tide in the evening was the ideal time. At 4 P.M. as the tide began to rise, the ship was moved to the chosen position by the use of ropes and by the sheer physical strength of the men working the capstan. As the tide rose farther, the lightened ship, rising too, could be pulled higher up the bank. Near the mangrove bushes she lay, her bow on the bank and her stern sloping well into the water. At low tide she was half in and half out of the river.

On this shortest day of the year, the ship at last was in a position where she could be repaired. Cook went below to inspect, from the inside, the timbering that had been smashed by the reef. By the light of a handheld lamp, he could see that the damage was more than he had anticipated. Fortunately the false keel had taken much of the impact.

Miraculously the ship had been saved primarily because a lump of the reef had wedged itself in her bottom timbers. This lump, firmly embedded on the starboard side, had prevented the sea from pouring in once the ship was liberated from the reef and able to sail away. While the ship was at sea the water could still enter. But the hole was not so dangerous as long as the lump of reef was neatly wedged. Cook's further examination revealed that four stout planks of timber had been smashed and several more planks had been "wounded." The way in which these planks were damaged was "hardly credible" to Cook: "scarce a splinter was to be seen but the whole was cut away as if it had been done by the hands of Man with a blunt edge tool." Banks echoed this description, saying that the hole almost seemed to have been roughly shaped by an axe.

The lump of coral, no larger than a man's fist, had served as a plug in the hole in the ship's timbering. It fitted the hole more tightly by virtue of smaller rocks and the grains of coarse sand that had wedged themselves in at the joins. The tight fit was aided by the intruding pieces of oakum and wool that the fothering process had ingeniously injected after the ship was refloated.

Those officers and men who inspected the leak—and everyone must have tried to inspect it out of curiosity—marveled at their good fortune in escaping its effects. Banks, who was not emphatically religious, confided to his journal that Providence had "worked in our favour." Parkinson, more religious, found a neat philosophical way to summarize the whole experience. The same coral rock that had endangered us, he vowed, also turned out to be "the principal means of our redemption." In the many discussions that followed the discovery of the extent of the damage, it was agreed that the ship had been in more danger than they realized at the time. Almost certainly she would have sunk but for the chance insertion of this "coral plug."

This river bank was the first place in Australia that could be called an industrial site. Here arose a shipbuilding yard along with a timber workshop and blacksmith's forge. Melted iron was converted into nails, of which thousands and thousands were needed for repairs. Sailmakers were active, their work spread out in front of them. The carpenters were soon at work replacing the damaged timbers, and it was a favorable time to make repairs to the rigging. Seamen were "scraping the ship's bottom" to remove the marine life that had clung to it.

As the other side of the ship had, in turn, to be repaired, preparations were made for "heeling the ship." A new anchor was put in place to act as anchorman in the ensuing tug-of-war, for the seamen—when all was ready—had to pull steadily on the ropes and so edge the ship into a new position. In short, the port side having been repaired, the ship now had to lie on her other side. The coming of the high tide aided this process.

The task of heeling was no sooner accomplished than more damage was found in the timbers on the other side. So the task of repairing went on. When the high tides came up the river, it was temporarily impossible to continue the repairs. And yet in the space of a few weeks almost all was in readiness for the *Endeavour* to return to the ocean when winds and tides became favorable.

A TOUCH ·OF THE SCURVY

As soon as the ship was safely in the river, a tent had been erected on higher ground to accommodate the sick. They were more numerous than any of the ship's journals had revealed during the previous fortnight. Maybe one in every dozen men was on the sick list. Certainly a few were suffering from scurvy; one was probably Green the astronomer and another was Tupaia the Polynesian. Tupaia had "livid spots on his legs," and his gums were soft and sore. He preferred to live in a tent pitched for him by Banks some distance from the main tent.

A small boat was sent out in the hope of netting fish, but a gale sprang up, and not one fish was trapped in the large net. Not content to lie in the tent, Tupaia set out to catch his own fish and probably ate much of what he caught. Banks, who was already engaged in botanical excursions, happily reported after a few days that Tupaia was "surprizingly recovered."

Once the ship had been unloaded and heaved onto what was her own sickbed, the pressures were eased for Cook and his crew. As not many men were needed to repair the ship and her equipment, other needs took priority. Fresh greens and fresh fish were sought for those who were sick and those who were well. The surgeon went up the river "to get beans for the sick," picking them from a native plant. More greens were gathered and tossed in the soup pot and served to all. Cook was indefatigable, continuing his disciplined regime that insisted the men should wash themselves, wear clean and dry clothes, and air their bedding. There was also a psychological advantage in being on shore, as the sick Frenchmen had realized when resting ashore at Doubtless Bay during the previous Christmas.

The tropical place where the ship lay was as close to the equator as Rangoon in Burma, Martinique in the West Indies, and Dakar in West Africa. For the crew of the *Endeavour* the big advantage was that this was the coldest time of the year; in short, the days resembled a mild English summer.

THE HARE WITH A GREYHOUND'S TAIL

On the expeditions made almost daily in search of fresh food, far from the beached ship, several sailors were open-mouthed at what they saw or thought they saw. A party shooting pigeons came back with stories of a strange animal. As Banks and Solander were busy collecting and drying botanical specimens near the ship they did not see the animal, but with puzzlement they heard that it was "as large as a grey hound, of a mouse color and very swift." It was not easily described, its movement being partly concealed by thick vegetation. On the following day the creature was seen moving with large leaps, but this sounded so incredible that Banks doubted—the sailors could not always be believed—the description given him. One seaman vowed that he had seen something as black as the devil and crowned by two horns; it was probably a flying fox or fruit bat with projecting wings.

It was clear to Cook that the mysterious leaping animal was a freak. On Sunday morning, June 24, he was walking not far from the ship when he must have blinked. Here was a wild dog that did not walk on all fours but "jumped like a Hare or dear." Losing sight of it, he inspected the ground where it had stood. He could detect no footprints; the ground was too hard. Back in the ship, several others who had seen the creature argued that its footprint resembled that of a goat. Certainly it was startlingly different to any known animal. Indeed, when the Americas had been first explored by Europeans more than two centuries earlier, nothing so startling was discovered.

Cook was the first to paint a detailed picture of the animal, not because he saw it for longer than anyone else but because he was a skilled and quick observer. He reported that it was "the full size of a grey hound" and the same shape. The way it carried its long tail also resembled a greyhound. That it should be so likened was understandable, for Banks kept two greyhounds in the ship. In the many discussions about the creature Banks must have been the court of appeal; but he could not adjudicate until he too glimpsed this strange beast. No creature, vowed Banks, "nothing certainly that I have seen at all resembles him."

The animal would have remained a mystery if the weather had been favorable. Wishing to sail away as soon as possible, Cook waited for the high tide and for the wind to blow from a suitable direction. Day after day he waited, giving Banks the opportunity to make, in three full days, an inland expedition bolder than any attempted since the ship had left England.

In a small boat Banks and Lieutenant Gore and the indispensable Tupaia set out like schoolboys on holiday. Along the winding Endeavour River, for so it had been named, they were rowed past the clumps of bushy mangroves, whose roots rose from the mud at lower tides. As the banks became steeper, the mangroves were replaced by grasslands and the chance to see the wildlife. Then Tupaia saw a dingo, and everyone saw a flying fox—as large as an English partridge. The mystery animal briefly appeared but proved too fast and too bounding to be hit by a musket shot.

At nightfall the mosquitoes descended on the men, who were now camped beside the river. Whereas at the beached ship the coastal breeze largely kept the mosquitoes away, here hardly a puff of wind was felt. Only smoke could repel the mosquitoes. Grasses and bushes were put on the fire, and in the smoky haze the men took shelter. But,

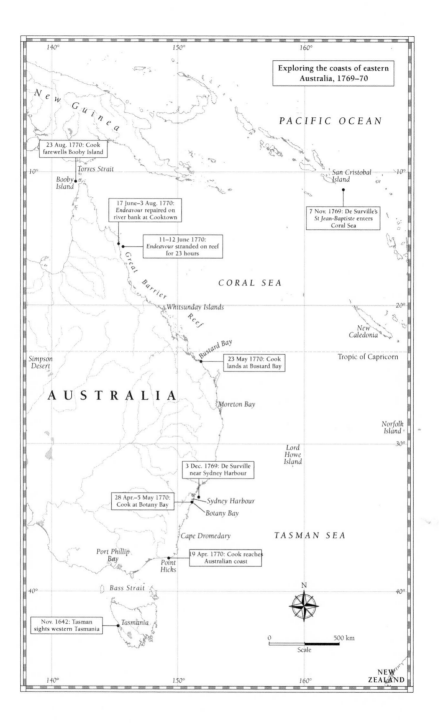

Exploring the coasts of eastern Australia, 1769–70

New Guinea

PACIFIC OCEAN

23 Aug. 1770: Cook farewells Booby Island

Torres Strait

Booby Island

17 June–3 Aug. 1770: *Endeavour* repaired on river bank at Cooktown

7 Nov. 1769: De Surville's *St Jean-Baptiste* enters Coral Sea

San Cristobal Island

11–12 June 1770: *Endeavour* stranded on reef for 23 hours

Great Barrier Reef

CORAL SEA

Whitsunday Islands

New Caledonia

Bustard Bay

23 May 1770: Cook lands at Bustard Bay

Tropic of Capricorn

Simpson Desert

A U S T R A L I A

Moreton Bay

Norfolk Island

3 Dec. 1769: De Surville near Sydney Harbour

Lord Howe Island

28 Apr.–5 May 1770: Cook at Botany Bay

Sydney Harbour

Botany Bay

Cape Dromedary

TASMAN SEA

Port Phillip Bay

19 Apr. 1770: Cook reaches Australian coast

Point Hicks

Bass Strait

Nov. 1642: Tasman sights western Tasmania

Tasmania

N

0   500 km

Scale

NEW ZEALAND

reported Banks, the mosquitoes "followed us into the very smoak, nay almost into the fire."

Soon after dawn the campers were rewarded. After walking across a wide expanse of grasslands they saw four of the strange animals. Shy and frightened, the animals ran away, but their heads and ears were clearly visible above the grass. It was a revelation to Banks who was the first to realize that these animals did not run on four legs but bounded on their two strong hind legs. At once Banks's greyhound gave chase but, obstructed by long and rank grass, she soon lost sight of the two animals she was chasing. Banks did not have to explain—all rural gentlemen of his day knew this fact—that a greyhound relied on sight rather than scent and so could not effectively chase animals that were obscured by tall grass. Muskets fired at the animals also missed their mark. Until an animal was shot and dissected, the mystery would remain.

At noon, after walking for miles, the men climbed into the boat and were rowed upstream. The tide began to ebb, and in shallower water they had to jump out and drag the boat along. Suddenly the sight of a column of rising smoke suggested that people were camped close by. Banks's desire to meet Aborigines remained intense, and yet it was an inexplicable fact that since leaving Botany Bay he had been close to none—except when he heard a loud voice on the beach of Palm Island in the evening darkness some weeks ago. Then an attempt had been made to contact the man. But, lamented Banks, he "ran away or hid himself immediately for we could not get a sight of him."

Now Banks had another chance. He and his men left the boat and approached the smoke. They found that the Aborigines had made a campfire beside a large tree, and their children had pulled down green branches in which to play. Near the ashes of the fire lay cooked yams or roots and the remains of shellfish. People had been present a short time ago: smoke was still curling from their fire, and human footmarks were freshly imprinted in the soft sand of the riverbank. With their acute hearing the Aborigines earlier must have heard the conversation of the boatmen and the splashing and swiveling sounds of the oars, whereupon they had vanished into the bush. Banks, disappointed at losing this opportunity to meet them, was puzzled by what he called their "unaccountable timidity."

That evening the Englishmen lit their own campfire on a sandbank surrounded by the little river. When bedtime arrived they made pillows from grass, placed a mattress of plantain leaves on the soft sand, and took off their coats to serve as a blanket. In the absence of mosquitoes they slept so soundly that the Aborigines could easily have launched a surprise attack and—said Banks—"caught us all Napping." He soon realized that if his party had slept on a sandbank farther downstream they might have been caught napping by another adversary for whom they were not alert: the saltwater crocodile. Rowing back to the *Endeavour* with the aid of a swift current, they saw a six-foot crocodile crawl across the mangrove mudflats and enter the river.

THE RIBBONED STRANGERS

To meet at least one Aborigine from this large land, and learn by questioning him, was a burning desire for Banks. Whereas the Maori had stepped forward boldly, the Aborigines everywhere had retreated. Two days after Banks returned to the ship, several Aborigines were seen on a sandy point on the opposite side of the river. Approached by a rowboat, they ran away "as fast as they could." Early next morning, before sunrise, a few more assembled at the same place and were spearing fish from a small wooden canoe equipped with outriggers. This was the most sophisticated boat that Cook had seen along the whole Australian coast; indeed it was learned, decades later, that such a canoe was used only in this corner of the continent and was almost certainly the result of contact with people living close to New Guinea.

The Aboriginal fishermen eventually paddled their outrigger canoe toward the beached *Endeavour*. They were now so near that gifts of paper, cloth and nails could be easily thrown toward them from the big ship. Gladly placed in the bottom of the canoe, they were probably the first gifts accepted so far by the Aborigines. Banks, who was more observant than Cook in these proceedings, noticed one turning point in the relations between blacks and whites. Someone aboard the *Endeavour*, as a gesture, threw down a small fish. The Aborigines promptly accepted it, and expressed "the greatest joy imaginable." The tide of suspicion was ebbing. They were receiving back their fish, caught in their own waters.

Sometime after the Aborigines paddled away—with the one gift they valued and the others they apparently didn't—they returned with another two kinsmen. Boldly they came alongside the ship, each carrying two spears and one spear-thrower for protection. Arranging themselves in a row, they faced the ship and the seamen who had gathered. Into this delicate confrontation Tupaia walked, almost as a referee. After he gestured successfully to the Aborigines to lay down their spears, they sat with him on the ground. Cook and some of his men walked over and joined the group on the ground, offering them beads, pieces of cloth, and other presents.

It was probably on this occasion that a colored riband, with a commemorative medal attached, was fastened around the neck of each Aboriginal man in the vicinity. Curiously, no mention of this ceremony was made in any of the journals at the time, and we know that it took place only because some Aborigines were to appear a few days later at the side of the ship, their ribands and medals still around their necks. During their absence they presumably spent many hours sitting or sleeping near a fire, for the ribands were now discolored by smoke.

The Aborigines seated alongside Tupaia remained alert, especially when one of the English sailors made a move. They had to be wary, for they were hopelessly outnumbered. Even so, the meeting was a firm step in amicable relations. This was the first time on the eastern Australian coast that whites and blacks had sat face to face, wary but friendly.

It was now midday, and the main meal was presumably piping hot and about to be served. Cook by gestures invited the four Aborigines to join him in eating. The invitation was declined, and they paddled "back to where they came from." Next morning more Aborigines appeared near the ship and handed over a fish, which was assumed to be in exchange for the fish given to them on the previous day. A spirit of tentative relaxation was in the air, and words were exchanged. Banks had the impression that the Aborigines were imparting their own names, one of which was Yaparico.

The Aborigines not only fingered the clothes worn by the Europeans but also touched their heads and skins. The Europeans in turn did their inspecting. Most Aborigines were coated with a film of smoke and dirt, for they slept on the ground and cooked at open fires, and the seafarers naturally wondered what was the real color of their skin. Banks stepped forward, spat on his finger and then rubbed the skin of one of the strangers. He discovered that it was as chocolate underneath as it seemed to be on the surface. A few Aborigines must have used the same moisture test to answer the question tantalizing them: was the skin of the Europeans naturally white, or was it concealed beneath cosmetics made of white clay?

The Europeans snatched every opportunity to satisfy their curiosity. Noticing that one of the black visitors, while not clothed on the body, was ornately clothed about the nose, they examined him intently. The bridge of his nose had been pierced, perhaps when young, and through the pierced hole was fixed the long bone of a bird. Cook observed that the bone was as thick as his finger, and far longer. All the Aborigines had similar holes in their noses. The one wearing the bone had difficulty with his speech, for his nostrils were blocked. It was also observed that the ears of Aborigines, like the noses, were pierced with a hole so large that a thumb could be poked through it.

With some merriment the sailors gave a seafaring name to the bone that pierced the Aboriginal nose. They called it the "spritsail yard," that being the yard or boom that was fixed at right angles to the bowsprit at the very front of the ship. It was already a nickname in use in the British Isles where some fishermen, annoyed when large fish damaged their nets, would catch an offender and cruelly thrust a bone peg through its gills so that it could not nose its way into the fishing nets again.

An attempt was made to measure the height of the Aborigines. Since there had already been a lot of touching and feeling by both peoples, the process of measuring caused little concern. The shortest Aboriginal man was measured at five feet two inches and the tallest—he was much the tallest—at five feet nine inches. Their average height was five feet six inches, but Banks did not add the comment—he perhaps should have added it—that such a height was probably little if anything below that of the average English sailor. Therefore his own conclusion, that this tribe of people was very small, is slightly puzzling. Admittedly their limbs and especially their ankles were probably thinner than those of the typical British sailor, and they were lighter in build, but probably they were the more nimble and active.

While they were virtually naked, the Aborigines usually wore a trinket or adornment. Some valued highly their necklace of shells, "neatly enough cut and strung together," and refused to hand it over as a gift when requested. On their upper arms most wore bangles or bracelets, woven out of twisted hairs. Around the waist a few wore a thin girdle made of human hair or the furry pelt of an animal, but the adornment that covered the widest area of the body was paint. Skilled painters, the Aborigines added a splash of red ochre to shoulders, chests, or breasts, and they so painted the face that the eyes seemed to be enclosed in an owllike circle, almost like a pair of spectacles. The legs and arms were often painted with a heavy white paint, reminding Banks of the white paint manufactured in Britain from lead—the mineral that had helped make his family's fortune. Always curious, he tried in vain to find the source of the clay from which these people mixed their white body paint.

While these social and medical inspections were being conducted with intense curiosity, a few officers strolled down to the river to examine the outrigger canoe. It was thin and narrow and, compared to the *Endeavour*, rather frail and makeshift. Paddles more than three feet long propelled the canoe in deep water while a long pole was used to punt it in shallow water. There was not much in the wooden canoe to examine, but the mere sight of the foreigners standing beside it ignited the suspicions of the nearby Aborigines. Realizing that if they lost their canoe they would be captives on that side of the estuary, they decided that the friendly meeting was over. Pushing the canoe into the river, they paddled it to the other side. In departing they said not a word.

The seafarers, having learned their lesson, were more circumspect toward those Aborigines who came across the river the following morning. In turn the Aborigines, seemingly more relaxed, were induced to visit the riverside tent where Tupaia lived, and were content to stay there a while. One canoeist even paddled across the river and returned with several other men whom he introduced by name—at least Banks thought this was the gist of his words and gestures.

On this day the ship's meals were being cooked in an open-air fireplace. The Aborigines, on being presented with several fish, accepted them in an offhanded way and apparently signaled their wish that the fish should be cooked for them. Some of the cooked fish they ate; the remainder they gave to one of Banks's long-tailed greyhounds, which was the focus of concentrated interest. The fact that the dog was so tame must have puzzled a people who owned no domesticated animals.

The morning visit was over. As the canoe was not capacious enough to carry away the six or so Aborigines, two trips had to be made. Meanwhile a woman, man, and boy appeared on the sand spit on the far side of the river. Until now the Englishmen had seen no women in the four weeks they had so far spent here. The news that she was standing on the sand spit, barely two hundred yards away, must have attracted every eye in the sex-starved ship and the neighboring tents and workplaces. The sailors who were busily carrying aboard the ballast, firewood, casks of water, and all the goods that had previously been unloaded in order for the repairs to take place, must have stopped work or slowed down so they could view what to them was almost a striptease show. Parkinson, the sharp-eyed artist, implied that the woman wore a headpiece consisting of a few feathers glued to the top of her hair by a piece of gum, but that the rest of her body was naked or almost naked.

The officers sent for their telescopes. Banks vowed that she was naked whereas the women they had met in Tahiti and New Zealand were not completely naked. "I allways before now," he confessed, "thought nature would have taught a woman to conceal" what he called these "parts" or "privities." The word *privities* was fashionable in the late Middle Ages and perhaps waning in usage by 1770. The Aboriginal woman probably was no less astonished that the white men had gone to such trouble to conceal their "parts."

In most countries of Europe in 1770, black-skinned people were scarce, and perhaps most of the English population outside London, Liverpool, Bristol, and the larger ports rarely encountered a black face. The crew's curiosity toward these Aborigines was persistent. Everything about them was discussed. It was widely agreed that their hair was black and lank, not frizzy or woolly, and that they sometimes cut it or singed it. One man was first observed to have longish straight hair, but the next day it was much shorter; the evidence suggested that he had used a firestick to singe the longer hairs.

Cook had first seen the Aborigines through the writings of William Dampier, who dismissed their bottlelike noses, wide mouths, and thick lips as ugly. Cook became more sympathetic the longer he viewed them. "Their features are far from being disagreeable," he concluded. Most displayed a sound set of teeth; and from nobody, male or female, had the two upper front teeth been knocked out in the way Dampier had reported. On the whole there was no looking down on the Aborigines on the grounds that they were untidy and unwashed. The seamen themselves, though Cook tried to insist on their cleanliness, were not always standing advertisements for soap and water.

Regretting that the Aboriginal men were wary of allowing their women to come near this ship filled with youngish men, Cook tried to offer a pithy description of the few who ventured near the ship: "They go quite naked both Men and women without any manner of Cloathing whatever, even the Women do not so much as Cover their privities." Cook went on to explain that the women's nakedness was probably complete, though "none of us were ever very near any of their women, one gentleman excepted." By gentleman he clearly meant an officer or a scientist. What exactly happened when the gentleman met the black woman is tantalizingly omitted from Cook's journal. Whether he happened to pass close to the woman while he was out strolling or busy hunting, and whether he made sexual advances to her, we do not know. That he was in a prowling state of mind is suggested by the delicacy with which Cook recorded the episode.

WHAT'S IN A WORD?

Cook had given up hope that Tupaia might know a few words of this strange tongue, which, in the family of languages, had no links whatsoever to his own Polynesian tongue. Nevertheless Cook hoped that names of plants, animals, and human limbs might be learned simply by pointing to them. He and Banks busily collected many words of what they called the New Holland language, not knowing that a maze of different languages were alive in the continent. The short list of collected words included various parts of the human body, extending from little finger and thumb to penis and scrotum. Cook also understood that a different word denoted the male from the female turtle. He learned how to say sun and sky in the local language. Decades later it was found, not surprisingly, that many words on the list had not been accurately understood. Thus the word thought to mean father was really the one used when referring to a sister's husband. The Aboriginal vocabulary, and especially the family ties it expressed, was more complicated than expected from such a seemingly simple people.

Banks was alert to the risks of pointing to a stone and hoping that an Aboriginal man would respond by providing the correct name. He knew that the response he received might rather indicate that the stone was sharp, or came from the beach or a remote hill, or was used for this purpose or that. Meanwhile the Aborigines chattered away as if their words would be instantly recognized by the visitors.

The sound of their voices was a little harsh in Banks's ears, though he later came to another opinion, dubbing the sound from one bearded face as shrill and even effeminate. Cook on the other hand thought the voices were "soft and tunable." As for the precision of the Aborigines' hearing and their ability to mimic, he was highly impressed. Being fine mimics, they probably learned more foreign expressions than did the English, and probably learned to pronounce them exactly.

Along the banks of the Endeavour River the relations between the clothed and unclothed peoples remained tentative, but not without promise. The two peoples met amidst a deluge of chatter, little of which could be understood by the other. The Aborigines willingly submitted to an examination of their matted hair and short beards, the paint and soot on their bodies, and the hole through the bridge of their noses. The British seamen submitted to the same inspection of their bodies. These inquisitive inspections, these strange meetings and the tentative respect they usually engendered, were of profound importance to the history of this continent. On the basis of the knowledge gained, the British were to make up their minds about the Aborigines, their way of life, and the ease with which a part of their lands might one day be occupied.

13

Kangaru

🪶 NATIVE ANIMALS, and the fleeting glimpses of them, fascinated the visitors. The bounding animal, so difficult to describe, continued to elude them. If only one could be captured. At last a small specimen was shot by that skilled marksman, Lieutenant Gore.

The sight of the dead kangaroo "that had so long been the subject of our speculations" drew breaths of amazement. The measuring of it drew further gasps. It was noted that its hind legs were nearly three times as long as its forelegs, and that its rump and tail were large but its head and shoulders small. The most engaging description came from Parkinson, who noted that it had four toes on its hind legs and five on its forelegs, and that its head was like a fawn's but its lips and ears like a hare's. He could not resist saying that, while it was not really like a greyhound, its tail tapered like that dog. After it was cooked he gave his studied opinion that it tasted like the flesh of the hare but had "a more agreeable flavor." That the species was a marsupial, and carried its young in a pouch or "purse," was probably not discovered while the expedition was in Australia.

THE MYSTERIOUS JUMPER

On July 14, 1770, Banks placed the name of the extraordinary animal on paper, spelling it as *kangaru*. Generations later it was discovered that kangaroo was not the local word for the species as a whole but for a kind of large, black kangaroo. In addition the word, when first pronounced in the presence of the English, was slightly misheard. The word spoken by their informant was actually *gaNurru* or *gan-gurru*. The name, unknown in most of the 250 languages spoken in other parts of Australia, belonged to the language of the local Gogo Yimidhir people. They contributed no other word to the English language, but it was a word that would circle the globe and appear in due course in a thousand other languages.

Most of the Aboriginal words widely used in present-day Australia come from a small area around Sydney where the Dharuk tongue was spoken. These words were not collected by Cook and Banks, for they had been unable to exchange any intelligible words with the Dharuk people, but by the Britons who later settled in Sydney. *Waratah*, the name of a distinctive tree, entered the language in 1788, and the Dharuk words for the animals *dingo* and *potoroo* entered a year later. In the year 1790 such nouns as *corroboree, boomerang, nulla-nulla, waddy*, and *warrigal* were adopted, while a few years later valuable Dharuk words such as *wombat, koala*, and *wallaby*, each denoting a well-known native animal, were borrowed.

The word *kangaroo* was perhaps the longest-lasting trophy carried away by the *Endeavour* from the Australian coast. No living kangaroo, however, was added to the European livestock on the ship. Banks would have loved to seize one and exhibit it in London as a novelty, but to capture alive this bounding animal proved impossible. As a second-best trophy, the skull of one kangaroo—probably a Great Grey Kangaroo—was taken to London and kept as a curiosity in the museum of the Royal College of Surgeons, where it was destroyed by enemy bombs in World War II.

It is easy to understand why the kangaroo, the largest of all living marsupials, eluded the visitors for so long. The Grey Kangaroo likes to hide among tree and scrub in the daylight and then, toward dusk, move into the open to feed on the grasses. They were elusive rather than rare. Their breeding rate was more than adequate, and the female Eastern Grey Kangaroo reached sexual maturity by the age of two years. Their joeys remained in the pouch month after month, not even protruding their head until they were nearly seven months old and not permanently leaving the pouch until they were over ten months of age.

How the kangaroo fitted into the categories and filing cabinets of zoology was a puzzle to Banks. The dead animal reminded him of the tiny jerboa—he called it Gerbua—a jumping rodent found in the Sahara Desert and the driest lands of northern Africa. Inhabiting burrows that it dug with the aid of its teeth and nails, it emerged at night, shy and alert and not easily captured. Its front limbs were short, its hind legs being six times as long, and it leaped. Like the kangaroo, its tail was much longer than its body. While in their acrobatics and physiology the jerboa and kangaroo did have strong similarities, they were different species.

For a crew of some ninety men relying on rations that might not last out the voyage to the next port of supply, even one kangaroo was a bonus. According to Banks's journal of July 15, "The Beast" that was shot on the grasslands was dressed and cooked "for our dinners." Many days later another kangaroo, twice as heavy, was shot. A final capture was made by one of Banks's greyhounds.

Kangaroo was supplemented by a more plentiful kind of flesh. On the same afternoon that Banks and Gore returned to the ship from their idyllic expedition along the river, boatmen exploring the maze of coral reefs noticed turtles on a tiny sandy island. Colored dark to light green, with a large shieldlike shell and a strong neck, these turtles swam long distances with their strong flippers. It has since been discovered that while the males stay at sea, the females breed on the sandy islands. Remarkably, nearly all return to the exact island on which they were born. As they are thirty or forty years old before they are ready to lay their first eggs, and as they normally wander over a large area of ocean in search of food, it is astonishing that they can find their birthplace, for it is only one sandy shoal among hundreds in the vicinity.

THREE CHEERS FOR THE "TURTLERS"!

Selecting a spot of sand well above sea level, the turtles used their front and hind flippers to dig a hole in which they laid more than a hundred eggs before covering them with sand. The eggs, each about as large as a Ping-Pong ball, were a prize for Aborigines who, during the breeding season, came in their canoes and burrowed to find them. The baby turtles were ready to be hatched from the remaining eggs after about two months alone in the warmth of the sand. Once hatched, with the aid of their flippers they found their way out of the sand and made their way to the sea. But many were seized and eaten by seabirds on the way. By then their mothers were back in the sea, feeding on the grasses and other plants growing on the seabed.

On the sand island, accidentally found by sailors in Cook's pinnace, were large edible turtles. With the blows from a heavy boathook wielded by a sailor, three of these green turtles were killed. Carrying the corpses into the shallow water and loading them onto the pinnace was the harder task, for together they weighed two-fifths of a ton, virtually equaling the weight of all the kangaroos and birds caught during the entire stay on the Endeavour River.

Cook did not know how long the ship, even after being repaired, would have to wait for the arrival of favorable winds. The fear was widespread that the southeasterly winds might persist month after month, imprisoning the ship in the river and preventing her from even attempting an outward voyage. Cook was worried about the adequacy of his total supply of food. So when the pinnace returned to the *Endeavour* with her first catch of green turtles, it felt almost like a miracle. One huge turtle, cut into scores of smaller pieces, was cooked for the next day's dinner. "This day all hands feasted on turtle for the first time," one diary revealed. One large green turtle was enough to provide not only a filling meal for every person in the ship but it was also a delicious treat, the taste being superior even to that of the small freshwater turtles occasionally served as a delicacy in England. The feast, Banks reported, "put every body in vast spirits," and they almost forgot that they were temporarily marooned on what they regarded as one of the remotest parts of the Earth.

The green turtles were so prolific on several of the islands that the pale-yellow sand was splashed with vivid green. On some days their numbers were "hardly to be credited." Many escaped as the seamen came near, and in rough water they were able to outstrip the oarsmen. The weather, wrote Banks, was "so boisterous that our boats could not row after them as fast as they could swim, so that we got but few." On several excursions only one turtle was killed; but those aboard the *Endeavour* rejoiced on several other days when they looked down on the approaching pinnace and saw as many as four large turtles and a stingray lying on her timbered bottom. Those seamen who nearly every day went out to the distant shoals and islands were given a special name: "the turtlers."

The prospect of killing more turtles was recompense for the loss of food stores after the *Endeavour* hit the reef. The seawater in the ship's hold had seeped into casks and barrels of foodstuffs; and the barrels of "bread"—the name given to ship's biscuits—were particularly affected. There was no thought of throwing away moldy biscuits: food might soon be scarce. The wooden lids of twenty-seven large barrels containing biscuits were opened, and the thousands of damaged biscuits were tipped out, arranged on sails spread on the ground, and heated and aired in the sunlight for a few hours. More than one-quarter of a ton of biscuits, after inspection, were left for the birds to eat. An equal amount, though "badly damaged," was hopefully declared to be edible.

The botanists were quick to test the plant foods growing here and there, for fresh vegetables were a recipe for good health. In addition to beans, which they boiled, they found a plantain and a variety of small native fruits, one of which resembled the pear and another the fig. One plant with small leaves smelled of lemon and orange and tasted like tea. Some sailors—the experimental tasters—felt sick after eating several new foods.

The turtles were only one of the attractions for the visiting seamen and scientists. The tall ant hills reminded them of Druids' monuments, and the butterflies in their garish colors were dazzling. Even the matter-of-fact Cook marveled at the gorgeous species of parrots. It also pleased him to recognize many seabirds including gulls, boobies, and noddies as well as herons and big-beaked pelicans.

Banks and Solander welcomed the sight of ducks, curlews, and noisy black crows, each of which resembled species familiar to them in England and Sweden. But most birds, especially the parrots and cockatoos and pigeons, were different to any they had seen in other lands; they also showed what Banks called an "extraordinary shyness." Even the crows of New Holland, he added, were very wary compared to the confident crows of Europe. The shyness of the native birds disappointed the scientists, who did not easily capture the specimens they wanted, either to draw or to be preserved and carried back to England.

Even at sea, when the ship was almost becalmed, sailors would go in rowboats in the hope of shooting any bird that seemed edible. In the weeks the sailors spent on Australian land, any men who could be spared from other tasks went into the bush to find birds for the cooking pot. Along the Endeavour River the hunters were crestfallen at catching at most a mere ten or twelve pigeons a day, when some vast flocks flying overhead were like a passing cloud. One of the Aboriginal skills that impressed the visitors was the ability, with such primitive equipment, to kill or capture a variety of birds, both swift and shy. That a white cockatoo—one of the wariest of all—could be captured was a surprise to the English observers.

A nature lover of today might express dismay at this killing of pretty birds, especially if the species is now in danger, but the men in the *Endeavour* had no alternative. They possessed no fresh meat in their stores: the casks of preserved mutton and beef were now old. Even when freshly packed in England the preserved meat, heavily salted, was not very palatable. While a few pigs and sheep did live in a roofed pen in the stern of the ship, they were held for an emergency or for a trading opportunity that might arise.

The crew relished any fresh fish and meat that was not salty. If meat or fish were free of salt, that was, in Banks's words, "sufficient to make it a delicacy." Banks, who lived in style at home, admitted that even the luxury of a partridge or pheasant, eaten in London or Lincolnshire, was perhaps less satisfying than the stewed flesh of a poor old Australian crow or hawk eaten aboard the *Endeavour* by those who had long been starved of fresh meat. Likewise, at sea, a meal consisting partly of the skinny flesh of shags and seagulls gave pleasure to those lucky enough to receive a serving. The oily and rank taste of "all that tribe of sea fowl" was temporarily forgiven. Those who missed out on a helping longed for their share when next an albatross or other large seabird was caught.

Cook's seamen did not marvel, as we might marvel, at the coral growing in the warm sea. Now one of the prized tourist resorts of the world, the Great Barrier Reef and its collection of living coral held no glamour for the men in the *Endeavour*. It was their enemy. They were not snorkelers or sightseers craving for a downward glimpse of the colored coral through a glass-bottomed boat. They simply wanted to locate a gap in the barrier reef through which their ship could pass safely.

Parkinson was one of the few to rejoice in the coral. When at last he stood admiringly on a reef, far from the shore, he marveled at the

"numberless variety of beautiful corallines of all colors and figures."
He compared the living coral "to a grove of shrubs growing under
water." The swift, brightly colored fishes were equally a marvel, and
at low tide he tenderly took a few by hand from a pool of water.

A FEW DROPS OF BLOOD

Until now, when invited aboard the ship, Aborigines had refused to
come. Now for the first time a few were bold enough to climb aboard.
In the atmosphere of goodwill they walked the deck, looking at almost everything with curiosity. But only one item excited them, and
it was familiar rather than novel. On the first day they came aboard,
they saw about ten or twelve green turtles lying on the deck. Returning the next day in larger numbers they tried to drag two of the heavy
turtles to the gangway and throw them overboard. Thwarted by the
crew, they tried again. In the words of Cook, now facing his most
serious confrontation on Australian soil, "they grew a little trouble-
some and were for throwing everything over board they could lay
their hands upon." Thinking they were hungry, Cook offered them
bread. The ten Aborigines were not interested in bread; they wanted
the turtles. Wishing to retrieve them, they left the ship and planned
their action.

One went to an English campfire where a kettle was being heated,
used the hot ashes to ignite a bundle of dry grass in his hand, and ran
around the perimeter of the ship, setting fire to the dry grass growing close to her side. The incendiary attack was performed with such
dexterity that the Marines and seamen barely had time to save the
adjacent blacksmith's forge and the tent in which Tupaia lived. They
were slow to defend the pig and her piglets kept in a small enclosure
on shore, and one little pig was scorched to death. In the swath of
long dry grass, the fire burned out of hand, spreading far from the
ship. Cook could only express his gratitude that the stock of gunpowder, stored on shore for more than a month, had recently been carried
back into the ship. On dry land the gunpowder might have exploded
in an instant, leaving the crew unable to use their big guns and all
their muskets until they reached a friendly port where gunpowder
could be purchased.

More Aborigines arrived at the place where the ship's fishing nets
and the crew's newly washed linen and clothes were laid out to dry,

and set fire to the grass. Cook, fearing that the ship would be the next target for the fire-lighters, ordered that shots be fired. One fire-lighter was wounded slightly; a few drops of his blood could be seen on the light-colored linen. That was the end of the Aborigines' visits to the ship and its vicinity.

A few days later a small party from the ship went into the country to gather greens. One seaman, straying from his companions, was walking through long grass when suddenly he came across an Aboriginal camp and fireplace. Meat had been recently cooked there, for the remains of a kangaroo were hanging from a tree. Several Aboriginal men and a boy were seated on the ground. That they did not run away as soon as they heard him approach—for their hearing was acute—was a sign of their confidence.

The seaman, taken by surprise, realized he was in a hazardous position. "At first," wrote Banks, "he was much afraid and offered them his knife, the only thing he had which he thought might be acceptable to them." In his eyes a valuable present—probably the most valuable the Aborigines had so far been given—it was initially accepted and duly passed from hand to hand. As they owned no metal object, and as the pocket knife was presumably sharp, their curiosity was aroused. The seaman's heart must have been pounding while they slowly examined it. Eventually they solemnly handed it back; their curiosity did not, apparently, extend to keeping the knife.

"They kept him about half an hour," recorded Banks, "behaving most civilly to him, only satisfying their curiosity in examining his body, which done they made signs that he might go away which he did very well pleased." Probably they had been interested in ascertaining whether, beneath those clothes, his skin and genitals were white too. Cook thought highly of these Aborigines and their final display of courtesy to the seaman. "They suffered him to go without offering him the least insult," he wrote approvingly. Indeed when the seaman left their company and began, in nervousness or confusion, to walk in the wrong direction, the Aborigines directed him toward the ship. No wonder that Banks in his journal referred to them as his friends "the Indians."

The impression of the British was that the Aboriginal women tended to be the hard workers. On the few occasions that women were seen, they were carrying wood to a fireplace or fetching shell-fish. The seamen, not observing the Aboriginal women using their sharpened sticks to dig for sweet yams, did not realize that the women were the diligent gatherers of those yams, greens, nuts, seeds, and fruits that were the main food for most Australians. What the Aboriginal women thought about these white-faced seamen we can have only a faint idea. At least they must have asked one another: wherever can the white women be?

THE INSCRUTABLE ONES

When Cook had examined the tiny bark canoes in Botany Bay, he concluded that the Aborigines were unable to sail in the open sea or, if able, did not venture far from land. His opinion changed when he reached the Endeavour River and examined the stronger, outrigger, hollow-log canoe. When his men began to hunt turtles on the distant islands and to look for passageways through the network of coral reefs, they realized to their surprise that the Aborigines were, at least sometimes, venturing far from land. On one isolated sandbank the seamen caught a turtle in which was embedded the remains of an Aboriginal hunting implement. In one place they found a wooden harpoon with a very long rope attached—a clever implement, which, until it was broken, they had used to catch turtles. On Lizard Island they saw simple huts or windbreak camps, which, being fifteen miles from the nearest point of the mainland, could have been reached only by a frail canoe in the open sea.

As his knowledge of the Aborigines increased, Cook was less scornful of their technology and their capacity as craftsmen. Their spear-throwers he admired: handheld, wooden launching pads, they were about as long as the human arm and rather "like the blade of a Cutlass." Over a distance of fifty-five yards, the wooden spears had about the same accuracy as a European-made musket. But the loading of a musket was a slow process, and skilled Aborigines could throw a second spear toward an escaping kangaroo long before the Marine could reload his musket and fire his second shot. In Cook's opinion, a spear launched from its spear-thrower was even more accurate than an iron ball fired from one of the ship's cannons. Even the Aborigines' fishing spears, simple at first sight, were skillfully designed. At the end of the wooden shaft were two, three, or even four sharp points or prongs which pierced a moving or still fish and occasionally a nearby bird. In essence the spear could either be used to stab the fish or, tied to a rope, it could be thrown at a fish just out of reach. The home-made rope enabled the spear and fish to be retrieved.

While the visitors were not generally impressed with what the Aborigines manufactured, they admired their skills and dexterity in daily life. Seeing the horizontal footmarks cut in the trunks of tall trees, they realized that Aborigines could climb skillfully to the top rather as the British seamen climbed into the rigging. Watching them create fire by rubbing two dry sticks together with gentle twirls of the palm of the hand—and so create a spark by friction—was "truely wonderfull," wrote Banks. The way they could set fire to the country—perhaps for hunting purposes, he assumed—was impressive. He saw a man running along the shore, holding a stick around which was wrapped dry grass, and every fifty or a hundred yards he would stoop down and set fire to leaves, grass, and twigs and so spread the fire. The ease with which those Aborigines living near the Endeavour River cooked food won the praise of the seamen.

Banks and Cook were tempted to call them "happy people." Their glory lay in the fact that they had no cravings for new possessions. Any European-made novelty shown to them was not worth keeping, in their view. Unlike the Polynesians, they stole nothing, and most of the things formally presented to them—an old shirt or a glass bead or an iron nail—were soon abandoned. When Banks wrote, at the end of his stay at the Endeavour River, that the Aborigines were content—"content with little nay almost nothing"—he was praising, not pitying, them. In his view it was perhaps God's design for the universe that those who were blessed with many possessions had the attendant disadvantage of wanting more, or of worrying that someone would steal what they owned. In contrast those Aborigines possessing so little were compensated by an absence of envy and discontent. Banks pointed to an English person's craving for tea, tobacco, spices, and alcohol: luxuries that soon became cravings and necessities. Whereas people who had never known them missed nothing, those who possessed them and were later deprived of them felt a sense of loss.

Those foreigners who are first to observe an exotic land will have contrary impressions and conclusions running side by side, jostling each other for dominance in their mind. Banks saw both harmony and violence in the daily life of the Aborigines. He wondered whether one reason why the population of this vast land was small was that the people were forever fighting one another with their simple but deadly weapons. The question of whether the Aborigines traditionally tended to encourage or condone violence is still a topic of unresolved debate. The evidence favors Banks's view that they frequently fought each other. In other words they were not as timid as he initially thought them to be.

WAS AUSTRALIA WORTH POSSESSING?

Would this vast land—or particular pockets of land—flourish if it passed into the hands or the control of people with more agricultural knowledge, or if the Aborigines learned how to farm rather than to forage? That crucial question was often on Cook's mind, especially in the weeks he spent near the Endeavour River. Initially his opinion of the land was cautious. While the western side of Australia, from what he had read, was dry and miserable, this eastern side was somewhat more promising. Anything would be superior, he implied, to the west coast. His own east coast, as far as he could judge, was very patchy, with fertile as well as poor soil. Probably he was inclined to assume that the barren land predominated. He regretted that he had seen no large rivers. In fact, by often sailing many miles from the shore, he had passed by several large rivers without being able to see their mouth.

Cook had the imagination and the vision to realize what might be done to the land, and how parts of it might be transformed if it were settled by Europeans. Admittedly in its present state, Cook wrote, the land "produces hardly any thing fit for man to eat." But if, in the years to come, European seeds and livestock were introduced, parts of this "Extensive Country" would flourish. Contemplating Australia's future, Cook almost sounded like a real-estate agent or the promoter of a new colony when he proclaimed that here was grass "for more Cattle at all seasons of the year than ever can be brought into this Country." In essence, if cattle were imported, they could eventually far outnumber those of the British Isles.

Banks's assessment of the land was more pessimistic. While it appeared green and fertile here and there, the soil appeared to deteriorate as the ship sailed north. There the soil was light and sandy and disappointing, and strands or tussocks of grass, and even trees, were not very close together. The word Banks used most often was "barren"; his summing up was that New South Wales was "the most barren countrey I have seen." No doubt exploration would yield many more fertile patches than he had seen in his short stay; but the proportion of fertile soil was tiny compared to the mass of rock and soil that was doomed, he thought, to be forever worthless. Admittedly the sea and land together could well yield enough food to keep alive "a company of people who should have the misfortune of being shipwrecked." It was a dismal assessment.

Recalling the long stretches of Australian coast he had recently glimpsed or seen, Cook thought the tropical part was slightly inferior: it grew trees that were smaller, and its vegetation covered less of the ground. As a former farm boy, who remained alert for signs of fertile soil and fresh water, he preferred Botany Bay to the tropical Endeavour River, now the site of Cooktown. And as a navigator he infinitely preferred Botany Bay and its safer harbor. But if he and Banks had been asked in 1770, which place was the most suited to an inflow of British settlers?, they would have pointed to New Zealand.

On the vital question of whether eastern Australia received enough rain to support herds and flocks in many places, Cook was more the optimist. He recalled that he could usually find water for the refilling of the *Endeavour*'s casks when he was rowed ashore, with the notable exception of Thirsty Sound, a mangrove estuary dissected by salty creeks. Banks was gloomier. In his eyes this was a dry land; but he imbibed hope by noting—from the damage left behind by scouring floods—that he was probably experiencing the coast at the dry season of the year. If Banks is read carefully, he is not quite as pessimistic as he first appears. Nine years later he was to be the European who more than any other extolled the possibilities of Botany Bay as a place of European settlement.

These discussions of eastern Australia's grasslands, rainfall, and climate, recorded in two handwritten journals, were of importance to Europe in the long term but disastrous for the Aborigines. In Europe more and more land was needed simply to feed the people; and more land was also needed to produce the fibers that clothed the people in winter and summer. Wool and flax—the raw material for linen and for sails too—were the main fibers used in the textile industry and were still far more important than cotton. All were grown largely in Europe. But the day would come when Australia would produce far more wool than any other country, and most of it would be sold to England and converted into cloth in those Yorkshire cities that were becoming a home of the new industrial revolution.

A COOK-TOWN ARISES

The repaired *Endeavour* prepared to sail. Soon the tropical valley and river mouth, where the crew had spent seven weeks, would show faint signs that they had ever been there. The grasslands burned on the day of dissent recovered after the next rainy season. Within a few years there was almost no sign that the ship had ever lain on her side on the river bank. At the places where the tents had been pitched, where food and gunpowder had been kept away from the rain, and where the blacksmith's forge had made nails to repair the ship's bottom, nearly all the evidence of the British occupancy vanished. The local Aborigines who returned to the site to catch fish and gather yams must have occasionally looked out to sea, just in case the *Endeavour* was returning. For them the weeks had been dislocating because their own supply of food was diminished while the visitors were trying as much as possible to live off the same land and fishing grounds.

One hundred three years after the *Endeavour* sailed out to sea, the estuary came to life again. Gold was discovered in the interior, at the Palmer River, and the Endeavour River became a harbor again. Wharves and warehouses arose close to the spot where the *Endeavour* had lain for repairs. Steamships and sailing ships arrived, at first with Australian gold-diggers and then with Chinese from Canton. By 1877 there were seventeen thousand Chinese men at the port and goldfield and the road that linked them.

Close to the river bank where the *Endeavour* had been beached, a tent town sprang to life. Soon transformed into a permanent town with banks, shops, halls, and dozens of hotels and grog shops strung along a wide main street, it even had a Catholic cathedral and a Chinese temple, a public botanical garden that would almost have satisfied Joseph Banks, and an official harbormaster whose presence would have pleased James Cook. The local Aborigines, now dislocated, sometimes came into the town to find food or to beg. In 1885 the town council imposed a curfew on them, and they were not allowed to remain in Cooktown after dark.

The gold, sold by miners to the local banks, was exported from Cooktown in ships steaming mostly to southern ports but sometimes returning to Canton. By the end of the 1870s perhaps a million ounces of gold had been won from the district. The port soon passed its peak, but at the end of the following decade it was still wealthy enough to honor Captain Cook by building a costly monument on the shore.

14

A Happy Puff of Wind

⚓ HAVING ESCAPED from a reef-dotted sea, the *Endeavour* must return to it. There was no alternative. The crew did not yet realize that their ship was almost locked inside a narrow arm of the sea, with Australia forming a barrier on one side and the outer edge of the Great Barrier Reef forming a long but intermittent wall of coral on the other side. That wall was covered by the sea at high tide, and usually a rowboat could safely cross it, but the *Endeavour* would have to find one of the gaps in the wall.

It is easy for us—we have the large-scale map—to see the layout of land and sea and coral reef, but Cook did not know the layout. Nothing like it exists elsewhere in the world. This rampart—he later called it a "Grand Reef"—ran for hundreds of miles, roughly parallel to the coast of Australia. If he could not find a safe passage through it or alongside it, he might have to return for hundreds of miles along the dangerous route he had recently followed.

As the *Endeavour* sailed in a strong wind close to the shore, a high island came into sight. Here was a natural lookout from which Cook might view the geographical puzzle of reef, sea, and coastline. Known as Lizard Island, it was low at one end and high at the other. Once the ship was anchored, Cook and Banks were rowed across the windswept sea to the beach, from which they set out to climb the prominent hill. The view unfolded dramatically as they climbed. From the peak in the late afternoon they were heartened to observe, not far out to sea, at least one channel or passage that seemed to cut through the long rampart of the reef.

Those who stand on that isolated hill on a calm, sunny afternoon—the sweeping panorama before them and the line of white waves spotlighting the length of the reef—can share the hope that Cook felt on seeing that channel. After descending the hill, Cook and Banks slept "under the shade of a Bush," the sandy beach making a soft mattress. Cook decided that he needed a second view of the reefs, and next morning he climbed the hill in the half-light, reaching the summit at sunrise. Alas, he wrote in his private log for Sunday, August 12, a haze had descended, blurring his view. Already he had despatched a boat to inspect the channel that he had vaguely glimpsed from the high hill. Cutting cleanly through the rampart of coral, it might be too narrow or too shallow to carry the *Endeavour* through. The reef, on inspection, looked formidable on this windy day. On both sides of the channel "the sea broke vastly high." The master of the small boat, while optimistic, did not dare attempt to pass through the channel and estimate its depth.

Cook and Banks rejoined the *Endeavour*, and she edged her way toward the gap in the coral reef. Cook saw with misgivings the breakers rise high before crashing on the reef. With everybody sharing in the tension, the ship at last approached the opening and the noisy breakers on either side. Meanwhile the master went ahead in a boat and, once he passed safely through the channel, signaled that it was safe for the *Endeavour* to follow. In a few minutes she passed through a gap that, in Cook's opinion, was surprisingly wide. Now known as Cook's Passage, it is frequently used by large ships.

Outside the wall of coral Cook found the open ocean suddenly so deep that the sailor heaving the long leadline could not find the seabed. The ship had escaped from her prison of coral.

On the following morning the *Endeavour* was out of sight of land for the first time in more than three months. "Satisfaction," wrote Banks, "was clearly painted in every mans face." Nothing could disturb that satisfaction for a day or two. Although the ship began to leak as a result of the force of the ocean swell, and one pump had to be operated, this was a light burden compared to the emotional burden that had been felt for weeks.

THE NEW PUZZLE: IS AUSTRALIA AN ISLAND?

Cook must often have been consulting the detailed maps inserted in Charles de Brosses's history of Pacific voyages, published in the French language just a dozen years before the *Endeavour* sailed from England. One map, drawn by Robert de Vaugondy of Paris, showed a strait clearly separating northern Australia from New Guinea. It also indicated that the south coast of New Guinea had already been explored, for Dutch and Spanish names dotted those parts of its shoreline facing Australia. On the nearby coastline of Australia, however, the map was deceptive. It gave not a hint of the Great Barrier Reef. It depicted that great bulge on which stood the site of New Jerusalem, but Cook had just disproved the existence of that bulge. While Vaugondy's map gave a hopeful outline of the dividing strait as a whole, it was perilously short of other information that a navigator required. It did not even indicate where the shipping channel—if it existed—could be found.

To add to the puzzle, in the course of his two volumes of narrative Charles de Brosses did not even mention the existence of Torres Strait. It was as if Vaugondy's map had been discovered by de Brosses at the very last moment and attached, without comment, to his book in the final stage of the process of printing and binding. The book was silent; the map was loud-voiced.

Cook's additional source of information about that strait was the nautical Scot and ardent advocate for the existence of the mysterious southern continent, Alexander Dalrymple. While residing as a young man in the Indian port of Madras, Dalrymple had seen a Spanish maritime document revealing that as long ago as 1606 the Spanish navigator Torres had passed through the strait which now honors his name. It was Dalrymple who presented to Joseph Banks a "Chart of the South Pacifick Ocean." The chart showed roughly the route taken by Torres across the southwest Pacific and through the narrow strait. Although Cook does not specifically mention examining the Dalrymple chart, he must have seen it and looked at it intently.

Cook cannot have been instantly impressed by the chart. He and Dalrymple were rivals, not friends. Moreover Cook's futile search for the unknown continent during the preceding twelve months had not enhanced his opinion of Dalrymple as a geographical theorist and mapmaker. We now know that Dalrymple's chart was deficient in nearly all the detail that a navigator needed. His sketch of the island of New Guinea was more like a thin sausage than the irregularly shaped island now depicted on maps of the world. The eastern part of New Guinea was elongated partly because Dalrymple had pinned to it the separate Guadalcanal, which is a vital part of the Solomon Islands. His chart has other defects, too. The Gulf of Carpentaria was clearly marked, but the position of the northeastern tip of Australia was astray. Not one of the strait's major islands—a danger to ships—was marked. That unique nightmare, the maze of coral reefs, was entirely absent from the chart. These criticisms are not intended to dismiss Dalrymple's brave chart as worthless. Like Vaugondy, he positively depicted the existence of Torres Strait.

On leaving his retreat at Cooktown, Cook had decided that his patched-up ship should attempt to resolve the question of whether Australia and New Guinea were joined. "I firmly believe," he wrote, that a strait separated them. Why was he reaching this belief? He was guided not wholly by the maps. The long northwestern trend of the Australian coast, a trend rarely faltering since he passed Bustard Bay and Moreton Bay, also pointed toward the site of the short strait marked on the chart in the French book. If the strait existed, then in his predicament—his ship was damaged—he had every incentive to use the strait in order to reach the Dutch East Indies and the Cape of Good Hope and the final homeward stretch along the Atlantic. The strait would certainly be shorter than the alternative route around the east and north of New Guinea.

A speedier voyage to Java was vital to Cook for another reason. His ship held only three months' supply of some foodstuffs and a smaller stock of others. Any unforeseen delay, Cook told his officers, "might prove the ruin of the Voyage." To save time was the potential attraction of Torres Strait. Moreover Cook could take advantage of the southeast monsoon in those couple of months before it annually changed direction and turned against his ship.

THROUGH THE FOAMING BREAKERS

It might have been easier for Cook's peace of mind if he had refused to attempt to find a way through Torres Strait. He had just escaped from the coral prison, but now he probably would have to find his way back. He guessed or assumed that he could not enter Torres Strait without first finding another opening in the Great Barrier Reef—that low wall often pounded by what Cook called "the vast foaming breakers." For hours he sailed north and northwest, hoping the long reef would come to an end. It did not end.

In fact the reef was dangerously near, and the *Endeavour* was being driven toward it by the waves and the southeasterly swell. On the morning of August 16, in the first light, the ship's predicament was stark. She was too close to the reef, and there was no opening. The wind was light, hardly a breath at times, and so it could not be enlisted to push the *Endeavour* back into safer waters. As the help of muscle power and oars was needed, the longboat and the yawl were lowered into the water in the hope that they might haul the *Endeavour* out of danger. The third boat, the pinnace, was being repaired by the carpenters just when it was urgently needed.

Meanwhile the *Endeavour* was at the mercy of the ocean swell and the tide. Like a rising and falling cork she was driven toward the main reef. One wave lifted her so high that the sailors could see, right across the hollow of sea in front of them, a mighty wave smashing against the reef. The hope of many seamen was that anchors could be dropped in order to hold fast the ship. The sea, however, was too deep for an anchor. For some time the ship seemed likely to crash into the reef. At 5:45 A.M. she was only forty yards from the breakers.

The nearest land was thirty miles to the west; what if the ship sank, and sank speedily? This sobering thought was in the mind of all who were called upon to work the oars in the hope of saving the *Endeavour*. Nonetheless the calmness and determination of everyone warmed Cook's heart. In this "truly terrible situation not one man ceased to do his utmost." Few were calmer than Green the astronomer who, with two assistants, was taking observations in order to determine the ship's longitude at the very minute when the swell seemed to be "heaving us right on" the reef that stood just ahead.

Nothing was so effective in preventing the *Endeavour* from hitting the reef than muscle power. The ship's own long oars, since sunrise, had intermittently been worked by relays of seamen. Known as sweeps, these oars protruded from the portholes in the gun room. Vital in the turning around of the ship, they also pushed her bow toward the wind and current, thus presenting a smaller front to the force of the sea. But human strength was not enough.

When all seemed lost, the wind came to the aid of the men working the big oars in the *Endeavour* and the small oars in the two towing boats. A light puff of wind began to blow from the right quarter. The wind barely tickled the sails, but it was enough. Remarkably, as Cook noted in his private log, the ship was just out of peril when the wind "fell again quite calm."

It was increasingly a day of tension. Another wide opening in the rampart of coral became visible. A boat was sent to inspect the opening, with the ship soon following in the hope that the wind and tide were favorable. And then, unexpectedly, the tide turned against the ship as she approached the gap in the coral wall. Through this gap the seawater gushed toward the ship like "a mill race"—a phrase evoking the rush of river water turning the waterwheels that, just before the age of steam, drove many English mills and mine pumps. The combination of the ebb tide and the powers of the oarsmen in the small boats removed the *Endeavour* from danger. By noon she was two miles out to sea.

In this part of the world the tidal changes were frequent. Before long, the flow of water would be reversed. Cook would have to exploit this incoming tide if he were to find an opening through the reef into the calmer inshore waters that were his goal. At about 1 P.M. Lieutenant Hicks, setting out in a rowboat to investigate the opening, reported that it was only a quarter of a mile in width and therefore risky but feasible. In the middle of the narrow gap rose a large rock, like a warning sign.

At mid-afternoon the time seemed ripe. A light easterly set in, and two boats did their best to turn the head of the *Endeavour* toward the opening while other sailors sat in a boat near the bow, their oars at the ready. Caught in the moving tide the ship was soon in the very jaw of the channel, a captive of the swift-flowing stream. It was a startling and reassuring moment. One minute the ship was in the turbulent, fast-running current; almost the next instant she was in smooth water.

At 4 P.M. she was safe. The water was calm, for the reef protected it from the swell in the open ocean. The following day became a minor celebration as parties of seamen went to the exposed reefs and returned to the *Endeavour* with such a collection of shellfish that three pounds could be served to every man.

In the entire voyage this had been the most dangerous day, even more hazardous in Cook's opinion than the time when the ship hit the reef. Cook wrote breathlessly about those few ticks of the clock when "we had hardly any hopes" of saving the ship or the seamen's lives. He did not think that God frequently intervened in human affairs, but in his first draft of the story he humbly wrote, "It pleased GOD at this very juncture to send us a light air of wind." Later he had second thoughts and, rewriting a few sentences, placed God in the vague background. But he still felt sufficiently humbled by the experience to name this opening the Providential Channel.

Richard Pickersgill vowed it was "the narrowest escape we ever had." Without God's help, he declared, "we must inevitably have perished, for the ship must have sunk alongside the rocks, which were as steep as a wall, and there would have been no hopes of saving one single life in so great a surf." Even the smaller boats might have been dashed to splinters by the high waves smashing against the coral reef. And if by chance a few men had been saved and had managed to paddle on planks of timber to the coast, which could be seen in the distance, what then would have been their future? Another two years might have passed before the Admiralty in England decided that their ship was lost and that a naval vessel, perhaps two, must be sent out to search for survivors.

We know how slow and frustrating a vigorous search for lost ships could be in that era. J. F. G. de La Pérouse, in the decade after Cook's death, was to lead one of the boldest of French expeditions. In an audacious sweep of the Pacific his two ships visited harbors as far apart as Easter Island, Monterey in California, Alaska, Siberia, and the Chinese port of Macao. In January 1788 his two ships were briefly in Botany Bay before setting out on the next phase of the long voyage, which, it was planned, would take them to de Surville's discoveries in the Solomon Islands and even within a hundred miles of the Providential Channel where Cook had almost lost his ship.

The French ships were not seen again. A relief expedition of two frigates, sent from the French port of Brest under the command of Vice Admiral Bruny d'Entrecasteaux, was still searching without success nearly six years after La Pérouse had disappeared. In the following century, reports that the vanished ships had hit a coral reef at Vanikoro, fifteen hundred miles due east of Cook's Providential Channel, eventually came to light. A band of the shipwreck survivors had managed to sail away from the coral island in a small boat in search of a friendly port. Somewhere in the open ocean they vanished. This medley of tragic news did not reach France until five decades after the disaster.

If Cook had lost his ship at that channel through the Great Barrier Reef, his fate might have been similar to that of La Pérouse. A search for his whereabouts would have been long delayed, and when finally organized from London it would have been slow. The commander of the English vessels finally sent by the anxious Admiralty in search of the vanished *Endeavour* would have had no alternative but to sail first to Cape Horn and search the southerly coasts of South America. The ships would then have approached Tahiti and its adjacent islands, hoping to find the survivors there. Once those likely places had been exhausted, the commander—if his crew had mostly escaped the scurvy—probably would have sailed south, in keeping with Cook's secret instructions, hoping to find the wreck of the lost *Endeavour* somewhere in the vicinity of the missing continent. Perhaps in desperation or boldness, the commander might have then voyaged toward New Zealand. Finding no survivors there, after learning of the *Endeavour*'s visit, he would have given up the search. He would not have contemplated searching for survivors in Tasmania or on the east coast of Australia. Those lands were not mentioned in the secret instructions that Cook carried in his cabin.

This was the terrible dilemma facing Cook if he lost his ship but saved his life near the coral jaws of the Great Barrier Reef. His very success as a navigator in traveling far beyond his expected goals would have jeopardized any search for him. Much of the history of Australia and New Zealand might have been different had the *Endeavour* not received, in that moment of peril, what some eyewitnesses called a "happy puff of wind."

WALES AND YORK: THE CHRISTENINGS

Cook was back in the kind of seascape where, two months earlier, his ship had run onto the reef. Smaller reefs lay here and there, some showing their teeth at low tide. For some days the ship, with the low-lying coast on one side and the Great Barrier Reef on the other, crept north, a boat or two sounding out the tricky path ahead. Cook now insisted on an anchorage during the hours of darkness. He had learned his lesson.

At last they reached the cape at the northeastern tip of the continent. One of the best-known points on the long coast, it is now called Cape York but was initially christened by Cook as York Cape. From the sea it is not a dramatic sight, but those who are fortunate enough to stand on the cape—and it is not easily reached by land—are usually stirred by the sight of the tiny rock-island opposite and the constant rush of turbulent sea between island and cape.

Just west of the cape, on the afternoon of August 22, Cook and Banks and Solander landed on an island crowned by round, rock-strewn hills. Assuming that this could be the last piece of Australian soil they would stand upon, Cook organized a simple ceremony on a hill. In the name of the king he hoisted the British flag on a makeshift pole, and the Marines who were with him stood in line, raised their muskets, and fired three volleys. Other Marines, waiting on the deck of the *Endeavour* to hear the sound rolling toward them from the island, responded with three more volleys. The chorus of shots must have been heard with surprise by the few inhabitants going about their tasks.

Cook was confident that the whole coast he had traversed "was never seen or visited by any European before us." He thought it appropriate, at this place that the Aborigines called Bedanug and he christened Possession Island, to make a formal claim to the whole coast extending back to the latitude of thirty-eight degrees south. The sites of the later cities of Brisbane and Sydney were inside that claimed territory, though whether Melbourne lay inside is open to doubt. Cook gave no hint of how far inland his claim extended. A man of the sea, he was essentially claiming possession of the coast and a vague hinterland.

While Cook's official instructions forbade him to claim land without the consent of the Aboriginal inhabitants—and he did not seek their consent—he was probably laying out his claim primarily against those of Holland, Spain, and other naval powers. He was not completely convinced that Britain would find it worthwhile to occupy any part of this vast land. This was the fortnight when he and Banks, writing a short summary in their journals, stressed that nothing of immediate value could be found on this entire coast. How mistaken they were. Some of the nearby "Indians" they met were actually wearing around their necks a gleaming ornament made of pearl shell. The *Endeavour* had chanced to enter a part of the coast rich in pearls; and in the following century a pearl fishery would be established on the shore of the very island where Cook formally claimed possession.

In referring to the coast he had followed for the best part of two thousand miles, Cook employed the familiar name of New Holland. He did not doubt that he was on the eastern side of the same vast land that had been seen by many Dutch captains far to the west. He did not think of using the name Australia, though that name was already circulating a little, even in his own ship, long before Matthew Flinders the navigator began, in 1804, to popularize it. Already in the *Endeavour*'s big cabin, Sydney Parkinson employed Australia as a general name for various lands of the southern hemisphere. Indeed several of his sketches and finished drawings of landscapes, seascapes, and people are inscribed with the word *Australia*.

At first Cook thought of giving the name of New Wales to the whole coastline he had explored. He was familiar with the Europeans' habit of conferring their homeland names on the southwest Pacific: thus the names of New Holland and New Zealand reflected the Dutch influences, while northeast of New Guinea stood the large islands of New Britain and New Ireland. Cook's tentative name of New Wales for this long Australian coast was therefore in keeping, though curiously the same name was already claimed by a Canadian district north of Ontario. At first it seems surprising that Cook did not prefer the name of New Yorkshire; he knew that English county whereas Wales was not familiar to him. But the Prince of Wales was the heir to the British throne, and Cook presumably decided that the prince should be indirectly honored even if the result was geographical confusion.

More than two months later Cook finally bestowed the longer name "New South Wales." The additional word "south" presumably denoted a new Wales sitting in the southern hemisphere rather than the old South Wales, of which Cardiff and Swansea were ports. Whatever the precise mixture of ideas in Cook's mind, the princely word Wales was much to the fore; next day an adjacent cluster of islands received the name of Prince of Wales Islands.

The round hill on which Cook raised the flag and fired the salute commanded a wide view, especially to the west. Drinking in the sight of that sunlit sea stretching away, he concluded that it must be part of the strait separating Australia from New Guinea. By weaving past the coral reefs and sand spits and submerged rocks, his ship could surely pass safely through the relatively short strait. "I did not doubt but that there was a passage," he wrote.

With the aid of intermittent breezes, the *Endeavour* sailed west, initially hugging the Australian coast. Here and there lay shoals, reefs, and sandbanks, and the rowboats had to show the way, testing the depth of the water. To cope with the fast-flowing tides, the *Endeavour* occasionally had to anchor even in hours of daylight. Cook now had extreme trouble pinpointing his ship's true position at noon each day. Usually so meticulous in his chartmaking and so skilled in defining his ship's position, he was not alive when his errors were finally discovered. They proved to be huge. His longitude was now astray by seventy-seven miles. Sometimes, however, Cook entrusted the calculating of longitude to astronomer Green, and later events would reveal that Green, in his fondness for rum and water, was not always accurate.

Safely through the strait and into an open ocean that Cook called "the India Sea," he looked to the southwest and saw the swell rolling steadily toward him. It had no accompanying wind, and he realized that such waves could arise only in a wide expanse of ocean. In his journal he rejoiced that "the dangers and fatigues of the Voyage was drawing near to an end." His satisfaction came also from his success in confirming that New Holland and New Guinea were separate lands.

He did not claim for one moment to have *discovered* the strait between them. He had merely confirmed what several French and Dutch mapmakers had proclaimed before he was even a naval officer. Nonetheless he deserved more praise than he sought for himself. Undoubtedly Torres the Spaniard deserves the highest praise, but his discovery could hardly be called a secure addition to seafaring knowledge because the rulers of Spain largely kept the existence of the strait a secret. They were determined that rival maritime nations should not know of this potential shortcut to their own kingdom's trading empires in the Philippines on the one side and South America on the other side. A few Dutchmen must also have known of the strait, though it is not certain whether any of their ships had ventured through it. In effect this vital corridor for ships had remained unused for nearly two centuries after its discovery.

A strait between major lands, whether it is the Persian Gulf or the Strait of Dover, is usually an open sea, offering few obstacles to careful pilots. Torres Strait, however, is risky. Of all the major straits in the world, it remains one of the most hazardous. It consists of separate, distinctive, and dangerous channels, each of which called for its own discoverer—a mariner willing to face high risks. The channel found by the bold Torres is still subject to debate. Cook did not know how to locate Torres's channel because no detailed chart was available to him or even to Spanish captains of the time. Therefore he found his own channel, close to the coast of Australia and near the point at which his ship first approached the vicinity of the strait.

It is possible that Cook used, unknowingly, the same strait that Torres had found. Captain Brett Hilder, an experienced pilot in these waters, spent years studying Spanish maps and writings in order to decide which channel Torres had used. In 1975, toward the end of his career, Hilder piloted a small cargo ship through Cook's route, now called Endeavour Strait, and convinced himself that it was the same route that Torres had found.

Long after the *Endeavour*'s voyage, the entire strait was shunned as risky by the captains of sailing ships. Eventually the safest passage, the Prince of Wales Channel, was discovered. Requiring the services of a professional pilot even today, this serpentine channel was ultimately marked by iron buoys, ringing bells, lighthouses large and small on rocky islands nearby, and floating beacons that flashed at night. The larger ships employing this channel sometimes have to wait for high tide before they can move at slow speed through the strait, and even then they are almost within a stone's throw of ships sailing in the opposite direction.

THE BOOBY ISLAND

After traversing the strait, wrote Cook, "we lost sight of land." How wonderful was the sensation to be ten or twenty miles from land, encircled by sea, and to feel relatively safe from the coral reefs and hidden sandbanks and rocks. Less than three weeks had passed since the ship had left her refuge and makeshift dockyard on the Endeavour River, and now she approached an isolated island that marked the end of her long period of exploration.

This flat-topped island, from which Cook was to look optimistically toward the open sea, deserves a dramatic name. Instead it is simply called Booby Island. The telltale signs of these brown birds with their yellow bill and white underwing were everywhere. From the ship the steep cliffs and slopes seemed strangely pale, until Banks discovered, to his amazement, that they were "white with the Dung of Birds." Ashore for an hour or two, the landing party shot so many boobies, presumably big enough to merit a place in the ship's big cooking pot, that the muskets ran out of ammunition. There was just enough time for a little botanizing in the hot sun before the specimens of new plants and the dead birds were rowed back to the waiting ship.

Almost two and a half centuries after Banks and Cook went ashore, the little island is an exotic sight for those walking the deck of the few passenger ships passing by. The bareness of the island is relieved by the cluster of palm trees waving when the seawind blows. Prominent is a white lighthouse with a red-painted dome, from which each night a white light flashes, eight times to the minute.

Until an automatic light was installed in recent years, the lighthouse keepers and their families lived in three or four houses that still stand on the bare plateau. Their only frequent visitors were birds, which landed while migrating to New Guinea or northern Australia. The last of the children who lived here received their school lessons by radio from Australia. They would remember, long after they left the island, warm days when the tide was out and they could walk on the wet rocks and fish for Red Emperor and Coral Trout and gather oysters from the rocks. In clear weather they could see, across the ocean, the mainland of Australia; and after darkness descended with its tropical speed they saw the lighthouse's long beam slanting on an ocean usually peaceful but sometimes turbulent.

Now the island is as deserted as it was in Cook's time. But nearly every day and night ships pass by, carrying Australian wheat to Indonesia or China, or Queensland copper to distant refineries. There is one other passing cargo that might have caught Captain de Surville's fancy. Australia is now the world's largest exporter of coal by sea, and large tonnages pass through Torres Strait toward the Indian Ocean, the Bay of Bengal, and the shallow Indian coastline he knew so well. Some of the coal might even be generating electricity in Pondicherry, the port de Surville had left in search of the Jewish land.

Leaving Booby Island behind, the *Endeavour* was entering a sea that often had been traversed before—a sea in whose harbors the Dutch and Portuguese regularly traded. This contrast between the sea ahead of Cook and those seas that he had left behind was stark. Since his departure from Tahiti he had been sailing into the unknown. He had spent a whole year in the realm of danger, part of it in the roaring forties, which has few rivals for howling winds and mountainous seas, and part of it in navigating the longest reef in the world. This was Cook's real triumph: he had sailed through a wider expanse of dangerous seas and followed more hazardous lines of coast than probably any previous explorer during a single voyage.

15

The Guns of Mourning

🖿 IN PONDICHERRY they waited for news of de Surville and his
ship loaded with textiles and spices. More than a year had passed since
he sailed away. While that was not a long time for such an ambitious
voyage, it was a long time for his supporters to be totally without news
of him. There were French merchants and officials resident in India
who had invested a large sum in the ship's cargo and now awaited
a financial dividend, and there were colored and white residents of
the French ports on the Indian coast whose family and friends were
aboard the absent ship. Above all, high French officials in India held
the hope that de Surville would launch a new commercial empire to
replace the one that France had virtually lost to Britain on the shores
of the Bay of Bengal.

We last observed the *St. Jean-Baptiste* far out in the South Pacific,
thousands of miles to the east of New Zealand. It was February 1770,
and she was all alone in the tempestuous seas, around the latitude of
forty degrees south. The missing continent remained missing. Captain de Surville's present aim was to exploit the strong westerly winds
to reach as quickly as possible a favorable position in the east Pacific,
from which he could veer north in search of Davis Land.

THE MYSTERIOUS LAND OF DAVIS

Some seven weeks after leaving New Zealand, de Surville began to
alter course and deliberately sail toward the land reportedly seen by

Dampier's shipmate more than eighty years earlier. Davis Land, or David Land, was believed to be large. If it were not a continent, it was a very large island. It was said to lie close to the Tropic of Capricorn, and it was thought by some to lie somewhere west of Easter Island. Vaugondy's map, a copy of which was in de Surville's possession, specifically showed the elusive David Land as lying in the latitude of twenty-seven or twenty-eight degrees south, and far out from the coast of what is now Chile. That squiggle on Vaugondy's map was maybe a thousand miles from the ship's current position, but such a distance did not deter de Surville.

On February 22 the *St. Jean-Baptiste* was thirty-five degrees south. By the start of March she was only about thirty degrees south, and moving closer to the equator. On March 5 she was near twenty-seven degrees, the same latitude in which David Land was reported to lie—according to Vaugondy's map. The long-sought land, if it existed, could not be far away.

The sea ceased to be cold and windswept. Headwinds replaced the tailwinds that had favored the ship. In the warmer air the scurvy again spread among the crew, and Ranginui, the Maori, was among the ill. Drinking water was so scarce that one pint became the meager daily ration. The cooks now had only a small daily portion of food to put into the big pots. To his credit de Surville insisted on giving away some of his own allowance of food.

Why he should have been short of food is a puzzle. The *St. Jean-Baptiste* was said to have been well stocked in Pondicherry, and she must have set out with at least one year's supply of basic foods. Moreover the death of nearly one-third of her crew by the time she sailed from New Zealand meant that fewer mouths had to be fed each day. Why then was the daily food of the officers and seamen now severely rationed? Presumably a large amount of grain had been spoiled by the inflow of seawater into the hold in the Tasman Sea. In addition, de Surville relied, as did Cook, on gathering as much fresh food as possible along the sea route; but he was unfortunate in calling at two harbors in the Philippines and the Solomons where food was difficult to procure. In contrast Cook had been more fortunate. In Tahiti he had enjoyed a culinary paradise, a tropical food bowl into which the ninety British seamen could dip week after week without endangering the food supply of the local inhabitants. He had also acquired supplies of fresh and smoked fish, and green and root vegetables, at several New Zealand harbors. Nowhere during the entire voyage did he face the scarcity of drinking water now facing de Surville.

The bay where de Surville had found shelter in New Zealand was, in retrospect, vital to the success of his voyage. In one sense it served him well. Greens were abundant, and fresh fish was initially delivered to him by the Maori. The root crops, however, were not yet ready to be dug, and there was no meat—not even pork—to be bought or bartered. At that time of year the soil around the wide bay was not productive enough to support the local population quite adequately, let alone divert food to nearly 140 members of the French crew. Admittedly firewood and fresh water were plentiful on shore, but not many fit seamen were available to cut the wood and carry aboard the casks of water during their fortnight's stay. Above all, the stay in Doubtless Bay was cut short by the devastating gale. As a result the contrast between the two captains and their fortunes was sharp. Here in the emptiness of the Pacific was the Frenchman, face to face with a severe scarcity that the Englishman, partly through good fortune and partly through good management, had to face at no stage of his voyage.

For de Surville there was hope. From the lookouts in his ship, whenever the weather cleared, the ocean stood out like a big plate, with nothing to be seen but sea and the circling horizon. And yet Davis Land might suddenly appear. The ship now was in the latitude of 27 degrees south and the longitude of 102 degrees, west of the meridian of Paris, and close to the position where land had reportedly been seen nearly a century ago. But the men on watch remained silent.

It was daybreak on March 6, and the squalls rushed past and flashes of lightning were seen in the east. Toward 10 A.M. the captain declared that he would call his officers together in council and seek their opinion—a rare request. It was a time for earnest discussion and flowery oratory. Did they all have "the constancy and steadfastness so necessary for exploration"? Did they cherish "la gloire du Patriotisme"? In essence, should the *St. Jean-Baptiste* continue to search for Davis Land? Or should she change direction and sail toward the nearest colonial port in Spanish South America and seek supplies there? One by one the opinions were given; the captain listened closely.

Everyone agreed—even the captain—that help for the disabled, and food and water for the able, were urgently needed. The captain recorded with his own hand that "to my great regret, we could no longer amuse ourselves looking for Davis land." Amuse ourselves? He must have had a wry turn of mind.

It is now certain that the hoped-for Davis Land and its exotic inhabitants did not exist. They were simply the fleshed-out examples of the well-argued faith in the existence of a rich and populated continent, just waiting to be discovered in the warmer zones of the South Pacific.

THE RIDDLE OF THE JEWISH COLONY

The long voyage had so far been inspired partly by myth and rumor. The theory that a colony or enclave of Jewish traders flourished somewhere in the South Pacific probably arose from errors of eye and ear and a leap of the imagination during the last hectic evening spent by the *Dolphin* and her British crew in Tahiti in 1767; but the theory was buoyed by the inescapable fact that the Jews were probably the world's most enterprising and most scattered merchants.

Something about the dress of certain Tahitians also conveyed a Middle Eastern air. On Cook's second voyage to the Pacific he carried with him a talented landscape artist, William Hodges, who painted a remarkable picture of the north coast of Tahiti, called *View of the Province of Oparree*. Described by several art critics as one of the notable British paintings of the eighteenth century, it depicts a canoe carrying two men, a paddler and a passenger. Both are wearing white turbans or turbanlike headgear, and both have beards and mustaches. Their dress and facial appearance might be described as somewhat Semitic.

The theory that a colony of mysterious strangers lived near Tahiti could have an additional explanation. Forty-five years previously, the *African Galley*, one of Roggeveen's three tiny Dutch ships, had been wrecked on the nearby island of Takapoto, only a short canoe voyage from Tahiti. The Dutch quartermaster and four sailors safely reached the shore and, refusing to be rescued by their kinsmen in another ship, obstinately remained behind. Perhaps they or their descendants were the strange men seen in the canopied canoe by those standing on the deck of the *Dolphin* years later. This explanation is feasible. The more likely conclusion, however, is that no Jewish merchants lived in this balmy corner of the South Pacific.

"LAND, LAND!"

Six days after de Surville abandoned his anxious search for the continent, he found that he was no longer sailing in unknown seas. Masts and sails could be seen near the horizon. This was probably the first European ship seen by de Surville's crew in more than half a year. The field glasses were not powerful enough to pick out her flag, but any ship in that remote ocean was likely to be Spanish. Nearly a fortnight later, on March 24, came another shout: "Land, land!" A volcanic peak could be just seen in the distance, a dramatic shape in this seemingly empty sea. It was the Frenchmen's first glimpse of land in nearly three months.

The peak belonged to the most westward of the islands in the Juan Fernández archipelago, Mas Afuera, meaning "farther out." Soon the archipelago's more important island, with its port and Spanish garrison, came into view. In the *St. Jean-Baptiste* the officers talked of sending boats ashore in the hope of gathering emergency supplies of food and water; but the coast of South America, only about four hundred miles away, was the more tempting goal. The captain decided that his ship should sail with all possible speed toward tropical Peru and the main Spanish colonial ports.

Meanwhile Ranginui, ailing and homesick, became gravely ill. For several hundred years, it is almost certain, no other Maori had sailed so far from his homeland. And yet in his last days, so far from home, he was near islands that were probably first discovered by other members of his own Polynesian race. Attempts were made to save him. The captain tried to keep him alive by offering him part of his own allowance of food. But Ranginui simply faded away. He died just as the Juan Fernández archipelago was sighted. In the journal of the second officer, Jean Pottier de l'Horme, appears the simple entry, "*Mort le Sauvage*" or "Death of the Savage."

Eleven days later, a few lofty crags drifted faintly into view. Mountains of uneven height, the Andes slowly took shape across the sea. After their cap of fog and mist was lifted, the crags could be seen

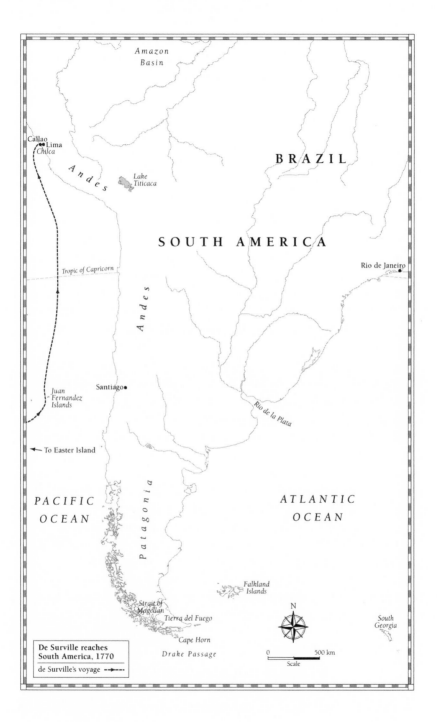

Amazon
Basin

Callao
Lima
Chilca

Andes

Lake
Titicaca

BRAZIL

SOUTH AMERICA

Rio de Janeiro

Tropic of Capricorn

Andes

Juan
Fernandez
Islands

Santiago

Rio de la Plata

To Easter Island

PACIFIC
OCEAN

Patagonia

ATLANTIC
OCEAN

Falkland
Islands

Strait of
Magellan

South
Georgia

N

Tierra del Fuego

Cape Horn

Drake Passage

0   500 km
Scale

De Surville reaches
South America, 1770

de Surville's voyage

sharply from the *St. Jean-Baptiste*. The sight of these continental mountains brought a feeling of quiet jubilation to the sailors. The long crossing of the Pacific was almost completed. The prospect of finding help in a Spanish colonial port for all those craving water and fresh food was only a few days away.

On Sunday, April 8, 1770, the minor port of Chilca, twenty-five miles south of the busy port of Callao, came into sight. On the coastal plain grew orchards with their lifesaving fruit, and just out to sea stood an island that was painted white by the droppings of thousands of seabirds. The *St. Jean-Baptiste* came to the edge of a bay, the water of which was colored like "green ooze," and put down her small kedge anchor. De Surville ordered the firing of his big guns—almost a distress signal—in the hope that a Spanish official would be rowed out with an offer of help. But from the sleepy port of Chilca came no response.

Desperate to obtain fresh provisions and water for his ailing seamen, and new anchors and other equipment for his ship, de Surville sat down with his quill pen and formally wrote to the viceroy of Peru a plea for help. Aware that a French ship in a Spanish colonial possession would be treated with suspicion, de Surville wished to show all respect. His fear was that his ship might be seized and that her valuable cargoes might be impounded.

To placate the Spanish authorities was the French captain's urgent desire. Accordingly he instructed Guillaume Labé, his first officer, to take the letter ashore in the hope that it would be received with courtesy and quickly forwarded to the Spanish viceroy's palace at Lima, not far from the coast. Setting out with several sailors in a small boat, the officer was soon disappointed to see the waves breaking over the bar at the mouth of the harbor. He decided that the crossing was hazardous and returned at noon with the letter undelivered. De Surville resolved to deliver the letter himself, hoping to purchase food and obtain fresh water at the same time.

THE FATE OF THE CAPTAIN

To emphasize his own position of command, de Surville put on his best naval uniform and his decorations. Fully dressed, he was almost weighed down by the heavy cloth and braid, and by his medals and ceremonial sword. Familiar with the sandbars and the sometimes treacherous waves that guarded the entrance to the Indian ports of Madras and Pondicherry, he realized the risk in rowing a small boat across this turbulent entrance. His decision was later said to be imprudent and even foolhardy, but he accepted the risks, for so many of his crew were ill.

So that the messages might be carried safely ashore even if the boat capsized, de Surville placed his official letter and other papers in a bottle, the throat of which he sealed firmly with a cork. If the sea remained choppy, a swimmer might be called on to jump overboard at the harbor's entrance and swim ashore with the bottle tied around his neck. An athletic seaman was chosen. Joachim Joseph, a dark-skinned helmsman who had stowed away in the ship in India, was trusted to reach the shore. He had the advantage of being a native of Pondicherry, and so would not be too dismayed by the sight of waves breaking on the tempestuous bar.

De Surville climbed down the rope ladder from his ship at 1:15 P.M. Two young French sailors, natives of Brittany, rowed him and Joseph toward the entrance to the harbor. The first officer standing on the deck watched the captain and the small boat approaching the treacherous stretch of sea at the entrance. "I was watching with a glass when he reached the bar," said the officer. "I saw the boat in extreme danger and then saw no more of it for a long time." He feared the boat had been swamped by the waves or even overturned.

The little boat certainly was in danger. Joseph, ready to fulfill his duty, removed his clothes before jumping overboard, "perfectly naked." As he swam, the message bottle, which was awkwardly tied to him, was tossed about by the rough sea, repeatedly hitting him in the face. After loosening the string to make the bottle less of a hindrance, he swam ahead. For one moment, looking over his shoulder, he saw the three Frenchmen struggling in the water, trying to stay afloat.

Succeeding in reaching the shore, Joseph lay there for half an hour, exhausted and perhaps initially unconscious. Eventually stirring himself, he stood up and looked out to sea but could see no swimmers. He suddenly thought of his precious bottle. It lay near him, on the beach, dumped by the waves. He salvaged it, along with the drenched ceremonial hat of Captain de Surville. Finally he walked or stumbled to one of the town's churches where he handed the letter to the parish priest. Given clothes and food, he was escorted overland to Lima. A speaker of Portuguese and French, he told his story to the viceroy and handed over the sealed bottle containing his captain's message.

Guillaume Labé, the deputy captain and a native of the French port city of Saint-Malo, was now in charge of the ship. His instructions were to wait outside the entrance of the little harbor and, if by chance Captain de Surville did not return, to sail the ship to the port of Callao a short distance to the north. The busiest port along the whole western coast of the Americas, it would surely provide food and water for the crew and perhaps new anchors and sails for the ship. The port was also close to Lima, the capital city, to which the message-carrier from the *St. Jean-Baptiste* was, unknown to Labé, on his way.

The *St. Jean-Baptiste* reached Callao just after dark and dropped her surviving big anchor in the muddy bottom of the harbor, close to other ships. As she urgently required a smaller anchor and another cable, the port's officials provided them. Food and water were also carried aboard. It came as a surprise to the French that they had been keeping the incorrect time. Labé had thought it was April 10, but he had recently crossed the International Date Line, and so in America it was only April 9.

From Spanish officials came, by word of mouth, the news that all had feared. Captain de Surville and the two Breton sailors had been drowned when their small boat was overturned on the bar at the harbour mouth. The captain, it was learned, had been formally buried in a cemetery close to the beach where his body had been washed ashore. His uniform, his high decoration—the Cross of Saint Louis—and a lock or two of his hair were now in the hands of Spanish officials. Formally they were entrusted to the care of the acting captain of the *St. Jean-Baptiste*, who in due course would carry them to France.

The ship's company conducted its own ceremony soon after sunrise. After firing a salute of fifteen guns in honor of the Citadel of Callao, which frugally conserved its gunpowder by firing only seven shots in return, the Frenchmen lowered their ship's flag to half-mast. Every five minutes, as if in a solemn procession, the "mourning guns" of the *St. Jean-Baptiste* were fired. At 8 A.M. the crew, including those sick sailors who were capable of coming onto the main deck, assembled to take part in the requiem mass conducted by the chaplain, after which a fifteen-gun salute was fired in homage to Captain de Surville. The shots echoed across the harbor. Months would go by before their first echoes reached Pondicherry and Paris.

In this widespread empire strictly guarded and regulated, the French ship and her crew were considered to be trespassers. The crew were virtually imprisoned in their own ship, though from that prison a few dozen men did escape. Even the chaplain, forgetting his duties as pastor, abandoned his flock and went inland with the intention of searching for silver and gold. Meanwhile a report was sent by slow ship to Spain, seeking official advice on how to handle these French intruders.

There was one consolation for those who remained aboard their floating prison in the harbor of Callao: they were infinitely healthier and safer than they had been during their thirsty voyage across the wide Pacific.

THE SECRET GOALS

There remains a mystery surrounding de Surville's voyage. The full instructions he received with the blessings of French officials were retained in his mind as a secret, and during no stage of the long voyage did he tell Labé, his next in command, what those instructions were. Although he carried a copy in writing, that copy was probably destroyed by Labé when the Spanish authorities in Peru seemed likely to search the ship. So far no other copy has been found in archives in France.

It is almost certain that Captain de Surville intended, if the opportunity arose, to lead a smuggling expedition to Acapulco in Mexico. He kept that plan a secret; he had no trouble keeping secrets. After his death, evidence of the plan was found among his papers. If the Spanish busily searching the ship in Callao were to find such an incriminating document, they would possess a strong argument for confiscating the whole cargo and escorting the senior French officers across the ocean to Spain to face trial. Preventive action was therefore taken in the ship. "I tore his document into a thousand pieces," wrote Labé, "and had them thrown in the fire."

While we do not know the main points set down in de Surville's instructions before he left Pondicherry, it is possible that by and large they specified the route that he in fact did follow. Occasionally he gave the impression that the turning points in that route were dictated by unexpected events, whether the warfare in the Solomons, the grave onset of scurvy in the Coral Sea, or the loss of anchors in New Zealand. But possibly he used most of these events and disappointments as pretexts to explain to his fellow officers, who were feeling frustrated, a sudden change of route which in fact was preordained by his secret instructions.

De Surville probably followed a course that his backers and the French minor officials broadly approved in advance—trading at ports unfamiliar to the French in the Malay peninsula and the northern Philippines, and then making a hurried search for those islands that de Quiros had found, it was believed, near or on the coast of what is now known as northern Queensland. Perhaps too he had been instructed to voyage into the Tasman Sea until the ship reached the latitude of New Zealand, then turn east in order to reach more easily—in an era when ascertaining one's longitude was a dilemma— that coastline of New Zealand that Tasman had found. And then finally came his secret instruction to make the long passage toward Spanish America, searching along the way for the rumored Jewish colony and David Land, which were the main goals of the voyage. And if he was unable to find the Jewish land? He should then sell his cargo, either illegally in a remote port in Spanish America, or legally in East Asia while on his way home.

The Spanish, after seizing the ship and questioning her crew, realized that the mysterious, endlessly discussed David Land was one of the French goals. Convinced that the *St. Jean-Baptiste* had actually found it, the Spanish authorities in Callao promptly sent out a naval expedition to investigate. They soon found the isolated Easter Island, which was not a new discovery, and returned to Peru with the news that at last they had found the long-lost David Land. This island, however, was a pathetic substitute for the missing continent.

A MEDAL FOR DE SURVILLE

We usually applaud the discovery of new lands, but the discovery of prevailing winds and currents and sea routes can be equally vital. De Surville was the first to traverse much of the Coral Sea, though he was disappointed to find no large islands in its center. He was also the first to make a west–east crossing in the temperate zone of the South Pacific, thereby discovering what was to become a vital sea route.

Other French explorers now began to harness the westerlies, entering the Pacific Ocean from the west rather than, as in previous voyages, from Cape Horn and the east. Captain Cook was also to exploit to the full the westerly winds of this route during his later expeditions. The westerlies were vital to the later European settlements that arose in eastern Australia and New Zealand. Thousands of sailing ships carrying their migrants from Europe, and then their gold and wool back to Europe, used these westerlies. In 1854 the new passenger clipper *Red Jacket*, carrying migrants to Australia, harnessed these westerlies and a new Great Circle route to sail from the South Atlantic to the entrance to Melbourne in just over seventeen days. The remarkable fact was that similar sailing ships, setting out from Liverpool or London, could often reach distant Melbourne in a faster time than they could reach the Indian ports of Bombay and Madras.

One curiosity is that European ships used a completely different route to go to Australia as to come home. They harnessed the westerlies in both arriving and departing. Thus the *Red Jacket*, after her amazing passage to Melbourne, set out with the same westerlies for England on her return voyage, and on the first leg she reached Cape Horn—5,600 nautical miles away—in exactly three weeks. Ultimately the steamships altered this formula. They based their route on the location of coaling ports and eventually on the presence of the new Suez and Panama canals rather than on the prevailing winds.

The life of Garibaldi, a founder of modern Italy, contains an episode that remains mysterious to European historians who do not know about these west winds. In 1852, during a period of exile from Italy, Garibaldi was captain of a vessel that left Callao on a trading voyage to Hong Kong and Canton. On his return voyage to Callao, he called for water at the Three Hummock Island, northwest of Tasmania. There he spent a brief idyllic time which, in the opinion of his English biographer G. M. Trevelyan, ultimately persuaded him to choose his permanent home on the small island of Caprera, near Sardinia. But why was Garibaldi sailing so far away from what seems, on the surface, to be the shortest route between China and Peru? He was venturing far into the southern hemisphere to use the route that de Surville had discovered.

To search in unknown oceans and to find no land is to be a discoverer. It is a tradition to honor a land explorer who found nothing but a desert—the desert was usually given his name. Honor should be equally conferred on an explorer who found a desert of sea and recorded the winds prevailing on that sea. For an empty sea, more than a desert, can become a busy pathway.

Back in France, those who loved Jean de Surville, or the two sailors who had drowned alongside him in 1770, or the many who died in his ship, were to know nothing of their loss until the following year. The families in India and Africa, the heaviest losers, were to wait even longer. For the news of de Surville's voyage in distant oceans was slow to reach Europe and India, and the extent of his voyaging is not fully recognized even today.

16

Deadly Cloud Over Java

ON THE MORNING of September 1, 1770, when the *Endeavour* was anchored within a spacious bight in western New Guinea, there came a surprise: the strong smell of land. In the warm morning air the smell was blown from the tropical shore by a light breeze. It was a perfume rather like that which the French in the *St. Jean-Baptiste* had sniffed near Sydney just nine months earlier. It must have been the talk of Cook and his sailors, for they had rarely experienced such an event during their voyage. Likening the smell to that of gum benjamin, Banks reported that the smell of land faded away "as the sun gathered power."

Cook decided to land on the coast, which was just visible. After a boat was lowered, he, Banks, and Solander took their seats, and nine or so sailors and Marines went with them. The shore they approached was muddy, and everyone had to walk gingerly ashore after leaving the boat.

Finding a grove of young coconut trees, and "wishing for the fruit," they knew that—unlike the nimble Papuans—they were incapable of climbing the vertical trunk to gather the half-ripe coconuts. They might have remained longer but for the arrival of numerous Papuans carrying a variety of weapons.

"OUR CROAKERS" LONG FOR HOME

After the *Endeavour* sailed away and the coast of New Guinea receded, most men must have sighed with relief. Faces were transformed. Even the glum, the sick, and "the melancholy looked gay." It was the fervent hope of most seamen that no further discovery should be made in this sweltering region—no river that Cook must explore, no exotic animal or bird that Solander must investigate, and no clash with native inhabitants to delay their sailing.

Nostalgia was a new word in the English language, used mostly by doctors of their patients. Banks enlisted the word to describe the new mood in the ship. Most seamen, he added, were "pretty far gone with the longing for home." Any cause for delay was resented, and those sailors whom Banks called "Our Croakers" were even complaining when the *Endeavour*, after gaining from the southeast monsoon, ran into trickier winds. Two days later "Our Croakers" nervously scanned the horizon for any new source of delay.

Even Banks thought of his homeland more than usual. Observing the seawater near New Guinea, he decided that it was as "muddy as the Thames at Gravesend." When the island of Timor came into sight he recalled that "our countrey man Dampier" had visited it seventy years earlier. Just the thought that another Englishman had once been in this region made Banks a little homesick. Seeing flocks of birds flying across the warm sea, he remembered that they were the same birds that Dampier had seen and christened as the New Holland Noddies.

Everyone in the *Endeavour* longed for news from home. Whereas Byron's and Wallis's recent voyages of exploration in the Pacific had lasted just under two years, Cook—after two years—was still far from home. Since the ship had sailed from Plymouth, its officers and crew had heard virtually no English news, public or private. After leaving Brazil they had seen not one European ship, though they had almost met de Surville's ship fourteen months later. Those *Endeavour* men who were married thought about children and wives, not even sure whether they were still alive. Unknown to Cook, at least one of his children had died since he had last kissed them. And there was Banks's girlfriend, with whom he had spent many hours on the eve of his departure. Had she married in his absence? Some seamen had left behind old parents, who might now be dead. For a sailor, absence was normal, but the absence of the *Endeavour's* men was abnormally long.

In coming a little closer to home, they could not help feeling slightly nervous. Britain and France, at peace for seven years, might again be at war. Even while the *Endeavour* was at sea, new wars had begun. Turkey and Russia were at war, with British officers helping to lead the Russian fleet and the French monarchy quietly backing the Turks. When the *Endeavour* was being repaired on the banks of Cook's River, Britain and Spain had almost gone to war over possession of the Falkland Islands. Cook knew, from his own experience in the most recent war against France, how volatile was the naval world.

Whereas a large French battleship, firing all the guns lined on one side of her deck, could direct toward the enemy a broadside of about fifteen hundred pounds of shot, the *Endeavour* at her most powerful could offer less than one-thirtieth of such firepower. With most of her heavy guns lying on the seabed near the Great Barrier Reef, she was virtually defenseless. Even that last resort—to escape when she met a superior French or Dutch ship—was not available to the *Endeavour*, for she was too slow.

In the third week of September the *Endeavour* reached the Indonesian island of Savu, lying several hundred miles from the northwest coast of Australia. A boat was sent to the beach to contact the Dutch officials. The agent of the Dutch East India Company, the first European they had met for two years, stepped forward, but he was not sure whether to greet or warn these intruders, who had caught him by surprise. On his isolated island he was not accustomed to seeing Englishmen. He spoke with Cook—a strange conversation. He was dubious of what he was told, and understandably, for Cook was careful to conceal the zigzag route his ship had taken and the discoveries he had made during the last two years. In the eyes of the European, the ragged sails and rigging and the strange shape of the *Endeavour* did not resemble a naval vessel.

When the agent and the local rajah agreed to come aboard the *Endeavour* for dinner, they insisted, being suspicious, that two Englishmen be held ashore as hostages. At the table in the big cabin the main language of discourse was Dutch, which fortunately Solander could understand, but Cook's craving for the latest news from Europe was not satisfied. As the island of Savu was remote, its latest news from Europe could well have been a year old.

The *Endeavour*'s stay was entangled in mutual suspicion until gifts were produced: the rajah took pleasure in accepting the gift of a greyhound from Banks and the very last English sheep from Cook. The English in turn did not want gifts; they simply wished to buy fresh food in order to keep the dreaded scurvy at bay. At last, on the eve of his departure, Cook was allowed to purchase jars of palm syrup, a small amount of fresh fruit, and a little zoo of livestock that included eight stunted buffalo, a few pigs and sheep, and some scrawny fowls. He also welcomed aboard a collection of hen eggs, of which half proved to be rotten.

SLAYING THE SCURVY

While Cook was still successful in coping with scurvy, he could not yet explain *why* he was successful. It can now be stated with certainty that the success of Cook's struggle against scurvy did not arise from most of the remedies provided by the Admiralty and carried in his ship. He was not a disciple of Dr. Lind and did not think citrus juice was vital. While folklore now maintains that he regularly dispensed rations of lime juice, his ship carried only a tiny quantity of citrus juice, little of which was lime and much of which was worthless lemon *rob*. Wort made from malt, which Cook saw as vital, is not useful according to the latest medical opinion, though Cook would again rely on it in his next world-circling voyage. The slabs of "portable soup," in which he had faith, were really of little worth, though they may have made the frequent supplement of greens more palatable to the average seaman. Sauerkraut, made from white cabbage and rich in Vitamin C, was certainly a valuable aid in his war on scurvy; and he rightly appreciated the value of the casks of sauerkraut provided by the Admiralty.

There was one quiet palliative which, from this distance in time, can be recognized. Cook managed to bring aboard, again and again, supplies of fresh vegetables and, sometimes, fruit. At the *Endeavour*'s first port of call, on the island of Madeira, he had bought a load of onions, even though he did not have the financial authority to pay for them. The onions, usually eaten raw, were useful in combating scurvy, and Lord Nelson was to order them for his ships in large quantities one-third of a century later.

The longer legs of a voyage, where no port of call was available, were the most conducive to scurvy. Cook was fortunate that he could dawdle at Madeira and Rio de Janeiro. He had time on his hands before he had to sail toward Tahiti to prepare his makeshift observatory in advance of the transit of Venus. Meanwhile, approaching Cape Horn, he allowed the botanists to go ashore at Tierra del Fuego, where they snatched the opportunity to find native plants. In the bleak landscape they soon found scurvy grass, of a kind that also grew near Britain's shores, and a native celery that was rather like English celery in appearance, though its taste was more like that of parsley. At first Cook was inclined to smile at the variety of new plants the botanists found, hinting that their only value was that they were not known in Europe. But next day his seamen brought back various greens as well as bundles of "winter's bark," stripped from the trunk of a tree bearing a green, laurel-like leaf. The bark was used to enrich the seamen's diet. Cook was beginning to understand that his two botanists could be very useful.

The ship's arrival in Tahiti gave the crew another opportunity to supplement their biscuits and preserved meat with fresh fruit, yams, and greens in plenty, and fresh fish and meat. But again the signs of scurvy appeared just before New Zealand came into sight. Fortunately, while exploring its long coastline, Cook's seamen had opportunities to gather wild celery, a kind of cress, fern roots, an herb known in England as lamb's quarters, and other greens. The scurvy vanished. Whenever the ship was anchored on a friendly coast, edible plants were carried aboard and either eaten raw or tossed into the big pot containing the portable soup.

Botany Bay provided the crew with fresh fish and selected greens, as did tropical Queensland, where the ship was repaired amidst an abundance of turtles and a variety of greens. Ironically the near wreck on the coral reef was in one sense a benefit, enabling the *Endeavour*'s company—after scurvy had reached several of its members—to recover in a river estuary where the diet was more healthy than it would have been at sea. Later came the few hours' stay at Booby Island, where the tame birds were shot and cooked, and the longer halt at the island of Savu. Few global voyages up to that time had enjoyed so many ports of call. With the help of Banks, Cook had made full use of them.

Today some of Cook's admirers with some validity tend to portray Banks as a wealthy dilettante, an amateur scientist who placed his own desires before those of the captain. And yet the determination of Banks and Solander to make excursions ashore, whenever Cook would allow them, did much to help the captain cope with scurvy. The excursions enabled the seamen to scythe fresh greens and collect fresh water. Again and again in the coastal countryside, some seamen scavenged their own simple sources of Vitamin C. At dinner Cook insisted that all the seamen eat the fresh greens and fresh meat placed before them. Early in the voyage there was a strange episode when he ordered a flogging for two seamen who refused to eat the fresh meat on their plates.

The lands that Cook chanced to visit assisted his campaign against scurvy. He called at no continent or island where the people were so hostile as to prevent him from gathering or buying fresh plant foods. De Surville endured the opposite experience. Cook's ship was like a train that stopped at all stations. De Surville did not have that luxury; usually in a hurry, he halted at few places and then only briefly. He neglected or mishandled most of his early opportunities to gather fresh food. Even his stay in Doubtless Bay, and the chance to provide his sick seamen with vitamins, was too short. Likewise, if Cook had been conducting his voyage in the name of commerce rather than science, he would have been in a constant hurry and, in consequence, his crew probably would have suffered severely from scurvy.

The health of the crew was the crucial difference between the rival French and British voyages. If many of Cook's seamen had died of scurvy, he would have turned back, perhaps before he reached New Zealand and certainly before he reached Australia. On the other hand, if de Surville had coped more effectively with scurvy in his big ship, he might have discovered a harbor in New South Wales and received much of the acclaim that Cook was later to receive for a similar discovery.

Cook is now acknowledged as the conqueror of scurvy, though he made no such claim for himself. A quarter-century later, in 1795, the campaign against scurvy was to win a major victory: Dr. Lind's theory was adopted by the Royal Navy, which tried henceforth to give a ration of lime or lemon juice to each sailor. As a result the Haslar Hospital near Plymouth quickly ran out of scurvy patients. Nonetheless, during the Napoleonic Wars many ships of the Royal Navy still suffered from scurvy. They were impeded by outbreaks of the disease even in the Mediterranean Sea, the home of lemons and oranges. Moreover the juice of limes—bought cheaply by the Royal Navy in the islands of the West Indies in the nineteenth century—proved to be far less effective than lemons in curbing scurvy. It was finally realized that the lime contained less Vitamin C. As late as 1900, celebrated European doctors still set out their own contradictory theories on the causes of scurvy, though they agreed on the value of lemon juice. During World War I in Europe the disease again flourished on battlefields such as Gallipoli and in the refugee camps in eastern Europe, but rarely at sea where the faster voyages of steamships had done much to reduce its incidence. The fact that scurvy survived into the twentieth century made Cook's achievement all the more remarkable.

LIES AND SECRETS

The *Endeavour*'s battle with scurvy was not yet over. Tupaia was again ailing when, at the start of October, the coast of Java and a steep volcanic cone came into view. A rowing-boat was sent to the nearest Javan village to buy fruit—Tupaia is "very ill," wrote Cook—and to fetch fodder for the remaining buffaloes penned on deck. The boat returned, almost empty. All Cook could do was to reach the port of Jakarta as quickly as possible.

For Cook the proximity of Jakarta, and the likely questioning of him by the Dutch authorities, was a nervous time. While he craved news from the outside world, he did not wish to divulge his own news, and least of all to reveal the seas in which his ship had sailed. As a precaution he gathered from his officers and crew the journals, diaries, and notebooks they had kept during the voyage, and locked them away so that prying Dutch officials could not easily discover where the *Endeavour* had been.

When the officials did come aboard the ship, Cook entrusted Lieutenant Hicks with the answering of the more forthright questions. Where, he was asked, did the ship come from? Hicks's confident reply was that the ship had come from Europe. At this answer the Dutchmen obviously voiced surprise. The ragged ship and her weather-torn sails gave every impression that she had not seen a European shipyard for years. As the ship had virtually struggled through hell to reach the Dutch East Indies, and showed the scars of her long ordeal, an alert official could not readily believe the claim that she had come straight from Europe.

When another Dutch official climbed aboard he handed over a formal printed document setting out nine questions, of which the most pointed was the ninth: did any "News worth of Attention" happen during the voyage? What a question to ask! Capable of filling fifty sheets of paper with details of his discoveries of lands and his encounters with strange peoples, Cook's answer revealed virtually nothing. The Dutchmen, apparently content with these evasive answers, casually announced that Jakarta could be reached in less than one day of sailing time. Never had a port been so eagerly awaited.

Europe, whose latest news Cook longed for, was filled with the humdrum and the everyday, with here and there an exceptional event. Joseph Black was applying his condenser to revolutionize the steam engine, which would eventually make the *Endeavour* and her species redundant; in Germany a Mrs. Beethoven—the surname was Dutch—was about to give birth to a son named Ludwig; the first volume of the first edition of *Encyclopaedia Britannica* was about to be printed, though it contained no entry for "New Holland"; and the River Thames was about to freeze as far upstream as Fulham. But the tiny morsels of news that Cook first received were of upheavals or warfare in Constantinople, Boston, and Poland.

Cook hoped that the sojourn in Jakarta would be just long enough to permit minor repairs to the hull of the *Endeavour* and the collecting of fresh water, vegetables, meat, and other supplies. The harm inflicted by the coral reef, however, was more serious than had been realized; and both the false keel and the real keel were damaged in a place not visible when the ship lay on her side at the river estuary in Queensland. Marine worms had almost devoured some planks of timber, and the coral had damaged others. The ship was leaking, and one of the pumps was quite "useless." Official permission was granted for the ship to make her way to a repair yard on the adjacent island of Onrust, but first all cargo and ballast had to be unloaded by hand, and most of the crew had to move to the tents erected for them near the Dutch warehouses at Kuypers.

The town of Jakarta was exciting and exotic for those visiting it for the first time. Parkinson thought it must be the most cosmopolitan of the larger towns in the world, with its crowds of Chinese, brown-skinned people from remote parts of the Indonesian archipelago, people from India and Africa, merchants from Armenia and Persia, and the mixture of Europeans. The Dutchmen, masters of the town, were presiding over the grander buildings such as the castle, town hall, and the octagon Calvinist church whose dome could be seen from afar, but they were outnumbered by the cavalcade of Germans, Danes, Swedes, and even—it was said—the Hungarians.

In this polyglot crowd the two Polynesians from the *Endeavour* wished to be seen as distinctive. Tupaia, presumably now wearing the clothes of dead English sailors, requested that he be clad in his own islander clothes, and was delighted when Banks purchased enough "South Sea cloth" to enable him to dress appropriately.

Banks and Solander rented a house in downtown Jakarta, and even hired a pair of open-air carriages with a local driver presiding on a coach box. Soon the two Polynesians were staying with them, and of course a few servants. In this cosmopolitan setting a Polynesian seemed the most exotic of all, and Banks was hardly surprised when "a man totally unknown to me ran out of his house" and inquired whether his exotically dressed friend was not on his first visit to the port. Of course Banks gave his answer that Tupaia was a total newcomer. The stranger replied that Tupaia rather reminded him of another brown man, so similar in appearance, who some eighteen months earlier had visited Jakarta with the French exploring ships. Banks was almost flabbergasted by such news. What, he asked, were the names of these French ships, and who was their commander?

AN ECHO OF ANOTHER FRENCH EXPLORER

There is so much that we know that many navigators of the eighteenth century would love to have known. At that time nearly all news traveled slowly, and any news from the deep Pacific traveled to Europe with snail-like speed. What Cook and Banks did not know, until their visit to Jakarta, was that a French expedition had recently been exploring parts of the same Pacific Ocean they had visited. They had not even heard of de Surville, but now, for the first time, they heard of Bougainville.

Chevalier Louis-Antoine de Bougainville, a high-ranking French soldier and a fine mathematician, was a hero in the Seven Years' War against Britain. At Quebec he had been fighting not far from Cook, though on the opposing side. During the subsequent peace he was selected to lead an official voyage combining diplomacy, discovery, and science. Assigned two naval vessels, of which the largest was the frigate *Boudeuse*, he departed from the French port of Nantes in November 1766, almost two years before the *Endeavour* sailed from England. Reaching the Falkland Islands in the stormy South Atlantic, Bougainville completed his formal mission to surrender the French settlement and allow Spain to take over. His ship, accompanied by the *Etoile*, then entered the Pacific Ocean.

His first goal was Davis Land, said to lie about twenty-seven degrees south of the equator. Bougainville was as well informed as he could be about this mythical land, having read Dampier, de Brosses, and the same authors whom de Surville and Cook perused. Finding no evidence of this land, the French ships sailed more or less west, eventually seeing the volcanic peaks of Tahiti that Wallis in the *Dolphin* had discovered in the preceding year.

After barely ten days in Tahiti, where they planted a vegetable garden and presented geese and turkeys to villagers, the French sailed away, thinking that Tahiti was their discovery. Following roughly the same route as the *Dolphin*, they knew it was safer to sail toward the equator and so reach the Dutch East Indies. Bougainville was in possession of Vaugondy's map showing the existence of Torres Strait and also the Land of the Holy Spirit, which the mapmaker had mistakenly placed on the north Queensland coast. Presumably they were his goals as he sailed west across the Pacific.

It must have been a tense hour when, late in the evening of June 4, 1768, the frigate *Boudeuse*, just ahead of her sister ship, "fired several shots, which is the signal of danger." Land, probably a small island or reef, was visible. Quickly the two ships changed course, veering to starboard. Fewer than thirty-six hours later they saw the white froth of a line of breakers possibly marking the outer edge of the Great Barrier Reef. One small coral reef, named after Bougainville, lies not less than a hundred nautical miles from the North Queensland coast. Sticks of wood, bunches of seaweed, and pieces of fruit floated by, suggesting that land was not far away. Fortunately Bougainville abandoned his attempt to enter the maze of coral and so approach Torres Strait. Instead his ships made the long detour around the east and north shores of New Guinea.

Diligent in curbing the fatal spread of scurvy—only seven sailors died from various illnesses in the space of twenty-eight months—Bougainville was less effective in staving off hunger. The ship's biscuits were putrid, and the salted meat stank after the coating of salt was removed. The last captive dog was cooked and eaten, with some smacking of lips by those who were apportioned a taste of it, and then a Dutch trading post on the Indonesian island of Buru gave them relief. Eventually the two French ships called at Jakarta, where their Polynesian passenger, Aotourou, strolled the streets and drew the attention of nearly all eyes. Then late in 1768 they reached the French-governed island of Mauritius where the sound of their own language, spoken ashore, was sweet music. In due course Bougainville reported personally to his masters in Paris, where Aotourou was a social sensation: almost a pop star, he was two centuries ahead of his time.

Of this globe-circling expedition by the French, Cook initially knew almost nothing. His *Endeavour* had sailed from England many months before Bougainville's *Boudeuse* returned from her global voyage to the French port of Saint-Malo. In Tahiti Cook at first detected no evidence, not even an empty brandy cask, of the brief French visit. After some months, however, the Tahitians casually informed him that some time ago two foreign ships had visited another part of their island, and that the foreign seamen had brought with them venereal disease. Cook closely questioned one of these eyewitnesses, even showing him a colored print displaying the flags of the various seafaring nations. To the display of flags the Tahitian had responded with misleading enthusiasm: "he at once pitched upon the Spanish Flag and would by no means admit of any other." Cook accepted his word. So neither at that time nor in the next eighteen months did he know that Bougainville was somewhere ahead of him.

Another snippet of news that Cook learned from his informants in Tahiti was quite true: the European ship had sailed away with a Polynesian man, said to be the son of a chief. Aotourou, handsome and rather amorous, was the one seen disporting himself in the streets of Jakarta. All these pieces of information, new and old, suddenly made sense to Cook after he reached Jakarta. He realized then that the ship calling at Tahiti was French and not Spanish.

The news of Bougainville's recent arrival in Java worried Cook. Until now he had no idea that a French expedition—indeed two such expeditions—had been exploring in the Pacific and even crossing his own route. As Cook himself had voyaged in as much secrecy as possible, he was entitled to assume that Bougainville, likewise intent on secrecy, had concealed from Dutch officials, as far as he could, his own route and discoveries. Cook naturally wondered where exactly Bougainville had been. What if the Frenchman had actually found the southern continent, sailed its shores, and seen some of its treasures? What if he were now in Paris, reporting his discoveries and preparing to depart on an expedition that would place a French town on the shores of the missing continent?

When Cook reached his next port of call he was to hear more about the French and their expeditions to the Pacific. They were the great economic power of Europe, the perpetual rivals of Britain, and whatever they did at sea was Cook's concern. Having lost, only seven years ago, most of their colonial empire in North America and India, the French had perhaps discovered the nucleus of another empire in an ocean where Cook had thought his *Endeavour* was sailing alone. In Jakarta, and later in Cape Town, Cook was entitled to ask himself whether his voyage was really a failure.

DEATH IN JAKARTA

They were enchanting days in Jakarta for all those British seamen who longed to be ashore; but then the wet season arrived. The city's fine, tree-shaded canals, constructed in imitation of Amsterdam, were a paradise for malaria-carrying mosquitoes. At the same time dysentery spread here and there. Some of those British visitors living in the scientists' rented house and in the ship's tents across the bay felt decidedly seedy.

Banks had had a foretaste of this unhealthiness when, upon arrival in Jakarta, he encountered a party of Dutch boatmen. Whereas the seamen in the *Endeavour* "truly might be called rosy and plump," the faces of the visiting boatmen were a ghostly white. The British seamen, looking down on the Dutchmen in their small boat, had jeered at their intensely pale faces. Now, just a month later, some of the British too were displaying anemic faces.

In the steamy heat of tropical Java, death stalked the British crew in their makeshift tents. Monkhouse the surgeon, gravely ill, died on November 5, Guy Fawkes Day. Three sailors and a servant were to die before Christmas came. Banks and Solander, sensibly retreating to a riverside house in higher terrain just beyond the suburbs, hired several female Malay nurses and a bevy of slaves and free helpers to care for them, but these helpers could not prevent illness from taking its grip. Solander, normally cheerful, felt a strong premonition of death until a Dutch doctor arrived to calm him. The doctor applied mustard plasters to Solander's feet and "blisters to the calves of his legs," and after a time the patient arose from his bed and tottered about.

In the sodden climate—it rained every afternoon—the sick botanists found something new to stir them a little. Banks, drained of much blood by the attentive Dutch surgeon and hardly able to leave his sickbed, was nonetheless sufficiently seduced by nature to marvel at the noisy song rising from the frogs crouching in the ditches when rain was about to pelt down. No European frog, he vowed, could match their chorus. Cook, looking after the repaired ship on the far side of the bay, thought less of himself than of others, and even sent his personal servant to the riverside house to attend to the two sick botanists. When Cook's own health deteriorated, the servant returned to care for him.

Of the cause of the illnesses that affected so many of the officers and crew, Cook and his assistant surgeon had no clear idea. Malaria was a new word in the English language, probably first used when Cook was a boy, and its cause was not known. The general diagnosis was that the malady came with the infectious air rising from a swamp or lowland; the word *malaria* stems from the two Italian words signifying bad air. Cook, perhaps wondering at first whether the disease weakening his men was a form of scurvy, invoked one of his favorite cures: at the local market he spent heavily on buying "an extraordinary quantity of vegetables every day."

One seaman, keeping his head during this despondent time, began to think it was time to desert. It so happened that Cook and his officers had offered an astonishingly high reward—fifteen guineas and a supply of arrack rum—for information leading to the detection of the man who had cut Orton's ears many months ago. After Cook had cleared the name of the original suspect, suspicion turned toward young Patrick Saunders, who reportedly came from Bangor in Wales. His conduct had long been erratic. In the course of the voyage he had been an ordinary seaman and then a midshipman, before being demoted back to seaman and then apparently reinstated. Perhaps fearing denunciation and punishment, he vanished into the crowded streets of Jakarta and was seen no more.

The first bouts of illness in Jakarta did not seem to harm the two Polynesians. Initially they were excited by the cosmopolitan sights. The young teenager Taiata, friend and kinsman of Tupaia, marveled at the sight and sound of horses drawing the carriages in the streets—he had never seen a horse—and danced with pleasure at other rousing scenes. Then he became seriously ill, his lungs inflamed. Death came to him with speed. His master, Tupaia, whose health had been intermittently impaired by the scurvy, had requested that he be allowed to sleep in a tent on an island where he thought the sea breezes would resuscitate him. But he too fell ill; he seemed to be overwhelmed by the loss of his fellow countryman. He died five days before Christmas.

Cook was inclined to argue that Tupaia had not looked after his health and that careless conduct had brought on his death. There must have been rivalry between the two men, for both were navigators and leaders, but only one could be supreme. The rivalry was possibly intensified by Cook's misjudgment on the coral reef. Thereafter it would be surprising if Tupaia had not argued that he, rightly or wrongly, should have been the navigator in those tropical seas.

Unfortunately Tupaia had already lost face. As his gift for languages, formerly so persuasive, proved to be useless in Australia, his prestige and even some of his self-esteem declined. Earlier in New Zealand, as the independent and vital interpreter, he was important; he had even succeeded in persuading the Maori that he and not Cook was the real captain of the ship and the head of the expedition. More than two years later, when Cook was to return to New Zealand, he heard on several occasions the Maori voices asking the whereabouts of Tupaia and *his* big ship. In their eyes he was the captain of the

Endeavour. There was sadness when they were told of his death in faraway Java.

The *Endeavour*, repaired with impressive skill and speed in the shipyard near Jakarta, was almost ready to sail. A full crew was needed for the next phase of the voyage. Fortunately most European ports in the tropics were the equivalent of today's hiring agencies, and sailors who had deserted one ship were often, after a period of holiday or hiding, persuaded to join another ship about to depart for Europe. To replace the *Endeavour* seamen who had died or were too sick even to tie a knot, nineteen men were recruited in Jakarta; and at least one of these men was to become a faithful follower of Cook and serve in his ships for years to come.

After more than two months in the harbor, the *Endeavour* sailed from Jakarta on Boxing Day 1770. In the open ocean the heat of the air by day and night, and the stuffy steamhouse atmosphere below deck, frustrated the seamen and even the gentlemen inhabiting the airy quarters of the big cabin. The sea breeze was too irregular to give relief. The drinking water brought from Jakarta was foul, and mosquitoes were actually breeding on the surface of the casked water. Mistakenly it had been expected that the sea winds would blow away the infections carried from Jakarta.

Passing slowly through the Strait of Sunda, the ship anchored off Princes Island to take on fresh food, firewood, and especially fresh water. On January 16, 1771, an air of resignation slipped into Banks's journal: "This Morn we wakd in the open Ocean, nothing in sight but sea and sky. The winds tho fair continud yet so gentle that we hardly knew whether we went on or stood still." The following day was windless until evening, "when a pleasant breeze sprung up and gave us hopes of soon gaining the trade wind, which we impatiently longd for, especially myself who had my fever every day." In the sultry weather of the Indian Ocean, illnesses continued to spread. More seamen were laid low by the malaria, dysentery, or some other infection.

Death became the ship's figurehead. Green the astronomer, the indefatigable teacher of others, was ill beyond hope. After he died it was discovered that the measurements and calculations he had made of the transit of Venus, nineteen months earlier, were in a mess, so untidily had they been recorded. The main purpose of the voyage seemed at risk until his records were reviewed and finally patched up.

Several of the ship's most trusted characters died. Reliable seamen of middling or upper rank—*esteemed* was the word conferred on them in death—they were sewn into their hammocks and cast into the deep. Truslove, the corporal of Marines, and Satterly the carpenter, whose skills had been crucial whenever the ship was repaired, were mortally ill. Thompson the one-handed cook, the preparer of tens of thousands of plates of food, presided no more over his hot stove. Death came silently along the quarterdeck and down the ladderway to beckon young Jonathan Monkhouse, whose idea it had been to fother the ship when she was battered and leaking. Sydney Parkinson the artist, who had already made more than a thousand drawings, many of which were meticulous in their accuracy, was seriously ill. He was intensely religious and was not bewildered by the approach of death. He did not recover. In this same bout of illnesses, Solander lost his Swedish friend Hermann Spöring, the obliging jack-of-all-trades who repaired nautical instruments and sometimes practiced the medical skills he had learned in the Finnish province of Sweden.

In Jakarta one of the few who had seemed hearty, physically and mentally, was the grandfather of the crew, John Ravenhill the sailmaker. At least seventy years old—maybe close to eighty in Cook's estimation—and an artisan from the port of Hull, he seemed indestructible. Cook marveled that he was "more or less drunk every day" but still competent at his craft. Friends thought that his high daily consumption of alcohol gave him an immunity to tropical disease. But now he lost his immunity: he fell ill after leaving Java and died on January 31, 1771, the same day the cook died.

Several seamen who had just joined the ship in Jakarta, seemingly vigorous, fell ill and quickly died. They were sewn firmly into their hammocks with the help of old Ravenhill's three-sided needles before being buried at sea. One-quarter of the crew died during the voyage between Jakarta and the coast of South Africa. When at last the trade winds blew regularly, the health of the surviving seamen improved. Whether the reason was psychological or medical did not matter; most seamen thanked the brisk, salt-laden wind.

The ship's rigging and the miles and miles of intertwined ropes had been renewed or mended at the Onrust repair yard; but now barely a dozen sailors were fit enough to take their place aloft. Cook was facing the crisis that had almost crippled the *St. Jean-Baptiste* early in her voyage. Indeed in the space of three months the *Endeavour* lost about the same proportion of her crew as the French ship had lost in her most miserable three months. Even some of Cook's seamen who survived were not in their full senses. Drunkenness carried some of them into fantasy land or made them aggressive. Rossiter, the Marine who was also employed as the ship's drummer, was punished for beating the sick and for defying orders.

In the face of the numerous deaths occasioned by the long stay in Jakarta, Cook must have regretted, more than ever, the *Endeavour*'s collision with the coral reef near the Australian coast. If she had not hit the reef, she would have arrived in and departed from Jakarta long before the season of humidity and diseases. Indeed, but for that accident she would not have made the detour to Jakarta at all but instead would have steered toward the southern tip of South Africa. In a powerful and pithy sentence Cook ultimately weighed the high price he had paid for striking the ledge of rocks: "this prov'd a fatal stroke to the remainder of the Voyage."

17

Is There War in Europe?

🦋 ACROSS CHOPPY SEAS the majestic and mighty flat-topped Table Mountain came slowly into view. As the harbor of Cape Town was not easily entered in the face of the fierce wind, the *Endeavour* had to ride with a scattering of other ships in the roadstead just outside. Cook was delighted to see that one of the largest of the waiting ships was English. A fast ship, *Admiral Pocock* had just arrived from Bombay; when her captain saw the Union flag flying on Cook's incoming ship, he ordered the firing of three volleys in formal salute. It was a stirring moment for Cook to hear that gesture by a sea captain of the nation from which he had long been parted. Thankfully, Cook entrusted to the captain, for safe delivery to England, letters he had already written to his masters and sponsors, the Admiralty and the Royal Society.

AT THE DUTCH INN

This was Cook's first visit to the dusty streets of Cape Town, now a century old and flourishing, and he was initially puzzled. Here were barren mountains overlooking a plain that seemed to him to be little better than an expanse of dry sand. In the vicinity of the port, the patches of fertile soil were so far apart that most of the orchards, vineyards, and kitchen gardens sat in isolation. Beyond Cape Town a traveler could walk for days before reaching some of the faraway farms that supplied rural produce to the ships that called at the harbor. Banks, who did not travel more than a few miles from the port but asked question after question of those who did, shared this puzzlement. He could see that even around the port the land was mostly bare sandhills or poor expanses like the moors of Yorkshire and Derbyshire. He was told that farther inland some farmers lived some five days' travel from their nearest neighbor, so sparsely peopled was the poor countryside.

The country, he concluded, was one of "immense barrenness" except for the few fertile patches. And yet this inferior countryside, by dint of the hard work of the Dutch and their rural servants and slaves, produced wine, flour, beef and mutton, and all kinds of luxuries, and offered them at prices that were often cheaper than those in Europe's ports. The abundance squeezed from this miserable corner of southwest Africa was hard to believe.

Here was an unrivaled port of refreshment for passing ships. In Cook's neat turn of phrase, here was a busy inn ready to dine and wine "all comers and goers." In terms of today's travel, Cape Town was like an international airport sitting in the heart of a vast desert but supplying nearly all its travelers with all they needed. Cape Town's success was all the more surprising because it suffered during the winter from a strong northwesterly which, blowing straight toward the harbor's entrance, could temporarily imprison deep-sea ships in its harbor.

These observations about the Dutch-owned colony were to be of high importance to the subsequent history of Australia. Cook vowed that "no country we have seen this Voyage" was as unpromising as the area around Cape Town. Banks said almost as much. This was really another way of saying that even New South Wales was not as barren as Cape Town's own hinterland. And yet Cape Town—and perhaps New South Wales too—was capable of rising above its grave defects. True, it had too much barren or hungry soil. But that defect was redeemed by tiny patches of fertile soil which, with the ingenuity of the Dutch settlers and the hard labor of their Malay servants and their various slaves, were supplying passing ships with the most nutritious grains, greens, fruit, meat, milk, butter, and wine. True, the Cape's homemade cheese was hardly worth tasting, and the beer was a disgrace. But its local produce on the whole was so abundant that each year many foreign ships carried away "a prodigious quantity" of food to that vital and populous French colony and naval base then called Isle de France but now called Mauritius. Banks feared that this strong French colony might, "in the beginning of a future war," be a sea base for launching an attack on England's possessions in India. But Mauritius remained strong only because Cape Town partly fed it. What a tribute to Cape Town and its people's energy! Here was a new way of looking at the soils around Botany Bay.

In Banks's eye there was another symbol of the Dutch colonists' ability to pluck prosperity from their rare patches of rich soil: the buxom, big-petticoated Dutch housewives with their impressive kitchens and dinner tables, their clear skins and ruddy complexions, and their large broods of lively children. Banks admired them. This charming twenty-eight-year-old philanderer confided to his journal: "had I been inclined for a wife I think this is the place of all others I have seen where I could have best suited myself."

For long, historians have wondered why Banks, who had dismissed the soil of Botany Bay when he was there, altered his opinion fewer than ten years later and enthusiastically recommended to his government that a settlement be made. What transformed his view? The likely answer is his visit to Cape Town. If so much could be achieved in that barren region, what might be achieved by someday cultivating a similar patchwork of soils near Botany Bay? If Banks had turned to the earlier pages of his journal and read his words, he might have taken up his pen and altered the rather pessimistic opinion he had set down on paper when the ship was finally leaving the Australian coast. But he was not one to revise his voluminous daily journals, and that is why they remain untidy, ill-spelled, but always alive.

TOWARD THE HOME STRAIGHT

After a stay of one month, the *Endeavour* was almost ready to sail for home. Sickness, however, was still stealing her crew. Three men died in the ship or in the tent hospital erected on the shore. Solander, so ill with violent bowel pains that his death seemed imminent, at last began to ease himself from his cabin and gingerly walk the stairs and ladders just before the ship sailed. But Robert Molyneux, the master, who was in charge of much of the daily running of the ship, was no longer capable of supervising his men. One of those alert and diligent leaders who had given much to the success of the voyage, it was Molyneux who, after the *Endeavour* struck the coral reef, had set out in his boat "with inimitable coolness" to report on the condition of the ship. He was soon to be buried off the coast of Africa.

The *Endeavour* sailed from Table Bay in mid-April, anchoring near Robben Island after leaving the harbor. Approaching the island in a small boat in the hope of buying a few fresh provisions, the boatmen were warned by armed guards that the nearby stone quarries were worked by prisoners, and that the whole island was out of bounds to foreigners. Two hundred years later that same island was the prison of Nelson Mandela before, finally released, he began to create a new regime in South Africa.

The riskiest leg of the *Endeavour*'s voyage seemed to be over, now that she was sailing in the vastness of the Atlantic Ocean, but no ocean was entirely secure in the eighteenth century. A new naval war between Britain and Spain seemed possible, according to news received by Cook from a ship that had recently arrived in Cape Town. Thus the *Endeavour*, when she reached the North Atlantic, might well be attacked by heavily armed Spanish ships plying the familiar trade route to their empire in central America. If Spain were at war, France might be fighting on her side, and the heavy guns of a first-rate French warship—a floating monument made of the timber from some three thousand mature trees—might be turned against the little *Endeavour*. In Europe the war years were about as frequent as the years of peace. In half the years since Cook was a ten-year-old, Europe had been at war.

Cook's crew resumed their naval drills, practicing with what he called the "Great Guns" as well as the small muskets. An air of alertness prevailed. On approaching the English-held island of St. Helena, the officers on deck could see, through their field glasses, the masts of a fleet of big, distinctive "Indiamen." Whose flag did they carry? It was impossible to tell from a distance. Through their glasses the Englishmen could make out a warship among them. There must be a war in Europe, Cook exclaimed: "we took it for granted that it was a war." On coming closer to the anchored ships, however, he felt a sense of relief. An English flag could be seen. This was an English convoy returning from India; it might even offer protection to the *Endeavour* if she proved fast enough to keep up with the bigger ships. For a time the *Endeavour*, though a very slow sailer, did keep the convoy in sight.

Not far from the equator, Cook sent across a boat to one of the closest ships in the straggling English-bound convoy, requesting that he might briefly borrow her surgeon for an urgent consultation. Lieutenant Zachary Hicks, who had been the first to set eyes on the east Australian coast, was ill. Like Forby Sutherland who died at Botany Bay, the lieutenant had long been suffering from tuberculosis, and now he was fading away. In his narrow cot he lay, uplifted by the hope that he might see his native land before he died. But the visiting surgeon, climbing aboard the *Endeavour*, saw that the patient was beyond help. Hicks died on May 25, soon after midday, and "in the evening his body was committed to the Sea with the usual ceremonies."

There was to be one more casualty in a ship that had witnessed so many. On the evening of July 4, Banks's surviving greyhound, known as Lady, was preparing to sleep in her master's cabin, taking her favored place on a large stool. "She had been remarkably well for some days," wrote Banks in a journal to which he now committed few sentences. But while he himself presumably lay asleep in the big cabin, his dog gave a loud yelp. Then there was silence.

Before this only a few dogs and cats had sailed around the world. In zoological history the departed Lady was unusual, for she had discovered and chased a kangaroo.

After Lady's death, just one other female remained aboard the male world of the *Endeavour*. A nanny goat, she had some claims to be the world's most traveled animal. She had sailed around the globe in the *Dolphin* with Captain Wallis, and then again with Cook, performing her duty of supplying milk to officers and those whose health was frail. She was one of the few creatures in the ship with her own servants, for at each landing place one or two of Cook's seamen had been at her service, cutting grass so that she could be fed.

The days passed, each becoming longer. The steamy heat gave way to cooler winds. The familiar sea lanes from Europe to the Americas were reached, and more ships were sighted in the distance. There lingered the fear that the *Endeavour* might be captured or even sunk by an enemy, and that all her journals and prized specimens might be confiscated or lost in the sea. One day a whaling schooner flying the English flag came into view and, after signals were exchanged, one of the *Endeavour*'s boats was rowed across to gather news. Coming from the British colony of Rhode Island in North America, the whaler carried slightly later news than any ship had conveyed to Cook since his departure from Cape Town two months earlier. Waiting on deck to watch his rowers return, Cook thankfully heard their report and recorded it in his journal: "all was peace in Europe."

It was Wednesday, June 18, 1771, and the promontory at Land's End and the English coastline lay only about three weeks away. The voyage—its hardships and dangers, its quarrels and carousals, and its failures and triumphs—was almost over. The failures could be forgotten. The triumphs would live.

LONDON AWAITS THE WORD

Britain, a seafaring nation, was accustomed to receiving no news or long-delayed news from ships that had set out for the far rim of the Earth. As the *Endeavour* was known to be exploring exotic seas and, perhaps, unknown lands, a long absence of news was only to be expected. But in London after two years, the total absence of news was causing some unease. And in its place, rumor inevitably stepped in. In London on September 28, 1770, when Cook in fact was near the island of Java, a disturbing report was published in *Bingley's Journal.* It was "surmised," reported the London journal, that the Spanish were preparing to go to war with Britain and were on the alert for any English ship trespassing in what they considered their own seas. Indeed they had already sunk "the Endeavour man of war which was sent into the South Sea." Probably everyone in the ship, said the report, had gone down: "Mr. Banks, and the famous Dr. Solander, were on board the above vessel, and are feared to have shared the common fate with the rest of the ship's company." Significantly, Cook's name was not mentioned. In the public imagination the scientists were all-important, and Cook was their pilot.

How such a rumor begins will never be known. Once launched, it circulates with breathtaking speed. Those who carry the rumor, passing it on to others, gain prestige from conveying their dramatic news. Those who hear the rumor feel proud that they too are able to pass it on. When questioned about the source of the "news"—it is no longer a rumor—they simply answer that in London everybody is talking about it.

Three months after the rumor of the *Endeavour*'s loss first circulated in London, ships arrived with news or rumors that the ship was safe. Appearing in at least four newspapers, this information was devoured by readers. In the Admiralty, however, it was not accepted as true. The high naval officials pointed out that they had not yet received a message from Cook. It was surely one of his duties, when he returned to the land of the living, to report speedily where exactly he had been and where he now was. But no official letter from him had so far reached London.

In May the long-circulating rumors that the *Endeavour* had sunk were replaced by favorable news. A ship arrived with another report that Cook's ship had reached Jakarta. Indeed his ship had reached that plague-tormented city exactly seven months ago. This news, printed in various London newspapers, included the message: "all well on board." By that time all on board were not well. More news of the voyage dribbled into London. The captains of several faster ships reported that they had seen the *Endeavour* at anchor in Cape Town and therefore assumed she would soon be sighted off England's southern coast.

Cook was within a week of home when he heard one of the gloomier rumors about his ship. On July 7, far from land, he exchanged news with a ship on her way from England to the West Indies. He learned that in England there lingered doubts whether the *Endeavour* would ever return home. In London's gambling circles the bets were still being laid—some for and some against the likelihood of her safe return.

With the aid of friendly winds the *Endeavour* finally approached the cliffs of Dover, reaching the Downs on July 12. In the afternoon Cook went ashore at the port of Deal and trod on English soil. Boarding a horse-drawn vehicle for the journey overland to the office of the Admiralty in London, he took with him his precious charts, drawings, and the heavy journal packed with handwritten pages. He had been away for almost three years.

COOK'S ACHIEVEMENT: NOT THE "UNFITEST MAN"

For months Cook had wondered how his extensive voyage would be finally assessed by the Admiralty. Long before reaching England he had pondered that question so vital to his naval career, for in the Royal Navy his rank was one of the lowliest of all those commanding a ship at sea. Occasionally, when provoked by events, he did confide his judgment of himself in his journal. But he did not like to boast; it was not in his nature.

He must have been tempted to single out and announce one potential victory: he had almost triumphed over scurvy. His voyage was not unique—others had made extended voyages without experiencing a death from scurvy—but his voyage could be called one milestone in the history of that disease. At first, however, this particular victory was almost irrelevant because so many of his crew, during and after the visit to Java, had died from other diseases. In no way could the whole voyage be viewed as a medical success, and it paled in comparison to Bougainville's recent voyage around the world.

And then there were Cook's geographical achievements. He was an explorer, but what exactly had he found? After leaving his haven at the Endeavour River in north Queensland he had privately expressed the hope that the Admiralty would acknowledge his exploration of an incredibly long coast. That Australian coast was so lined with dangers that for about a thousand nautical miles his sailors had been constantly "heaving the lead" in order to assess the depth of water— "a circumstance that I dare say never happen'd to any ship before." Three days later, engaging in another soliloquy, he told himself that he had willingly confronted higher risks "upon this coast than may be thought with prudence I ought to have done with a single Ship." Undoubtedly an explorer with only one ship—and so with small hope of rescue if that ship were wrecked—had to be cautious. On the other hand he conceded that if he had taken no risks he would have been condemned as "the unfitest man in the world" to lead what was intended to be a voyage of discovery.

Weeks later, in the tropics, he justifiably became more assertive. Drafting a report that he intended to forward to the Admiralty at the first opportunity, he concluded that his voyage of exploration "will be thought as great and as compleat if not more so than any Voyage before made in the South Seas." Again his humility grasped the pen and deleted the word "great." Just before he reached England, boldness again took up his pen. There was something Cook decided he had to say. He had explored, he wrote, a long expanse of coastline which "I am confident was never seen or visited by any European before us." Almost as if to cancel out that self-praise, he humbly explained to the highest naval officials that he had made no important discoveries. In his eyes the unseen continent was the only discovery worthy of the title of *great*, and so far it had eluded him.

The coasts of eastern Australia and New Zealand, which he had explored so diligently, and the coastal regions he had discovered, seemed to be the minor prizes. They were not yet of burning importance to any European nation, not even his own. But their day would come: Australia and New Zealand would become havens for immigrants from Europe and then from nearly every part of the world. Two and a half centuries later they would together hold a population almost equal to that held by France in 1770, when it was the most populous nation in Europe. That the local inhabitants would be disturbed and their way of life endangered by the new colonists were not widely envisaged. The prevailing view in Paris and London, Berlin and Philadelphia was that they would gain from the arrival of Western civilization. In fact the losses for them would at first be devastating. Having been isolated for so long from the rest of the world, the Aborigines and Maori were about to be subject to smallpox, measles, influenza, and other novel infections carried to their lands by new European settlers. The voyage that had largely conquered scurvy was indirectly to expose native peoples to a new form of conquest: all those European infections to which they had no immunity.

18

Two Voyages and Their Ripples

THE VOYAGES were over; but the ripples flowed, and still flow.

In the summer of 1771 the newly arrived captain of the *Endeavour* was seen in the streets of Greenwich and London, where no doubt he was personally hailed by the few people who knew or recognized him, but his role as a major discoverer was not yet appreciated. The instant heroes of the voyage were Banks and Solander, who were publicly praised less as naturalists than as astronomers sent to observe the transit of Venus. In science their triumph was almost beyond dispute. On this expedition they had increased by about one-fifth the known plant species of the world. In marine life and zoology their discoveries were also remarkable, and none more so than the kangaroo. It was Banks and Solander who were first invited to discuss the voyage with King George III at his residence near the Thames at Richmond on August 10, just one year after the *Endeavour* lay in danger near the Great Barrier Reef.

Cook had his own duties to fulfill and letters to write. They included a letter to Penrith in Cumberland, where Mr. George Monkhouse had just been informed that he had lost two sons during the voyage. Their personal possessions, as the custom was, had been auctioned on board the *Endeavour*, except for surgeon Monkhouse's instruments and medicines. The considerable sum waiting for his father was 229 English pounds, 17 shillings, and six and a half pence; so Cook wrote.

Cook went home to the London suburb of Mile End to greet his wife, Elizabeth, and surviving children—two fewer than when he was last in their presence. At least Elizabeth could congratulate him for laying out the naval carpet for their eager sons, James and Nathaniel. In the southern hemisphere, in their absence, they had been placed in the *Endeavour*'s books as junior members of the crew. Although they received no pay on their imaginary voyage, their presence in the ship's books meant that they had already acquired some seniority in the Royal Navy before they actually joined it. What Cook did to promote his sons was illegal and out of character but not unique in the navy of his day.

From the Admiralty, Lieutenant Cook received a formal letter thanking him for a mission "extremely well" performed, and congratulating his officers and men for their cheerfulness and alertness in "the fatigues and dangers of their late voyage." There also arrived, one Sunday morning, a pleasing message from Joseph Banks, who had resumed his place in the capital city as a young man with high connections, informing Cook that he was to be promoted to the position of captain. Cook replied with words of thanks from a coffee house in Charing Cross. Finally Cook was summoned to meet King George III, with whom the transit of Venus was the topic of animated discussion. Without the king's enthusiasm, the voyage to Tahiti might not have taken place. That he was central to one of the important voyages in the history of the world is now largely forgotten.

NO SEA CAN HURT HER

Meanwhile, in London, Cook assumed that if his own work deserved praise, so did his three-masted *Endeavour*. To a questionnaire handed to him by the navy, he replied that his square-sterned bark steered faithfully and rode well in a gale. She also rolled "easy" in the trough of the sea when the heavy waves came rolling past. Pondering the question— did she hold her own when in the company of other ships?—he gently had to remind his superiors that in the endless expanses of the Pacific Ocean he did not once meet another ship. Only once, in the Atlantic, did he have "the opportunity to try her" when sailing in the same direction as other ships. This must have been the occasion near St. Helena when briefly he trailed the convoy of large English ships returning from India. He also had to report that her fastest speed was a mere eight knots. And how did she perform in gales, many of which had assaulted her? In "a topgallant gale," and carrying little sail, she ran at about five knots.

Another test of the *Endeavour* was her behavior when lying to, when the bow or head of the ship had to be pointed in such a direction "that a heavy sea may not tumble into her." How did the *Endeavour* perform in such tempestuous conditions? "No Sea can hurt her," Cook answered—so long as the appropriate sails were in place.

The *Endeavour's* days of exploration had ended. There was no thought of employing her again on dangerous coasts. One of the most effective of exploring ships, she now returned to her old career as a simple carrier. Initially she was fitted out for a voyage to serve the few British colonists living in the Falkland Islands, where supplies were needed; but a few years later, under the new name of the *Lord Sandwich*, she conveyed troops to North America, where they were to fight the rebelling colonists. In 1778 at Rhode Island the ship was once more a servant of her country but in a slightly demeaning way. With other ships she was deliberately sunk in Newport Harbor, in the hope they would together present an obstacle against any enemy fleet trying to enter the harbor. At that time the significance of her voyage around the world was not fully appreciated, and the opportunity to convert her into a floating museum was lost.

She had so fulfilled the tasks demanded of her that when two ships were needed for another long exploring expedition to the Pacific, Cook's praise of her could not be ignored. Another two Whitby colliers—new versions of the *Endeavour*—were selected by the navy to explore the seas that Cook had left behind. Eager to lead the new expedition, he was comforted by the thought that he would be in command of two ships instead of one.

His mission was to sail to Cape Town and enter again the southerly parts of the vast oceans in search of the missing continent. It must be emphasized that the missing continent, though no one seems to have openly said so, could no longer be so glamorous if by chance it were belatedly found. The romance, the magic of that land, had depended on much of it intruding into subtropical seas. But Tasman had shown in the southern Indian Ocean and Cook and de Surville had proved in the southern Pacific that the missing continent, if it really existed, would probably lie to the south and therefore experience a cooler climate than had been hoped. It certainly would not be rich in spices or new tropical plants, whether a new form of cotton or an alternative kind of tobacco or cocoa. It would not, judged by a prevailing geological theory, even be rich in gold or silver. If the missing continent were to be found to lie only in the far southern parts of the globe, it would also be smaller than the one that Cook and de Surville had expected to find.

Banks had contributed enormously to the voyage of the *Endeavour*. And while he must sometimes have vexed Cook, his presence helps explain Cook's success in coping with scurvy. In contrast, if Banks had been voyaging in the *St. Jean-Baptiste* and exerting his influence on her captain, the results from the French expedition might have been very different. It was also Banks who suggested that the Polynesian priest and navigator Tupaia be invited to join the *Endeavour*; and Tupaia's skills as an observer and interpreter enabled the explorers to acquire in New Zealand the kind of knowledge they could not acquire in Australia. Thanks to Banks and his companion Solander, this was an extraordinary voyage in the history of the natural sciences. Above all, the voyage is widely known because of the two voluminous but contrasting journals kept each day, one by Cook and the other by Banks.

Banks looked forward to accompanying Cook on this second search. Indeed he expected to bring aboard the *Resolution* an entourage of a dozen scientists, artists, and servants, for all of whom accommodations now had to be built. That two of Banks's party were musicians and servants—"two French horn men" was how Cook described them—and another was a personal cook, distinctly gave the impression that the voyage would be a fashionable picnic as well as a scientific excursion. Cook was slightly peeved at the sight of stylishly dressed ladies and gentlemen coming to the docks to see the extensions to what they viewed as "Mr. Banks' ship." He also feared that his ship was becoming less seaworthy under the pressure of demands for more and more accommodations.

Cook did not openly voice these complaints. They made themselves apparent when the ship, with her enlarged accommodations, weighed anchor at Gravesend and began to sail down the Thames on her way to Plymouth Sound. The pilot in charge was aghast at his ship's unpredictable behavior. While several light coal ships swept past, standing upright, the *Resolution* was heeled over as if about to capsize!

Having traveled the world in second class, this time Banks had insisted on first class and was willing to pay for it. There was to be no first class, however, in any ship commanded by Cook. Moreover the doubts about the seaworthiness of the *Resolution* and her new superstructure were officially endorsed, and "the penthouse" was condemned as a danger to the safety of the ship. Alterations were made under Cook's supervision. The space for the Banks entourage soon disappeared.

So Banks and Solander abandoned Cook's second voyage just as it was about to begin. One month later, on June 12, 1772, they were cheerfully sailing down the River Thames on a scientific voyage to Iceland, all their luggage having been transferred to this vessel. By that time Cook's two ships *Resolution* and *Adventure* were almost ready to leave Plymouth for Madeira, where they were to take on four thousand gallons of wine and then to "proceed upon farther discoveries toward the South Pole."

In her house at Mile End, Elizabeth knew that she must again say farewell to her wandering husband. In her care was left one keepsake: the nanny goat who had been twice around the world. Various visitors wished to set eyes on this remarkable creature; and to impress them, an inscription was composed for the goat's silver collar by the compiler of the new English dictionary, Dr. Samuel Johnson. The celebratory verse was in Latin, of course, but it was translated with charm and dignity into English:

> *In fame scarce second to the nurse of Jove,*
> *This Goat, who twice the world had traversed round,*
> *Deserving both her master's care and love,*
> *Ease and perpetual pasture now has found.*

The reference to the "nurse of Jove" reminded many readers that Jove or Jupiter, when living as an infant in a cave in Crete, had been reared by a goat. Unfortunately the inscribed collar of this English globe-trotting goat was not worn for long. On March 28, 1772, nine months after her return to England, she died at the Cooks' home.

FAR SOUTH: A NEW WAVE OF EXPLORING

The chances of the missing continent being found in a warm or mild climate of the South Pacific had vanished. The lesser hope remained that somewhere at the colder, southern end of the Indian Ocean a large area of land might still be found. It was almost a last hope.

The search was renewed. Two French ships under the command of Marion du Fresne, a native of Saint-Malo, left Cape Town in December 1771, fewer than six months after Cook's *Endeavour* had reached home. With the aid of the strong westerlies, they quickly explored the south Indian Ocean, surveying much of that vast zone in the roaring forties and beyond. They found lonely islands, including Prince Edward and the Crozets, but there was not a hint of a continent nearby. They then spent a few days on the east coast of Tasmania, at Blackman's Bay, before sailing to New Zealand. There in June 1772 in two separate incidents, the French experienced the fighting skills of a people who had no gunpowder. Marion du Fresne and twenty-four of his officers and seamen were killed.

Cook on his second exploratory voyage was also on his way to New Zealand. From Plymouth he sailed in his converted collier, the *Resolution*, accompanied by the Royal Navy officer Tobias Furneaux in command of the *Adventure*. After calling at Cape Town they sailed into the unknown. In the cold reaches of the Indian Ocean, Cook ventured farther south than any navigator before him; on January 17, 1773, his ship crossed the Antarctic Circle. His sister ship *Adventure* was now on her own. In a New Zealand bay, just before Christmas 1773, eleven of her men were gathering timber and filling water casks when they were attacked and killed. Hitherto Cook had thought the Maori were pliable and usually willing to negotiate. After these bloody episodes it was realized that New Zealand, in contrast to eastern Australia, would not easily be colonized by Europeans.

In the entire world only one inhabited island of moderate size and some commercial potential was still waiting to be found by Europeans. It was the tropical island of New Caledonia, a mere one-fifteenth the size of New Zealand. De Surville went close to it while sailing the Coral Sea in 1769, and Cook found it on his second global voyage five years later. There remained to be discovered that icy uninhabited land, the continent of Antarctica, which no one was to see until the following century.

A FRENCH WIDOW

Mme. Marie de Surville was still living in the walled town of Port-Louis in western France when she heard of her husband's drowning, almost a year after he died. Longing to know more about the voyage and about his last days, she hoped that the ship's surviving officers would be permitted to come home to France. But the *St. Jean-Baptiste* was held for three years as captive in the port of Callao, only a few miles from the harbor where de Surville had drowned. It was as if Spain wished to impart a lesson: intruders were not allowed in Spanish colonial seas. At last, with the aid of sixty Spanish sailors, the ship prepared to depart on the long voyage to France.

In April 1773 the *St. Jean-Baptiste* finally sailed from her prison on the shores of the Pacific Ocean. Facing hail and snow south of Cape Horn, she made her slow way to the Atlantic, passed within sight of the Falkland Islands, and then crossed the equator. Although scurvy reappeared—the first death was that of a Spanish sailor—the presiding fear now was not scurvy but war. The apprehension in Captain Labé's mind was that Europe might again be at war, and that his ship might be recaptured just when his homeland was almost in sight. Gunnery practice was begun. On August 1, 1773, an English ship, on her way from New York to West Africa, slipped into sight and seemed harmless enough to be approached with safety by the heavily armed French ship. When the two ships were within earshot, the question was nervously asked by Labé and cheerfully answered across the water: Europe was at peace!

A few weeks later the French members of the crew of the *St. Jean-Baptiste* saw the coast of their homeland. The sight was stirring; there were lumps in their throats when the aroma of summer came to them with the east wind. Past the mudflats and sand shoals the ship slowly approached the walled citadel of de Surville's home port, Port-Louis, and the wide estuary that led to the newer port of Lorient. But the sea was rough, the wind was blustery, and the tide did not favor the vessel. If only the wind would blow from the hoped-for direction! In clear sight of French soil, the returning seamen were still captive of that powerful force which, in the Bay of Bengal and the Indian Ocean, the Coral Sea and the Tasman Sea, in gale-swept Doubtless Bay and the harbor mouth of Chilca, had teased and frustrated them and played with their hopes. For a few hours the homecoming ship was stranded on a shoal while the people of Port-Louis watched and waited, almost within shouting distance.

Mme. de Surville was relieved to hear that the ship's captain, Guillaume Labé, was ready to meet her. It was a memorable moment when she received in her hands a few of her husband's keepsakes, brought all the way from Peru: a lock of hair snipped from his head after his corpse was washed ashore, his ceremonial suit made of velvet and decorated with gold braid and crimson silk, a few of his books and his Cross of St. Louis. From the gruffly spoken but kindly French officer who handed over these belongings she heard about the strange voyage and her husband's last day.

Like Labé, Marie de Surville's family's fortune was largely tied up in the voyage of the *St. Jean-Baptiste*. So she was heartened that the ship, safely home again, could now release its unsold cargo in readiness for an auction. Although the cargo had gone around the world, most of it was in fair condition on the sale days. So the silks and cottons and carpets found a home, not in the Jewish bazaars of that imagined Pacific land but in shops and houses in France.

A REUNION: THE LIVING AND THE DEAD

Cook did not yet know of de Surville's remarkable voyage of exploration. Five years after their near meeting off the coast of New Zealand, he remained ignorant.

It was on the homewards leg of his second voyage of exploration, in March 1775, that Cook called at Cape Town, where his ship anchored near French and Dutch merchant ships. It so happened that one of the French ships was on her way to Pondicherry. Her commander, Captain Julien-Marie Crozet, had been second-in-command of a recent expedition to New Zealand, the first to arrive since Cook's *Endeavour* had sailed away. It was Crozet who had marveled at the accuracy of Cook's maps of New Zealand, likening them to the existing maps of France.

Thus these two celebrated navigators met for the first time, and Cook invited Crozet to dine with him. "Captain Crozet seemed to be a man possessed of the true spirit of a discoverer and to have abilities equal to his good will," wrote Cook in his journal.

How the reminiscences flew! They touched the oceans familiar to both captains. Vital geographical knowledge changed hands. Crozet, as a friendly gesture, even handed to Cook, for quick examination, a chart of the Pacific that was soon to be published in France. One of the long voyages marked on the chart was that taken by Captain de Surville more than five years earlier. The information on the chart obviously surprised Cook, who had not heard of the French ship. In his journal written at the Cape in the next few hours, he could not even remember the precise name of the ship and simply referred to her as under the command "of one Captain Surville."

Quickly glancing over the French chart in the presence of Crozet, and no doubt observing the route of his own *Endeavour* marked clearly on it, Cook saw with some amazement that he and de Surville had at one point been incredibly close to each other. Cook even jumped to the conclusion that de Surville was actually in Doubtless Bay when he had passed it in the *Endeavour* in December 1769. In fact de Surville was not in the bay on that day; but a day or two later the two ships were almost within sight of each other, at a time when each captain had every reason to assume that no other European ship was within several thousand miles.

Toward de Surville, Cook instinctively felt the respect that one maritime discoverer usually feels toward another. It is now widely believed that de Surville discovered little of importance, but Cook would not have agreed. Although he knew more than anybody about the seas and shores of the southwest Pacific, he discovered something new on reading the French chart placed before him. It was Cook who had recently placed New Caledonia on the map. He had then sailed away with the conviction that a dangerous zone of coral reef extended almost all the way westward from New Caledonia to Queensland and its Great Barrier Reef. He had believed—until he saw the route of de Surville right through that zone—that a wide expanse of the Coral Sea was too dangerous to navigate. While Cook did not exactly say so, he must have realized that de Surville was bolder in entering unknown seas than most of his recent predecessors in the South Pacific.

Around the cramped dinner table there must have been more discussion of de Surville's voyage. Crozet and de Surville actually came from the same French town, and indeed were born only a few doors from each other in Port-Louis, though in different years. Accordingly Cook learned something about de Surville the man, and heard how he had been drowned on the day he reached Peru. So on this memorable day in 1775, Cook and Crozet amicably dined in the ship riding at anchor, with Table Mountain looming above them, and their minds together revisiting faraway Pacific harbors that both had recently explored.

FATE OF THE GREAT ONES AND THEIR FRIENDS

In the following year Cook set out on his third voyage into the vast unmapped parts of the Pacific Ocean. It was to be his final voyage. In Hawaii in February 1779, on hearing that one of his boats had been stolen, he acted as de Surville had acted in a similar clash on the shores of New Zealand nearly ten years earlier: infuriated by the loss of the valuable six-oared cutter, he retaliated decisively. Before long the order was given for the English muskets to be fired. Outnumbered, Cook's men were not prepared for the vigorous counterattack. He was on shore and waiting to be rescued by one of his own boats when he was hit by a club and stabbed by a dagger in both the neck and shoulder. He fell into the shallow sea and was dispatched with further blows. A little later his stolen jacket and trousers were seen to be adorning one of the armed Hawaiians lining the shore.

As a master of the seas, Cook deserved to be farewelled with the kind of grand ceremonial funeral that Lord Nelson, the hero of the battle of Trafalgar, was to receive a quarter-century later. Instead, in the confusion, the farewell was delayed, for where was his body? Eventually his head, his right hand, and many of his bones were recovered and ceremonially buried at sea. The news of his death did not reach London for another eleven months. Banks heard the sad news from his friend Lord Sandwich: "poor Captain Cooke is no more."

Long before word arrived of her husband's death, the year had been miserable for Elizabeth Cook. Her teenage son Nathaniel, a midshipman in the Royal Navy, was drowned when his ship went down in a hurricane off Jamaica. Only two of her six children were now alive. In old age, half a century later, she lived comfortably in the London suburb of Clapham, dressed expensively in black satin, and even kept a footman. She died in 1835, at the age of ninety-three, and was buried in the middle aisle of the church of Great St. Andrew in Cambridge.

Dr. Daniel C. Solander, the lover of plants and of most human beings, was not a seeker of fame. He had been content to allow his patron Banks to take most of the credit for those botanical and other discoveries for which he must have been equally responsible during the *Endeavour*'s voyage. In May 1782, still attending in his leisurely way to his plants and classifications in London, the jolly Swede was suddenly "attacked by paralysis." The doctors who visited his bedside said there was no hope. Joseph Banks was gratified that he alone was selected from "the innumerable Englishmen" who, along with the Swedish friends, wished personally to escort the coffin into the Swedish Lutheran church in Princess Square, London.

Solander's name sits on several points of the map of the vast Pacific. Today mariners entering Botany Bay see his name on a headland while those reaching the southwest corner of New Zealand pass a bleak and rocky island favored by seabirds and known as Solander Island.

Meanwhile, in France, many of de Surville's men who were lucky enough to return home had resumed their former occupations—de Villefeix the chaplain serving as a village priest, others as officers of trading ships, and some probably as rural laborers, having seen enough of the ocean. Marie de Surville continued to reside in the port from which her husband had sailed away, and was to live long enough to hear the first rumblings of the French Revolution.

In many English and French cottages were to be found the keepsakes of those voyages—perhaps a native weapon, a sea chest, a carved piece of bone from a whale or other creature, a shell necklace, or the dry cutting of a tropical plant. But one legacy of the *Endeavour*'s voyage was more influential than these solid souvenirs. By 1790 educated people in Europe and the Americas had infinitely more knowledge of other human societies and their diversity than they possessed when they were young.

A long life lay ahead of Joseph Banks. He would live until June 1820, exactly fifty years since he almost lost his life on the coral reef. He was a vigorous survivor, with his finger in a hundred pies. He had married a "comely and modest" bride who was just over half his age, but they were to have no children; Banks instead had his worldwide family of scientists and collectors whom he fostered or adopted. He built up his own wonderful library and herbarium at Soho Square in the heart of London and converted the Kew Gardens, farther along the river, into a botanical paradise. He was the uncrowned chief of British science in a great and ripening age of science; the correspondent of a thousand people in England and overseas; and the recipient of the latest foreign news, scientific and unscientific. Every oddity of nature was referred to him for comment; and in the space of fourteen years the presence of mermaids on three different parts of the Scottish coast was brought urgently to his notice. But a mythical Scottish mermaid, above or below the waist, could not possibly match the shapely young Tahitian women of whom he carried clear memories. His voyage in the *Endeavour* remained as magic in his mind.

A BRIEF ENCOUNTER AT BOTANY BAY

In the year of Cook's death, Joseph Banks for the first time began to advance the prospects of Botany Bay as a place where the British might make a settlement. For some sixty years Britain had sent or "transported" convicted criminals to some of the North American colonies where they were mostly bought by plantation owners. The traffic in convicts was not highly publicized but more than fifty thousand reached the colonies that became the United States; George Washington employed at least one. When the American colonies rebelled against England in 1775, they refused to receive shiploads of surplus convicts from the motherland. So the new British convicts remained at home, spent their nights in old ships or hulks close to the shore, and were employed in the daylight to build stone breakwaters and other public works. When the hulks began to bulge with convicted criminals, new prisons were built.

Soon arose the sensible idea that there must be some overseas harbor to which the convicts could be sent and usefully employed in such a way that they would assist Britain's commerce and naval strength. New Zealand might have been the first choice—at one time it had been Cook's favorite southern land—but its armed men and swift canoes were judged to be a military hazard. In 1779 Banks gave evidence to a government committee, suggesting that Botany Bay, "in the Indian Ocean," was the suitable place. He enthusiastically noted that its climate was rather like that of Toulouse in the south of France and that the convicts, when supplied with seeds and livestock, would soon be able to feed themselves. Their presence would be an advantage to the British Empire and merchant fleet, now expanding in that rich, vast ocean to the east of the Cape of Good Hope. So the seeds of a new empire were sown.

In January 1788 a fleet of English ships, carrying Marines as well as convicts, arrived safely in Botany Bay. They found the grass dry and fresh water hard to find. Unlike Cook, they had arrived in one of the less favored months of the year. As the wind and waves were sweeping into the harbor with a force Cook had not experienced during his week's stay, the newly arrived Englishmen decided that a superior harbor must be found. After several days the British fleet was ready to sail a few miles along the coast.

The rivalry of the British and the French on the Australian coast was not yet finished. De Surville had almost discovered Botany Bay and Sydney Harbor, months ahead of the British. Now another Frenchman was only days away. Jean-Francois de La Pérouse, exploring the Pacific with two ships, *Boussole* and *Astrolabe*, had been visiting one of those bleak Russian ports in the north Pacific when he received a message sent overland from Paris, instructing him to sail to the far side of the equator and see whether the British were making a settlement at Botany Bay. He set out on the long voyage by way of Samoa, where he lost a few of his crew in a fight.

The two French ships appeared on the horizon near Botany Bay just a few days after the arrival of the British fleet. They were seen from the sandstone cliffs, but at first their flags—their "colors"—were not clearly visible. As the wind blew from the shore, the ships were at risk if they came closer. For two days they rode the waves, sometimes out of sight, and perhaps not far from the position where, some eighteen years earlier, their countryman de Surville had smelled the land. These two French ships, the first in these waters since de Surville's fleeting visit, now came so close to Botany Bay that their men in the lookout could see the masts and colors of the British ships at anchor there.

On the morning of January 26, 1788, the day now celebrated annually as Australia Day, Captain John Hunter prepared to lead the convoy of British ships out of Botany Bay and guide them into Sydney Harbor. About to depart, he saw two large ships flying French colors and approaching the mouth of the bay that he was about to leave. He showed every courtesy to the French. He even decided to offer them help in entering the unfamiliar harbor. "I sent a boat with an officer to assist them in," wrote Hunter, and fortunately, "about an hour after, a breeze sprung up from the south-east." The French ships came inside in neat procession and anchored in the bay not far from the place where Cook's *Endeavour* had once been riding at anchor. Many of the French were suffering from scurvy, extreme lassitude, and other sicknesses; their chaplain was to be buried on the shores of the bay.

The Frenchmen remained in the bay for six weeks. A makeshift stockade and camp were erected near the beach, partly to protect a boat they were building. Several British naval officers, coming by sea from Sydney or walking overland, were welcomed and entertained, and information changed hands. The French, in return, were not invited formally to visit the new British settlement in Sydney Harbor, but a French captain did arrive in a rowboat with letters and despatches, which the British had promised to send to Europe by the next available ship.

The intention of La Pérouse was to sail first to New Caledonia and Tonga, perhaps revisit the discoveries of his fellow countrymen de Surville and Bougainville in the Solomons, and then venture through Torres Strait to inspect the Gulf of Carpentaria and the northern coast of Australia. He was entitled to assume that when he finally reached France his reports would be digested, debated, and acted upon. The French government would then decide whether or not to place a settlement somewhere in eastern Australia or New Zealand.

The French ships sailed from Botany Bay. When last sighted from the sandstone cliff, they resembled two tiny patches on the horizon. The white of the sails finally faded and was swallowed by the blue of the ocean. The ships were not seen again.

Who Was the Discoverer?

⛏ OF THE SEA EXPLORERS who have claims to the title of discoverer of Australia, the Aborigines come first: they were the finders, more than fifty thousand years ago, and they slowly settled the land they found. In New Zealand the Maori have an undisputed claim to be the discoverers and colonizers. Their discovery, requiring a long voyage into the unknown, was one of the finest feats in the history of seafaring. Centuries later came the Europeans.

Strictly speaking, the Europeans did not discover these lands; they rediscovered them, an equally arduous task. Which European discoverers deserve fame? In New Zealand it is the Dutch. In Australia the claimants are more numerous. The debate about their primacy is endless.

One school of thought argues that the Portuguese were the first to see the coast of Australia. This claim is expounded in Kenneth G. McIntyre's 1977 book *The Secret Discovery of Australia* and Peter Trickett's 2007 book *Beyond Capricorn*. Fascinating but difficult to substantiate, the theory of Portuguese discovery is rarely lacking in disciples. There is circumstantial evidence that the Portuguese, who were early settlers on the island of Timor, could have seen the northwest coast of Australia before the Dutch. But the argument that the Portuguese discovered eastern Australia is, to most historians, not yet convincing. Professor Alan Frost, a leading historian of Pacific discovery, summarizes that argument pithily and critically in pages 91–95 of *East Coast Country: A North Queensland Dreaming*, published in 1996. The debate about the Portuguese is far from over. But even if the Portuguese did discover part of eastern Australia, they did not publicize it. Other seafarers had to find it afresh and, more important, to explore and evaluate it.

There is scant academic support for the theory that the Chinese were the first outsiders to rediscover Australia and New Zealand. The theory that the Chinese visited those coasts in the fifteenth century was outlined by Gavin Menzies in his book *1421: The Year China Discovered America*, first published in 2003. Menzies' case, fluently written, continues to captivate many Australian and New Zealand readers, even after it has been torpedoed on the Internet. The reading public was often enthralled; historians were not. His evidence has not stood up to inspection. His key claim that the Chinese shaped a commemorative "pyramid" at the Queensland gold town of Gympie, a surprising distance from the coast, has no evidence in its favor. Someday a more documented case for Chinese exploration might well be put forward.

On the basis of present knowledge the Dutch deserve high praise. From 1606 onward they discovered many parts of the long coastline of Australia and made known their discoveries. Their fine explorer Abel Tasman also discovered Tasmania and New Zealand at the close of 1642. But praise for the Dutch cannot be extended too far. To discover is to see with both eyes; they saw with only one eye, for they were not prepared to venture inland and discover what lay behind the coastal reefs, cliffs, and dunes. They rejected their opportunities to explore the numerous coastal regions of Australia or New Zealand that they had been the first to see. The exception was western Australia's Swan River, which they did explore.

To discover, and to believe in the importance of one's discovery, usually leads to action. For valid reasons Holland did not act. A tiny republic, it was already overextended by 1650, possessing ports in many parts of the world. The Dutch merchants had their hands on more overseas trade than they could digest. For these reasons they did not explore farther along the coasts of Australia and New Zealand and then found a colony; but they placed signposts on maps so that others could follow them.

The Dutch claim to the title of discoverer of Australia is much stronger than any British claim. When Cook arrived off the east coast in 1770, only the eastern quarter of the continent had not been discovered. It was self-evident that an east coast must exist. Moreover the Spanish had seen the tip of the far north of that coast and the Dutch had virtually seen the far south, though they were mistaken, as was Cook, in thinking initially that Tasmania was actually part of the continent. Cook was the first to sail along the east coast. His voyage was important because that coast proved to be, in its combination of soil and climate, more attractive than the west coast. It was a coast worth discovering.

Cook's voyage in the southwest Pacific in 1769–1770 shows how inadequate is the word *discover*. In those years, by the orthodox definitions, Cook was not a notable discoverer. But in another sense he did nothing *but* discover. He investigated what earlier European navigators had been too hurried to inspect. On a vast stretch of coast, extending from the north and east capes of New Zealand to the coral reefs of north Queensland, he found harbors, straits, headlands, and coastal mountains and mapped them. He watched intently the sea winds and currents and speculated about the climate as best he could; and his resident scientists studied the flora, fauna, soils, and sweeping grasslands, and observed the habits, ways of life, and weapons of the inhabitants of the two distinct lands.

It is fair to suggest that the men in the *Endeavour*, in less than a year spent on these coasts, learned more about New Zealand and Australia than the Dutch had ever learned, and far, far more about eastern Australia than the Chinese, Portuguese, and Dutch could ever have learned if in fact they did once visit its coast. Cook and Banks brought home to London, without exactly saying so, the ingredients of a vague blueprint for the ultimate colonization of both New Zealand and Australia. Such a set of ingredients had rarely emerged from a single voyage of exploration in any major part of the world.

The controversy—did the Chinese or Portuguese, Dutch or British really discover Australia?—partly centers on the scarcity of facts. It is also a dispute about the meaning of one word—*discovery*. That magical word carries too many meanings. The dispute therefore is likely to continue. Meanwhile a few simple propositions can be put forward. While not resolving the debate, they will perhaps clarify it.

Discovery, to be worthwhile, requires layer after layer of observation. It calls for assessments over a wide area. A discoverer is not simply the first navigator to see a land and then sail away. A discoverer must recognize the significance of what he sees and indirectly persuade others to recognize it. Discovery, whether of a mining field or a new drug, calls for assessments on many fronts. Moreover a discovery becomes important and effective only if it leads to further action. In the story of inventions, historians ultimately give the prize to the inventor who produces results.

Little credit can be conferred on the inventor who makes his discovery in his secret laboratory and does not see its significance or tells no one about it. Likewise, in the history of mineral and oil discovery there was usually a prospector who came early and saw the resource but did nothing to exploit it. In science as in mining, credit usually goes to those discoverers—they might be the second or third in line of discovery—who investigate further. In the end they act on the basis of what they see and change the course of history.

Discovery is usually a collective more than an individualistic process. Cook could not have achieved so much without the help of Abel Tasman and earlier navigators. They erected vital signposts: they provided him with his first outline—something between a squiggle and a map—of long stretches of coast. Cook set out to multiply the signposts, and did so perhaps by the hundreds. He was a discoverer on a different scale from his predecessors. He took risks by going ashore again and again. His exploration had a perceptiveness and thoroughness matched by no earlier European explorer or group of explorers in these seas or probably in any seas.

Most of the significant discoverers in the southwest Pacific were assisted by earlier seafarers, seen or unseen. Just as Cook gained enormously from Tasman's discoveries, Tasman had profited from discoveries on the west and south coasts of Australia by earlier Dutch navigators. In their turn the earlier Dutch sea captains reaching western and northern Australia used landmarks and maps set down at the Cape of Good Hope, India, Java, and beyond by earlier Portuguese and Spanish navigators, who had been aided by Asian pilots and navigators. Vasco da Gama, in rounding South Africa and finally finding his way to India in 1498, had relied on a Muslim pilot whom he met in Mozambique. If one day it should prove true that the Portuguese or Chinese did discover parts of the coast of Australia and New Zealand, the question will then arise: how much were they assisted by the knowledge and guidance of southeast Asian seafarers, or by the sailors of the Indonesian archipelago or New Guinea whose vessels they chanced to encounter on their way to the new lands?

Some discoveries are significant rather than important. If it turns out to be true—though it is an unlikely event—that the Chinese discovered Australia and New Zealand, the fact will be a legitimate source of pride for China. But it will be of little importance in the history of Australia or New Zealand because it had no effect on the subsequent history of those lands. At sea there are dead-end discoveries as well as dynamic ones.

Another of our biases has to be recognized. In tracing the major discoveries in the southwest Pacific, we give too much weight to the finding of lands and not enough to the finding of narrow seas. The discovery of such vital shortcuts as Torres Strait (1606), Cook Strait (1770), and Bass Strait (1798) enhanced the value of the land discoveries. Likewise, to detect a prevailing wind could be as important as discovering a land. The Dutch discovery of the power of the westerly winds in the middle latitudes of the Indian Ocean actually led them to the west coast of Australia as well as opening the fastest sea route from Cape Town to Java. The discovery by de Surville of the value of the westerly winds and of the west–east route in the South Pacific was also crucial.

The concept of a single all-important discoverer may be applied more sensibly to an island than to a continent. A continent, by definition, is too large to be encompassed by only one discoverer. The coastline of the Australian continent runs for more than eleven thousand miles. Why should the grand title of discoverer be awarded solely to an explorer who visited only 1 percent of that coastline but knew nothing about the remainder of the coast, in all its variety, and nothing about the shape and size of the continent itself?

Subsequent political events help determine who should be given the title of discoverer. The continent of Australia in 1901 became the territory of just one nation; but if a different course of events in Europe had divided Australia permanently into three separate nations, each nation might now be giving credit to a different discoverer— namely the navigator who found that particular part of the distinct nation. So the nation of Northern Australia might recognize a Dutch discoverer, and the nation of New South Wales might recognize Cook as its discoverer.

In a big landmass, the first discovery does not automatically lead to the finding of the remoter parts. Sydney and its nearby coastline, as far as we know, was not found until more than a century and a half after the discovery of the north coast. The discovery of the Sydney coastline was delayed by at least two sea barriers. One barrier was the narrow and dangerous Torres Strait and the nearby coral reefs. A lesser barrier was Tasmania, a projecting headland on which stormy seas crashed. Just as the vast inland deserts and the Nullarbor Plain virtually cut the Australian landmass into two separate parts, so Torres Strait, the Great Barrier Reef, and the wild seas of the Great Australian Bight and the Southern Ocean virtually imposed two ocean barriers. Therefore it may be more realistic to divide Australia into at least two distinct lands—or even four—and allow each to honor its own discoverer.

Discover is a wonderful word but it is huge. It is also slippery and ambiguous. Too much is demanded of it. But we will continue to use it and overuse it because it is so simple and powerful. To return to the question: who—long after the Aborigines—rediscovered Australia? There is no simple and satisfactory answer, for the words *Australia* and *discoverer* are both elusive.

Selected Sources

It would have been impossible to write this book without the careful editorial work carried out many years ago by two New Zealand maritime historians, J. C. Beaglehole and John Dunmore. Beaglehole edited the journals of both James Cook and Joseph Banks, a massive task performed with patience and learning. I doubt whether in the region sometimes called Australasia there has ever been such an editorial marathon. Beaglehole also wrote a life of Cook, filled with careful detail and insights. Like many biographers, he became so close to his subject in spirit and sympathy that he was almost a disciple, and sometimes very reluctant to criticize him. In a few important places I disagree with Beaglehole while continuing to admire his work.

John Dunmore edited and translated from the French a large part of the journals of Jean de Surville and his deputy Guillaume Labé. His translations, published in 1981 in *The Expedition of the St. Jean-Baptiste to the Pacific, 1769–1770*, are in fluent and lively prose. He wrote a careful introduction to the book. He has also written other works on the French maritime explorers, including his two-volume *French Explorers in the Pacific* (1965 and 1969). In places I depart from his views, and in places I build on his work, while continuing to express my debt.

The journals of Cook and de Surville were published by the Hakluyt Society. (The Hakluyt Society was established in 1846 for the purpose of printing rare or unpublished Voyages and Travels. For further information, see their website at www.hakluyt.com.) I also acknowledge my debt to the State Library of New South Wales, which published the journal of Banks in two volumes. I express thanks to the Alexander Turnbull Library Endowment Trust of Wellington, New Zealand, which published in 1982, in a small print run, the careful translations by Isabel Ollivier and Cheryl Hingley of *Extracts from journals relating to the visit to New Zealand of the French ship St. Jean-Baptiste in December 1769 under the command of J. F. M. de Surville*. A revised edition was published in 1987.

In the following notes I refer often to two works and usually quote them in abbreviated form:

Banks's Journal: J. C. Beaglehole, ed., *The Endeavour Journal of Joseph Banks, 1768–1771*, two volumes for the Trustees of the Public Library of New South Wales "in association with Angus & Robertson," Sydney, 1962.

Cook's Journals: J. C. Beaglehole, ed., *The Journals of Captain James Cook on His Voyages of Discovery: Volume One, The Voyage of the Endeavour 1768–1771*, Hakluyt Society, Cambridge, England, 1968. The first edition appeared in 1955, but this new edition contains corrections and additional information.

The above journals, running to some eighteen hunded printed pages, are the main sources for my story of the *Endeavour*. It is usually easy to tell whether I am using information from Cook or from Banks, therefore I do not always cite these journals specifically in the selected notes set out in the following pages.

CHAPTER 1: TOWARD THE LAND
OF THE LONG CANOES

page

4 George Robertson and his missing continent: his journal is reprinted in Hugh Carrington, ed., *The Discovery of Tahiti: A Journal of the Second Voyage of H.M.S. Dolphin Round the World*, London, 1948, see pp. 130–136, 234.

4 People resembling Jews: Robertson in Carrington, *The Discovery of Tahiti*, p. 228.

6 Cook's father's cottage in Melbourne: inspected 2005–2007.

7–9 Cook's early career at sea: J. C. Beaglehole in Cook's *Journals*, vol. 1, pp. cvi ff.

7 Cook's spelling of Gibraltar: J. C. Beaglehole, *The Life of Captain James Cook*, London, 1974, p. 17.

9 Accident to Cook's hand: J. C. Beaglehole, "Cook the Man," in G. M. Badger, ed., *Captain Cook, Navigator and Scientist*, Canberra, 1970, p. 18.

9–10 Cook's astronomy in Canada: Beaglehole, *The Life of Captain James Cook*, pp. 87–90.

10 Eclipse of sun near equator, May 15, 1771: Cook's *Journals*, vol. 1, p. 469.

11 Appearance of Cook: C. Ryskamp and F. A. Pottle, eds., *Boswell: the Ominous Years 1774–1776*, London, 1963, pp. 308–309; portrait by Nathaniel Dance in National Maritime Museum, Greenwich, inspected 2007.

12–13 Observing the transit: R. J. Bray, "'Australia and the transit of Venus,'" *Proceedings of the Astronomical Society of Australia*, 1980, vol. 4, no. 1; a letter from Dr. Bray to me, May 6, 1981.

13–14 King George III and his enthusiasm for astronomy: Jeremy Black, *George III: America's Last King*, New Haven, 2006, pp. 181–183.

16–17 Sleeping and cooking arrangements: in addition to snippets coming from the various *Endeavour* journals, I gained from a visit to the full-scale replica of the bark *Endeavour*, which was in Melbourne, March 2006.

18 Thompson the disabled cook: letter from Cook to Navy Board, June 9, 1768, reprinted in Cook's *Journals*, vol. 1, p. 614; Beaglehole, *The Life of Captain James Cook*, p. 140.

21 Daniel Solander's career: Banks's *Journal*, vol. 1, pp. 24–26.

22 The world in 1768: *Muir's Historical Atlas: Medieval and Modern*, 10th ed., London, 1964, esp. p. 58 for "The World at the Treaty of Paris, 1763."

22–23 Banks being rowed around ship: Banks's *Journal*, vol. 2, pp. 309–314; Cook's *Journals*, vol. 1, pp. 55, 63n.

25 Solander tastes Brazilian fruits: Cook's *Journals*, vol. 1, pp. 200–201; Banks's *Journal*, vol. 2, p. 310.

26–27 Buchan's painting of "Watering-Place in the Bay of Good Success": Rüdiger Joppien and Bernard Smith, *The Art of Captain Cook's Voyages*, New Haven, 1985, vol. 1, p. 11.

CHAPTER 2: A MISSING CONTINENT

29 Passage past Cape Horn to the Pacific: Beaglehole, *The Life of Captain James Cook*, pp. 164–166.

30–31 Thieving in Tahiti: Arthur Kitson, *The Life of James Cook, the Circumnavigator*, London, 1911, pp. 93–98.

31 Tahitian shot "with the greatest glee": Parkinson, *Journal of a Voyage*, p. 15.

32 Observatory at Tahiti: Cook's *Journals*, vol. 1, pp. 86–87.

32 Green's calculations: G. M. Badger, "Cook the Scientist," in Badger, *Captain Cook*, pp. 38–39.

33 Warm temperatures at noon on most days: Sydney Parkinson, *A Journal of a Voyage to the South Seas in His Majesty's Ship Endeavour*, London, 1773, pp. 30.

33 Banks and three pretty girls: Banks's *Journal*, vol. 1, p. 285.

34 Cook's sealed "Additional Instructions": Cook's *Journals*, vol. 1, pp. cclxxxii ff. They are signed on July 30, 1768.

36–37 Dalrymple and his belief in a missing continent: Howard T. Fry, *Alexander Dalrymple (1737–1808) and the Expansion of British Trade*, London, 1970, esp. pp. 108–109, 123–126.

36 Dalrymple finds Colbert's book: Edward Duyker, essay on "Alexander Dalrymple and the English Text," in *Mirror of the Australian Navigation* by Jacob Le Maire, Sydney, 1999, unpaged.

36 Charles de Brosses: *Histoire des Navigations aux Terres Australes*, two volumes, Paris, 1756 (reprint, Amsterdam, 1967). Appended to the book is the important map by Robert de Vaugondy.

38 The wealth of the sugar islands: David Eltis, Frank D. Lewis, and David Richardson, "Slave Prices, the African Slave Trade, and Productivity in the Caribbean, 1674–1807," in *Economic History Review*, vol. 58, August 2005, pp. 671–680.

38–39 Estimated area and population of missing continent: Fry, *Alexander Dalrymple*, pp. 125–126.

39 Lord Morton and science: *The Dictionary of National Biography*, London, 1921–1922, "James Douglas," vol. 5, p. 1236.

39 Lord Morton views: manuscript letter of 1768, printed in appendix 2 of Cook's *Journals*, vol. 1, p. 516.

39 White inhabitants near New Britain: John Callander, *Terra Australis Cognita*, Edinburgh, 1768, vol. 3, p. 613.

41 Tupaia less burdensome than "lions and tigers": Banks's *Journal*, vol. 1, p. 312.

42 The clever diver: Alan Villiers, *Captain Cook: The Seamen's Seaman*, London, 1967, p. 124; a charming account of Tupaia's first weeks with the ship.

42 Cheshire cheese and English porter: Banks's *Journal*, vol. 1, pp. 388, 394.

43 New comet: Cook's *Journals*, vol. 1, pp. 160 and 160n.; Banks's *Journal*, vol. 1, p. 389.

43 Matra on the comet: Alan Frost, ed., *The Precarious Life of James Mario Matra*, Carlton, 1995, pp. 38–39.

CHAPTER 3: A FRENCH FLOATING BAZAAR

44 De Surville's secret instructions: John Dunmore, ed., "Introduction," in *The Expedition of the St. Jean-Baptiste to the Pacific 1769–1770*, London, 1981, pp. 17–19.

45–46 De Surville's career: Dunmore, *The Expedition*, pp. 1–5.

47 Ship and cargo: Dunmore, *The Expedition*, pp. 30–32.

47–48 Muslims in crew: Dunmore, *The Expedition*, pp. 226, 226n, 283.

48 Chevalier's letter of December 1768: translated and cited by Dunmore, *The Expedition*, pp. 21–22.

49 Robertson's glimpse of "Jews": his journal in Hugh Carrington, ed., *The Discovery of Tahiti: A Journal of the Second Voyage of H.M.S. Dolphin Round the World*, London, 1948, pp. 227–228.

50 Rochon hears rumor of Jews: cited by Dunmore, *The Expedition*, p. 23.

50 Jews in Canton: C. G. F. Simkin, *The Traditional Trade of Asia*, London, 1968, p. 80.

50 Jews in Aden: Elkan N. Adler, ed., *Jewish Travelers in the Middle Ages: 19 Firsthand Accounts*, New York, 1987, p. 102.

50 Cochin's synagogue: visit in November 1990.

50 Jews of Cochin: Ashin das Gupta, *India and the Indian Ocean World: Trade and Politics*, Delhi, 2004, pp. 1–2, 109, 117, 130–131, 177.

51 Jews said to be in New Guinea: Dampier cited in Dunmore, *The Expedition*, p. 26n.

51–52 Davis Land: Carrington, *The Discovery*, Appendix, pp. 274–277; Cook's *Journals*, vol. 1, p. xxii.

53 Banks and minerals: Banks's *Journal*, vol. 1, p. 472.

54–55 The lure of the Solomons: Colin Jack-Hinton, *The Search for the Islands of Solomon, 1567–1838*, Oxford, 1969, esp. ch. 1, p. 82.

57 Battle in Solomons: Dunmore, *The Expedition*, pp. 39–40, 193–196.

57 Kidnapped boy: Dunmore, *The Expedition*, pp. 198, 207.

57 The Arsacides: Dunmore, *The Expedition*, p. 105n; see also Bernard Lewis, *The Assassins: A Radical Sect in Islam*, London, 2003 ed., p. 7.

58 Lind and scurvy: Stephen R. Bown, *Scurvy: How a Surgeon, a Mariner and a Gentleman Solved the Greatest Medical Mystery of the Age of Sail*, Camberwell, Australia, 2003, ch. 5.

59 Cook's stock of sauerkraut: Beaglehole, *The Life of Captain James Cook*, p. 135.

59–60 Cabbage in the cask: Banks's *Journal*, vol. 1, pp. 249, 394; Dr. Hulme's lemon essence and malt: pp. 393–394.

60 Hygiene and scurvy in Anson's fleet: Glyndwr Williams, ed., *Documents Relating to Anson's Voyage Round the World, 1740–1744*, London, 1967, pp. 63, 83.

60 Long-preserved soup tablets: G. M. Badger, "Cook the Scientist," in Badger, *Captain Cook*, p. 48.

60 Byron preceded Cook in his treatment of scurvy: see his letter of February 1765 in Robert E. Gallagher, ed., *Byron's Journal of His Circumnavigation, 1764–1766*, Cambridge, England, 1964, p. 156.

61 Scurvy before *Endeavour* reaches Tahiti: Surgeon Perry to Lieutenant Cook, June or July 1771, printed in *Historical Records of New South Wales*, Sydney, 1893, vol. 1, part 1, "Cook 1762–1780," pp. 339–342. This information is not in the daily happenings recorded in Cook's *Journals*. Beaglehole's appendices in those same *Journals* (vol. 1, pp. 633–635) delete a vital part of the Perry report. Likewise Beaglehole, in *The Life of Captain James Cook*, p. 170, does not quote Perry and therefore draws optimistic conclusions about the relative absence of scurvy in the *Endeavour*.

62 Failure to gather fresh greens in Bashee islands: de Surville's journal, in Dunmore, *The Expedition*, p. 67.

62 De Surville needs fresh food: Dunmore, *The Expedition*, p. 124.

CHAPTER 4: YOUNG NICK'S DAY

63–64 Dutch exploring and colonizing: Günter Schilder, *Australia Unveiled: The Share of the Dutch Navigators in the Discovery of Australia*, Amsterdam, 1976, esp. chs. 7, 8, 14; Alan Taylor, *American Colonies: The Settlement of North America to 1800*, London, 2002, pp. 251–257.

64 Instructions to Tasman: Andrew Sharp, ed., *The Voyages of Abel Janszoon Tasman*, Oxford, 1968, pp. 30–39.

65 Tasman advised to disguise eagerness for precious metals: Sharp, *The Voyages*, pp. 36–37.

66 Tasman at Three Kings: Tasman's journal in Sharp, *The Voyages*, pp. 138 ff.

66 Three Kings Islands: personal sighting in February 2007.

67–68 Opinions that white people inhabit missing continent: John Callander, *Terra Australis Cognita: Or, Voyages to the Terra Australia . . .*, Edinburgh, 1766–1768, vol. 3, p. 613; Alexander Dalrymple, *An Historical Collection . . . South Pacific Ocean*, London, 1772, part 1, p. 53, part 2, p. 19.

68 Dr. Hulme's lemon remedy: Banks's *Journal*, vol. 1, p. 393.

68 Livestock in *Endeavour*: Banks's *Journal*, vol. 1, p. 394.

69 Banks and Solander converse in cabin: Banks's *Journal*, vol. 1, p. 396.

70 Cape Fly Away: Banks's *Journal*, vol. 1, p. 397.

70 Nick a "son of a Bitch": manuscript journal by John Bootie, cited by Beaglehole in Cook's *Journals*, vol. 1, p. ccxxxv.

71–72 Discovery of New Zealand: Banks's *Journal*, vol. 1, pp. 394–397; Cook's *Journals*, vol. 1, p. 167.

72 Distinctive canoes: Banks's *Journal*, vol. 2, pp. 11, 23.

73 English oarsmen's eyes in backs of heads: Beaglehole, *The Life of Captain James Cook*, p. 206.

74 Meetings at Poverty Bay: an illuminating interpretation comes from Nicholas Thomas, an anthropologist, in *Cook: The Extraordinary Voyages of Captain James Cook*, New York, 2003, pp. 86 ff.

75 Tupaia's opinion of the Maori: Banks's *Journal*, vol. 1, pp. 460, 469.

76 Killing a cloth-stealer: John Gascoigne, *Captain Cook: Voyager Between Worlds*, London, 2007, p. 87.

76–77 Transit of Mercury: Sir Frank Dyson, Astronomer Royal, "Planets" in *Chambers's Encyclopaedia*, London, 1926, vol. 8, p. 203; Beaglehole, *The Life of Captain James Cook*, pp. 205–207.

77 New Zealand commodities: Banks's *Journal*, vol. 1, pp. 9–11 for timber and flax; Cook's *Journals*, vol. 1, p. 204 for resin.

78 Potato thief and his legal action against Cook: Cook's *Journals*, vol. 1, pp. 216n2, 594.

79 Ship's narrow escape in moonlight: Cook's *Journals*, vol. 1, p. 219; Beaglehole, *The Life of Captain James Cook*, p. 208; Alan Frost, *The Precarious Life*, pp. 48–49; Banks's *Journal*, vol. 1, pp. 446–447; Parkinson, *Journal of a Voyage*, p. 210.

CHAPTER 5: THE SEA OF SURVILLE

83–84 Labé's confusion about Easter Island: his journal in Dunmore, *The Expedition*, p. 229.

85 De Surville's early decision to change course for New Zealand: his journal in Dunmore, *The Expedition*, pp. 126, 230.

85 Labé's hope of precious metals: Dunmore, *The Expedition*, p. 245.

87 Peru and the meadow smell: Herman Melville, *Moby Dick*, 1851, ch. cxxxii.

87 Smell of land: journals in Dunmore, *The Expedition*, pp. 131, 232.

87 Odeur de terre: *Journal du Sieur Pottier de l'Horme . . . sur le St. Jean-Baptiste*, National Library of New Zealand, Wellington (microfilm MS 56); original manuscript in Archives Nationale, Paris, p. 187.

87–88 Smell of land in 1852: William Howitt, *Land, Labor and Gold; Or, Two Years in Victoria* etc., London, 1855, vol. 1, pp. 1–2. His ship, when the smell of hay drifted aboard, could have been only thirty miles from the nearest land, though she was possibly ninety miles from the Port Phillip Heads lighthouse, which marked her official falling in with the land.

89–90 Pitiful inhabitants: de Brosses, *Histoire des Navigations*, vol. 2, p. 380.

90 Dampier on miserable Australians: Christopher Lloyd, *William Dampier*, London, 1966, pp. 85–86.

90–91 Closeness of coast to *St. Jean-Baptiste*: On this difficult question, Dunmore gives differing views. Thus he noted in *The Expedition*, p. 232n, that on December 4 the ship was, he believed, "not more than 200 miles from the coast of New South Wales—probably far less." In his introduction, on p. 42, he estimated that the ship came "possibly to within a hundred miles of the Australian continent." His map of the ship's route, on p. 34, suggested, however, that at that point she was three or four hundred miles from Sydney Harbor. My conclusion, based on the distance that the aroma of land can travel offshore, the presence of cuttlebone and seaweed, and the near-shore position of the continental shelf, is that the ship was much closer to Sydney than in Dunmore's estimates. The shipboard journals, and their disputable estimates of daily west–east distances sailed between Australia and New Zealand, posed another problem.

92 Buffon on civilization in Australian mountains: de Brosses, *Histoire des Navigations*, vol. 2, pp. 382–383.

93 "God knows": Labé's journal, in Dunmore, *The Expedition*, p. 233.

95–96 De Surville near North Cape on December 15–16: Dunmore, *The Expedition*, p. 239.

96–97 Closeness of two ships: Richard P. Aulie, *The Circumnavigation of New Zealand*, Captain Cook Study Unit, 1999, United Kingdom, <http://www.captain cooksociety.com/ccsu2514.htm>.

CHAPTER 6: TWO SHIPS WENT SAILING BY

98 Crisscrossing paths of two ships: see maps in Dunmore, *The Expedition*, p. 237, and Cook's *Journals*, vol. 1, opp. p. 161.

99 Maori chief in French ship: "Monneron's Journal," in McNab, *Historical Records of New Zealand*, Wellington, 1914, vol. 2, p. 269.

100–102 Parsley and cress for scurvy: Monneron's journal in McNab, *Historical Records*, vol. 2, p. 285.

102 De Surville on justice to Maori: his journal, cited in Dunmore, *The Expedition*, p. 5.

103 Seductive gestures "not made even in brothels": Labé's journal, in Dunmore, *The Expedition*, p. 249.

103 The French chaplain goes walking: de l'Horme's journal, in McNab, *Historical Records*, vol. 2, p. 331.

104–105 First Christmas in New Zealand: John Dunmore surveys the evidence in *The Expedition*, appendix C, pp. 289–291.

105 Christmases celebrated in *Endeavour*: Cook's biographer Beaglehole argues that Cook could hardly be expected to record the celebrations and drunken state of the crew at Christmas 1769, for "he is too busy with nautical detail"; see Beaglehole's editorial note in Banks's *Journal*, vol. 1, p. 449n. But the day probably was not very busy, thanks to the light and smiling breeze. In contrast the weather of the previous Christmas had been boisterous, and Cook must have been busier, but this same excuse had not prevented him from mentioning in his journal the celebrations—they were far from sober—and the bad steering they occasioned; see Cook's *Journals*, vol. 1, pp. 37, 226. Beaglehole sometimes felt the need to defend Cook from minor as well as major criticisms; nonetheless he remains a wonderful guide to Cook's journals.

106 When "our sick went walking": Labé's journal in Dunmore, *The Expedition*, p. 256.

106–108 Ship almost wrecked in gale: Isabel Ollivier and Cheryl Hingley, eds. and trans., *Extracts from journals relating to the visit to New Zealand of the French ship St. Jean-Baptiste in December 1769 under the command of J. F. M. de Surville*, Alexander Turnbull Library Endowment Trust, Wellington, 1987, rev. ed., pp. 27–32, 114–116.

108 "This good man": Monneron's journal in McNab, *Historical Records*, vol. 2, p. 277.

108 Scurvy deaths after gale: Labé in Isabel Ollivier and Cheryl Hingley, *Extracts from journals*, p. 83.

109 A "heavenly meal": De Surville's journal, in Dunmore, *The Expedition*, p. 155.

110 Ranginui kisses the feet: de l'Horne's journal in McNab, vol. 2, p. 315.

110 Four kidnapped passengers: Labé in Isabel Ollivier and Cheryl Hingley, *Extracts from journals*, p. 85.

111 Lauriston Bay as a future base: De Surville's journal, in Dunmore, *The Expedition*, p. 162.

112 De Surville's meeting with officers: Labé's journal, in Dunmore, *The Expedition*, pp. 264–265.

CHAPTER 7: WILD MUSICIANS AND WILDER SEAS

113 The succession of gales: facsimile of private *Endeavour* log, in McNab, vol. 2, pp. 155–157. The log is attributed to Zachary Hicks.

113–114 The wind's tunes: Joseph Conrad, *The Mirror of the Sea: Memories and Impressions*, London, 1946 (first published 1906), pp. 38–39; Ray Parkin, himself a seaman and one of the most alert observers of Cook and his *Endeavour*, wrote about the winds "making tunes here and there about the hull and rigging," in *H. M. Bark* Endeavour: *Her Place in Australian History*, Melbourne, 1997, p. 83.

114 The quest for accurate charts: Lord Blackett, "Captain Cook and the Royal Society" in Badger, *Captain Cook*, pp. 18–19.

115 Tasks at Queen Charlotte Sound: Cook's *Journals*, vol. 1, p. 244.

115 Bellbirds' concert: Banks's *Journal*, vol. 1, pp. 455–456, 461.

115 Singing of male and female bellbirds: Malcolm Wood, "Songlines," *Massey Magazine*, Massey University, Palmerston North, April 2006, issue 20, pp. 12–19.

115 Cooked human flesh: Banks's *Journal*, vol. 1, p. 455.

116 Visits to Maori camp: Banks's *Journal*, vol. 1, pp. 459–460, 463–464.

118 Gore and his "imaginary land": Cook's *Journals*, vol. 1, p. 254.

119 In "some books": Banks's *Journal*, vol. 1, p. 459; Cook's *Journals*, vol. 1, p. 255n.

120 High peak and extensive land: Cook's *Journals*, vol. 1, p. 256.

120 Hoped-for sight of new continent: Banks's *Journal*, vol. 1, pp. 469–472.

120 Port Egmont hens: Cook's *Journals*, vol. 1, p. 257.

121 Banks retains faith in the missing continent: Banks's *Journal*, vol. 2, pp. 38–39.

121–122 Ship almost crashes into the Traps: Alan Frost, *The Precarious Life*, p. 55.

121 No moon in early morning: Banks's *Journal*, vol. l, p. 472.

122 Parkinson and "providence": Parkinson, *Journal of a Voyage*, p. 121.

122 Eating Tahitian dog: Cook's *Journals*, vol. 1, p. 262n; Parkinson, *Journal of a Voyage*, p. 122.

122 Marble outcrops: Banks's *Journal*, vol. 1, p. 472, and vol. 2, p. 4; Cook's *Journals*, vol. 1, p. 262.

123 South Island "wild and romantic": Parkinson, *Journal of a Voyage*, p. 122.

124–125 Crozet praises Cook's charts: Beaglehole, *The Life of Captain James Cook*, p. 221n.

126 "God is merciful": Labé's journal in Dunmore, *The Expedition*, p. 245.

126 Ranginui as captive: Labé's journal in Dunmore, *The Expedition*, pp. 262–264.

126 Stormy weather: Monneron's journal in Dunmore, *The Expedition*, p. 289.

127 Officers and scurvy: calculated from the lists in Dunmore, *The Expedition*, pp. 275–276.

128 Morton and climate: manuscript letter of 1768, printed in appendix 2 of Cook's *Journals*, vol. 1, p. 516.

129 Size of Asia and America mistaken: *Encyclopaedia Britannica*, first ed., Edinburgh, 1771, vol. 1, p. 134, and vol. 2, p. 682; *Van Nostrand Atlas of the World*, Princeton, 1961, p. 9.

129 Height of Andes and Himalayas: *Encyclopaedia Britannica*, first ed., Edinburgh, 1771, vol. 1, pp. 134–135.

CHAPTER 8: WHERE ARE ALL THE PEOPLE?

131 Cook's secret instructions do not mention Australia, let alone Torres Strait: Cook's *Journals*, vol. 1, p. cclxxxii.

131 Wallis fears Cape Horn: Robertson in Carrington, *The Discovery of Tahiti*, p. 252n.

132 Scarcity of certain foods: Parkinson, *Journal of a Voyage*, p. 125. No other source seems to mention food scarcity or the relative speed of the Java route.

132 Cook mentions wish to explore eastern Australia in his *Journals*, vol. 2, p. 112n.

133 A towering sea: Parkinson, *Journal of a Voyage*, p. 132.

133 Portuguese navigators along the coast of eastern Australia: Professor Alan Frost, a historian of Pacific discovery, summarizes that evidence pithily and critically in *East Coast Country: A North Queensland Dreaming*, Carlton, 1996, pp. 91–95. The debate about the Portuguese is far from over. Even if the Portuguese did discover part of eastern Australia, they did not publicize it. Others had to find it afresh and, more important, to explore and evaluate it.

133 The Dutch and eastern Australia: In 1770 there was no knowledge of the existence of the strait that actually separated Tasmania from Australia proper. By 1788 the existence of Bass Strait was suspected but not proved. So when the first British fleet arrived in Botany Bay in 1788, well to the north of Tasmania, they were settling on land to which the Dutch could well have had a prior claim. By then, however, Holland was politically weak. The weak, in terms of practical politics, do not usually have effective claims to territory. The discovery of Bass Strait in 1798 would have seriously weakened any such Dutch claim.

134 The ship "wore" or "veered": the meaning of the verbs are defined in Admiral W. H. Smythe, *The Sailor's Word-Book*, London, 1867, pp. 710–711.

135 Hicks the real finder: Cook's *Journals*, vol. 1, p. 299n.

135 Hicks's journal for Thursday, April 19, 1779: *Historical Records of NSW*, vol. 1, part 1, p. 177.

135 Cape Everard was renamed Point Hicks in 1970: see *The Australian Encyclopaedia*, Sydney, 1977, vol. 3, p. 294. The date of its discovery is now given as April 20, 1770. Cook lost a day in crossing what is now called the international dateline, but on his calendar the day of discovery was Thursday, April 19.

137 Parkinson sees smoke: Parkinson, *Journal of a Voyage*, p. 133.

137 Pickersgill on blacks, *Historical Records of NSW*, vol. 1, part 1, p. 213.

138 Banks notes smaller fires and the absence of gardens: Banks's *Journal*, vol. 2, p. 50.

138 Prejudices from Dampier: Banks's *Journal*, vol. 2, p. 50,

138 Parkinson sees no canoes: Parkinson, *Journal of a Voyage*, p. 133.

138–139 Mount Dromedario: the Italian map, depicting this cape, was published by Antonio Zatta in Venice in 1774. The map is held by a private collector in Melbourne.

139 Pigeon House Hill: *Historical Records of NSW*, vol. 1, part 1, p. 213.

139 Aborigines' frugality with firewood: G. Blainey, *Triumph of the Nomads*, Melbourne, 1975, p. 72.

139 Aborigines' signaling: Parkinson, *Journal of a Voyage*, p. 133.

140 Attempted landing was at Collin's Rock, nine miles north of Port Kembla: Cook's *Journals*, vol. 1, 1968 ed., "corrigenda," p. 691.

142 Our "mother Eve": Banks's *Journal*, vol. 2, p. 54.

142–144 First clash with Aborigines: Banks's *Journal*, vol. 2, pp. 54–56; Cook's *Journals*, vol. 1, pp. 305–306; Parkinson, *Journal of a Voyage*, p. 134. It was Beaglehole who alertly pointed out that Maori exclamations were wrongly attributed to Aborigines. See his "textual introduction" to Cook's *Journals*, vol. 1, p. cclv.

CHAPTER 9: IN BOTANY BAY

145 Sutherland's death: Cook's *Journals*, vol. 1, p. 307; Parkinson, *Journal of a Voyage*, p. 136.

146 No man lost through sickness: Cook's *Journals*, vol. 1, p. 501.

146 Aboriginal canoes: Cook's *Journals*, vol. 1, pp. 305, 396–397.

148–150 Further conflicts and tensions with Aborigines at Botany Bay: Banks's *Journal*, vol. 2, pp. 54–55, 58, 60, 134; Cook's *Journals*, vol. 1, p. 310.

149 Pickersgill on Aborigines: *Historical Records of NSW*, vol. 1, part 1, pp. 213, 215.

149–150 Tupaia and "Indians": Banks's *Journal*, vol. 2, p. 58.

150 Aborigines' little-noticed skills: Blainey, *Triumph of the Nomads*, esp. chs. 8, 9, 11, 12.

151–152 Banksia plants: Alex George on "Banksia," in Richard Aitken and Michael Looker, eds., *Oxford Companion to Australian Gardens*, Melbourne, 2002, p. 73; *New Royal Horticultural Society Dictionary of Gardening*, New York, 1992, pp. 303–305.

152 Eye is the secret: Richard Jefferies, *The Gamekeeper at Home*, Collins, London, n.d. (but first published in 1878), ch. 4 and esp. p. 99.

153 Day-long inland excursion: see journals of Banks and Cook for May 1, 1770.

153–154 Cook's River and Chinese gardens: R. J. Haworth, "The Shaping of Sydney by Its Urban Geology," *Quarternary International*, 2003, pp. 49–50.

154 Gilbert White: *The Natural History of Selborne*, London, 1901, pp. 93–94 (May 12, 1770), 191–193 (January 29, 1774).

154–155 Wind exposure of Botany Bay: Alan Frost, *Arthur Phillip 1738–1814*, Oxford, 1987, p. 165.

155 Naming the bay of stingrays: Beaglehole, *The Life of Captain James Cook*, p. 230.

156 Plant specimens kept in tin chests: Banks's *Journal*, vol. 2, p. 62.

157 Rainbows: Parkinson, *Journal of a Voyage*, p. 136.

157–158 Cook misses harbors: Beaglehole, "Introduction" to Cook's *Journals*, vol. 1, p. cl. In making this fascinating observation about Cook, Beaglehole rather exaggerates Cook's errors of judgment. Newcastle and various other eastern Australian harbors were not natural harbors but required expensive harbor works.

CHAPTER 10: INTO THE CORAL JAWS

159–160 Orton's ear: Parkinson, *Journal of a Voyage*, p. 138n.

160 Matra's background: Alan Frost, *The Precarious Life*, pp. 1–6.

163 Stinging caterpillars: The Australian entomologist is Dr. Ian Common, *Moths of Australia*, Carlton, 1990, p. 37.

164 Habits of bustard: H. J. Frith, *Wildlife Conservation*, Sydney, 1973, p. 199; E. E. Morris, *A Dictionary of Austral English*, Sydney, 1972 (reprint), pp. 483–484; H. W. Wheelwright, *Bush Wanderings of a Naturalist*, London, 1861, pp. 61–62.

164 Sound of bustard: J. D. Macdonald, *Birds of Australia*, Sydney, 1973, p. 143.

165 Gum tree: Banks's *Journal*, vol. 2, p. 73.

165 Mount Morgan gold: G. Blainey, *The Rush That Never Ended: A History of Australian Mining*, Melbourne, 1963, pp. 241–244.

165 Rich ores: Parkinson, *Journal of a Voyage*, p. 141.

166 Whitsunday: Cook's *Journals*, vol. l, p. 337.

166–167 Cook and Easter: after calculating when Easter fell in 1769 and 1770, I scanned Cook's *Journals* but could find no visible sign that he recognized or celebrated it.

168 New Jerusalem and bulge on Queensland coast: de Brosses, *Histoire des Navigations*, vol. l, map appended. The map placed the site of the harbor of St. Philip and St. James about two hundred miles north of New Jerusalem, which was supposed to be on the shores of this same harbor.

168 De Quiros discovery of 1606: Miriam Estensen, *Terra Australis Incognita*, Crows Nest, New South Wales, 2006, ch. 13; Celsus Kelly, *La Austrialia Del Espíritu Santo*, Cambridge, England, 1966, vol. 1, pp. 115, 126, 221–222.

169 Cook "certain" about Quiros: Cook's *Journals*, vol. 1, p. 377.

169 Smell of "gum Benjamin"; Parkinson, *Journal of a Voyage*, p. 141; Robert Hunt, ed., *Ure's Dictionary of Arts, Manufactures, and Mines*, London, 1861, vol. 1, p. 294.

172 Apollo spacecraft: Dorothy Hill, "The Great Barrier Reef," in Badger, *Captain Cook*, p. 70.

172 Stormy nights near shoals: Banks's *Journal*, vol. 2, p. 74.

173 Coral at Green Island: Banks's *Journal*, vol. 2, p. 77.

CHAPTER 11: A SEDUCTIVE MOON

176–182 This story of striking the reef and the twenty-three hours of peril is reconstructed from Banks's and Cook's journals, with help from Pickersgill's journal, which was republished in *Historical Records of NSW*, vol. 1, pp. 221–222.

178 Dismantling upper masts and yards: for a masterly description of the technicalities of the tasks, see Parkin, *H. M. Bark Endeavour*, pp. 307–309.

181 Theory of very high tide on moonlit night: Cook to Sir John Pringle, April 1776, in McNab, *Historical Records of New Zealand*, vol. 2, pp. 129–130.

184 Cook to Captain Walker: Cook's *Journals*, vol. 1, p. 508.

184–185 Villiers on Cook's decision. Alan Villiers, *Captain Cook*, p. 137.

185 On "ideal conditions for night sailing": Beaglehole, *The Life of Captain James Cook*, p. 237.

185 Banks sees coral at Green Island: Banks's *Journal*, vol. 2, p. 77.

186–187 Visibility of submerged coral reefs: personal information from Captain John Foley, Torres Strait pilot; "Navigation Among Coral Reefs," *Pacific Islands Pilot* (Eastern Groups), U.S. Navy Hydrographic Office, Washington, D.C., 1916, vol. 2, pp. 42–43. See also *Australia Directory*, London, 1907, vol. 2, p. 539, for danger of approaching Elizabeth Reef in the face of morning sun.

187 De Quiros on sea's color: journal of Munilla in Celsus Kelly, *La Austrialia*, vol. 1, p. 149.

188 Horatio Nelson to First Lord of Admiralty in 1801: James Aitken, ed., *English Letters of the XIX Century*, London, 1946, p. 48.

188 Dutch wreck in moonlight: Günter Schilder, *Australia Unveiled*, pp. 113–114.

188 *Quetta* wrecked: G. Blainey, *Black Kettle and Full Moon: Daily Life in a Vanished Australia*, Camberwell, 2003, p. 14.

189 The "hair-breadth escapes": Parkinson letter, reproduced in Joppien and Smith, *The Art of Captain Cook's Voyages*, vol. 1, pp. 50–51.

189 Parkinson on reef: cited in Joppien and Smith, *The Art of Captain Cook's Voyages*, p. 51.

CHAPTER 12: IN COOK'S RIVER-CAMP

190–191 Entry into river: Cook's *Journals*, vol. 1, pp. 348–350.

193 The reef as "redemption": Parkinson, *Journal of a Voyage*, p. 143.

194 Scurvy: Surgeon Perry in *Historical Records of NSW*, vol. 1, part 1, "Cook 1762–1780," p. 342; Banks's *Journal*, vol. 2, p. 82.

195 Excursion upstream: Banks's *Journal*, vol. 2, pp. 88–90.

195 Greyhound's sight: Richard Jefferies, *The Gamekeeper at Home*, ch. 4.

201 Hole in ears: Alan Frost, *The Precarious Life*, p. 63.

201 Nose peg or spritsail yard: Banks's *Journal*, vol. 2, p. 125; Cook's *Journal*, vol. 1, pp. 358, 395. Joppien and Smith, the authors of the excellent book on the art resulting from the *Endeavour*'s voyage (*The Art of Captain Cook's Voyages*, vol. 1, pp. 46, 48), did not think any contemporary drawing of the people of the Endeavour River existed; but they actually print a Parkinson drawing of two nose-peg men who were almost certainly from that river.

203 Women wearing feathers: Parkinson, *Journal of a Voyage*, p. 147.

203–204 Aborigines' faces: Cook's *Journals*, vol. 1, pp. 358, 358n, 395.

203 "Privities": Cook's *Journals*, vol. 1, p. 395.

204–205 Voices, words, and translations: Banks's *Journal*, vol. 2, pp. 93, 124, 136–137; Cook's *Journals*, vol. 1, p. 358.

CHAPTER 13: KANGARU

206 Parkinson on kangaroo: Parkinson, *Journal of a Voyage*, p. 145.

207–208 Banks on kangaroo: Banks's *Journal*, vol. 2, pp. 93 ff, 116–167.

207 Aboriginal words: see R. M. W. Dixon, *The Languages of Australia*, Cambridge, 1980; Bruce Moore, ed., *The Australian Oxford Dictionary*, 1999.

207 Bombed in England: Beaglehole's editorial note in Banks's *Journal*, vol. 2, p. 94n.

207 Breeding habits of eastern grey kangaroo: H. J. Frith, *Wildlife Conservation*, Sydney, 1973, pp. 276–278.

210–211 Native birds: Cook's *Journals*, vol. l, pp. 394–395; Banks's *Journal*, vol. 2, pp. 117–119; Parkinson, *Journal of a Voyage*, pp. 144–145.

211–212 The coral's beauty: Parkinson, *Journal of a Voyage*, p. 156.

212–213 Aborigines and turtles: on this episode, see comments by Nicholas Thomas, *Cook*, p. 121.

213 Wandering seaman: Cook's *Journals*, vol. l, p. 363; Banks's *Journal*, vol. 2, p. 98.

215 Praise of simple life: Cook's *Journals*, vol. l, p. 399; Banks's *Journal*, vol. 2, p. 130.

216 Aboriginal warfare: Banks's *Journal*, vol. 2, p. 123.

216–217 Final assessment of land and its fertility: Cook's *Journals*, vol. l, p. 393; Banks's *Journal*, vol. 2, pp. 51, 113, 121–122.

218–219 Cooktown and Chinese: G. C. Bolton, *A Thousand Miles Away: A History of North Queensland to 1920*, Brisbane, 1963, pp. 53–57, 96.

CHAPTER 14: A HAPPY PUFF OF WIND

220–221 Lizard Island and Cook's Passage: Cook's private log, *Historical Records of NSW*, vol. l, part 1, pp. 69–70.

222 Vaugondy map: the last of three folding maps appended to the end of de Brosses, *Histoire des Navigations*, vol. 1.

222–223 Dalrymple map for Banks: Fry, *Alexander Dalrymple*, pp. 121–122.

223 Shortage of food "might prove the ruin": Cook's *Journals*, vol. 1, p. 374.

224 The "sweeps": Smyth, *The Sailor's Word-Book*, p. 669.

226 Cook and God: Cook's *Journals*, vol. 1, pp. 377, 545. See John Gascoigne, *Captain Cook*, ch. 6, for an impressive discussion of Cook's religious beliefs.

226 "Providential Channell": Cook's *Journals*, vol. 1, pp. 377–380, 545–546; *Australia Pilot*, first ed., 1916, vol. 3, p. 147.

226 Pickersgill's story: *Historical Records of NSW*, vol. l, p. 229.

226–227 Discovery of lost La Pérouse ships: Colin Jack-Hinton, *The Search*, pp. 295–296, 338–340.

229 Pearls on Possession Island: *Australia Pilot*, vol. 3, p. 219; Banks's *Journal*, vol. 2, pp. 108.

229 Parkinson and name "Australia": Beaglehole in Cook's *Journals*, vol. 1, p. cclxix n.

229 New Wales in Ontario: Beaglehole, *The Life of Captain James Cook*, p. 249; Cook's *Journals*, vol. 1, p. 388n. My deduction is that the site of Melbourne might well be outside the territory Cook claimed.

230 Cook's longitude seventy-seven miles astray: Geoffrey C. Ingleton, *Matthew Flinders: Navigator and Chartmaker*, Guildford, 1986, p. 202.

231 Hilder's research: Brett Hilder, *The Voyage of Torres*, St. Lucia, Queensland, 1980, pp. 87–89, 92–95.

232–233 Booby Island: Banks's *Journal*, vol. 2, pp. 110–111; Lighthouses of Australia Inc., 2007, Melbourne, <http://www.lighthouse.net.au/lights> with Rob Hindmarsh's reminiscences; *Australia Directory*, London, 1907, 6th ed., vol. 2, p. 492; Ken Simpson and Nicolas Day, *Field Guide to the Birds of Australia*, Camberwell, 2004, pp. 42, 301–302, 371–375.

CHAPTER 15: THE GUNS OF MOURNING

235 De Surville steers from forty south toward equator: *Journal du Sieur Pottier de l'Horme*, pp. 274–282.

235 Davis Land: Dunmore, *The Expedition*, pp. 18–19, 23–26, 51–53.

236 Water scarce: Monneron's journal in McNab, *Historical Records of New Zealand*, vol. 2, p. 291.

236 Ship's position at March 6: *Journal du Sieur Pottier de l'Horme*, p. 283.

236 Council summoned: *Journal du Sieur Pottier de l'Horme*, p. 283.

237 Hodges's painting of turbaned men: *View of the Province of Oparree . . .*, catalogue no. NMM BHC, 1936, in exhibition *200 World-class Paintings*, at National Maritime Museum, Greenwich, which I saw on June 22, 2007.

237–238 The shipwrecked Dutchmen: John Callander, *Terra Australis Cognita: Or, Voyages to the Terra Australis*, Edinburgh, 1766–1768, vol. 3, pp. 584–605. Written by a German Marine, this account of the voyage and wreck was first published at Leipzig in 1738.

238 A Spanish sail: Monneron's journal in McNab, *Historical Records of New Zealand*, vol. 2, p. 291.

240–241 Tragedy at Chilca: journals of Monneron and de l'Horme in McNab, *Historical Records*, vol. 2, pp. 293–295, 345–347.

241 "I was watching": Labé in Dunmore, *The Expedition*, p. 268.

245 Westerlies' route: Hugh Carrington, who died in 1947, was among the first to honor de Surville for pioneering the west–east route in the South Pacific. See his introduction to *The Discovery of Tahiti*, p. xxiii.

245 Red Jacket and westerlies: Colin Jones, "Documents for the Speed of Clippers," *The Mariner's Mirror*, August 2002, vol. 88, pp. 334–336.

245 Australia–Europe trade routes in the day of sail: Blainey, *The Tyranny of Distance*, Sydney, 2001, pp. 40–42, 183–186.

245 Garibaldi on Tasmanian island: G. M. Trevelyan, *Garibaldi and the Thousand: May, 1860*, London, 1928, esp. p. 29. Trevelyan, not knowing of the "Surville westerlies," could offer no explanation for Garibaldi's call at an island thousands of miles away from the direct Callao–China route.

CHAPTER 16: DEADLY CLOUD OVER JAVA

248 Nostalgia and the "croakers": Banks's *Journal*, vol. 2, pp. 145, 145n, 147.

249 European wars: Neville Willliams, ed., *Chronology of the Modern World: 1763 to the Present Time*, London, 1966, pp. 14–16.

249 Guns of warships, Max Adams, *Admiral Collingwood: Nelson's Own Hero*, London, 2003, p. 44; Roy Parkin, *H. M. Bark* Endeavour, p. 73.

250–253 Vitamin C in various foods: I am grateful to Dr. Keith Farrer, a Melbourne food scientist, for his comments on the relative efficacy of sauerkraut, lime, and lemon.

251 Tierra del Fuego and greens: Banks's *Journal*, vol. 1, pp. 216–217.

251 New Zealand's wild greens: Banks's *Journal*, vol. 2, pp. 8–9.

251 Scurvy at Botany Bay: G. Blainey, "Sydney 1788" in D. J. Mulvaney and J. Peter White, eds., *Australians: To 1788*, Sydney, 1987, pp. 422–423.

252 Flogging for two men who refused fresh meat: Cook's *Journals*, vol. 1, p. 7.

252–253 Scurvy targeted by Royal Navy: Bown, *Scurvy*, pp. 222–243.

253 Scurvy persists in navy: Janet Macdonald, "Two years off Provence: the victualling and health of Nelson's fleet in the Mediterranean, 1803–5," *The Mariner's Mirror*, November 2006, vol. 92, p. 443 ff.

254 Events in European winter of 1770–1771: Neville Willliams, ed., *Chronology of the Modern World*, pp. 14–18. For frozen Thames, see *Annual Register*, London, 1771, entry January 11, p. 6.

253–254 Cook evades Dutch questioning: Cook's *Journals*, vol. 1, pp. 429–430.

255 Cosmopolitan town: Parkinson, *Journal of a Voyage*, pp. 175–180.

257 Bougainville visits Jakarta: Banks's *Journal*, vol. 2, pp. 188–189.

257 Bougainville near Australia: John Dunmore, *French Explorers in the Pacific*, vol. 1, pp. 94–95.

257 French or Spanish flag in Tahiti: Cook's *Journals*, vol. 1, pp. 98–100.

259 Pale Dutchmen: Banks's *Journal*, vol. 2, p. 184.

259 Vegetables bought in Jakarta: Cook's letter of September 30, 1771, *Historical Records of New South Wales*, vol. 1, p. 344.

260 Death of Tupaia and opinions of him: Parkinson, *Journal of a Voyage*, pp. 182n; Cook's *Journals*, vol. 1, pp. 441–442; Banks's *Journal*, vol. 2, pp. 187, 190–191; Nicholas Thomas, *Cook*, pp. 134–135, 181–182.

262 Ravenhill's background and age: Cook's *Journals*, vol. 1, pp. 441, 448 n, 593; *Historical Records of NSW*, vol. 1, p. 335.

263 Voyage's "fatal stroke": Cook's *Journals*, vol. 1, p. 500.

CHAPTER 17: IS THERE WAR IN EUROPE?

264–265 Cape Town prospers with barren soils: Cook's *Journals*, vol. 1, pp. 463–465; Banks's *Journal*, vol. 2, pp. 248–249, 252–256, and also p. 113, n2, where Beaglehole wonders why Australian soil was more appealing to Banks in 1779 than in 1770.

265 One "great Inn": Cook's *Journals*, vol. 1, p. 465.

265 Harbor impeded in winter: Cook's *Journals*, vol. 1, p. 465.

267 Molyneux's "inimitable coolness": Banks's *Journal*, vol. 2, p. 77.

267 Fear of war with Spain: Cook's *Journals*, vol. 1, pp. 462, 468, 474.

268 Death of Hicks: Cook's *Journals*, vol. 1, pp. 470–471.

268 Death of Lady: Banks's *Journal*, vol. 2, p. 274.

268 Nanny goat: Beaglehole, *The Life of Captain James Cook*, pp. 147, 269.

268–269 Rhode Island schooner: Cook's *Journals*, vol. 1, p. 474.

269 *Bingley's Journal*: Beaglehole, *The Life of Captain James Cook*, pp. 269–270. For other London news reports, see Cook's *Journals*, vol. 1, appendix vii.

271–272 Cook's self-assessment: Cook's *Journals*, vol. 1, pp. 375, 387 ("I am confident"), 501, 501n, 504–505.

CHAPTER 18: TWO VOYAGES AND THEIR RIPPLES

273 New plant species: Harold B. Carter, "Sir Joseph Banks and the Royal Society" in R. E. R. Banks, et al., *Sir Joseph Banks: A Global Perspective*, Kew, United Kingdom, 1994, pp. 4–5.

273 Cook to Monkhouse: Cook's *Journals*, vol. 1, p. 634.

274 Cook promotes own sons: Beaglehole, *The Life of Captain James Cook*, p. 141.

274–275 Sailing qualities of *Endeavour*: Cook's *Journals*, vol. 1, p. 636.

275 End of *Endeavour*: information from the Australian National Maritime Museum, Sydney; see <http://www.anmm.gov.au>.

277 Banks's seaborne "penthouse": McNab, *Historical Records of New Zealand*, vol. 2, pp. 91–97.

277 Voyage to Iceland: *Annual Register*, 1772, pp. 116, 291n.

277 Cook's goat: Beaglehole's introduction to Cook's *Journals*, vol. 1, p. cxxxiii; James Boswell, *The Life of Samuel Johnson LLD*, London, 1931, vol. 1, p. 406.

279 *St. Jean-Baptiste* returns to France: John Dunmore, *The Expedition*, pp. 45–49; *Journal du Sieur Pottier de l'Horme*, pp. 387–388.

281 Cook finally learns of de Surville: Cook's *Journals*, vol. 2, pp. 656–657.

281 Former voyagers in France: Dunmore, *The Expedition*, pp. 7–8, 9, 48–49, 289.

282 Theft of cutter and anger of Cook: Christine Holmes, ed., *Captain Cook's Final Voyage: The Journal of Midshipman George Gilbert*, Manuka, Australia, 1982, pp. 105 ff.

282 Causes of Cook's death: why Cook was killed is the subject of much argument. For a brief illuminating summary, see Thomas, *Cook*, pp. 391–392, 442–443. While accepting that the event is complex, my feeling, in the light of de Surville's similar reaction, is to give more emphasis to the maritime implications of the loss of the cutter.

282 Death of Cook's children and wife: Beaglehole, *The Life of Captain James Cook*, pp. 689–695.

282 Mrs. Cook's death and burial: letter by Martin Riley, *The Times*, London, February 15, 1985.

283 Death of Solander: Banks's letter in Edward Duyker and Per Tingbrand, eds., *Daniel Solander*: Collected Correspondence 1753–1782, Melbourne, 1995, p. 414.

284 Banks and mermaids: Keith Thomas, *Man and the Natural World*, Harmondsworth, 1984 ed., p. 134.

284–285 Complex reasons for sending convicts to Botany Bay: Alan Frost, *Convicts and Empire: A Naval Question 1776–1811*, Melbourne, 1980, esp. pp. 121 ff.

285–286 La Pérouse at Botany Bay: John Hunter, *An Historical Journal of Events at Sydney and at Sea 1787–1792*, Sydney, 1968, p. 29; John Dunmore, *French Explorers in the Pacific*, vol. 1, pp. 275, 281; John Cobley, *Sydney Cove 1788*, Sydney, 1980, esp. pp. 33, 35–36, 50–51; John Dunmore, *Where Fate Beckons*, Sydney, 2006, pp. 247–249.

Picture Credits

Page 1 Jacob Gerritsz Cuyp, 1594–c.1651/National Library of Australia (nla. pic-an2282370-v)

Page 2 (top) Thomas Luny, 1759–1837/National Library of Australia (nla. pic-an2280897-v); (bottom) Dessinateur: Nicolas Marie Ozanne, 1728–1811; Graveur: Yvon Le Gouaz/Les Ports de France, La Citadelle du Port-Louis, vu de la pointe de Graves/Photograph © Musée National de la Marine (PH 79975)

Page 3 John Webber, c.1752–1793/National Portrait Gallery, Canberra (2000.25)

Page 4 Photograph by Lee Schiller/Australian National Maritime Museum, Darling Harbor, Sydney

Page 5 (left) Photo by Popperfoto/Getty Images; (right) Greg Elms/Lonely Planet Images (132-601)

Page 6 (top) "Man, Woman & Child, Natives of Terra del Fuego, in the Dress of That Country," Sydney Parkinson, *A Journal of a Voyage to the South Seas, In His Majesty's Ship The ENDEAVOUR*, London: Printed for Charles Dilly, in the Poultry; and James Phillps, in George-Yard, Lombard-Street, M DCC LXXXIV; (bottom) "A fortified town or village called a hippah, built on a perforated rock at Tolaga in New Zealand" (actually Mercury Bay)/Engraved from a drawing by J. J. Barralet after Herman Diedrich Spöring (1773)/National Library of Australia (nla.pic-an9184935)

Page 7 Photograph by Lloyd Homer/Institute of Geological and Nuclear Sciences

Page 8 (left) View in the Aurere area, Doubtless Bay, probably photographed by Arthur James Northwood between 1910 and 1939/Alexander Turnbull Library, Wellington, New Zealand (1/1-010957-G); (right) Scuba diver on the seabed at Doubtless Bay alongside the first of the three anchors of the *St. Jean-Baptiste* to be discovered/Photograph taken in 1974 by an unidentified photographer/Alexander Turnbull Library, Wellington, New Zealand (PAColl-0412-1)

Page 9 (left) Warwick Berry, 2007 http://www.flickr.com/photos/double-_you_ be/ (right) The entrance to Botany Bay, with Cronulla Headland in the foreground, 1974/National Archives of Australia (A6135, K23/10/74/10)

Page 10 (top) Bustards in Queensland, 1989/National Archives of Australia (A6135, K5/10/89/54); (bottom) William Byrne, 1743–1805 (engraving 1773)/ National Library of Australia (nla.pic-an9184938-v)

Page 11 "Two of the Natives of New Holland, Advancing to Combat," Sydney Parkinson, *A Journal of a Voyage to the South Seas, In His Majesty's Ship The ENDEAVOUR*, London: Printed for Charles Dilly, in the Poultry; and James Phillps, in George-Yard, Lombard-Street, M DCC LXXXIV

Page 12 (top) Great Barrier Reef, 1973/National Archives of Australia (A6180, 31/7/73/3); (bottom) © QT ong/terragalleria.com

Page 13 William Hodges, 1744–1797/© National Maritime Museum, Greenwich, London, Ministry of Defense Art Collection (BHC 1936)

Page 14 (left) Self-portrait, Sydney Parkinson, *A Journal of a Voyage to the South Seas, In His Majesty's Ship The ENDEAVOUR*, London: Printed for Charles Dilly, in the Poultry; and James Phillps, in George-Yard, Lombard-Street, M DCC LXXXIV; (right) "The Lad Taiyota, Native of Otaheite, in the Dress of His Country," Sydney Parkinson, *A Journal of a Voyage to the South Seas, In His Majesty's Ship The ENDEAVOUR*, London: Printed for Charles Dilly, in the Poultry; and James Phillps, in George-Yard, Lombard-Street, M DCC LXXXIV

Page 15 William Hodges, 1744–1797/© National Maritime Museum, Greenwich, London, Ministry of Defense Art Collection (BHC 1778)

Page 16 Antoine Cardon, 1772–1813 (engraving), 1810 / drawn by William Evans National Library of Australia (nla.pic-an6053449)

Every effort has been made to locate the copyright holders of printed and photographic material, and the publisher welcomes hearing from anyone in this regard.

Index